BELLE
BEAST HUNTER

In remembrance of **Angelo Ty "Bong" Dazo** who passed away on June 29, 2018.
Our heartfelt condolences go out to his family, friends, and fans.

zenescope

BELLE
BEAST HUNTER

Story **JOE BRUSHA, RALPH TEDESCO, & DAVE FRANCHINI**

Writer **DAVE FRANCHINI**

Artwork **ARIO MURTI** PROLOGUE & CH. 6 PGS. 143-150 **BONG DAZO** CH. 1-3

IGOR VITORINO CH. 4-6 PGS. 129, 130, 134, & 139-142 **EMAN CASALLOS** CH. 6 PGS. 131-133 & 135-138

Colors **IVAN NUNES** PROLOGUE **JUAN MANUEL RODRIGUEZ** CH. 1-6

Letters **TAYLOR ESPOSITO** (OF GHOST GLYPH STUDIOS) PROLOGUE **KURT HATHAWAY** CH. 1-6

Editor **DAVE FRANCHINI**

Art Direction & Design **CHRISTOPHER COTE**

Cover Artwork **IGOR VITORINO & KYLE RITTER**

Grimm Universe created by **JOE BRUSHA & RALPH TEDESCO**

This volume reprints Belle: Beast Hunter issues 1-6 and Grimm Fairy Tales: 2017 Armed Forces Edition short story 'Belle: Hunter of Beasts' published by Zenescope Entertainment. First Edition, January 2019 • ISBN: 978-1942275787

Joe Brusha • President & Chief Creative Officer
Ralph Tedesco • VP Film & Television
Christopher Cote • Art Director
Dave Franchini • Editor
Christina Barbieri • Assistant Editor
Ashley Vanacore • Graphic Designer

Lauren Klasik • Director of Sales & Marketing
Jennifer Bermel • Business Development & Licensing Manager
Jason Condeelis • Direct Sales Manager
Laura Levandowski • International Project Coordinator
Rebecca Pons • Marketing & VIP Coordinator
Stu Kropnick • Operations Manager

WWW.ZENESCOPE.COM

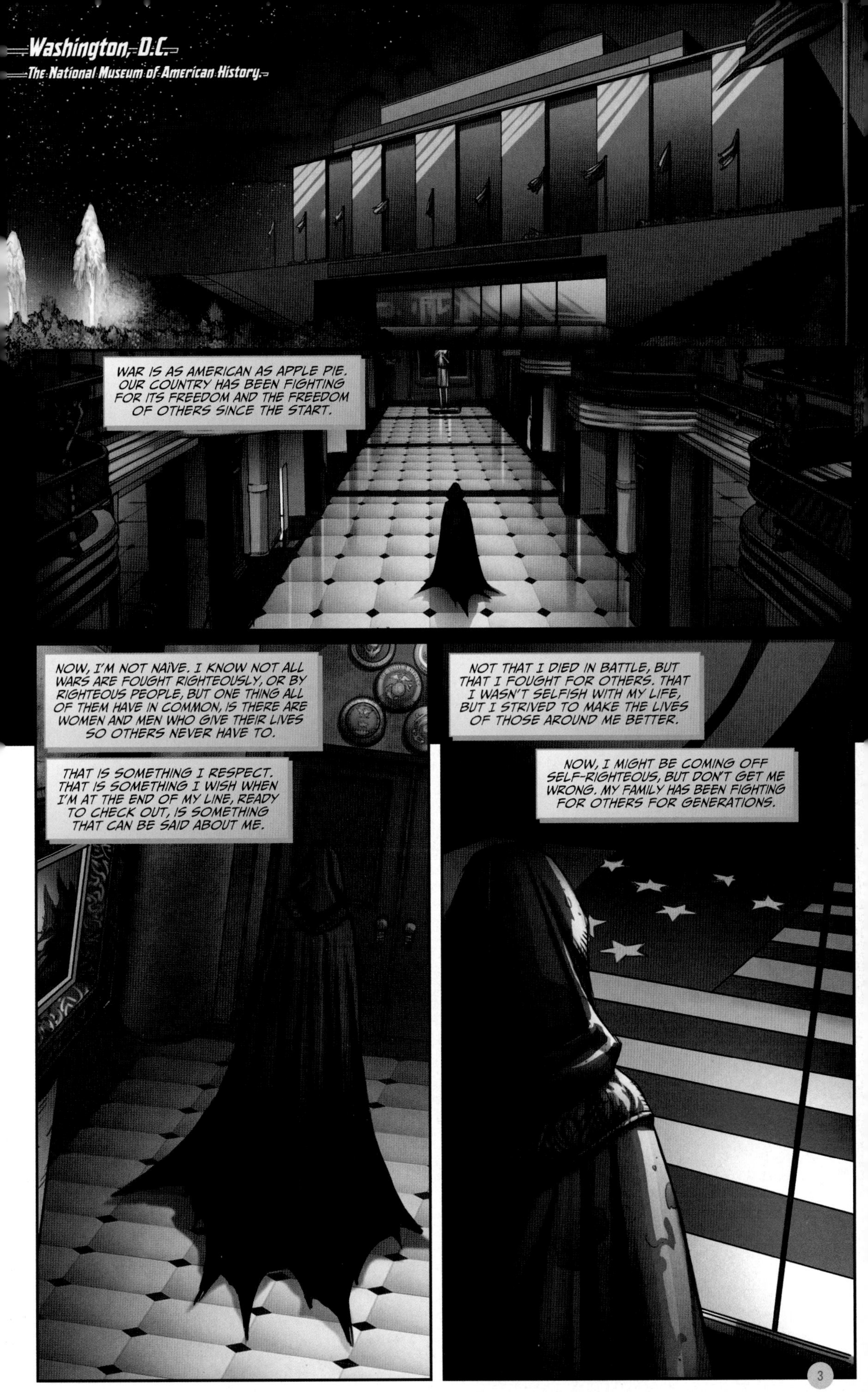
Washington, D.C.
The National Museum of American History.
WAR IS AS AMERICAN AS APPLE PIE. OUR COUNTRY HAS BEEN FIGHTING FOR ITS FREEDOM AND THE FREEDOM OF OTHERS SINCE THE START.
NOW, I'M NOT NAIVE. I KNOW NOT ALL WARS ARE FOUGHT RIGHTEOUSLY, OR BY RIGHTEOUS PEOPLE, BUT ONE THING ALL OF THEM HAVE IN COMMON, IS THERE ARE WOMEN AND MEN WHO GIVE THEIR LIVES SO OTHERS NEVER HAVE TO.
THAT IS SOMETHING I RESPECT. THAT IS SOMETHING I WISH WHEN I'M AT THE END OF MY LINE, READY TO CHECK OUT, IS SOMETHING THAT CAN BE SAID ABOUT ME.
NOT THAT I DIED IN BATTLE, BUT THAT I FOUGHT FOR OTHERS. THAT I WASN'T SELFISH WITH MY LIFE, BUT I STRIVED TO MAKE THE LIVES OF THOSE AROUND ME BETTER.
NOW, I MIGHT BE COMING OFF SELF-RIGHTEOUS, BUT DON'T GET ME WRONG. MY FAMILY HAS BEEN FIGHTING FOR OTHERS FOR GENERATIONS.

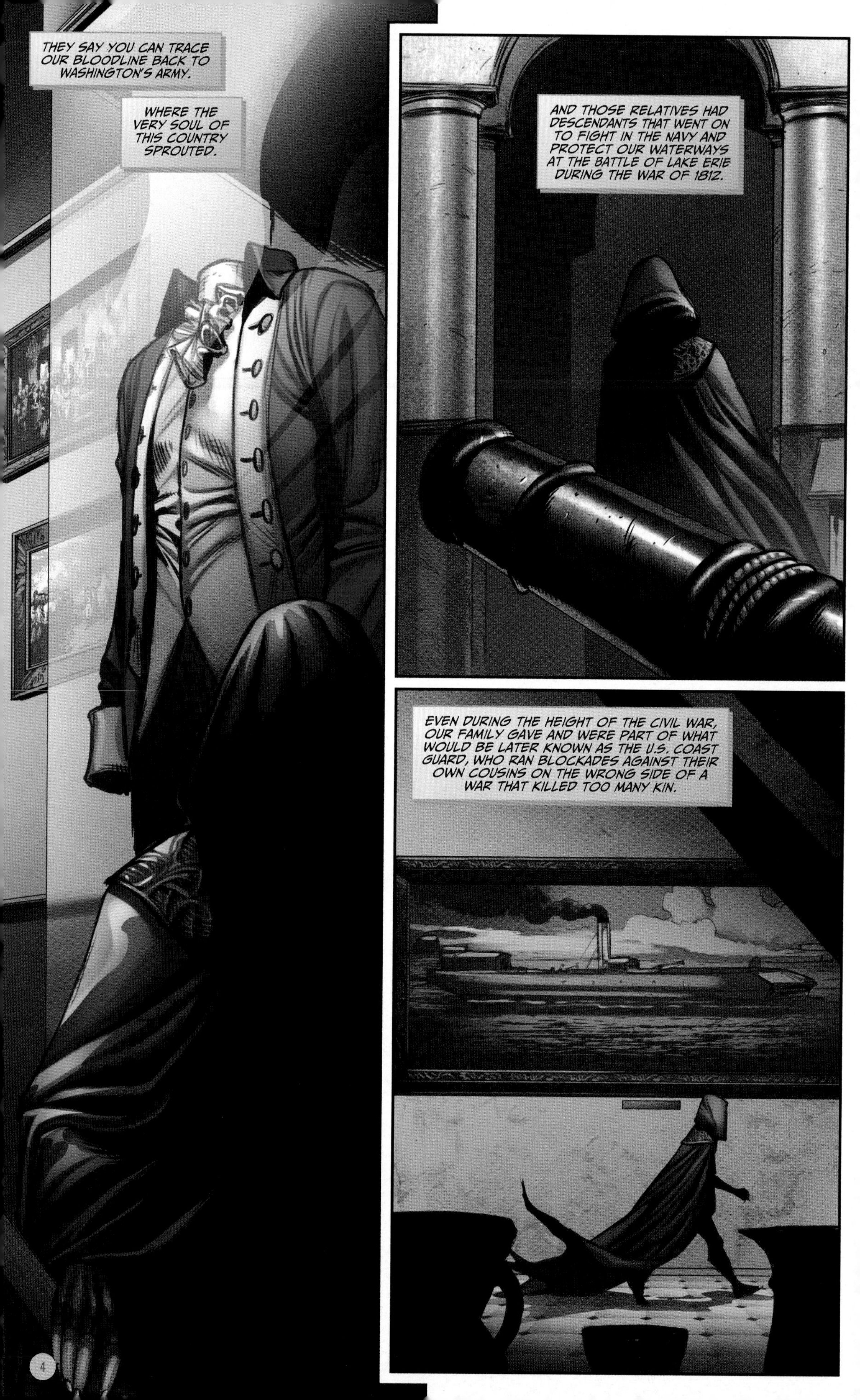
THEY SAY YOU CAN TRACE OUR BLOODLINE BACK TO WASHINGTON'S ARMY.
WHERE THE VERY SOUL OF THIS COUNTRY SPROUTED.
AND THOSE RELATIVES HAD DESCENDANTS THAT WENT ON TO FIGHT IN THE NAVY AND PROTECT OUR WATERWAYS AT THE BATTLE OF LAKE ERIE DURING THE WAR OF 1812.
EVEN DURING THE HEIGHT OF THE CIVIL WAR, OUR FAMILY GAVE AND WERE PART OF WHAT WOULD BE LATER KNOWN AS THE U.S. COAST GUARD, WHO RAN BLOCKADES AGAINST THEIR OWN COUSINS ON THE WRONG SIDE OF A WAR THAT KILLED TOO MANY KIN.

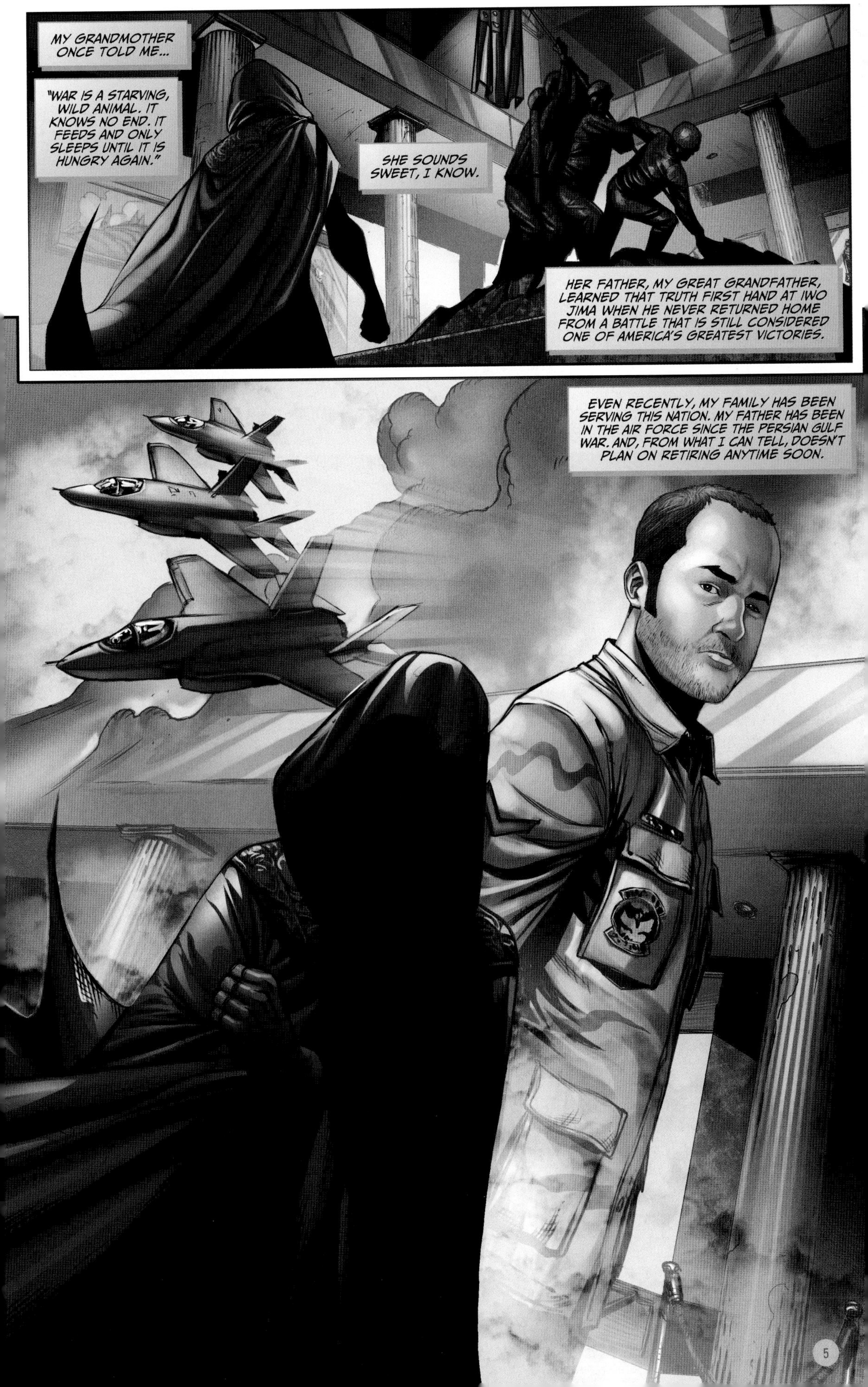
MY GRANDMOTHER ONCE TOLD ME...
"WAR IS A STARVING, WILD ANIMAL. IT KNOWS NO END. IT FEEDS AND ONLY SLEEPS UNTIL IT IS HUNGRY AGAIN."
SHE SOUNDS SWEET, I KNOW.
HER FATHER, MY GREAT GRANDFATHER, LEARNED THAT TRUTH FIRST HAND AT IWO JIMA WHEN HE NEVER RETURNED HOME FROM A BATTLE THAT IS STILL CONSIDERED ONE OF AMERICA'S GREATEST VICTORIES.
EVEN RECENTLY, MY FAMILY HAS BEEN SERVING THIS NATION. MY FATHER HAS BEEN IN THE AIR FORCE SINCE THE PERSIAN GULF WAR. AND, FROM WHAT I CAN TELL, DOESN'T PLAN ON RETIRING ANYTIME SOON.

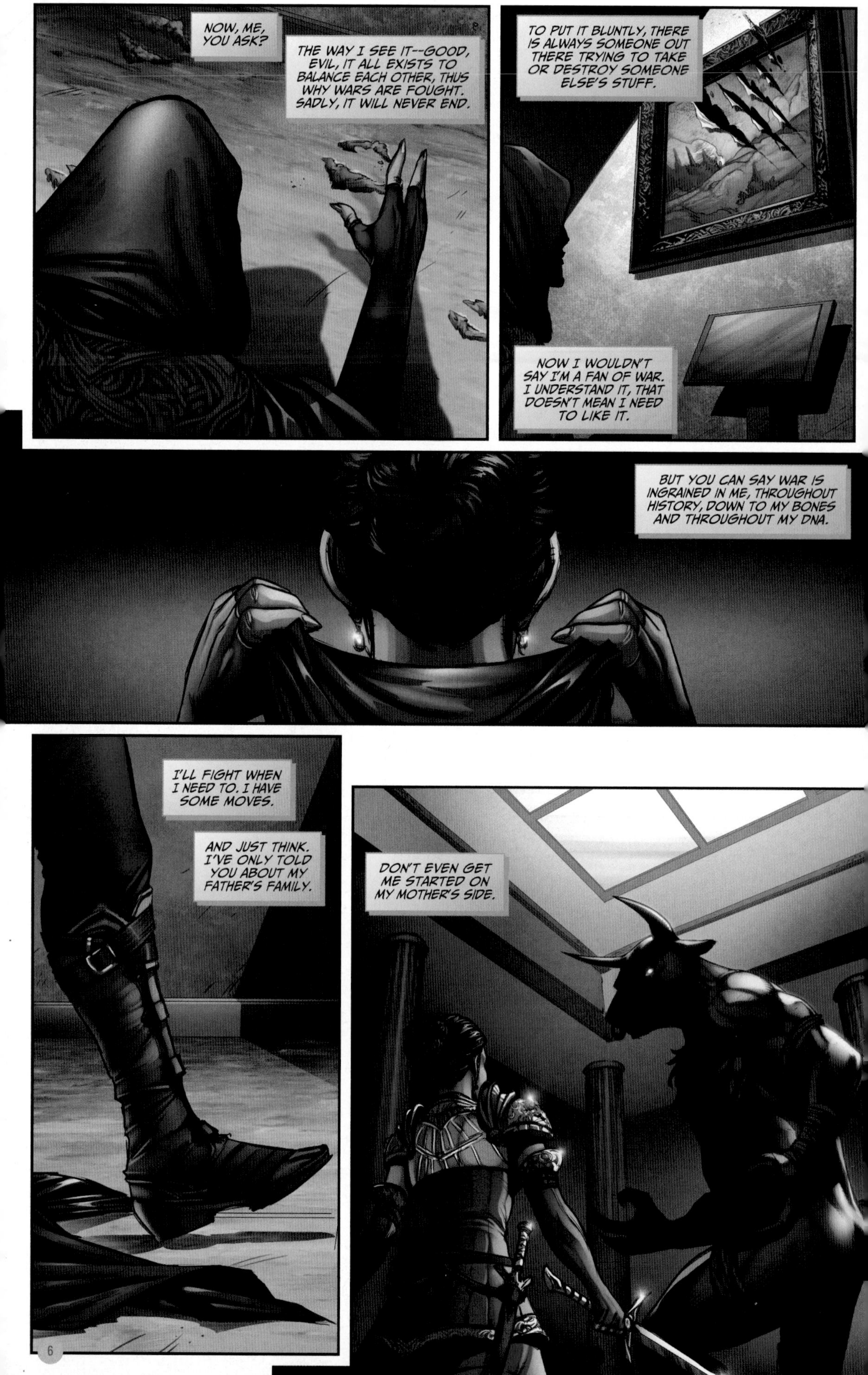
NOW, ME, YOU ASK?
THE WAY I SEE IT--GOOD, EVIL, IT ALL EXISTS TO BALANCE EACH OTHER, THUS WHY WARS ARE FOUGHT. SADLY, IT WILL NEVER END.
TO PUT IT BLUNTLY, THERE IS ALWAYS SOMEONE OUT THERE TRYING TO TAKE OR DESTROY SOMEONE ELSE'S STUFF.
NOW I WOULDN'T SAY I'M A FAN OF WAR. I UNDERSTAND IT, THAT DOESN'T MEAN I NEED TO LIKE IT.
BUT YOU CAN SAY WAR IS INGRAINED IN ME, THROUGHOUT HISTORY, DOWN TO MY BONES AND THROUGHOUT MY DNA.
I'LL FIGHT WHEN I NEED TO. I HAVE SOME MOVES.
AND JUST THINK. I'VE ONLY TOLD YOU ABOUT MY FATHER'S FAMILY.
DON'T EVEN GET ME STARTED ON MY MOTHER'S SIDE.

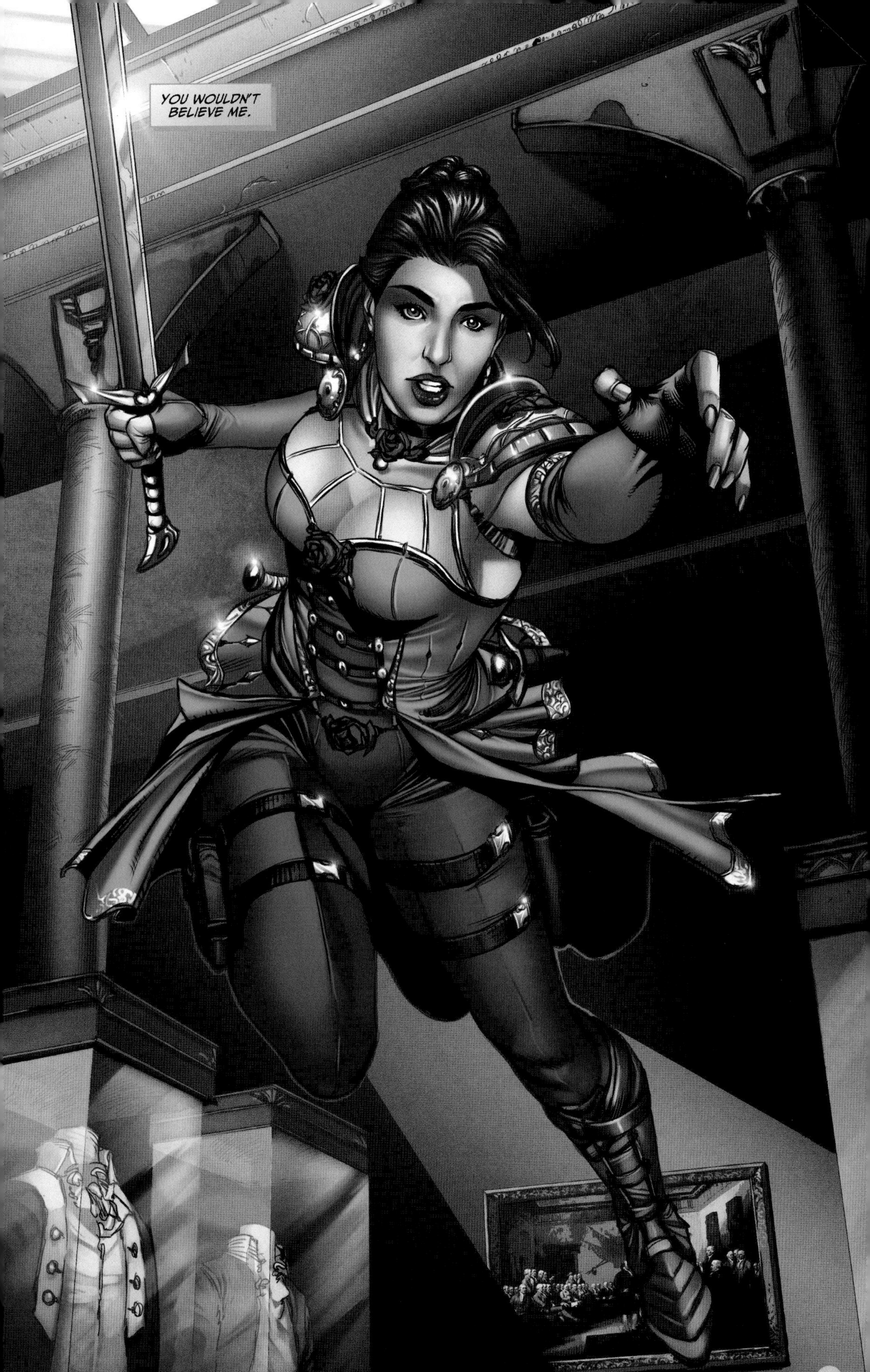
YOU WOULDN'T BELIEVE ME.

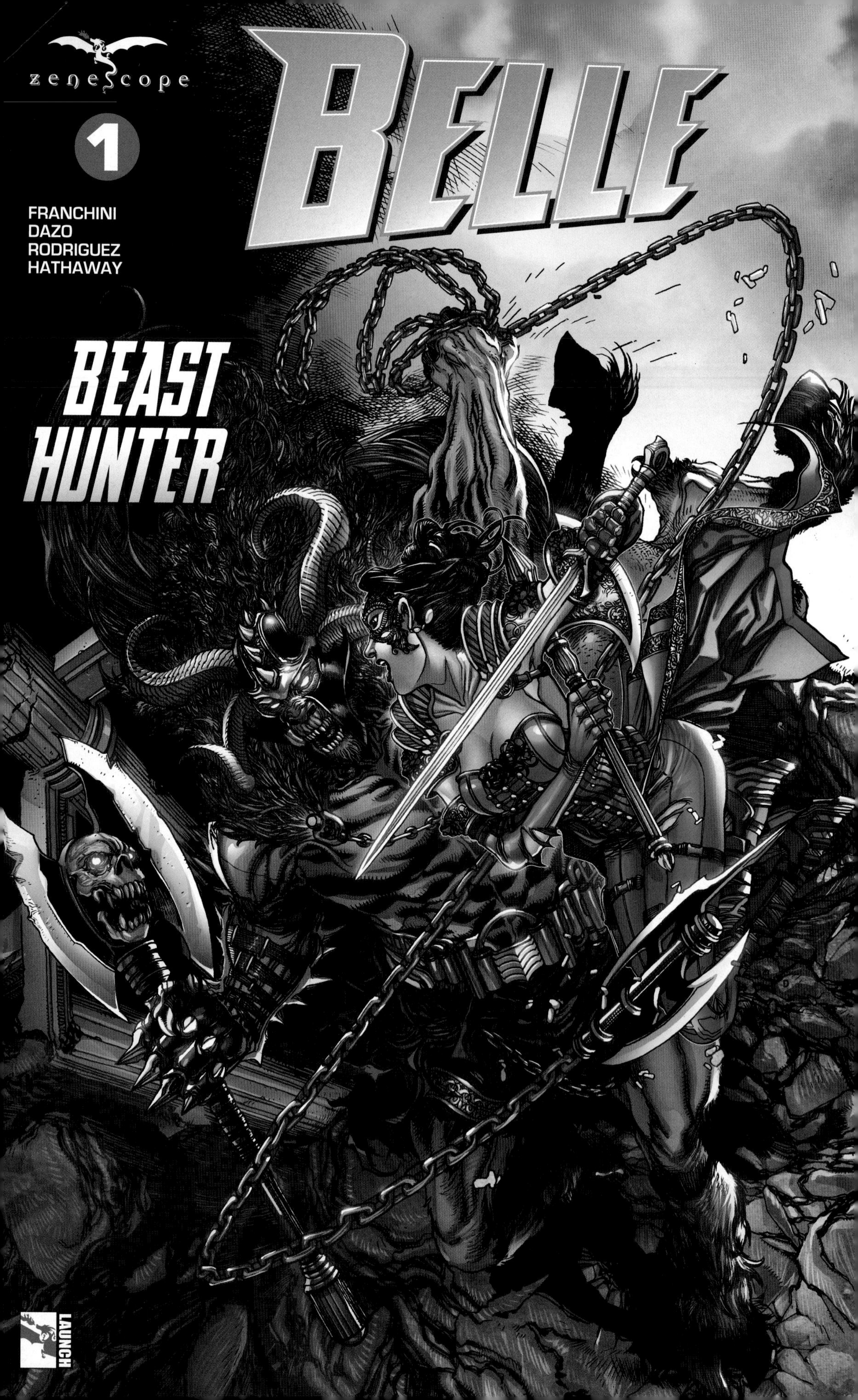
zenescope
1
BELLE
FRANCHINI
DAZO
RODRIGUEZ
HATHAWAY
BEAST HUNTER
LAUNCH

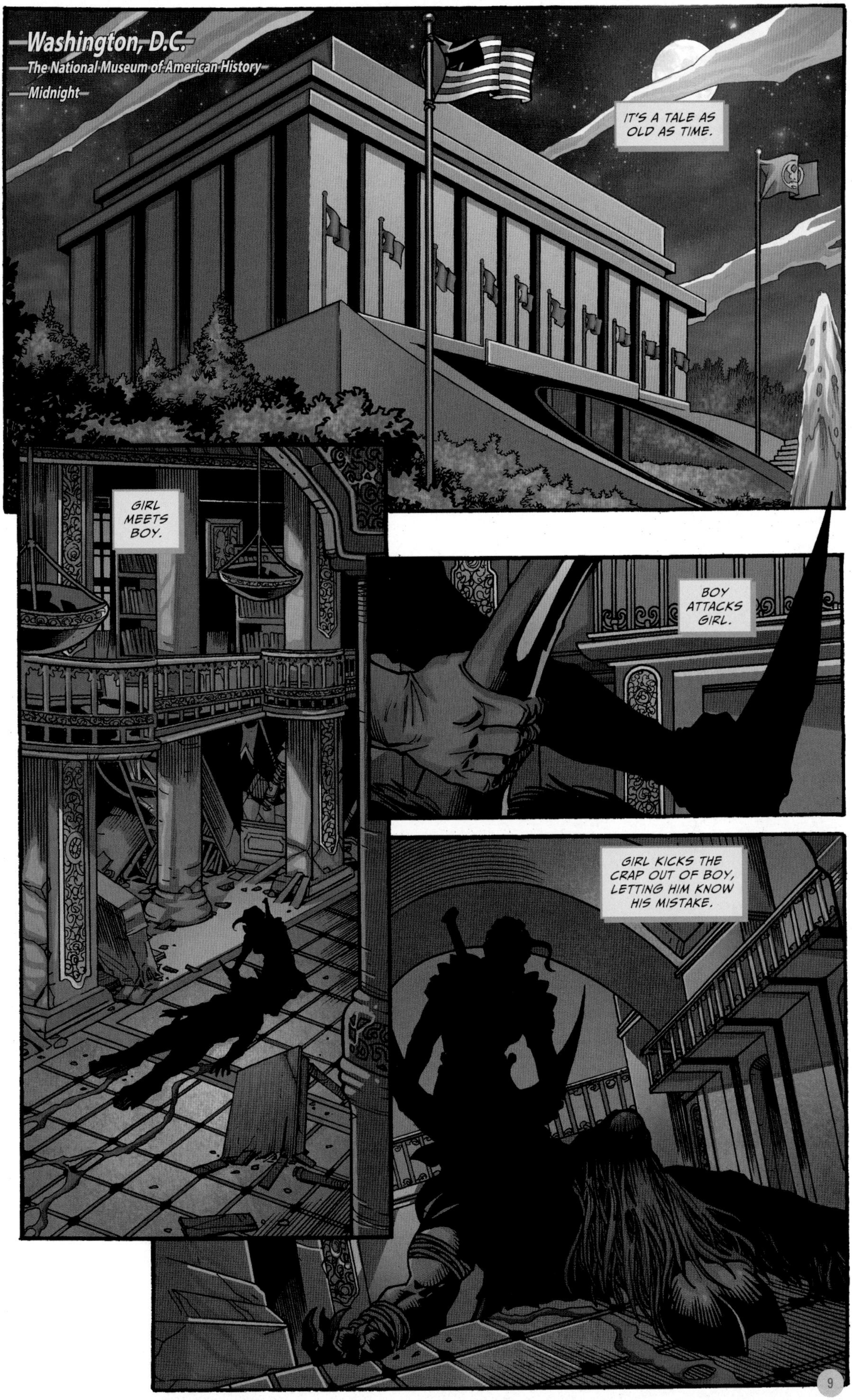

Washington, D.C.
The National Museum of American History
Midnight
IT'S A TALE AS OLD AS TIME.
GIRL MEETS BOY.
BOY ATTACKS GIRL.
GIRL KICKS THE CRAP OUT OF BOY, LETTING HIM KNOW HIS MISTAKE.

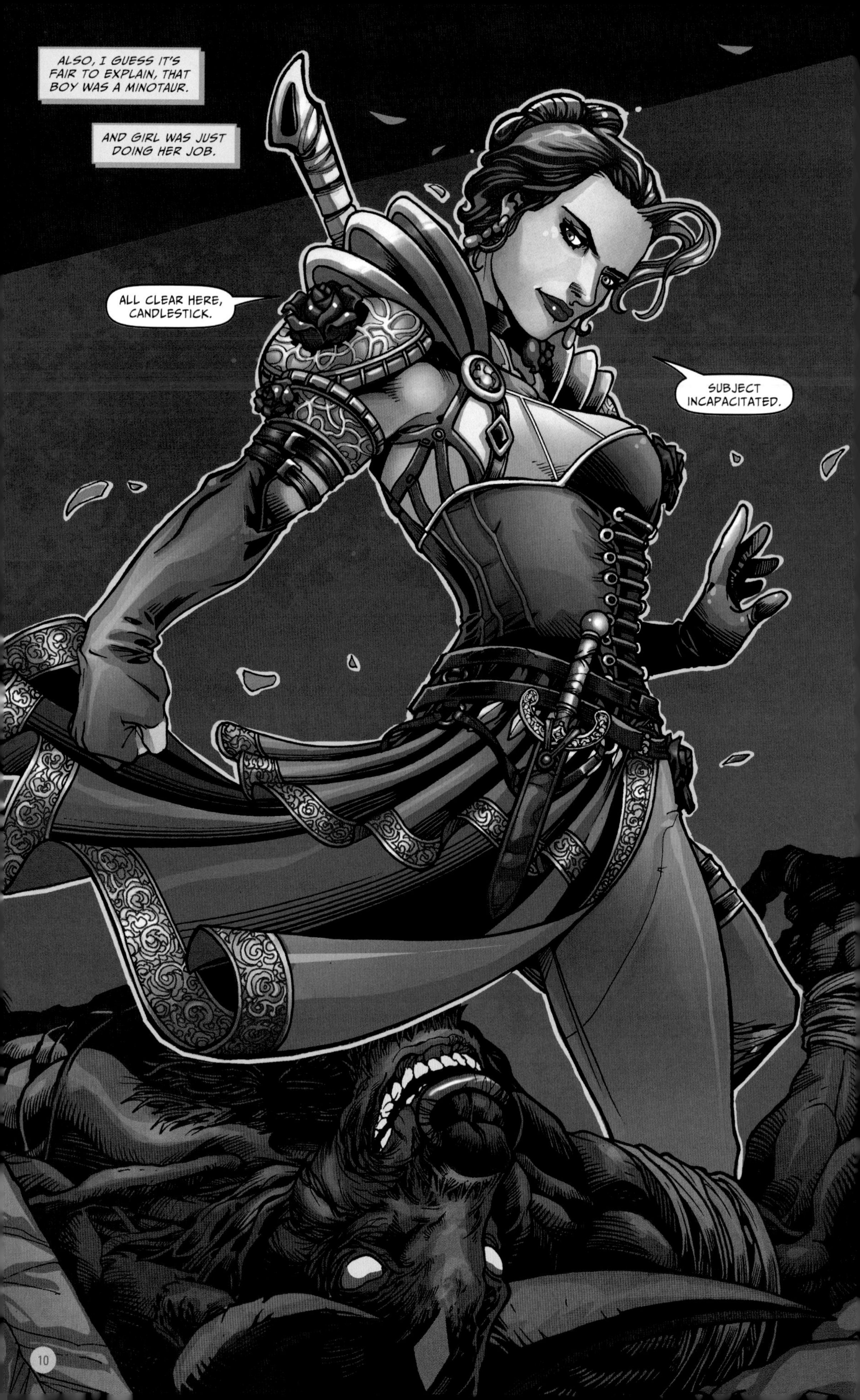
ALSO, I GUESS IT'S FAIR TO EXPLAIN, THAT BOY WAS A MINOTAUR.
AND GIRL WAS JUST DOING HER JOB.
ALL CLEAR HERE, CANDLESTICK.
SUBJECT INCAPACITATED.

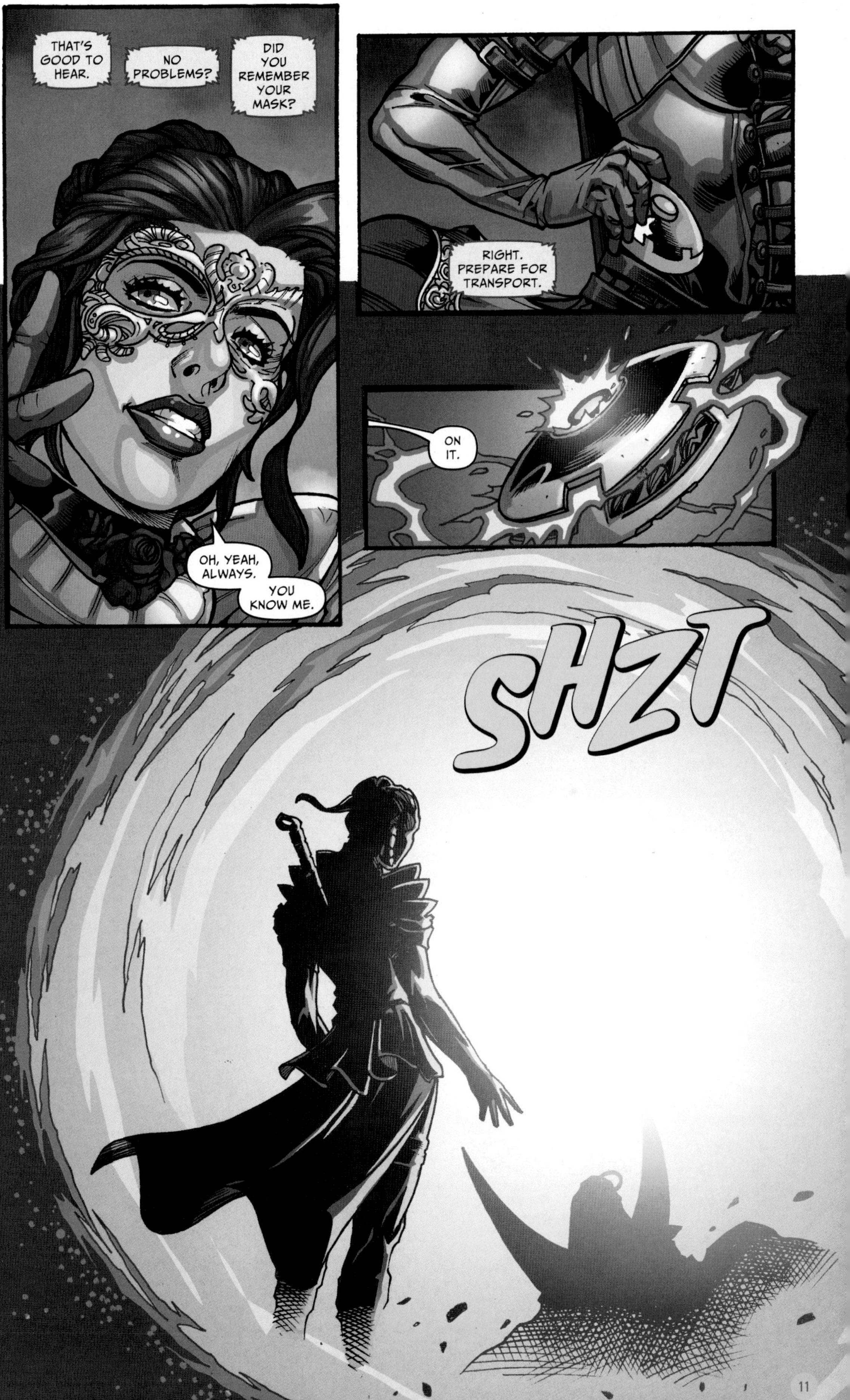
THAT'S GOOD TO HEAR.
NO PROBLEMS?
DID YOU REMEMBER YOUR MASK?
OH, YEAH, ALWAYS.
YOU KNOW ME.
RIGHT. PREPARE FOR TRANSPORT.
ON IT.
SHZT

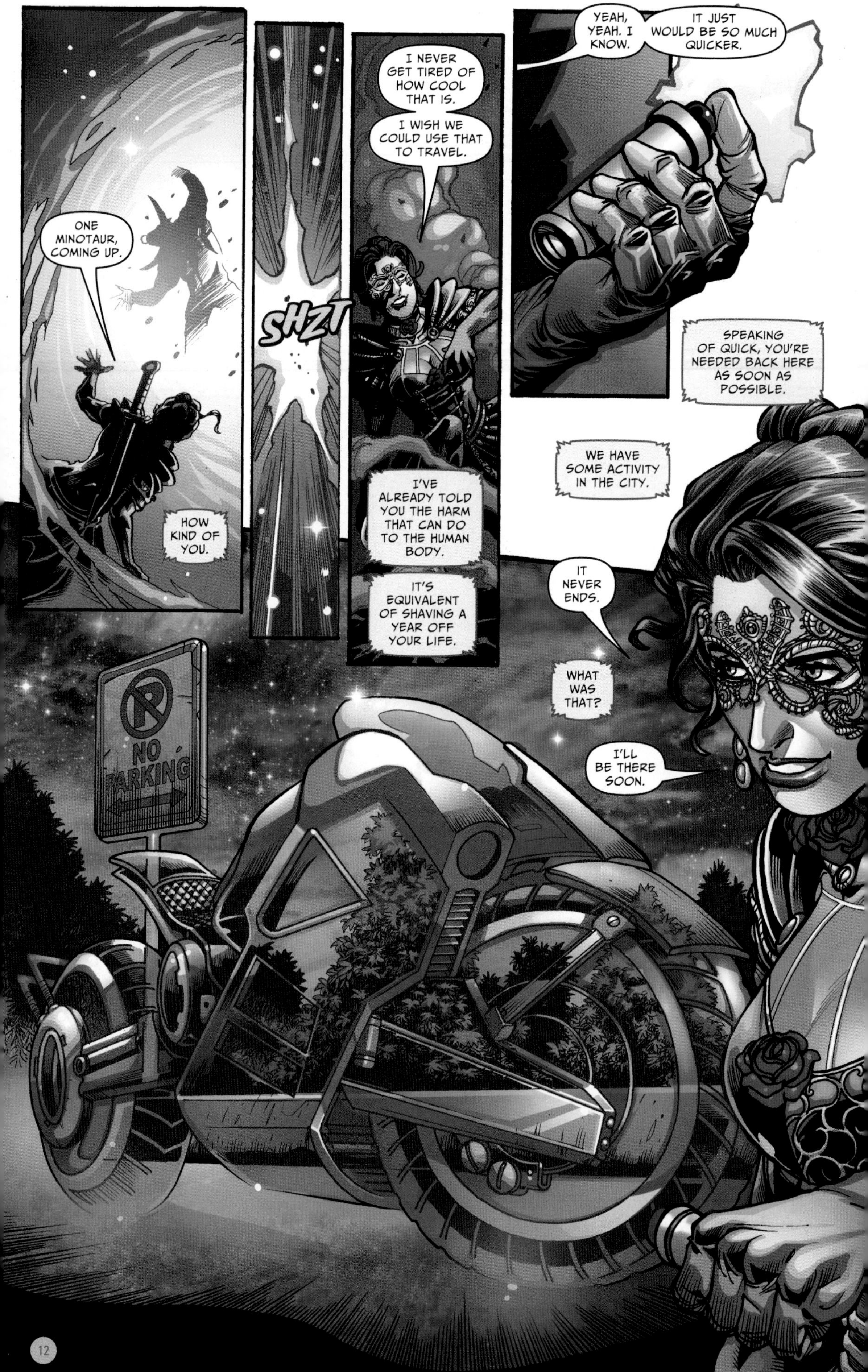

ONE MINOTAUR, COMING UP.
HOW KIND OF YOU.
SHZT
I NEVER GET TIRED OF HOW COOL THAT IS.
I WISH WE COULD USE THAT TO TRAVEL.
I'VE ALREADY TOLD YOU THE HARM THAT CAN DO TO THE HUMAN BODY.
IT'S EQUIVALENT OF SHAVING A YEAR OFF YOUR LIFE.
YEAH, YEAH. I KNOW.
IT JUST WOULD BE SO MUCH QUICKER.
SPEAKING OF QUICK, YOU'RE NEEDED BACK HERE AS SOON AS POSSIBLE.
WE HAVE SOME ACTIVITY IN THE CITY.
IT NEVER ENDS.
WHAT WAS THAT?
I'LL BE THERE SOON.
NO PARKING

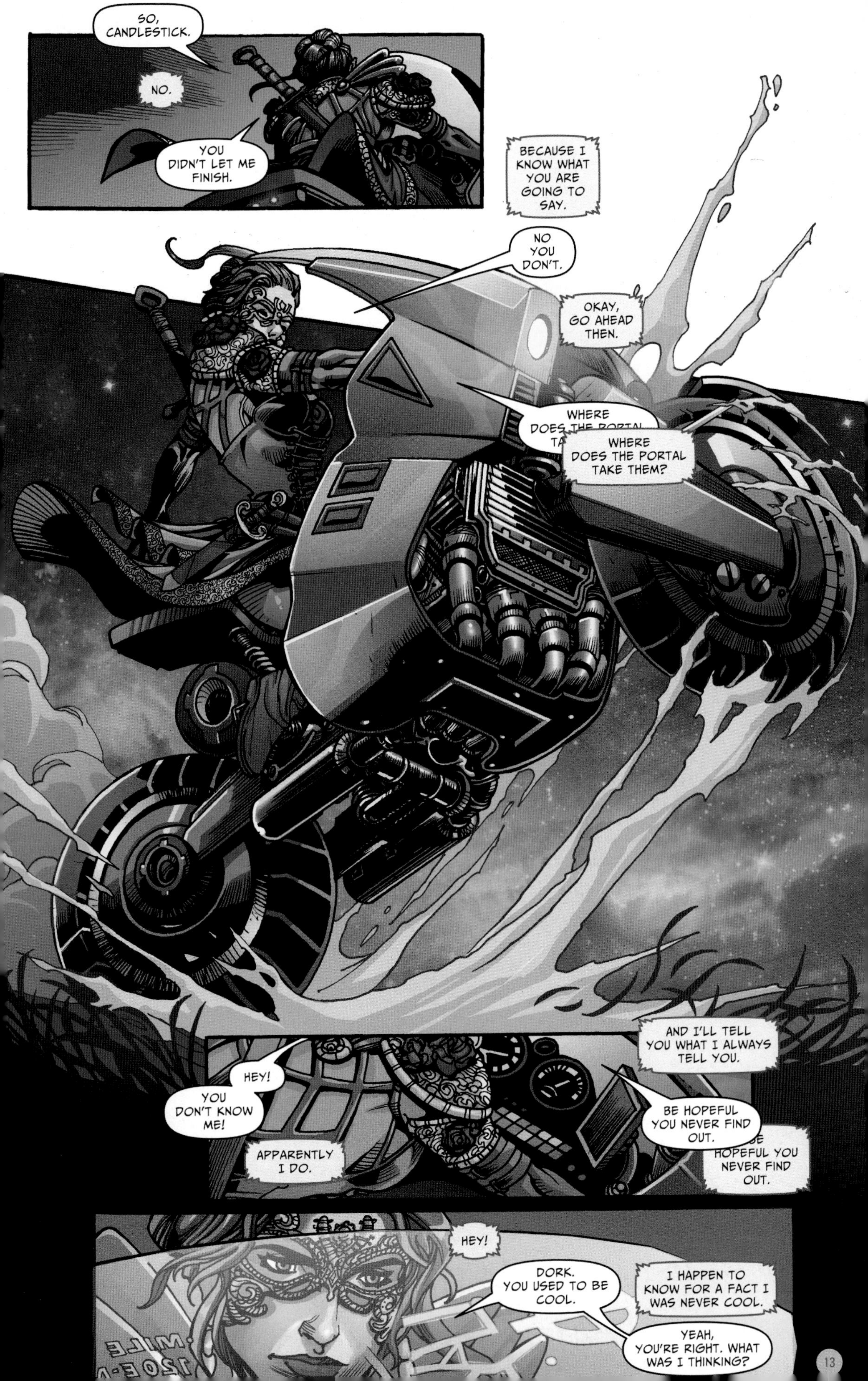

SO, CANDLESTICK.
NO.
YOU DIDN'T LET ME FINISH.
BECAUSE I KNOW WHAT YOU ARE GOING TO SAY.
NO YOU DON'T.
OKAY, GO AHEAD THEN.
WHERE
WHERE DOES THE PORTAL TAKE THEM?
AND I'LL TELL YOU WHAT I ALWAYS TELL YOU.
HEY!
YOU DON'T KNOW ME!
APPARENTLY I DO.
BE HOPEFUL YOU NEVER FIND OUT.
HOPEFUL YOU NEVER FIND OUT.
HEY!
DORK. YOU USED TO BE COOL.
I HAPPEN TO KNOW FOR A FACT I WAS NEVER COOL.
YEAH, YOU'RE RIGHT. WHAT WAS I THINKING?

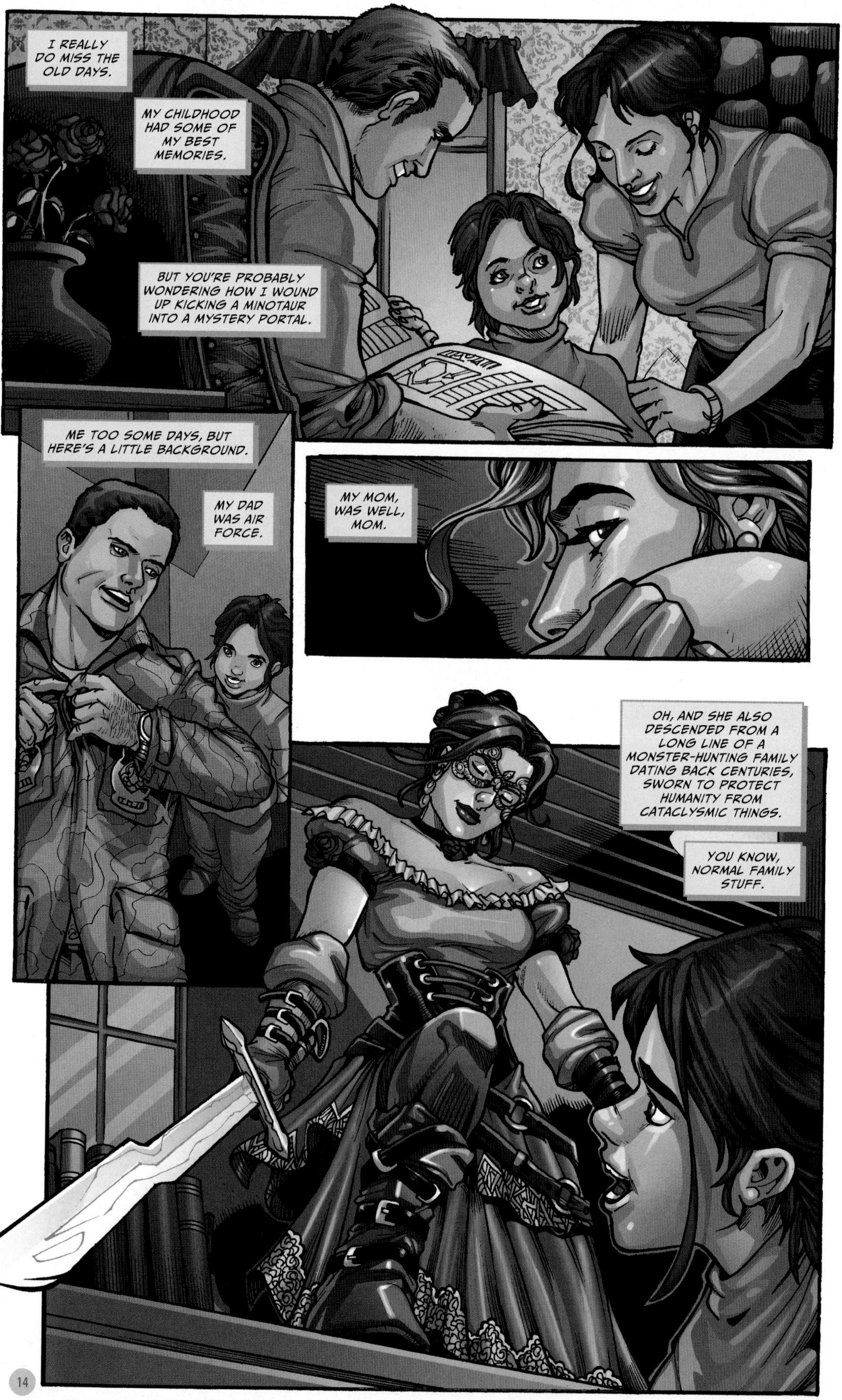
I REALLY DO MISS THE OLD DAYS.
MY CHILDHOOD HAD SOME OF MY BEST MEMORIES.
BUT YOU'RE PROBABLY WONDERING HOW I WOUND UP KICKING A MINOTAUR INTO A MYSTERY PORTAL.
ME TOO SOME DAYS, BUT HERE'S A LITTLE BACKGROUND.
MY DAD WAS AIR FORCE.
MY MOM, WAS WELL, MOM.
OH, AND SHE ALSO DESCENDED FROM A LONG LINE OF A MONSTER-HUNTING FAMILY DATING BACK CENTURIES, SWORN TO PROTECT HUMANITY FROM CATACLYSMIC THINGS.
YOU KNOW, NORMAL FAMILY STUFF.

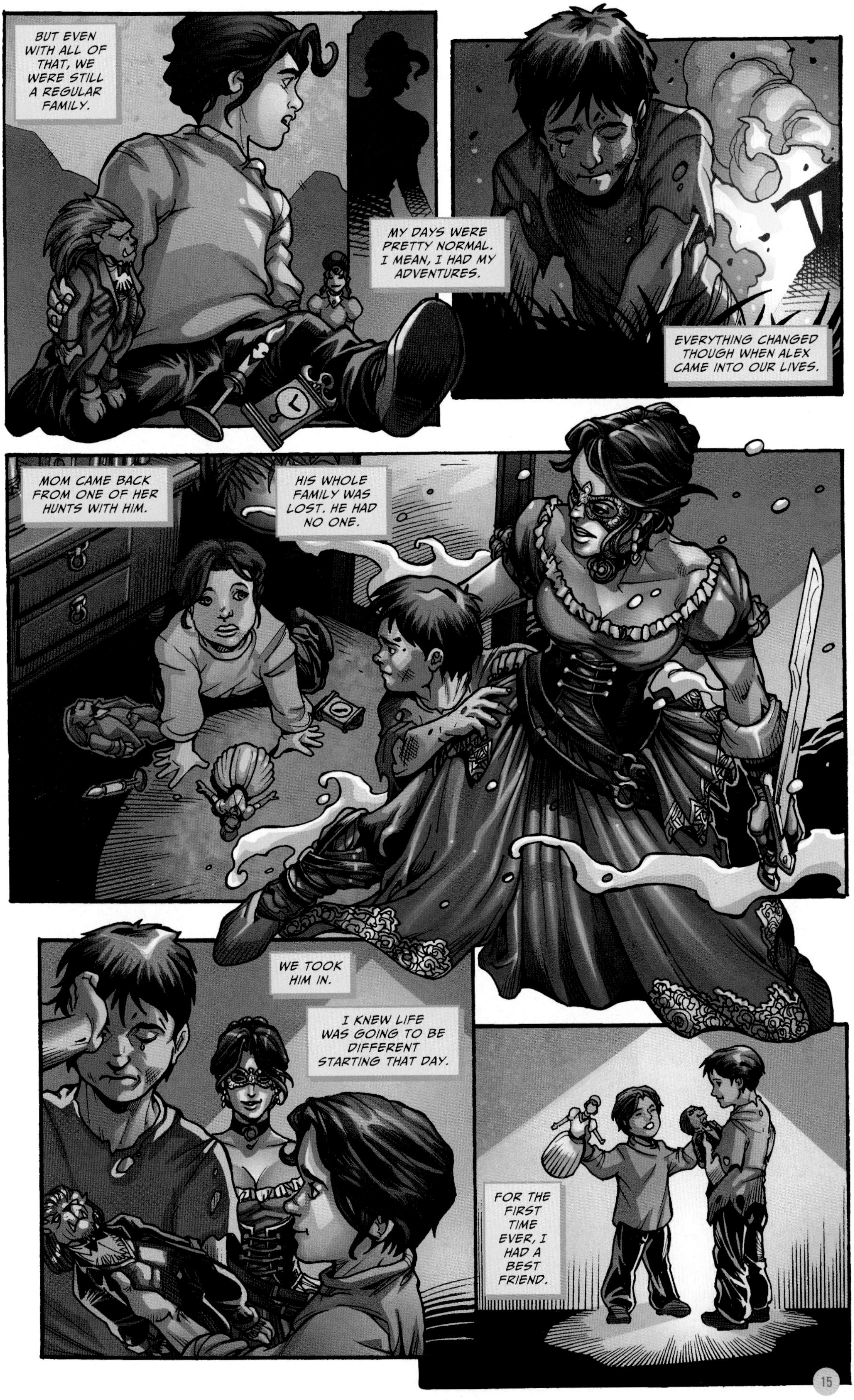
BUT EVEN WITH ALL OF THAT, WE WERE STILL A REGULAR FAMILY.
MY DAYS WERE PRETTY NORMAL. I MEAN, I HAD MY ADVENTURES.
EVERYTHING CHANGED THOUGH WHEN ALEX CAME INTO OUR LIVES.
MOM CAME BACK FROM ONE OF HER HUNTS WITH HIM.
HIS WHOLE FAMILY WAS LOST. HE HAD NO ONE.
WE TOOK HIM IN.
I KNEW LIFE WAS GOING TO BE DIFFERENT STARTING THAT DAY.
FOR THE FIRST TIME EVER, I HAD A BEST FRIEND.

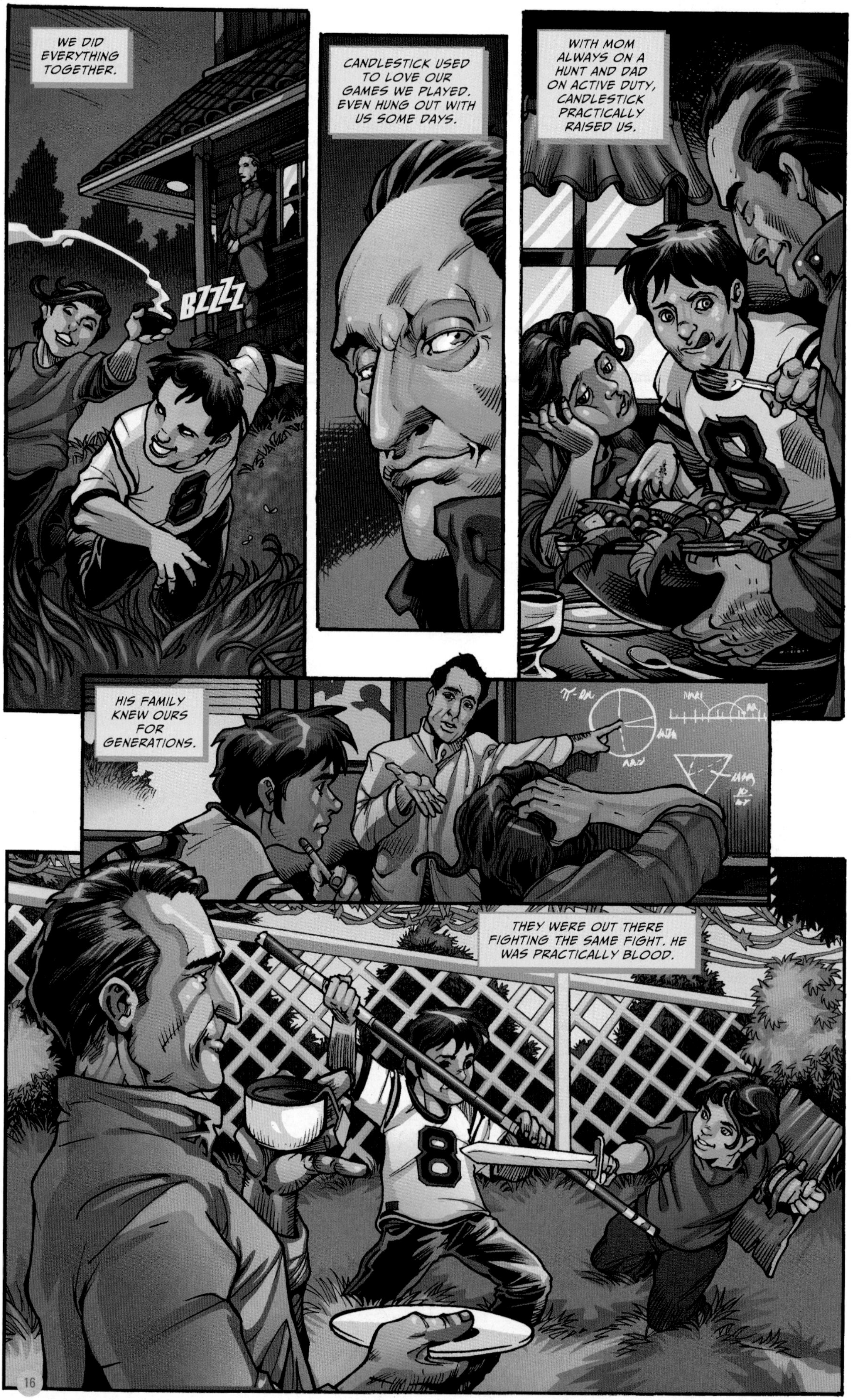
WE DID EVERYTHING TOGETHER.
BZZZZ
CANDLESTICK USED TO LOVE OUR GAMES WE PLAYED. EVEN HUNG OUT WITH US SOME DAYS.
WITH MOM ALWAYS ON A HUNT AND DAD ON ACTIVE DUTY, CANDLESTICK PRACTICALLY RAISED US.
HIS FAMILY KNEW OURS FOR GENERATIONS.
THEY WERE OUT THERE FIGHTING THE SAME FIGHT. HE WAS PRACTICALLY BLOOD.

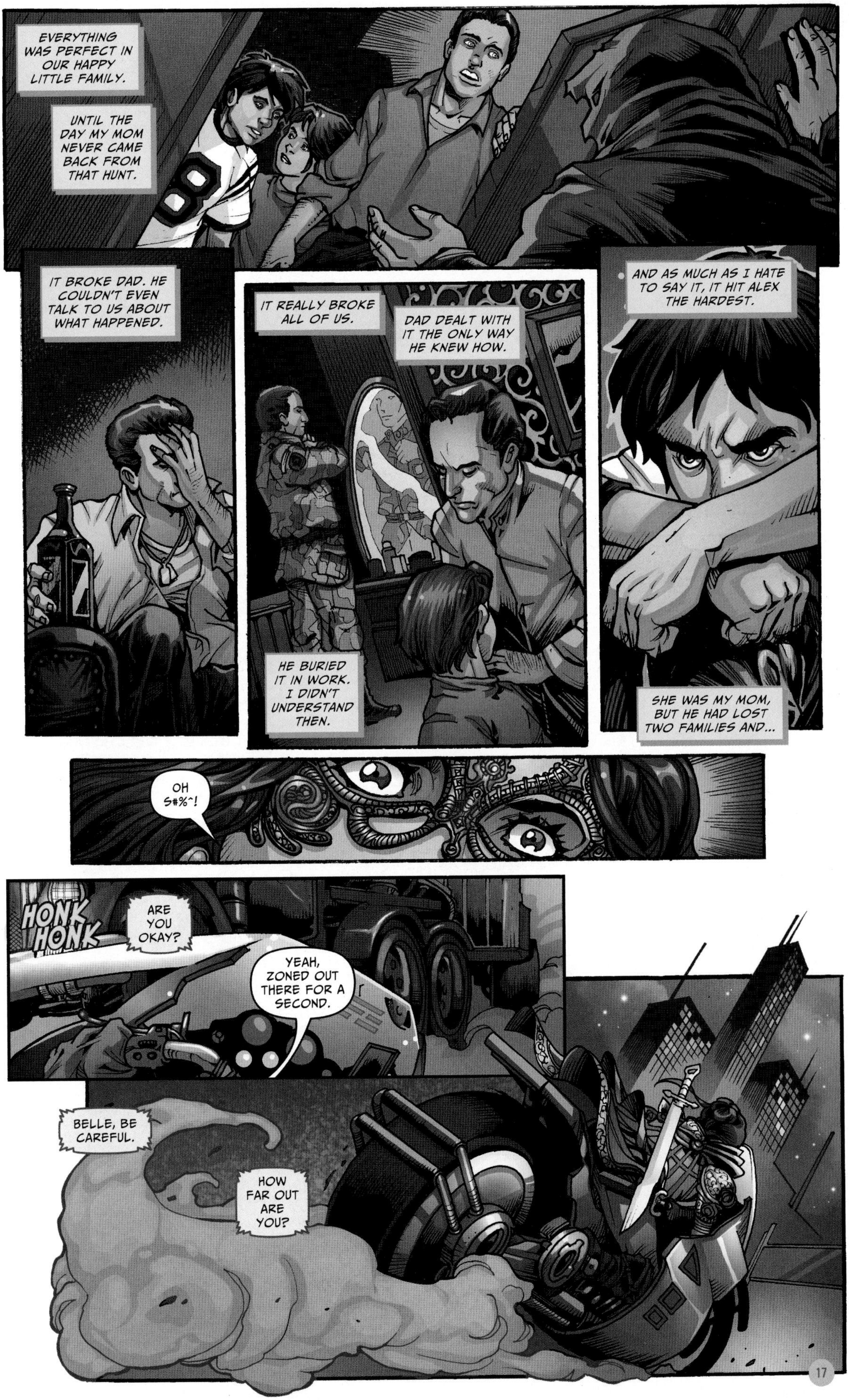
EVERYTHING WAS PERFECT IN OUR HAPPY LITTLE FAMILY.
UNTIL THE DAY MY MOM NEVER CAME BACK FROM THAT HUNT.
IT BROKE DAD. HE COULDN'T EVEN TALK TO US ABOUT WHAT HAPPENED.
IT REALLY BROKE ALL OF US.
DAD DEALT WITH IT THE ONLY WAY HE KNEW HOW.
HE BURIED IT IN WORK. I DIDN'T UNDERSTAND THEN.
AND AS MUCH AS I HATE TO SAY IT, IT HIT ALEX THE HARDEST.
SHE WAS MY MOM, BUT HE HAD LOST TWO FAMILIES AND...
OH S#%^!
HONK HONK
ARE YOU OKAY?
YEAH, ZONED OUT THERE FOR A SECOND.
BELLE, BE CAREFUL.
HOW FAR OUT ARE YOU?

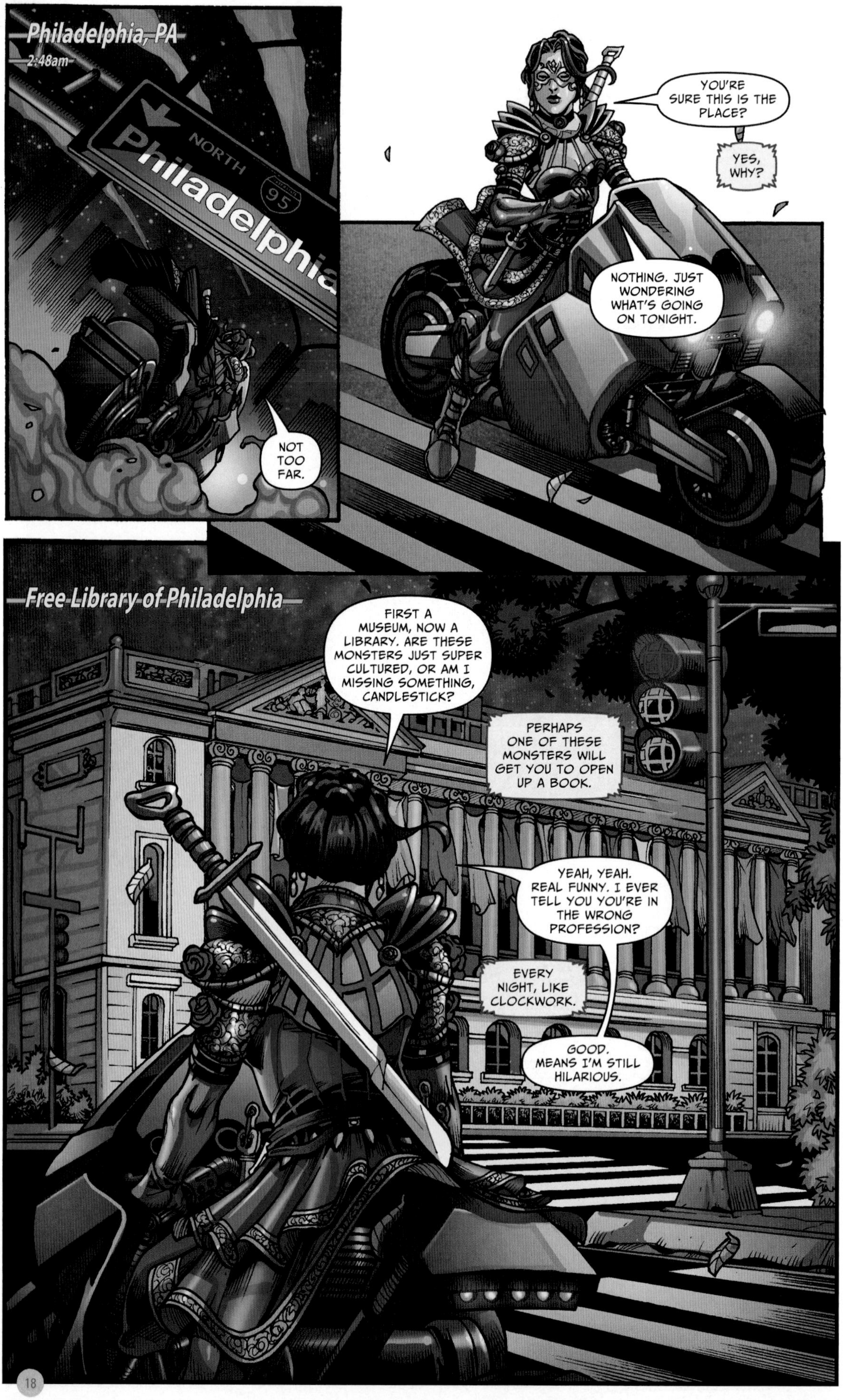
Philadelphia, PA
2:48am
NORTH
95
Philadelphia
YOU'RE SURE THIS IS THE PLACE?
YES, WHY?
NOTHING. JUST WONDERING WHAT'S GOING ON TONIGHT.
NOT TOO FAR.
Free Library of Philadelphia
FIRST A MUSEUM, NOW A LIBRARY. ARE THESE MONSTERS JUST SUPER CULTURED, OR AM I MISSING SOMETHING, CANDLESTICK?
PERHAPS ONE OF THESE MONSTERS WILL GET YOU TO OPEN UP A BOOK.
YEAH, YEAH. REAL FUNNY. I EVER TELL YOU YOU'RE IN THE WRONG PROFESSION?
EVERY NIGHT, LIKE CLOCKWORK.
GOOD. MEANS I'M STILL HILARIOUS.

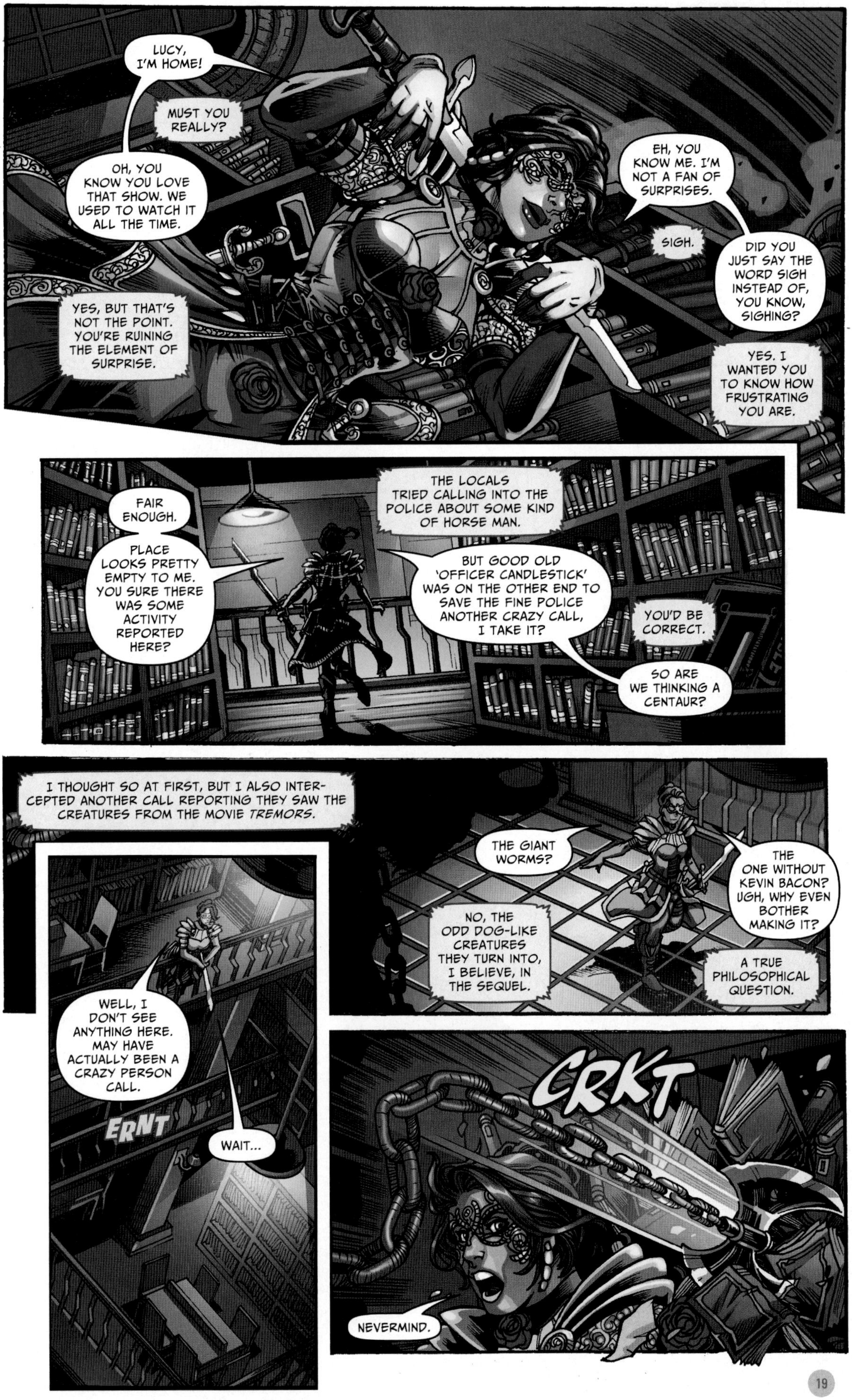
LUCY, I'M HOME!
MUST YOU REALLY?
OH, YOU KNOW YOU LOVE THAT SHOW. WE USED TO WATCH IT ALL THE TIME.
YES, BUT THAT'S NOT THE POINT. YOU'RE RUINING THE ELEMENT OF SURPRISE.
EH, YOU KNOW ME. I'M NOT A FAN OF SURPRISES.
SIGH.
DID YOU JUST SAY THE WORD SIGH INSTEAD OF, YOU KNOW, SIGHING?
YES. I WANTED YOU TO KNOW HOW FRUSTRATING YOU ARE.
FAIR ENOUGH.
PLACE LOOKS PRETTY EMPTY TO ME. YOU SURE THERE WAS SOME ACTIVITY REPORTED HERE?
THE LOCALS TRIED CALLING INTO THE POLICE ABOUT SOME KIND OF HORSE MAN.
BUT GOOD OLD 'OFFICER CANDLESTICK' WAS ON THE OTHER END TO SAVE THE FINE POLICE ANOTHER CRAZY CALL, I TAKE IT?
YOU'D BE CORRECT.
SO ARE WE THINKING A CENTAUR?
I THOUGHT SO AT FIRST, BUT I ALSO INTERCEPTED ANOTHER CALL REPORTING THEY SAW THE CREATURES FROM THE MOVIE *TREMORS*.
THE GIANT WORMS?
NO, THE ODD DOG-LIKE CREATURES THEY TURN INTO, I BELIEVE, IN THE SEQUEL.
THE ONE WITHOUT KEVIN BACON? UGH, WHY EVEN BOTHER MAKING IT?
A TRUE PHILOSOPHICAL QUESTION.
WELL, I DON'T SEE ANYTHING HERE. MAY HAVE ACTUALLY BEEN A CRAZY PERSON CALL.
ERNT
WAIT...
CRKT
NEVERMIND.

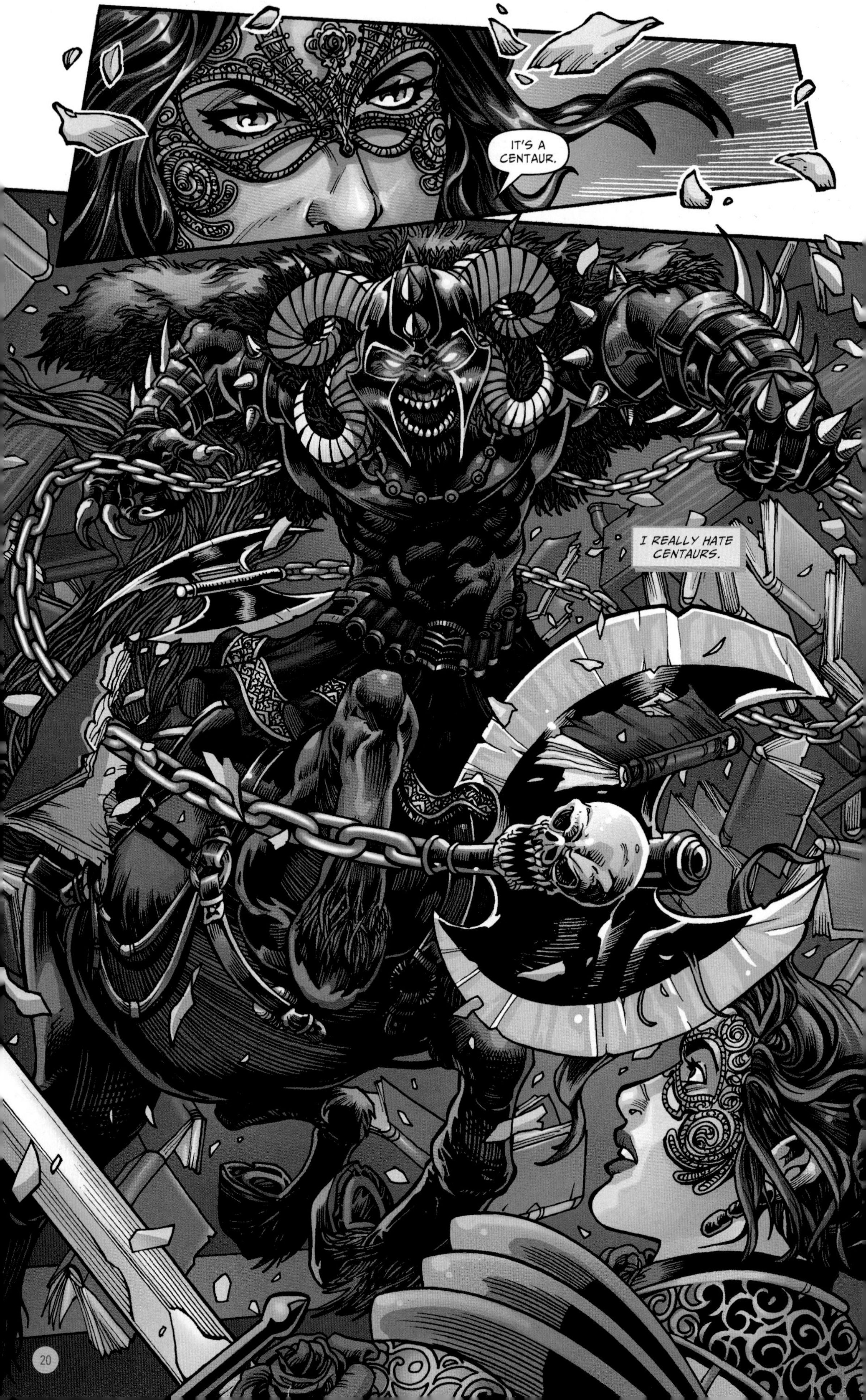
IT'S A CENTAUR.
I REALLY HATE CENTAURS.

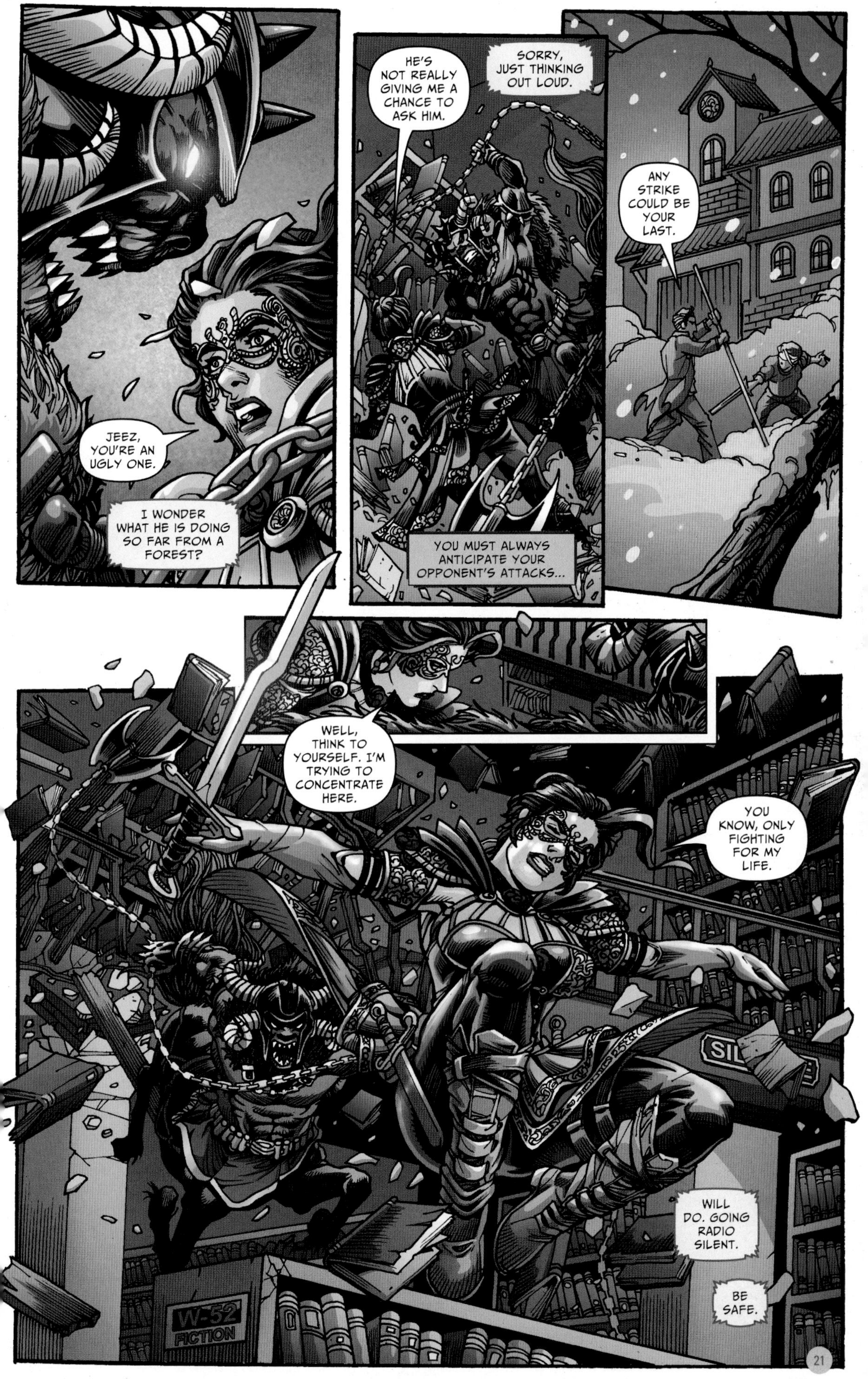
JEEZ, YOU'RE AN UGLY ONE.
I WONDER WHAT HE IS DOING SO FAR FROM A FOREST?
HE'S NOT REALLY GIVING ME A CHANCE TO ASK HIM.
SORRY, JUST THINKING OUT LOUD.
YOU MUST ALWAYS ANTICIPATE YOUR OPPONENT'S ATTACKS...
ANY STRIKE COULD BE YOUR LAST.
WELL, THINK TO YOURSELF. I'M TRYING TO CONCENTRATE HERE.
YOU KNOW, ONLY FIGHTING FOR MY LIFE.
W-52 FICTION
WILL DO. GOING RADIO SILENT.
BE SAFE.

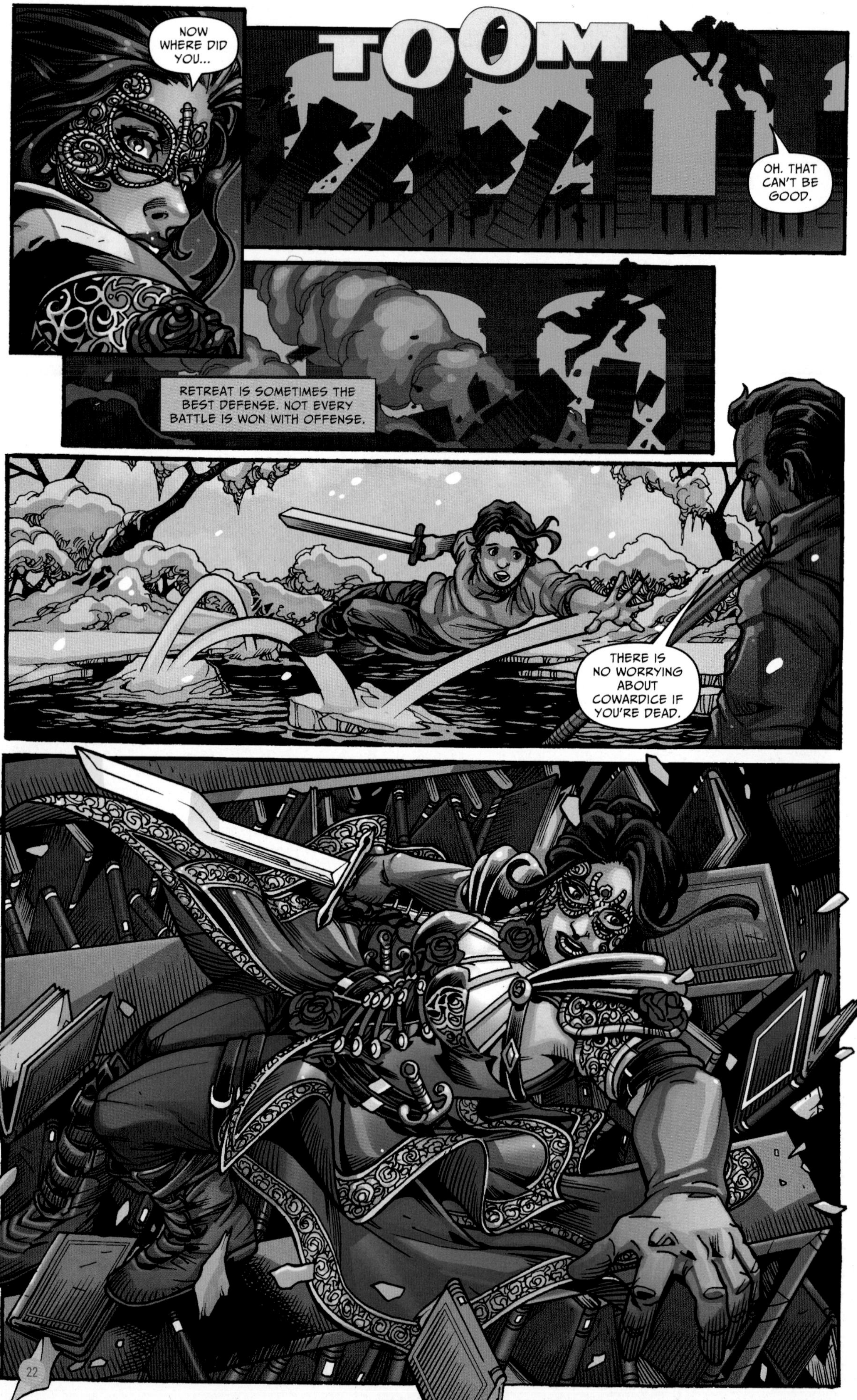
NOW WHERE DID YOU...
TOOM
OH. THAT CAN'T BE GOOD.
RETREAT IS SOMETIMES THE BEST DEFENSE. NOT EVERY BATTLE IS WON WITH OFFENSE.
THERE IS NO WORRYING ABOUT COWARDICE IF YOU'RE DEAD.

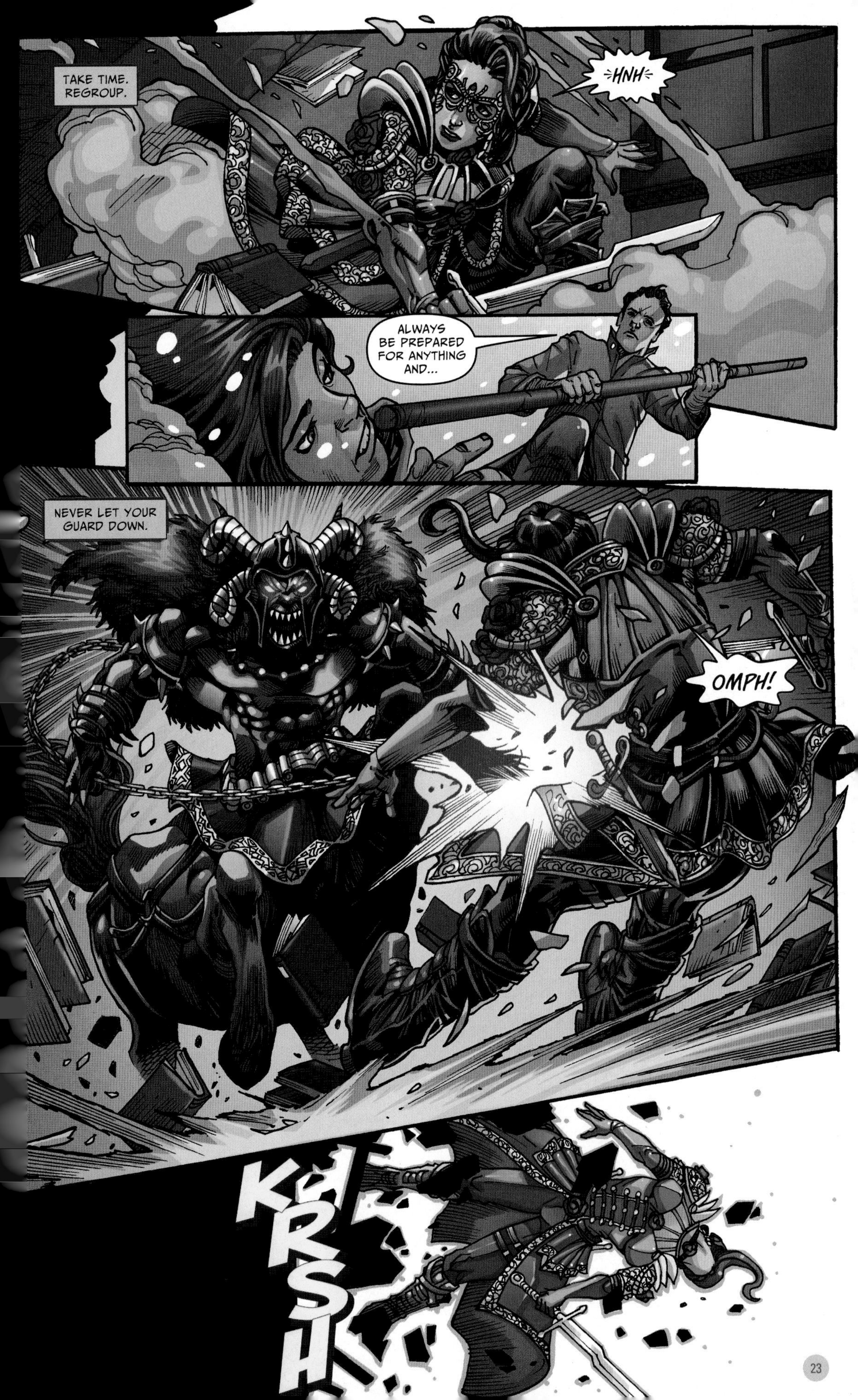
TAKE TIME. REGROUP.
HNH
ALWAYS BE PREPARED FOR ANYTHING AND...
NEVER LET YOUR GUARD DOWN.
OMPH!
KRSH

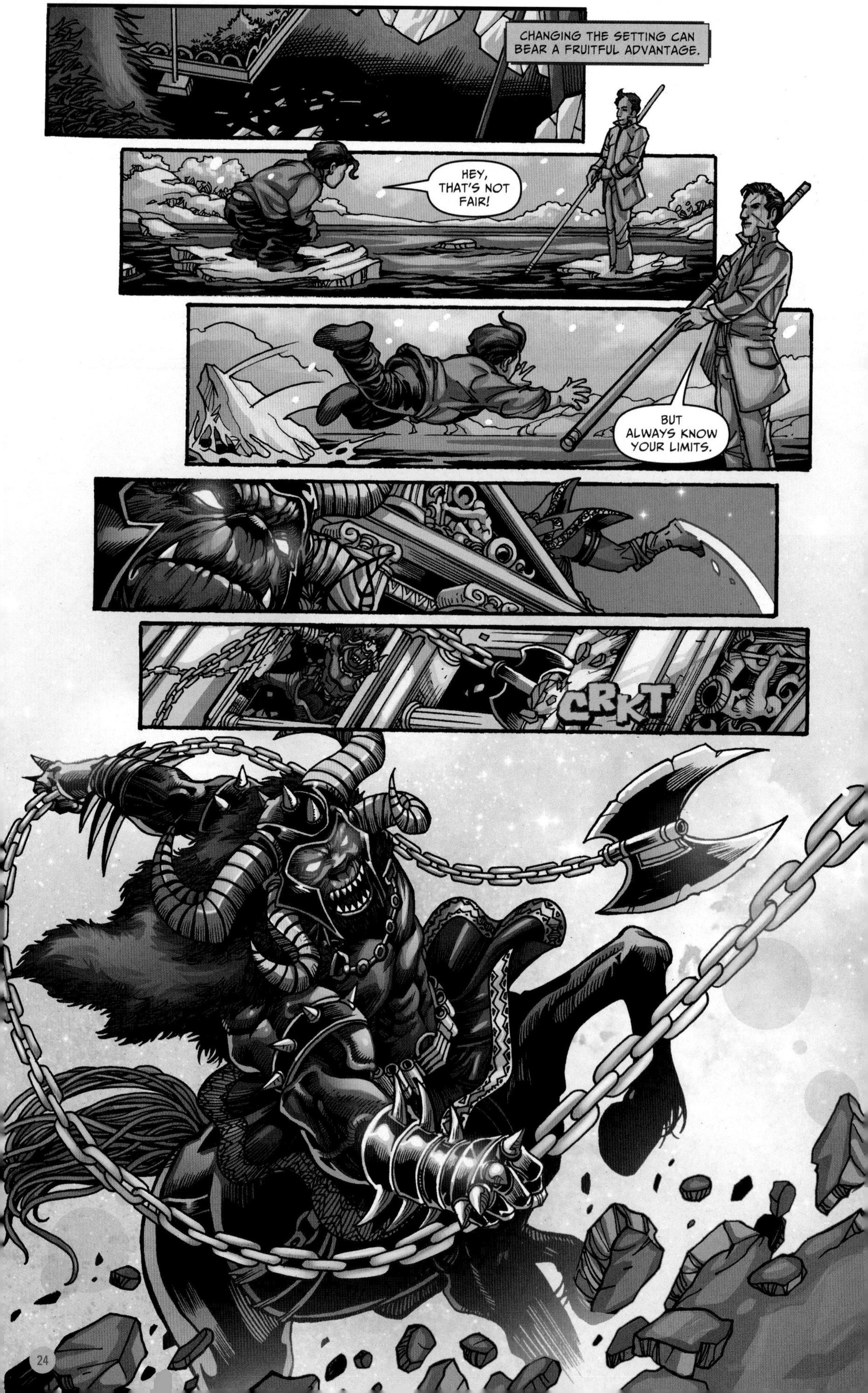
CHANGING THE SETTING CAN BEAR A FRUITFUL ADVANTAGE.
HEY, THAT'S NOT FAIR!
BUT ALWAYS KNOW YOUR LIMITS.
CRKT

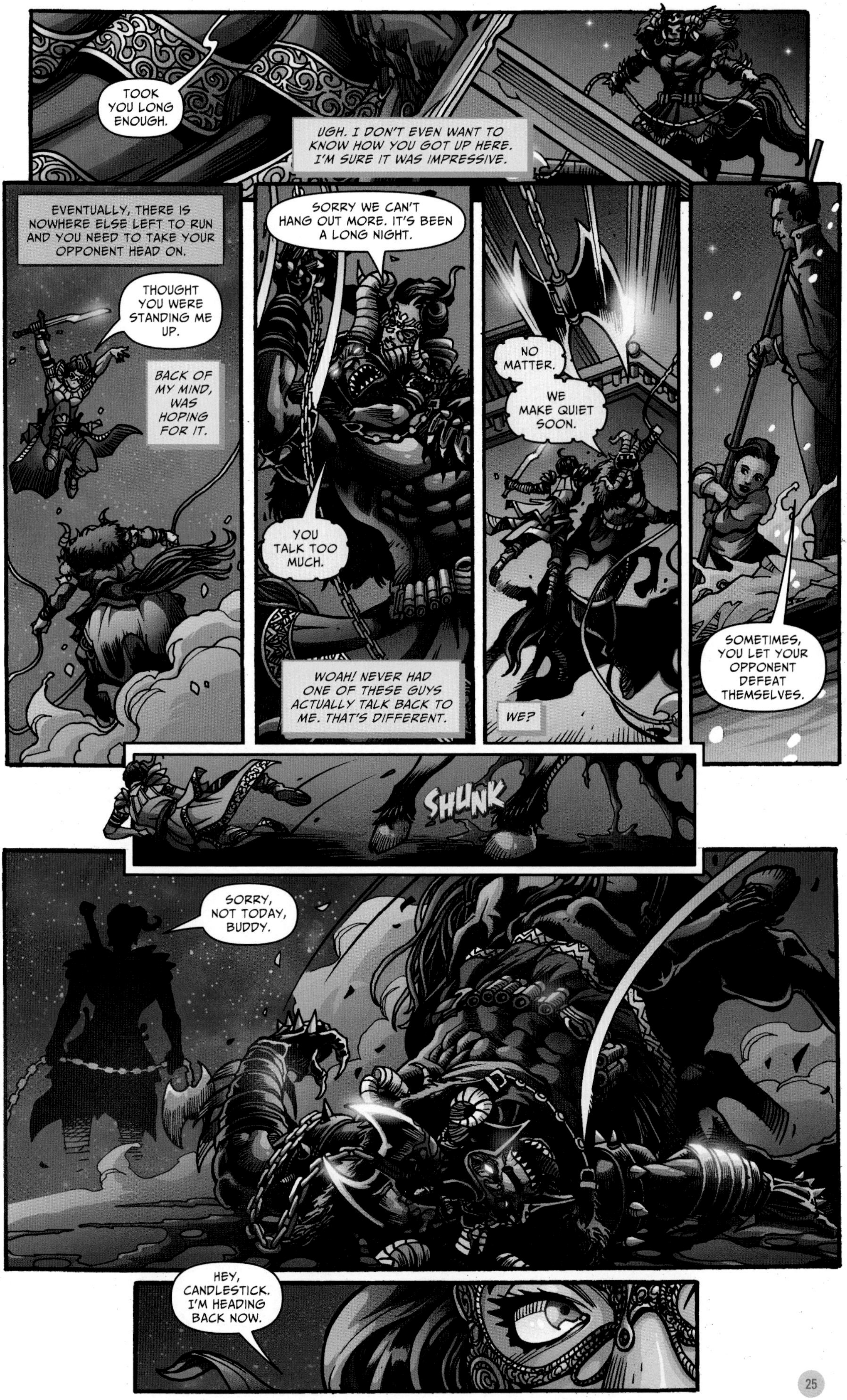
TOOK YOU LONG ENOUGH.
UGH. I DON'T EVEN WANT TO KNOW HOW YOU GOT UP HERE. I'M SURE IT WAS IMPRESSIVE.
EVENTUALLY, THERE IS NOWHERE ELSE LEFT TO RUN AND YOU NEED TO TAKE YOUR OPPONENT HEAD ON.
THOUGHT YOU WERE STANDING ME UP.
BACK OF MY MIND, WAS HOPING FOR IT.
SORRY WE CAN'T HANG OUT MORE. IT'S BEEN A LONG NIGHT.
YOU TALK TOO MUCH.
WOAH! NEVER HAD ONE OF THESE GUYS ACTUALLY TALK BACK TO ME. THAT'S DIFFERENT.
NO MATTER.
WE MAKE QUIET SOON.
WE?
SOMETIMES, YOU LET YOUR OPPONENT DEFEAT THEMSELVES.
SHUNK
SORRY, NOT TODAY, BUDDY.
HEY, CANDLESTICK. I'M HEADING BACK NOW.

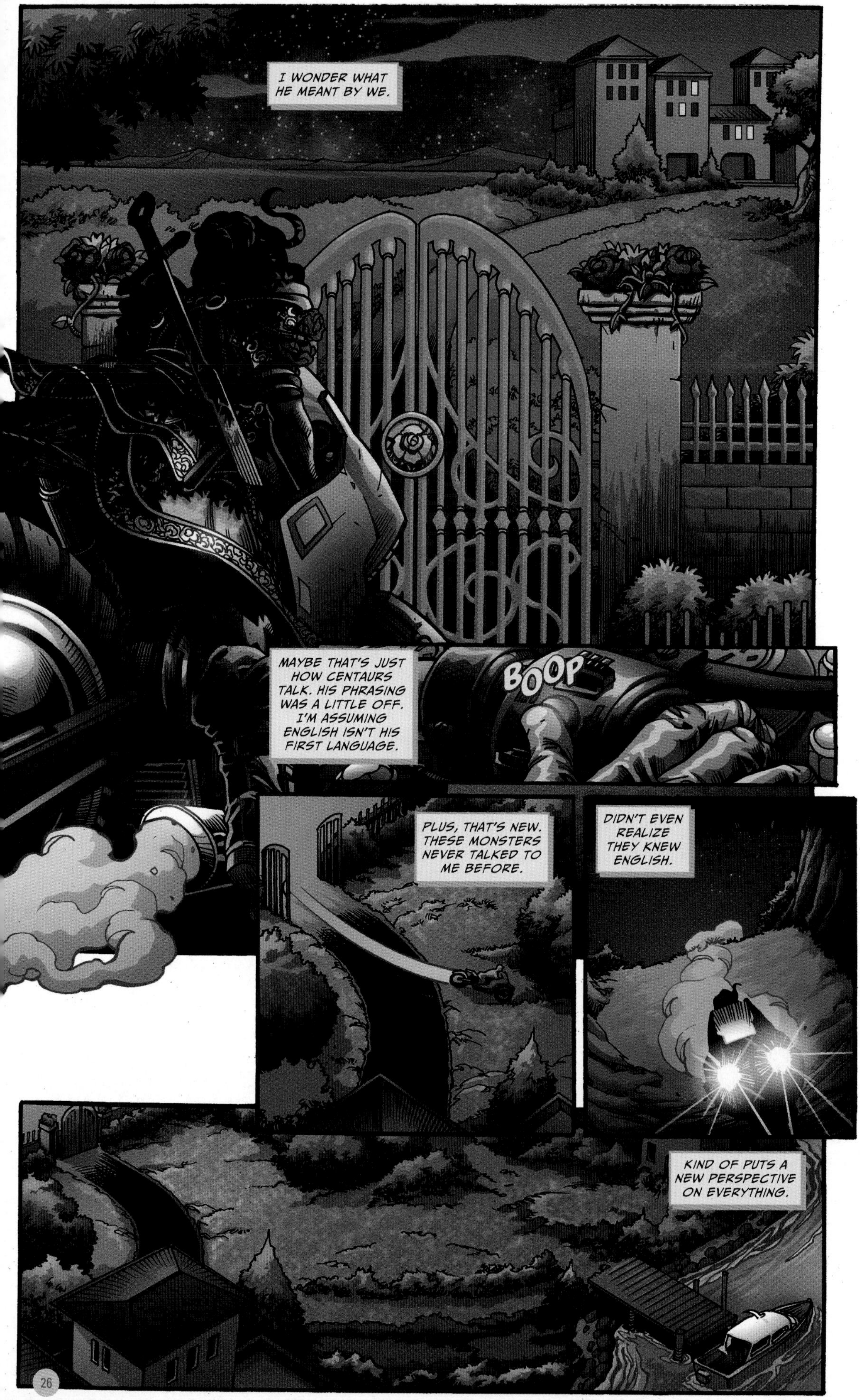
I WONDER WHAT HE MEANT BY WE.
MAYBE THAT'S JUST HOW CENTAURS TALK. HIS PHRASING WAS A LITTLE OFF. I'M ASSUMING ENGLISH ISN'T HIS FIRST LANGUAGE.
BOOP
PLUS, THAT'S NEW. THESE MONSTERS NEVER TALKED TO ME BEFORE.
DIDN'T EVEN REALIZE THEY KNEW ENGLISH.
KIND OF PUTS A NEW PERSPECTIVE ON EVERYTHING.

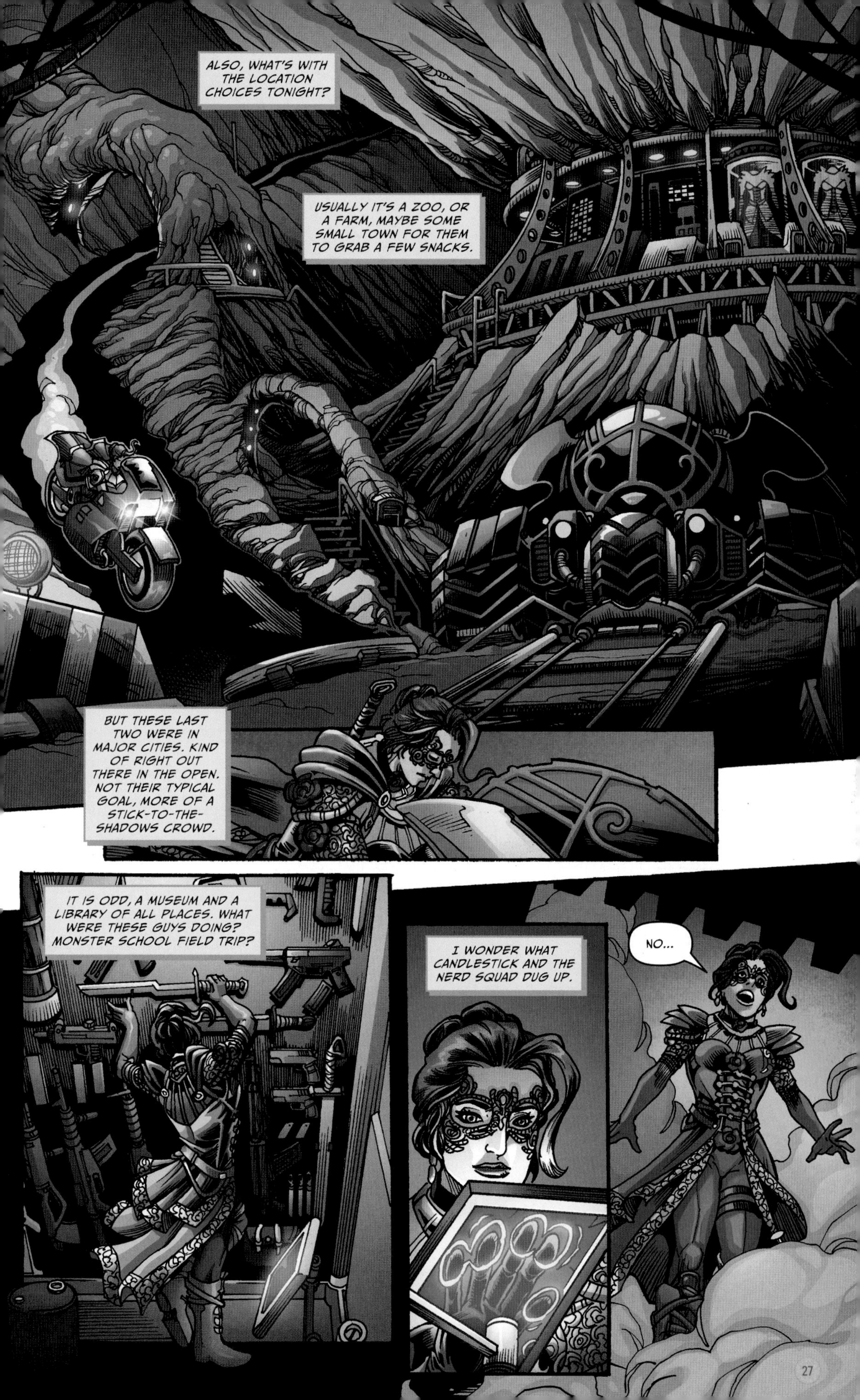

ALSO, WHAT'S WITH THE LOCATION CHOICES TONIGHT?
USUALLY IT'S A ZOO, OR A FARM, MAYBE SOME SMALL TOWN FOR THEM TO GRAB A FEW SNACKS.
BUT THESE LAST TWO WERE IN MAJOR CITIES. KIND OF RIGHT OUT THERE IN THE OPEN. NOT THEIR TYPICAL GOAL, MORE OF A STICK-TO-THE-SHADOWS CROWD.
IT IS ODD, A MUSEUM AND A LIBRARY OF ALL PLACES. WHAT WERE THESE GUYS DOING? MONSTER SCHOOL FIELD TRIP?
I WONDER WHAT CANDLESTICK AND THE NERD SQUAD DUG UP.
NO...

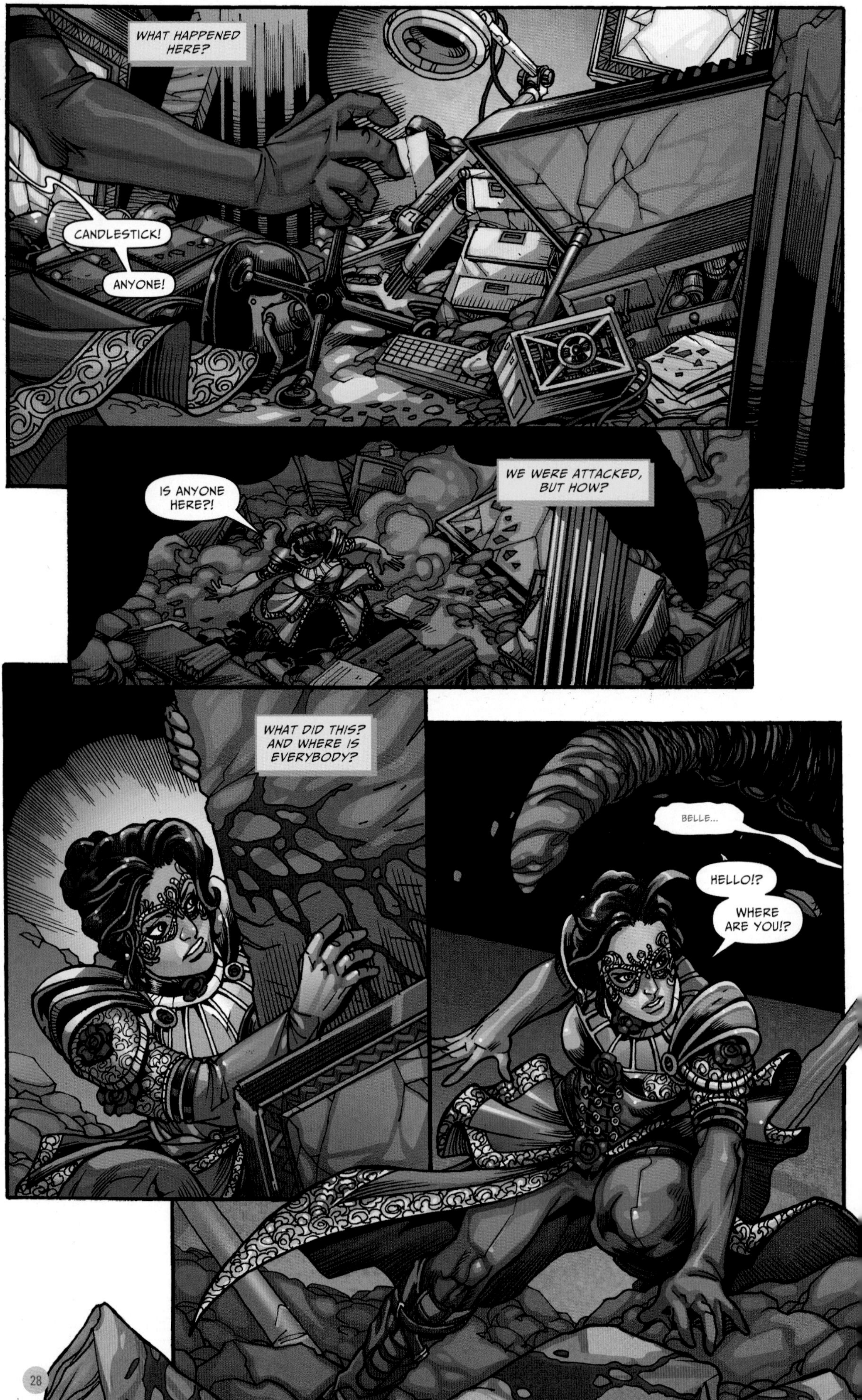
WHAT HAPPENED HERE?
CANDLESTICK!
ANYONE!
IS ANYONE HERE?!
WE WERE ATTACKED, BUT HOW?
WHAT DID THIS? AND WHERE IS EVERYBODY?
BELLE...
HELLO!?
WHERE ARE YOU!?

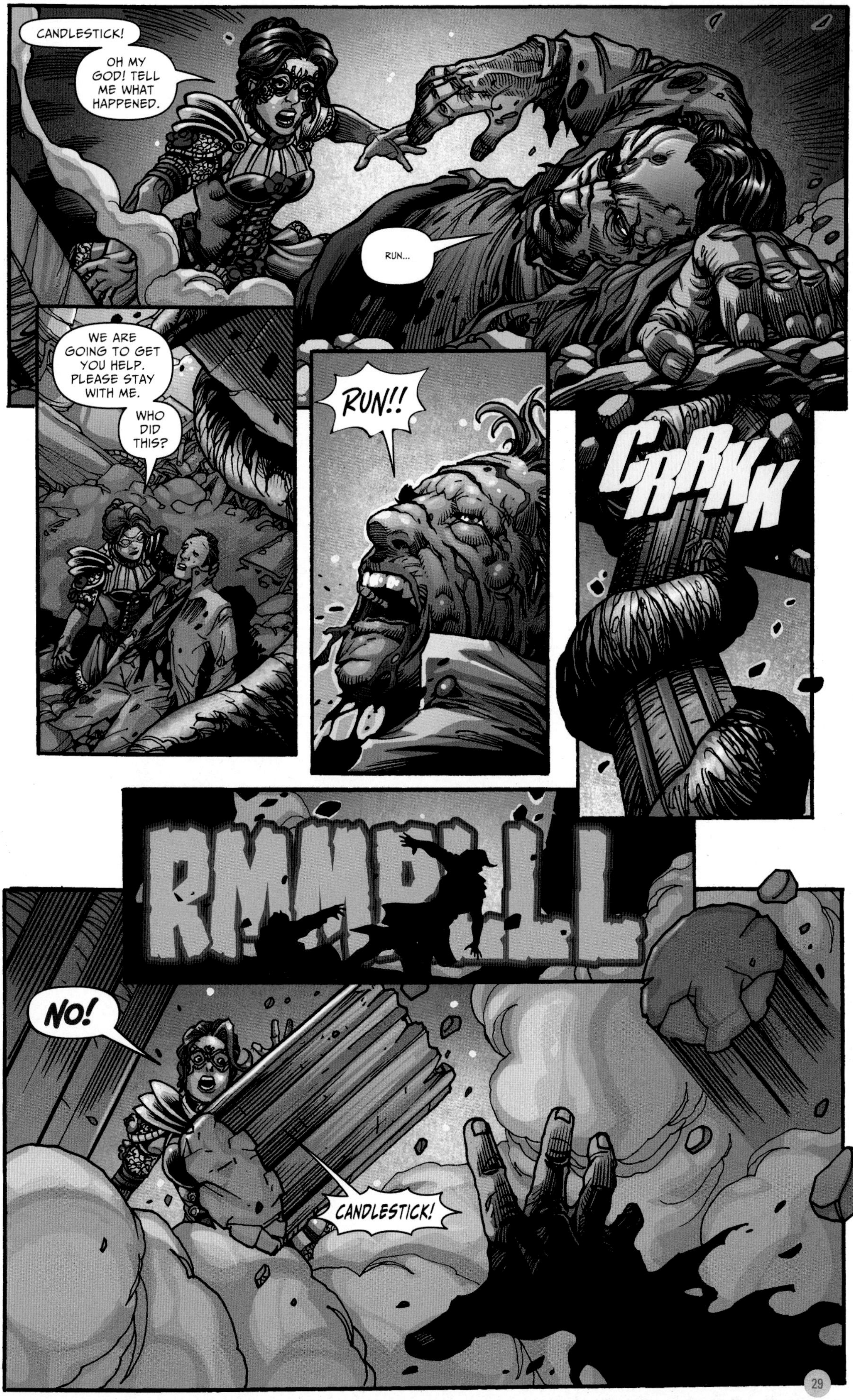
CANDLESTICK!
OH MY GOD! TELL ME WHAT HAPPENED.
RUN...
WE ARE GOING TO GET YOU HELP. PLEASE STAY WITH ME.
WHO DID THIS?
RUN!!
CRRKK
NO!
CANDLESTICK!

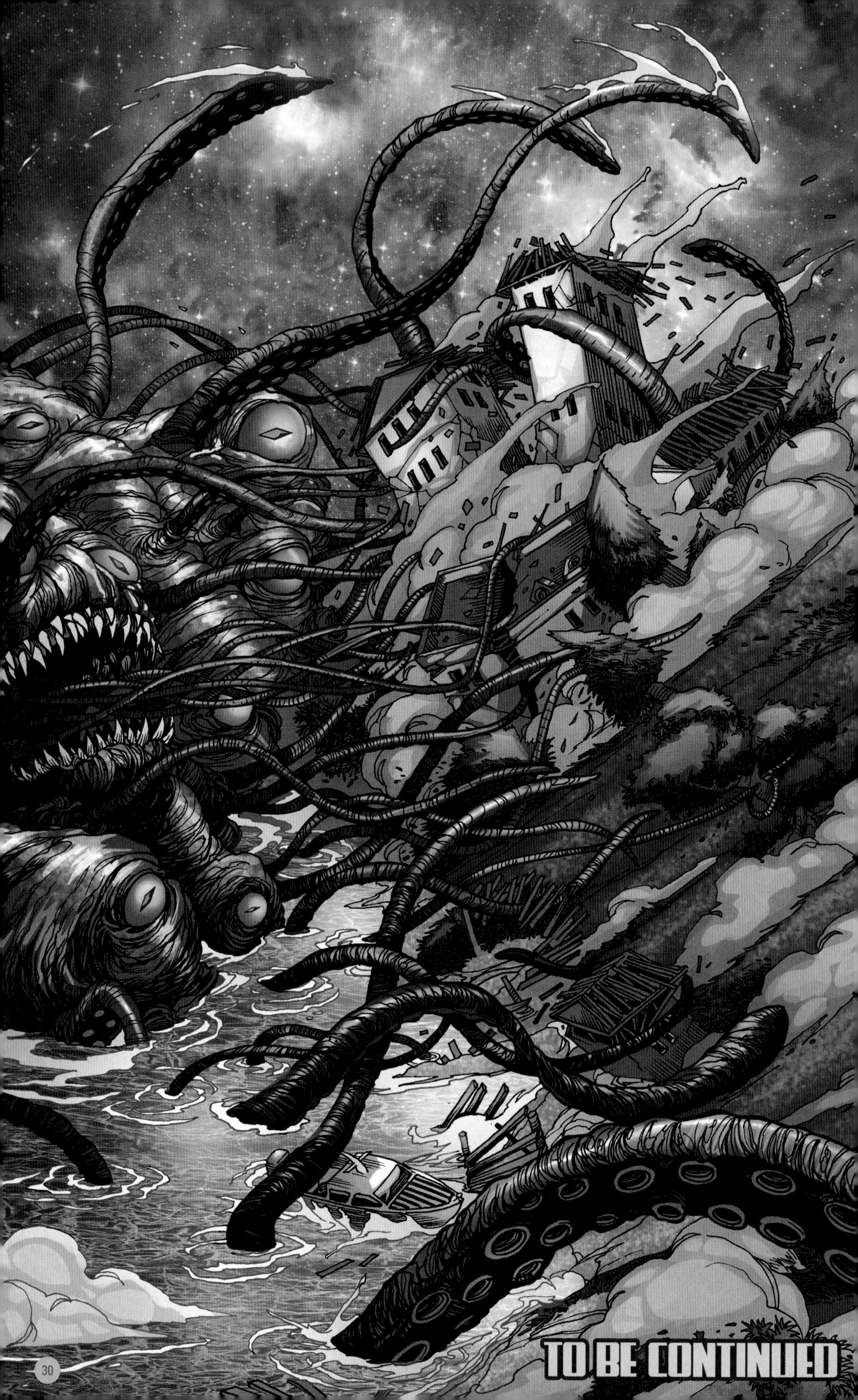
TO BE CONTINUED

BELLE
BEAST HUNTER

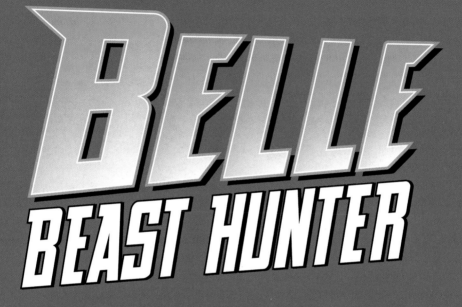

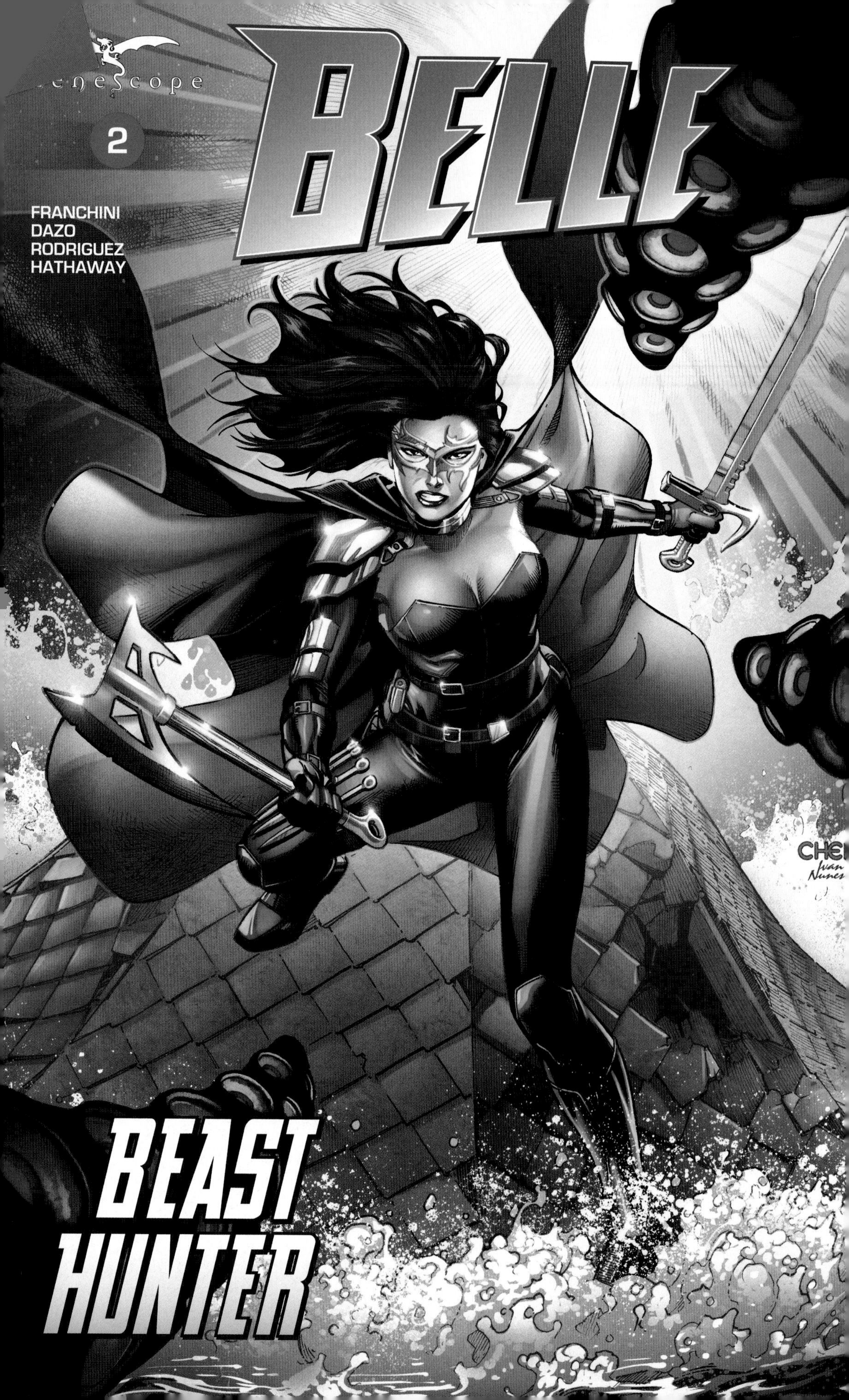
Zenescope
2
BELLE
FRANCHINI
DAZO
RODRIGUEZ
HATHAWAY
BEAST HUNTER

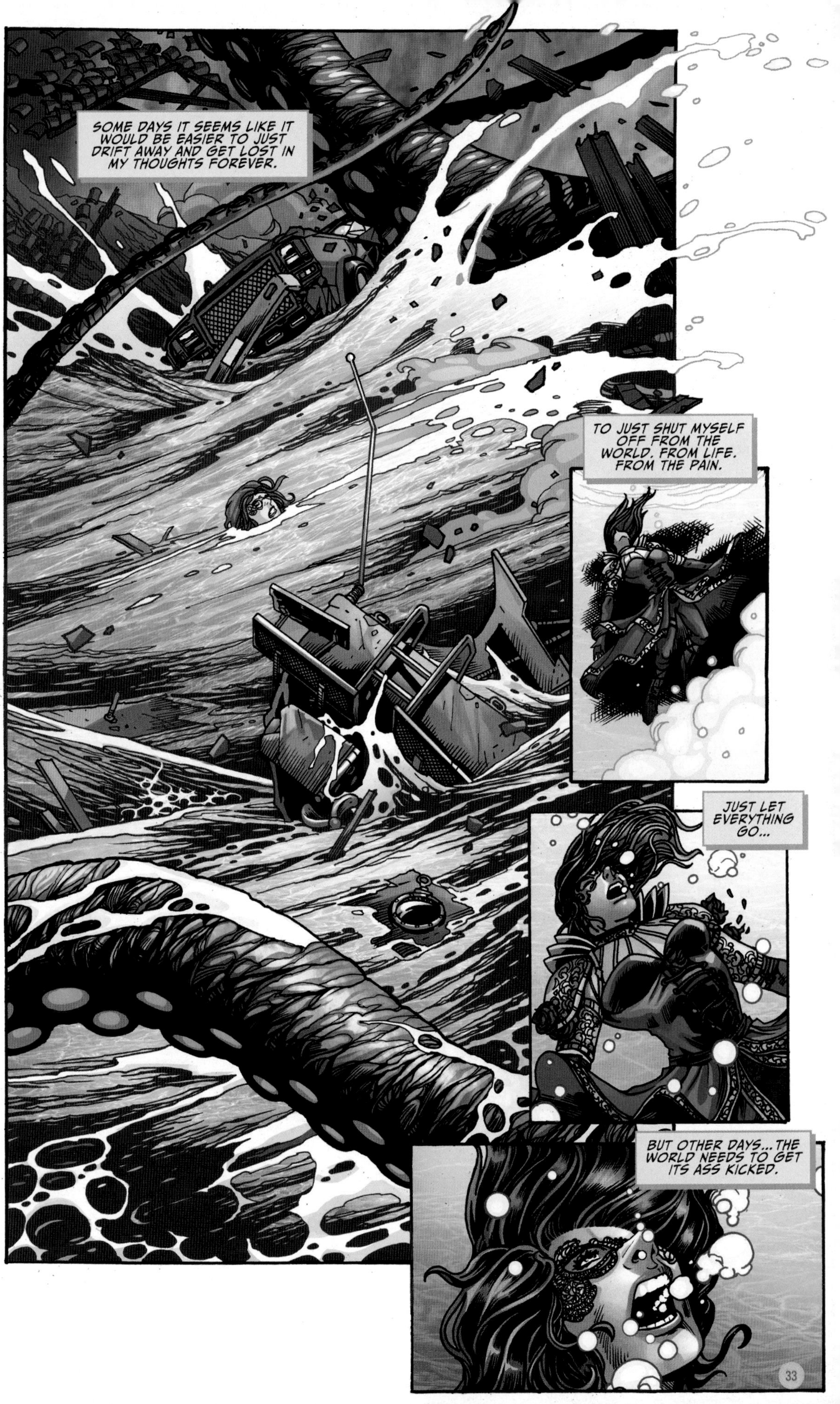
SOME DAYS IT SEEMS LIKE IT WOULD BE EASIER TO JUST DRIFT AWAY AND GET LOST IN MY THOUGHTS FOREVER.
TO JUST SHUT MYSELF OFF FROM THE WORLD. FROM LIFE. FROM THE PAIN.
JUST LET EVERYTHING GO...
BUT OTHER DAYS... THE WORLD NEEDS TO GET ITS ASS KICKED.

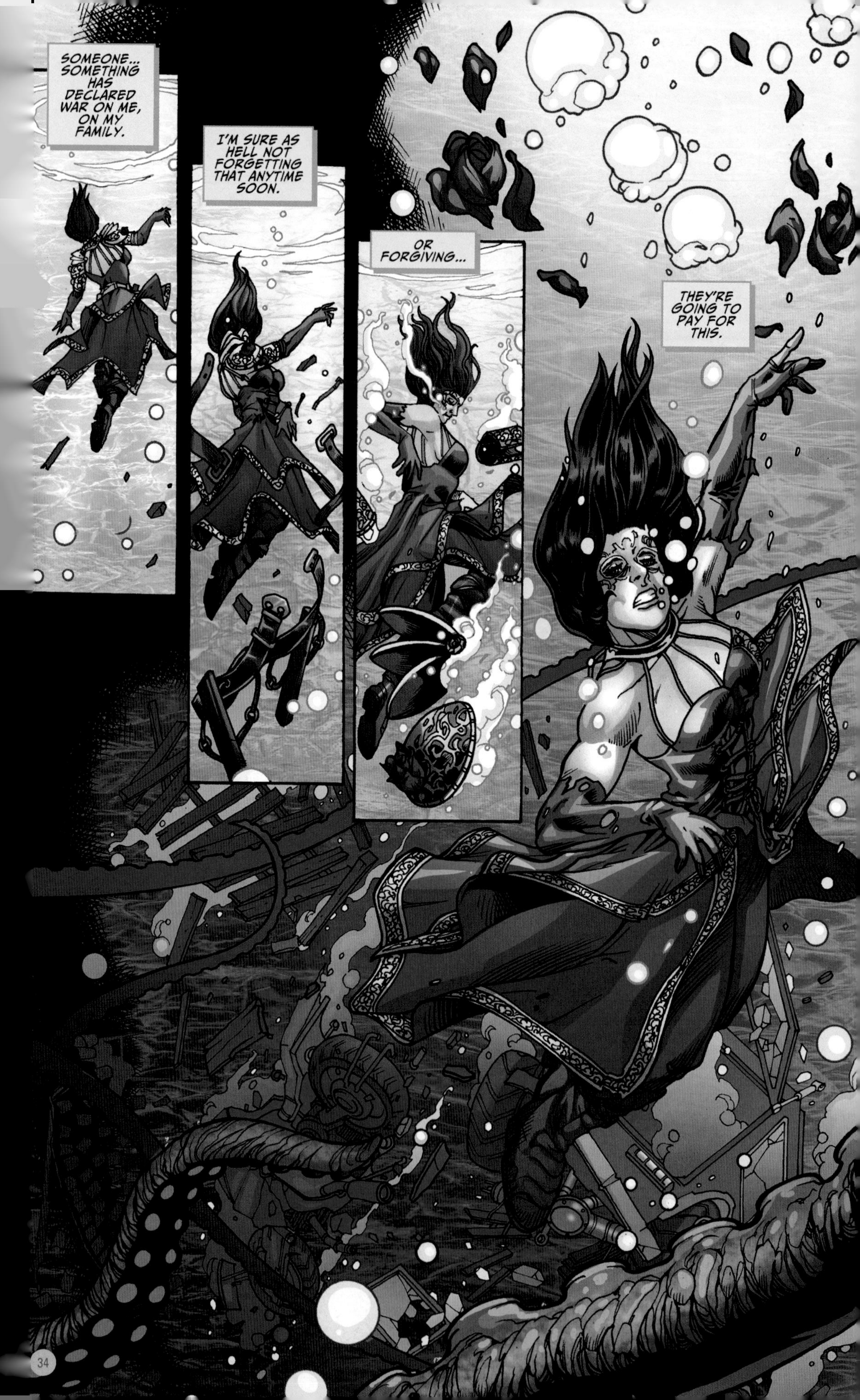
SOMEONE... SOMETHING HAS DECLARED WAR ON ME, ON MY FAMILY.
I'M SURE AS HELL NOT FORGETTING THAT ANYTIME SOON.
OR FORGIVING...
THEY'RE GOING TO PAY FOR THIS.

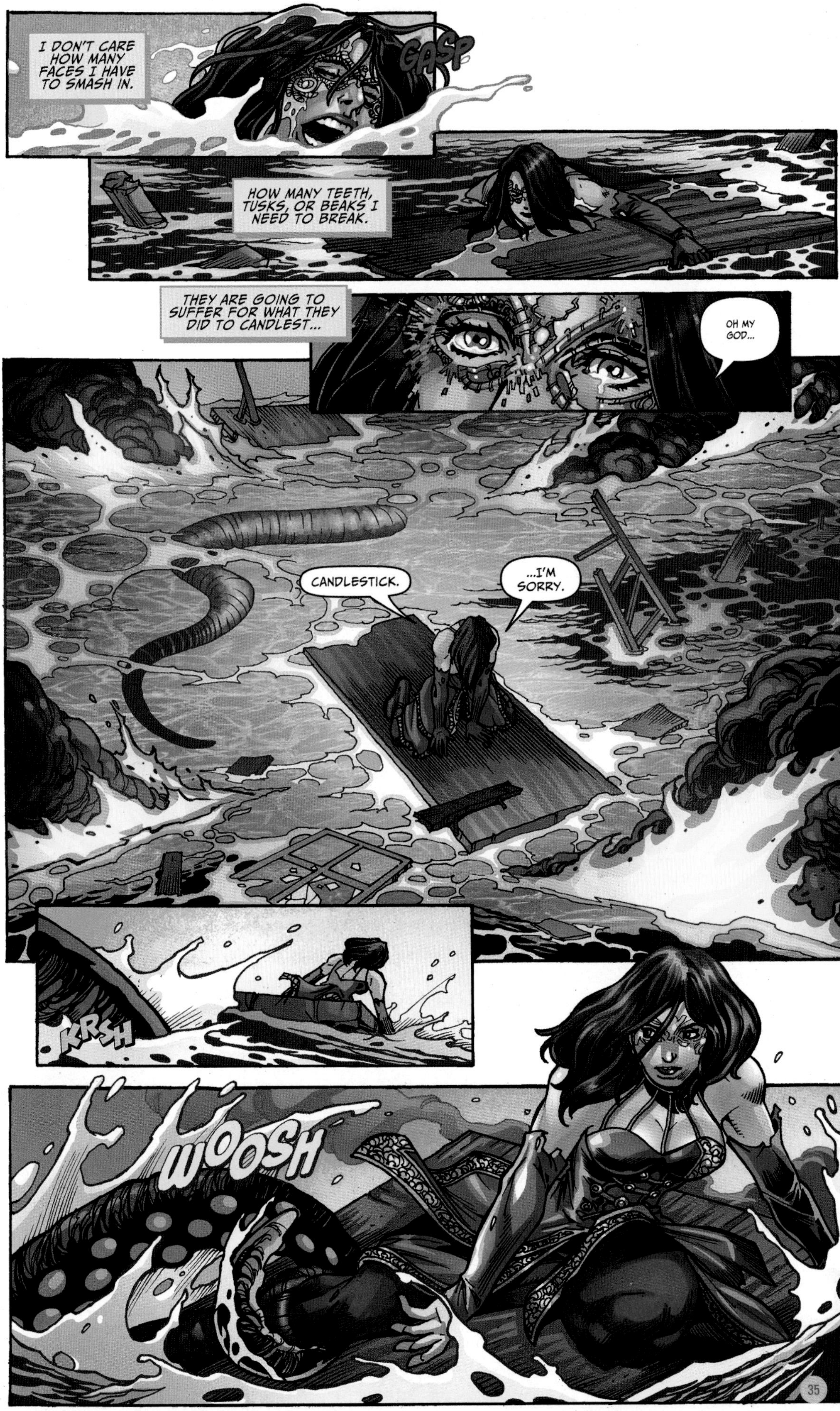
I DON'T CARE HOW MANY FACES I HAVE TO SMASH IN.
GASP
HOW MANY TEETH, TUSKS, OR BEAKS I NEED TO BREAK.
THEY ARE GOING TO SUFFER FOR WHAT THEY DID TO CANDLEST...
OH MY GOD...
CANDLESTICK.
...I'M SORRY.
KRSH
WOOSH

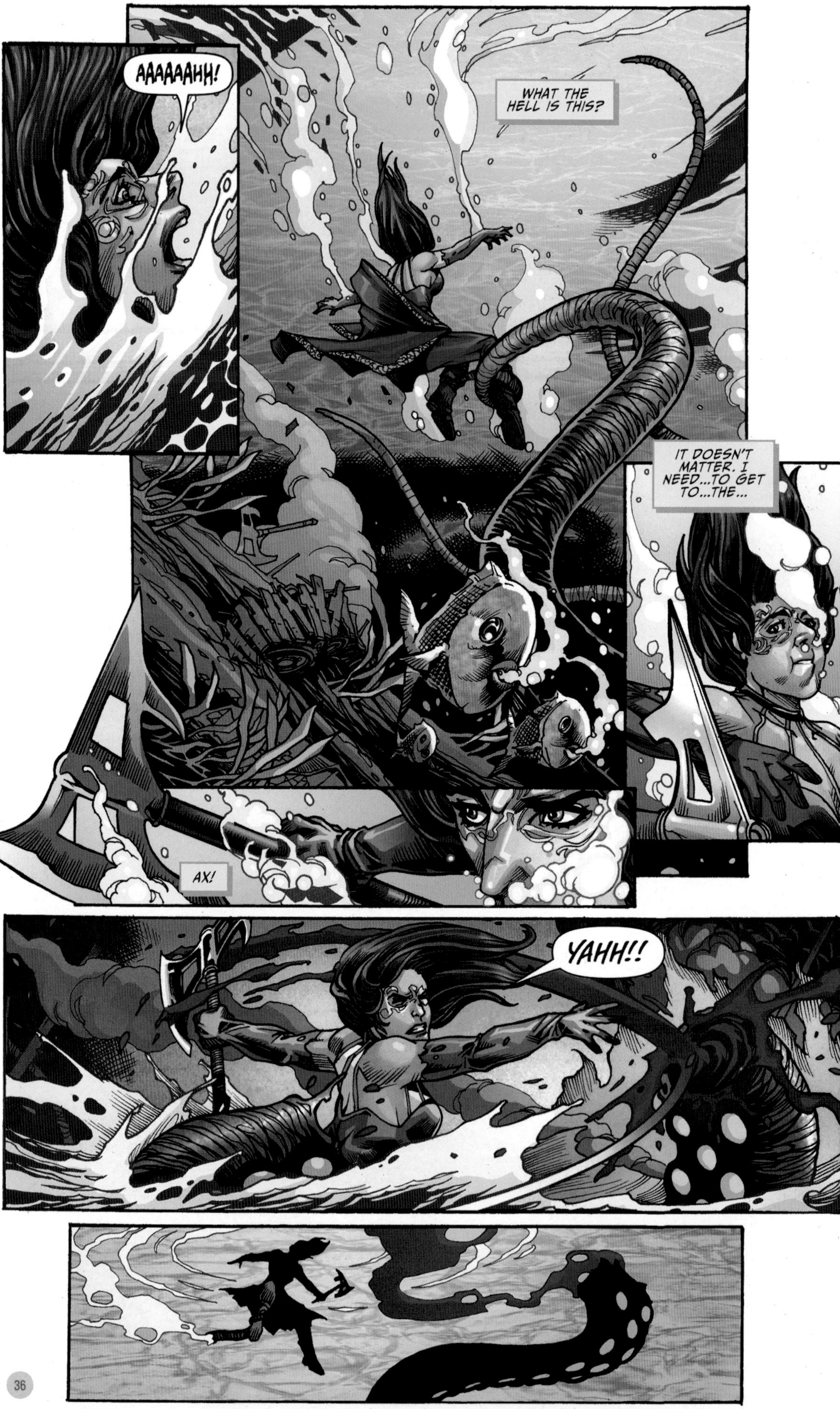
AAAAAAHH!
WHAT THE HELL IS THIS?
IT DOESN'T MATTER. I NEED...TO GET TO...THE...
AX!
YAHH!!

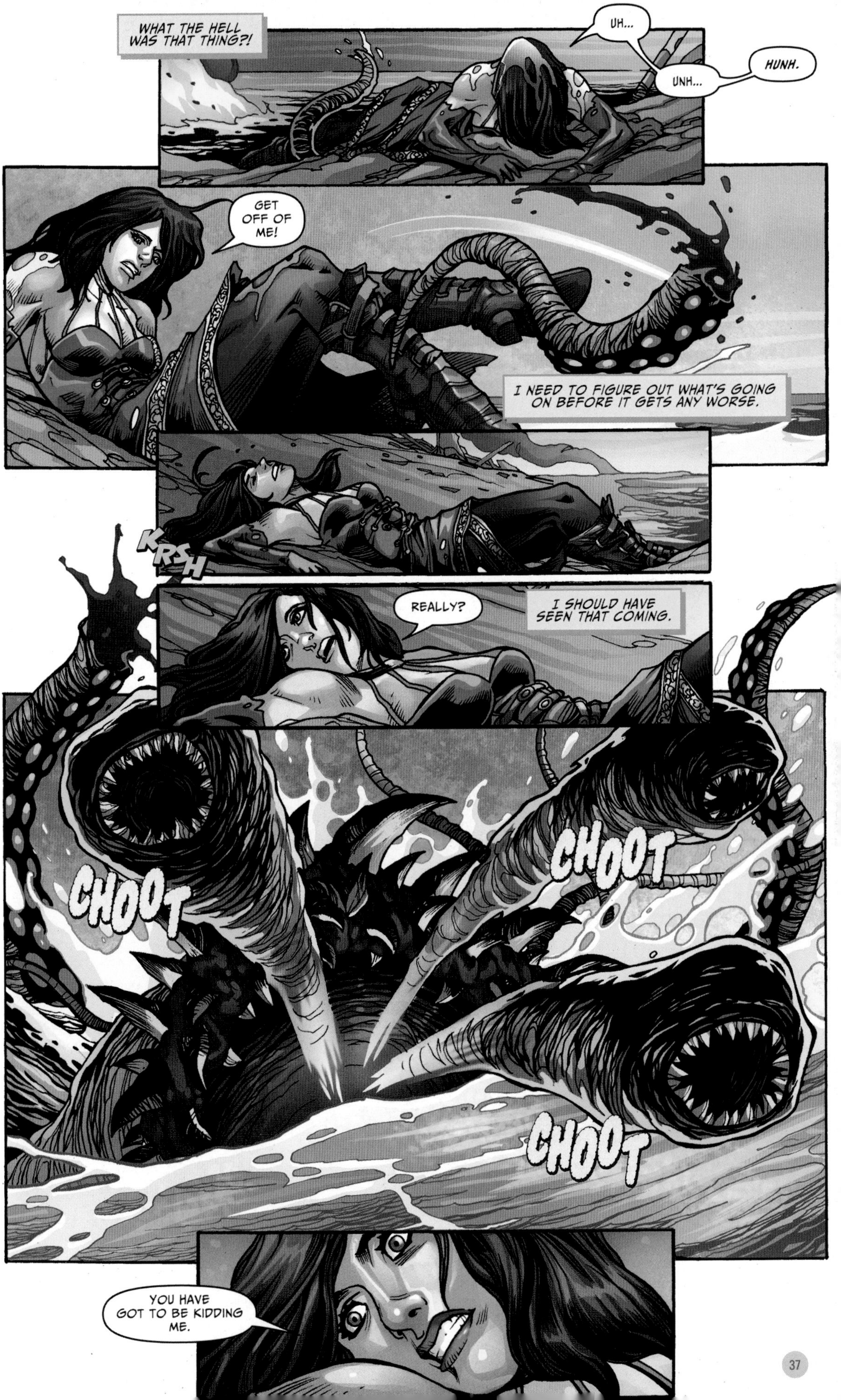
WHAT THE HELL WAS THAT THING?!
UH...
UNH...
HUNH.
GET OFF OF ME!
I NEED TO FIGURE OUT WHAT'S GOING ON BEFORE IT GETS ANY WORSE.
KRSH
REALLY?
I SHOULD HAVE SEEN THAT COMING.
CHOOT
CHOOT
CHOOT
YOU HAVE GOT TO BE KIDDING ME.

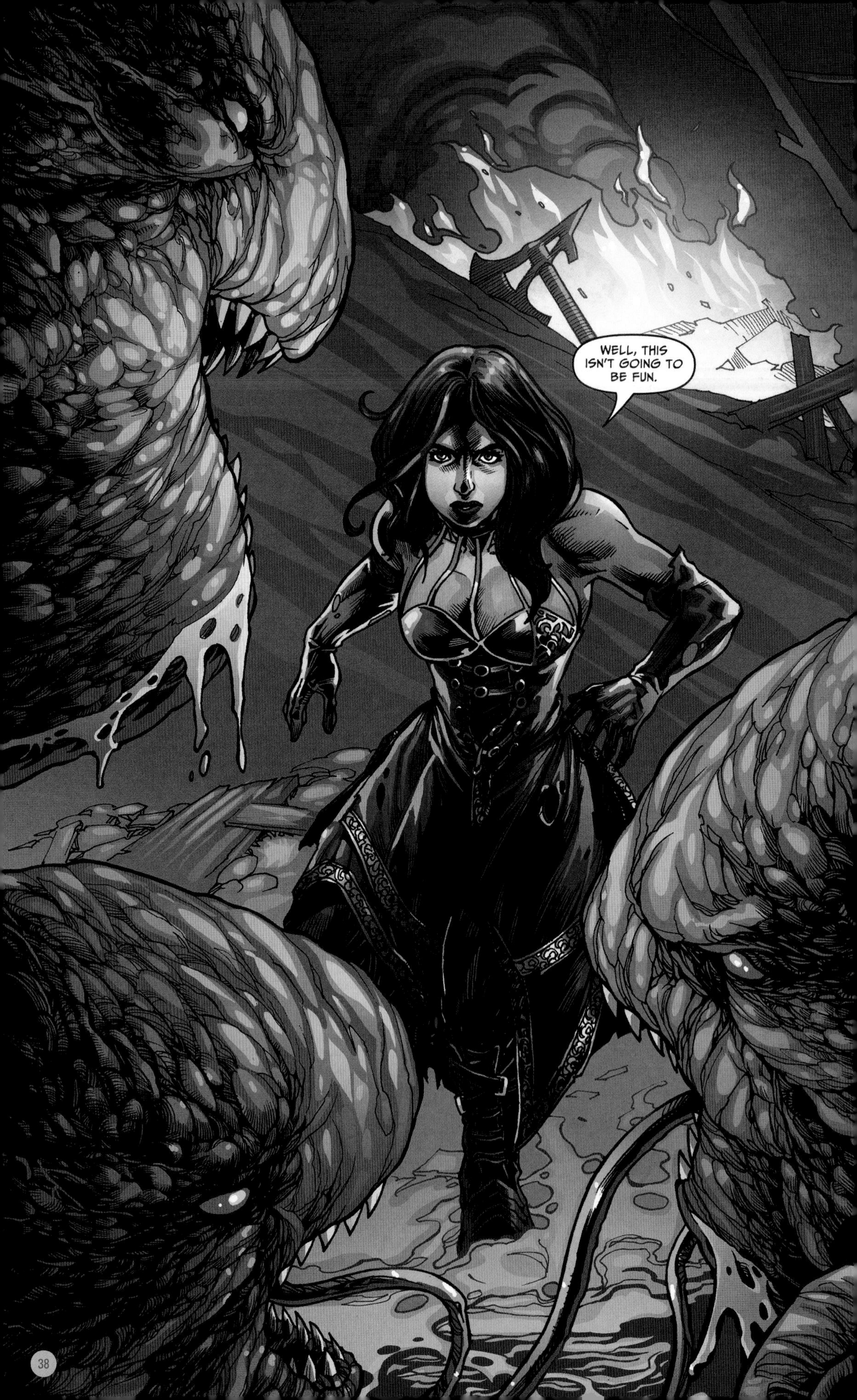
WELL, THIS ISN'T GOING TO BE FUN.

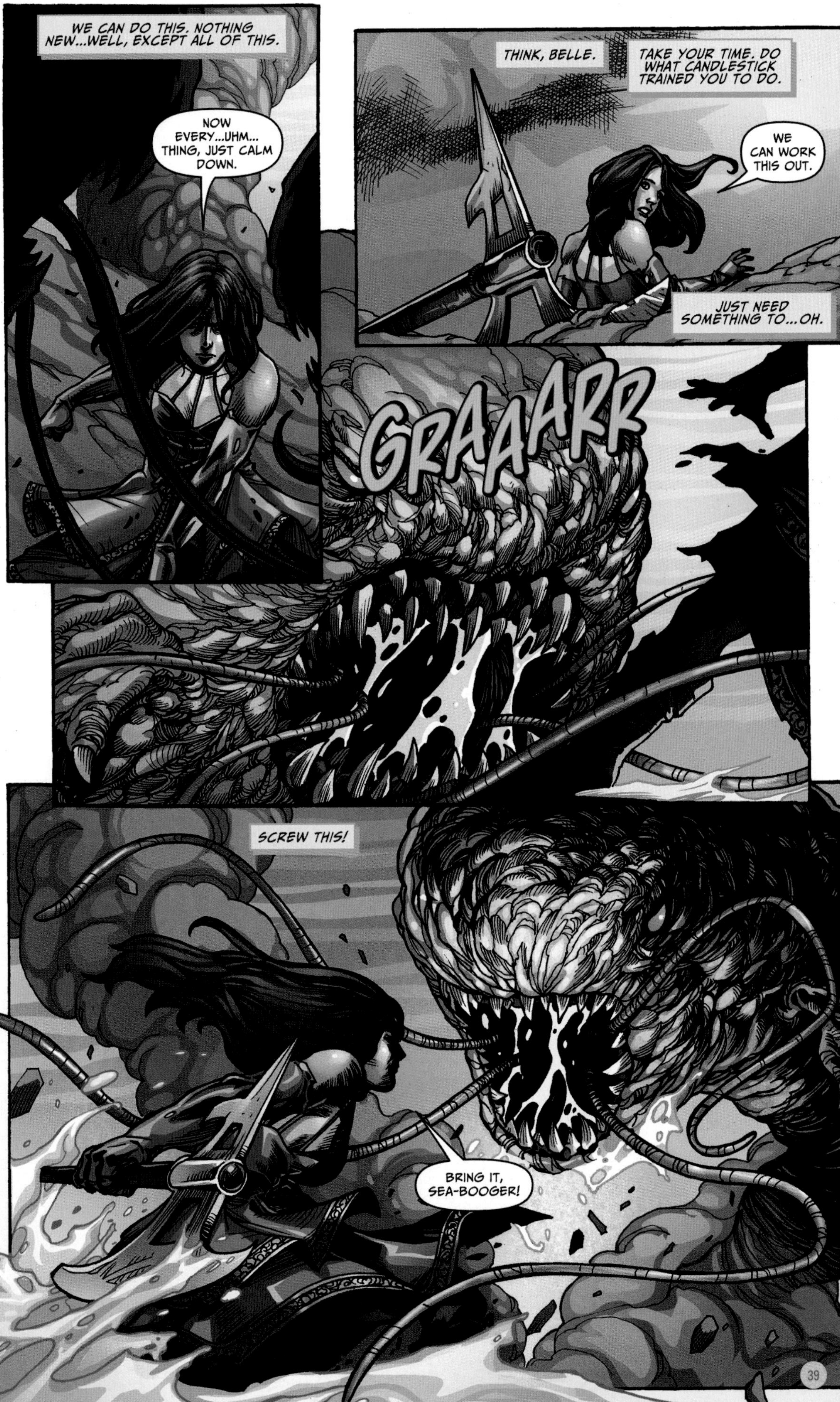
WE CAN DO THIS. NOTHING NEW...WELL, EXCEPT ALL OF THIS.
NOW EVERY...UHM... THING, JUST CALM DOWN.
THINK, BELLE.
TAKE YOUR TIME. DO WHAT CANDLESTICK TRAINED YOU TO DO.
WE CAN WORK THIS OUT.
JUST NEED SOMETHING TO...OH.
GRAAARR
SCREW THIS!
BRING IT, SEA-BOOGER!

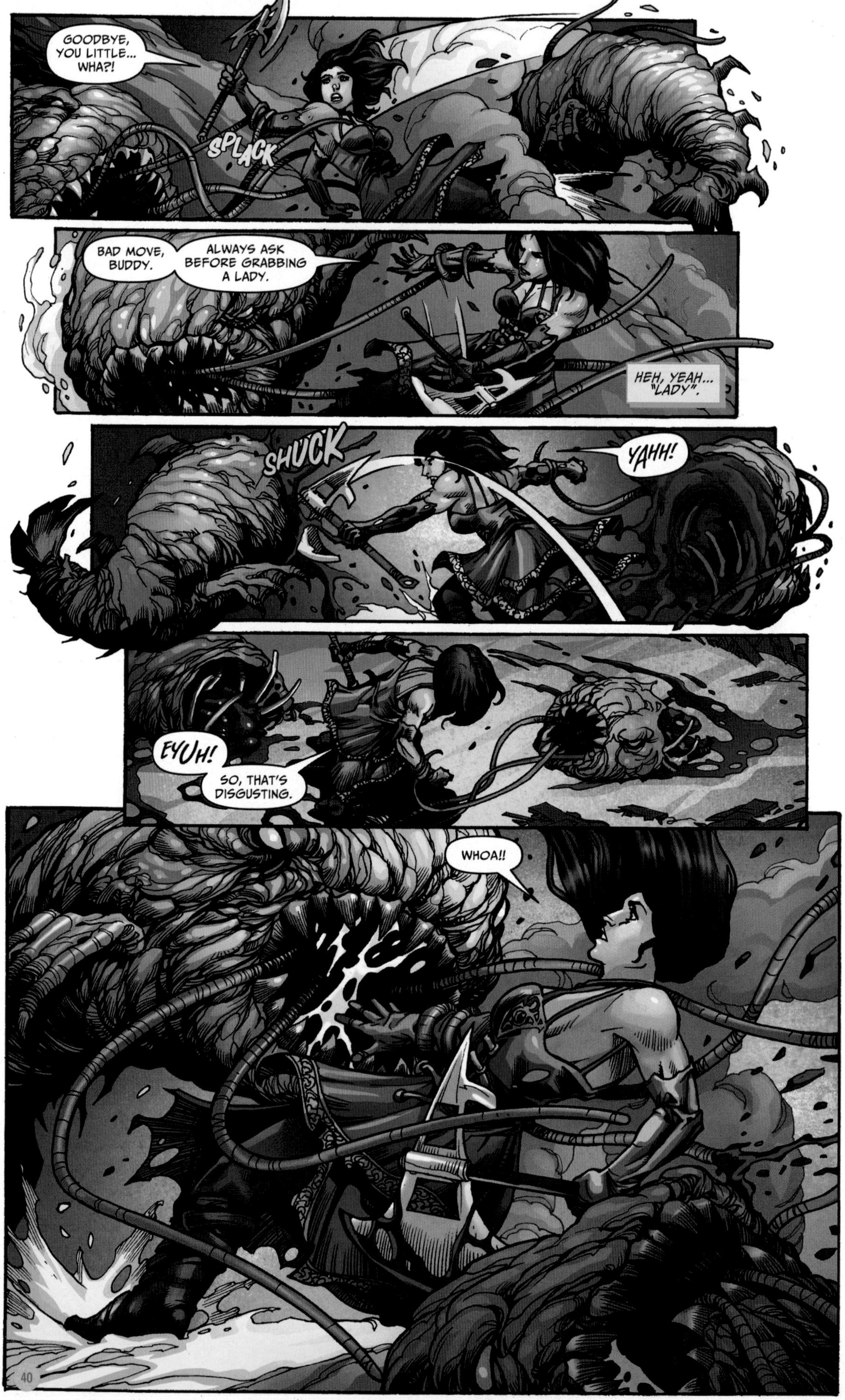
GOODBYE, YOU LITTLE... WHA?!
SPLACK
BAD MOVE, BUDDY.
ALWAYS ASK BEFORE GRABBING A LADY.
HEH, YEAH... "LADY".
SHUCK
YAHH!
EYUH!
SO, THAT'S DISGUSTING.
WHOA!!

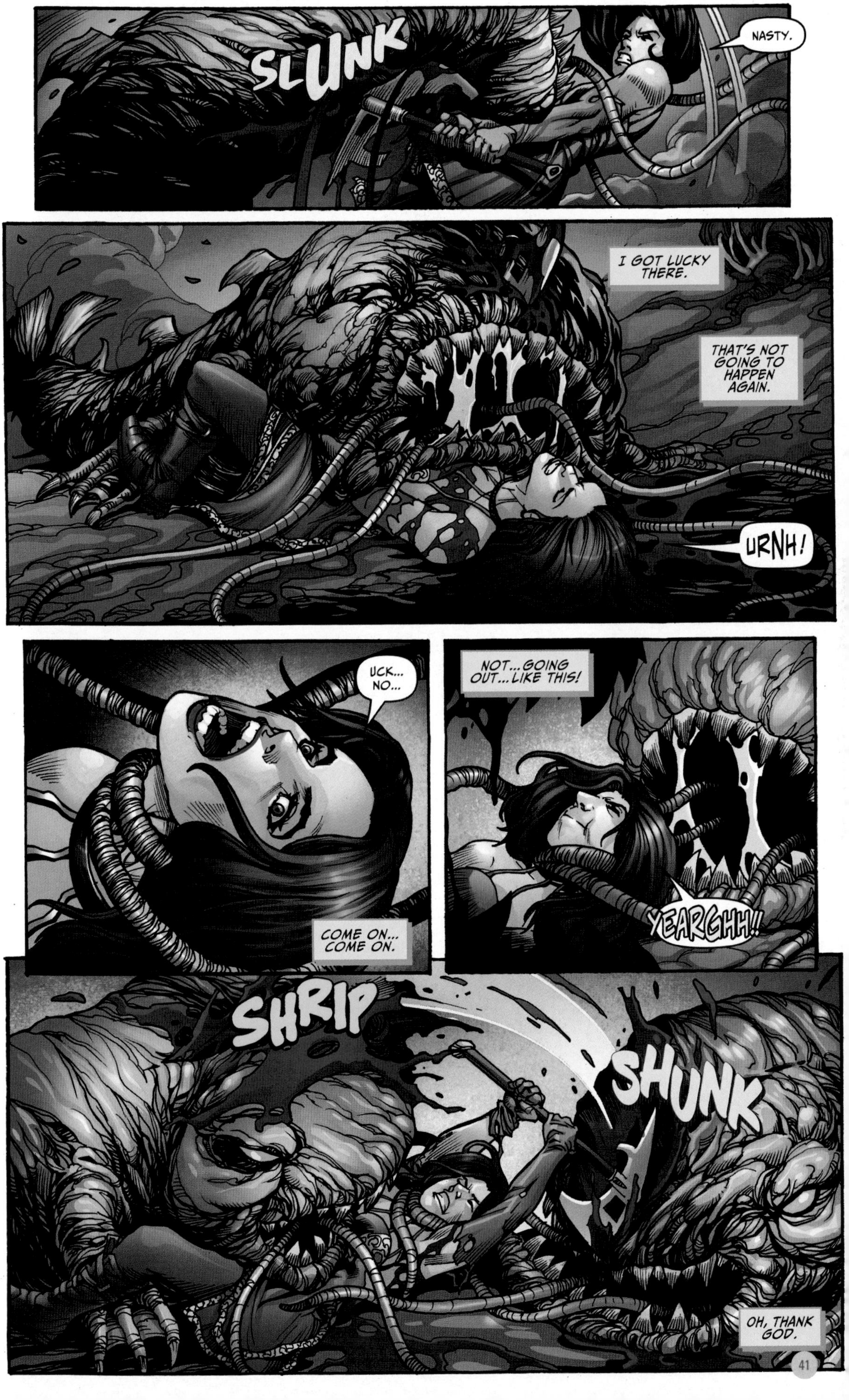
SLUNK
NASTY.
I GOT LUCKY THERE.
THAT'S NOT GOING TO HAPPEN AGAIN.
URNH!
UCK... NO...
COME ON... COME ON.
NOT... GOING OUT... LIKE THIS!
YEARGHH!!
SHRIP
SHUNK
OH, THANK GOD.

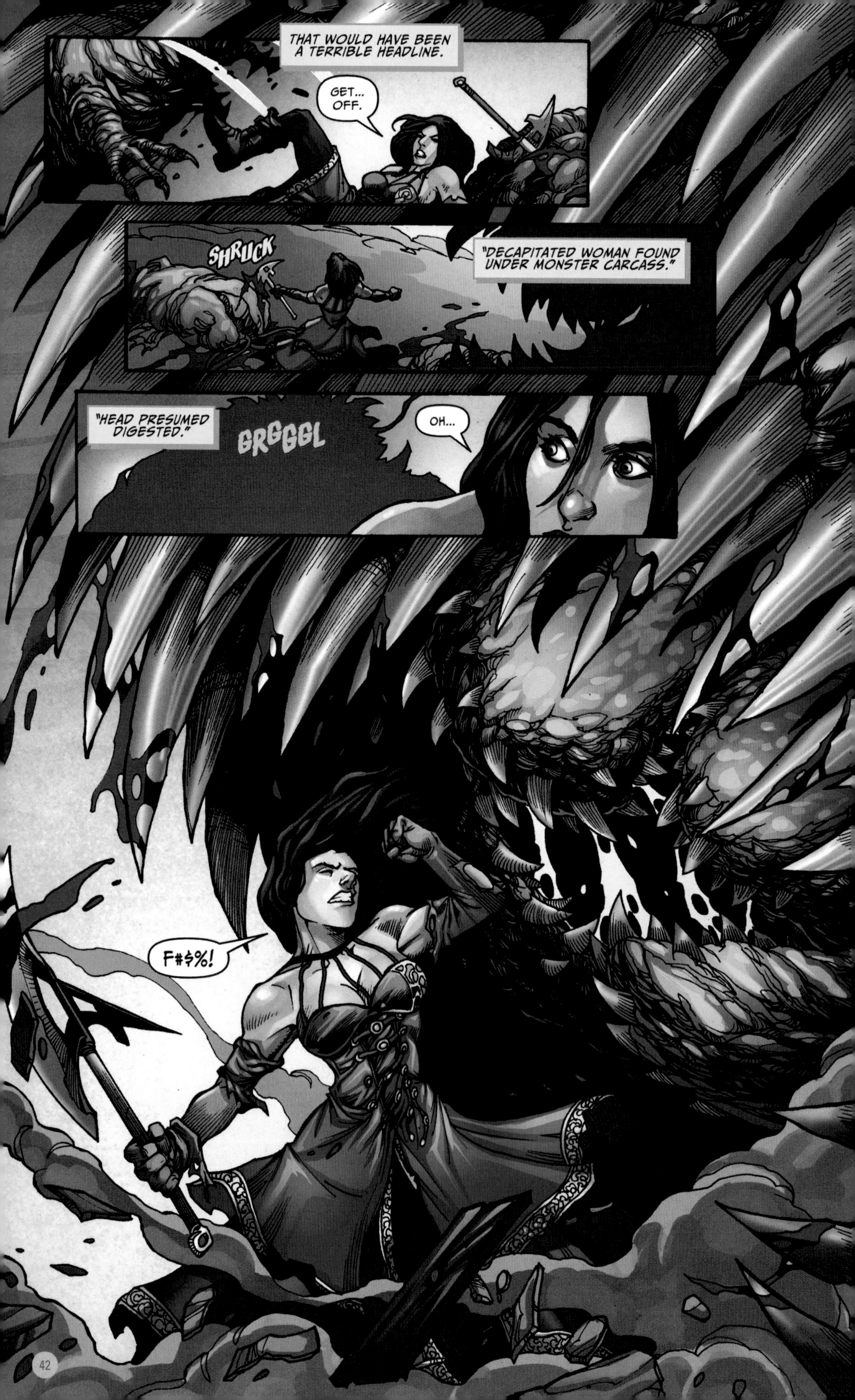
THAT WOULD HAVE BEEN A TERRIBLE HEADLINE.
GET... OFF.
SHRUCK
"DECAPITATED WOMAN FOUND UNDER MONSTER CARCASS."
"HEAD PRESUMED DIGESTED."
GRGGGL
OH...
F#$%!

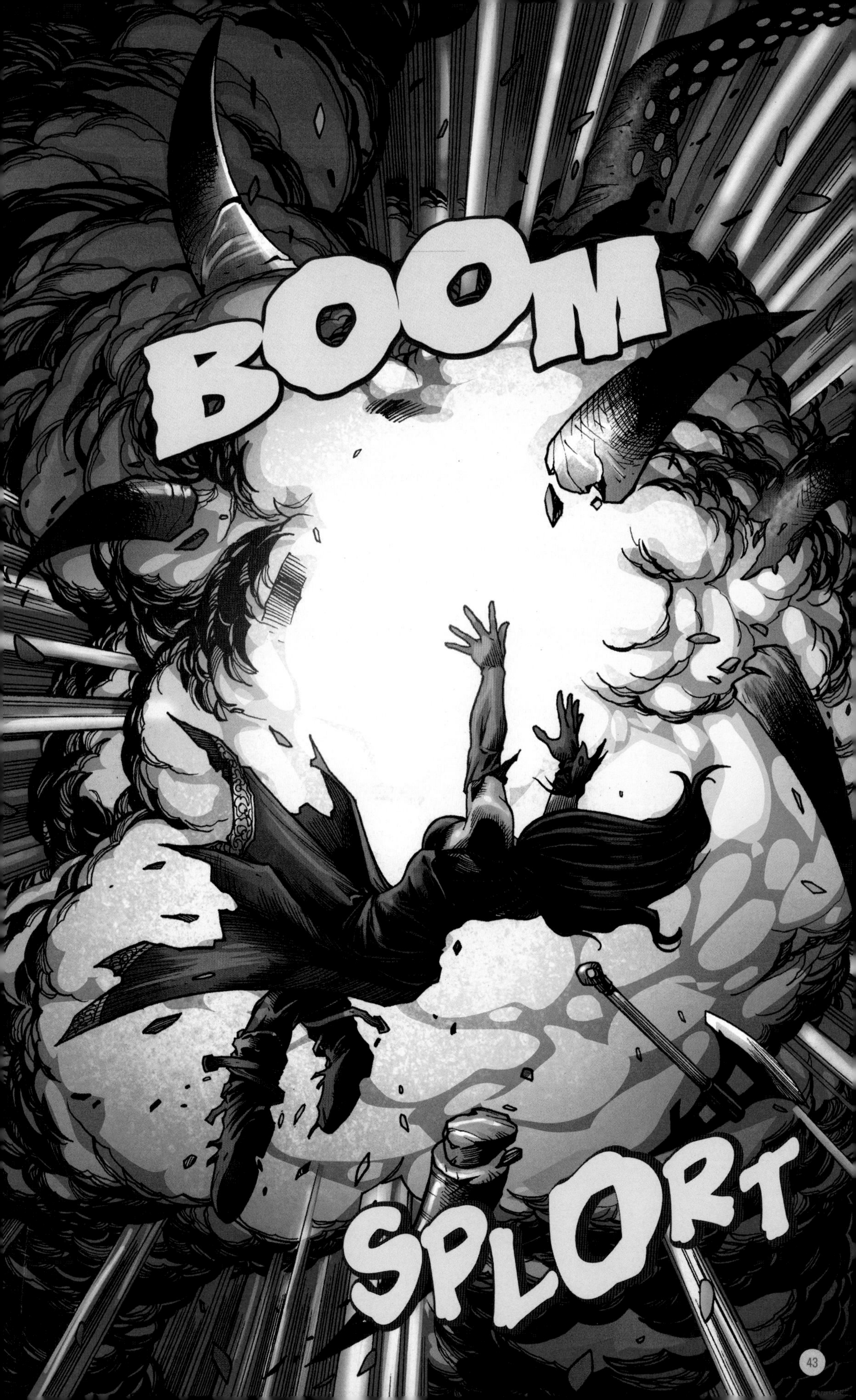
BOOM
SPLORT

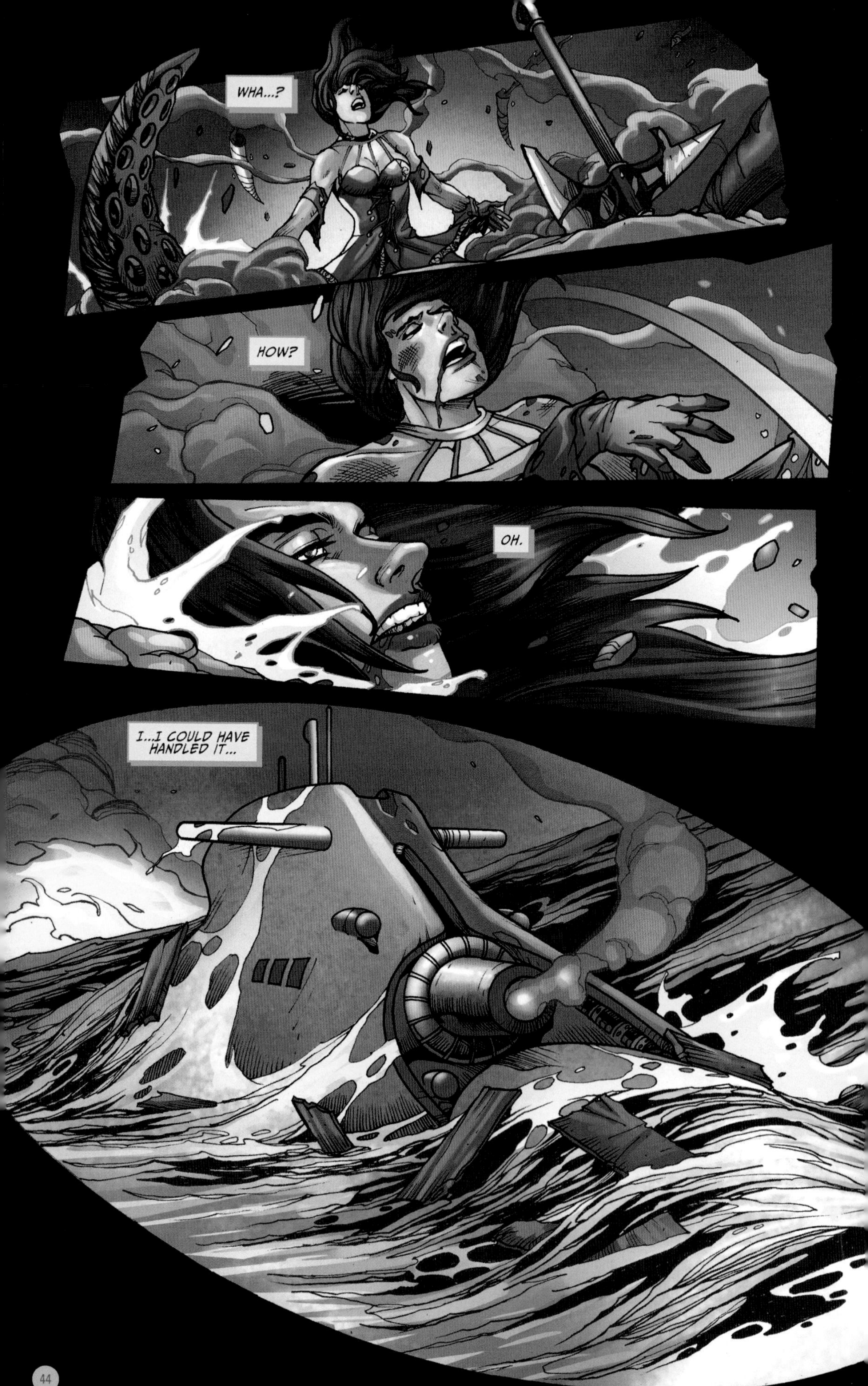
WHA...?
HOW?
OH.
I...I COULD HAVE HANDLED IT...

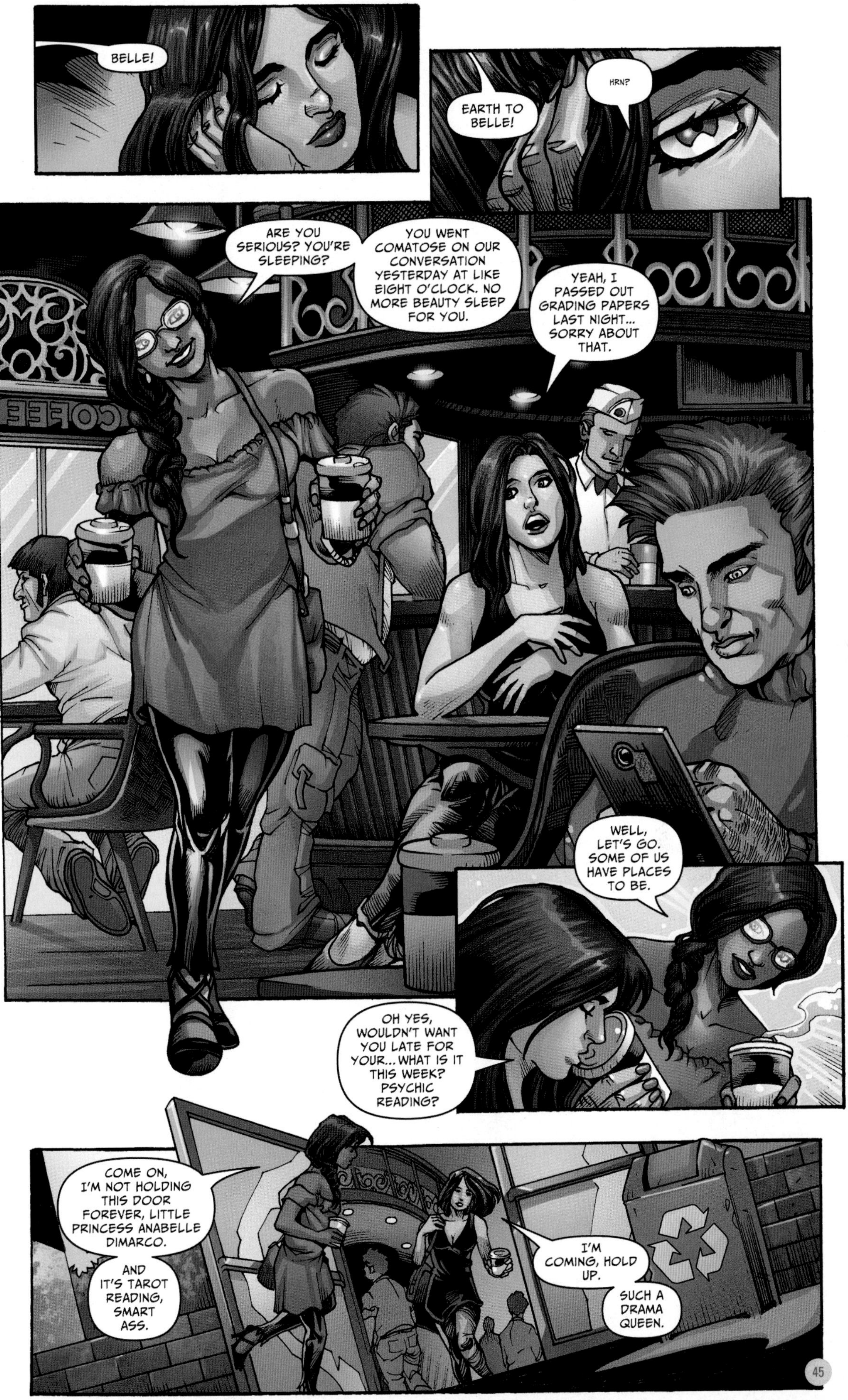
BELLE!
EARTH TO BELLE!
HRN?
ARE YOU SERIOUS? YOU'RE SLEEPING?
YOU WENT COMATOSE ON OUR CONVERSATION YESTERDAY AT LIKE EIGHT O'CLOCK. NO MORE BEAUTY SLEEP FOR YOU.
YEAH, I PASSED OUT GRADING PAPERS LAST NIGHT... SORRY ABOUT THAT.
WELL, LET'S GO. SOME OF US HAVE PLACES TO BE.
OH YES, WOULDN'T WANT YOU LATE FOR YOUR... WHAT IS IT THIS WEEK? PSYCHIC READING?
COME ON, I'M NOT HOLDING THIS DOOR FOREVER, LITTLE PRINCESS ANABELLE DIMARCO.
AND IT'S TAROT READING, SMART ASS.
I'M COMING, HOLD UP.
SUCH A DRAMA QUEEN.

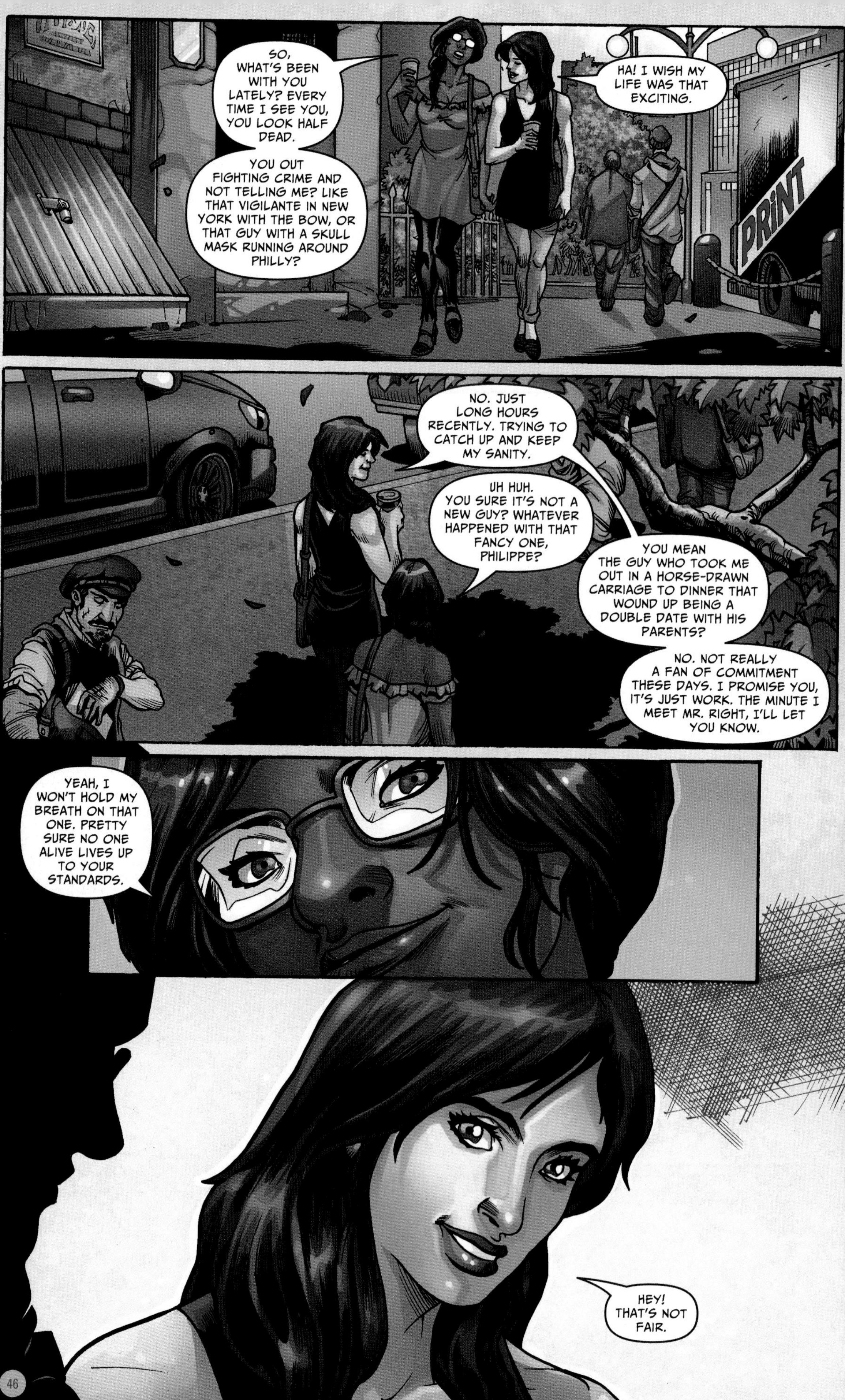

SO, WHAT'S BEEN WITH YOU LATELY? EVERY TIME I SEE YOU, YOU LOOK HALF DEAD.
YOU OUT FIGHTING CRIME AND NOT TELLING ME? LIKE THAT VIGILANTE IN NEW YORK WITH THE BOW, OR THAT GUY WITH A SKULL MASK RUNNING AROUND PHILLY?
HA! I WISH MY LIFE WAS THAT EXCITING.
PRINT
NO. JUST LONG HOURS RECENTLY. TRYING TO CATCH UP AND KEEP MY SANITY.
UH HUH. YOU SURE IT'S NOT A NEW GUY? WHATEVER HAPPENED WITH THAT FANCY ONE, PHILIPPE?
YOU MEAN THE GUY WHO TOOK ME OUT IN A HORSE-DRAWN CARRIAGE TO DINNER THAT WOUND UP BEING A DOUBLE DATE WITH HIS PARENTS?
NO. NOT REALLY A FAN OF COMMITMENT THESE DAYS. I PROMISE YOU, IT'S JUST WORK. THE MINUTE I MEET MR. RIGHT, I'LL LET YOU KNOW.
YEAH, I WON'T HOLD MY BREATH ON THAT ONE. PRETTY SURE NO ONE ALIVE LIVES UP TO YOUR STANDARDS.
HEY! THAT'S NOT FAIR.

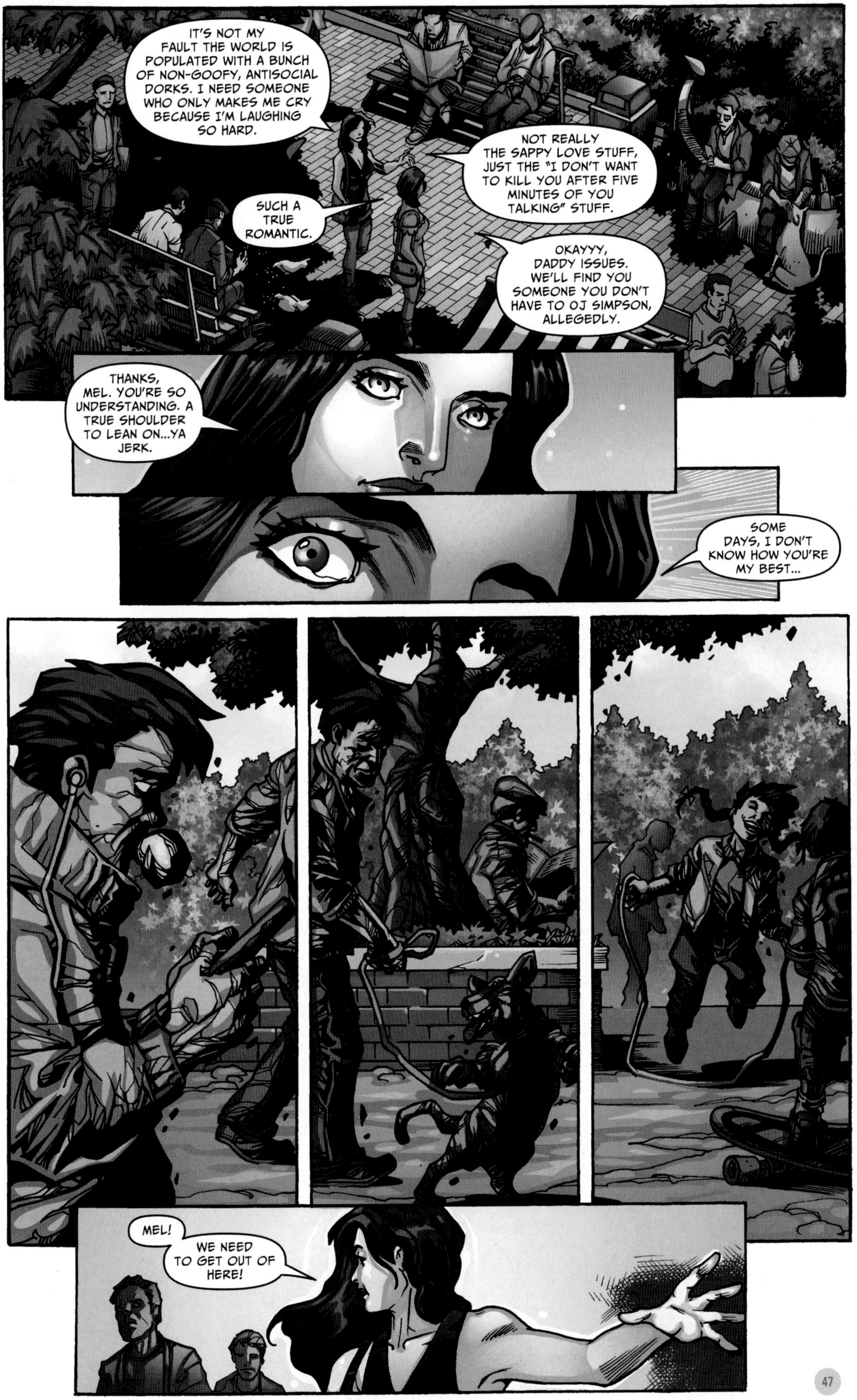
IT'S NOT MY FAULT THE WORLD IS POPULATED WITH A BUNCH OF NON-GOOFY, ANTISOCIAL DORKS. I NEED SOMEONE WHO ONLY MAKES ME CRY BECAUSE I'M LAUGHING SO HARD.
SUCH A TRUE ROMANTIC.
NOT REALLY THE SAPPY LOVE STUFF, JUST THE "I DON'T WANT TO KILL YOU AFTER FIVE MINUTES OF YOU TALKING" STUFF.
OKAYYY, DADDY ISSUES. WE'LL FIND YOU SOMEONE YOU DON'T HAVE TO OJ SIMPSON, ALLEGEDLY.
THANKS, MEL. YOU'RE SO UNDERSTANDING. A TRUE SHOULDER TO LEAN ON...YA JERK.
SOME DAYS, I DON'T KNOW HOW YOU'RE MY BEST...
MEL!
WE NEED TO GET OUT OF HERE!

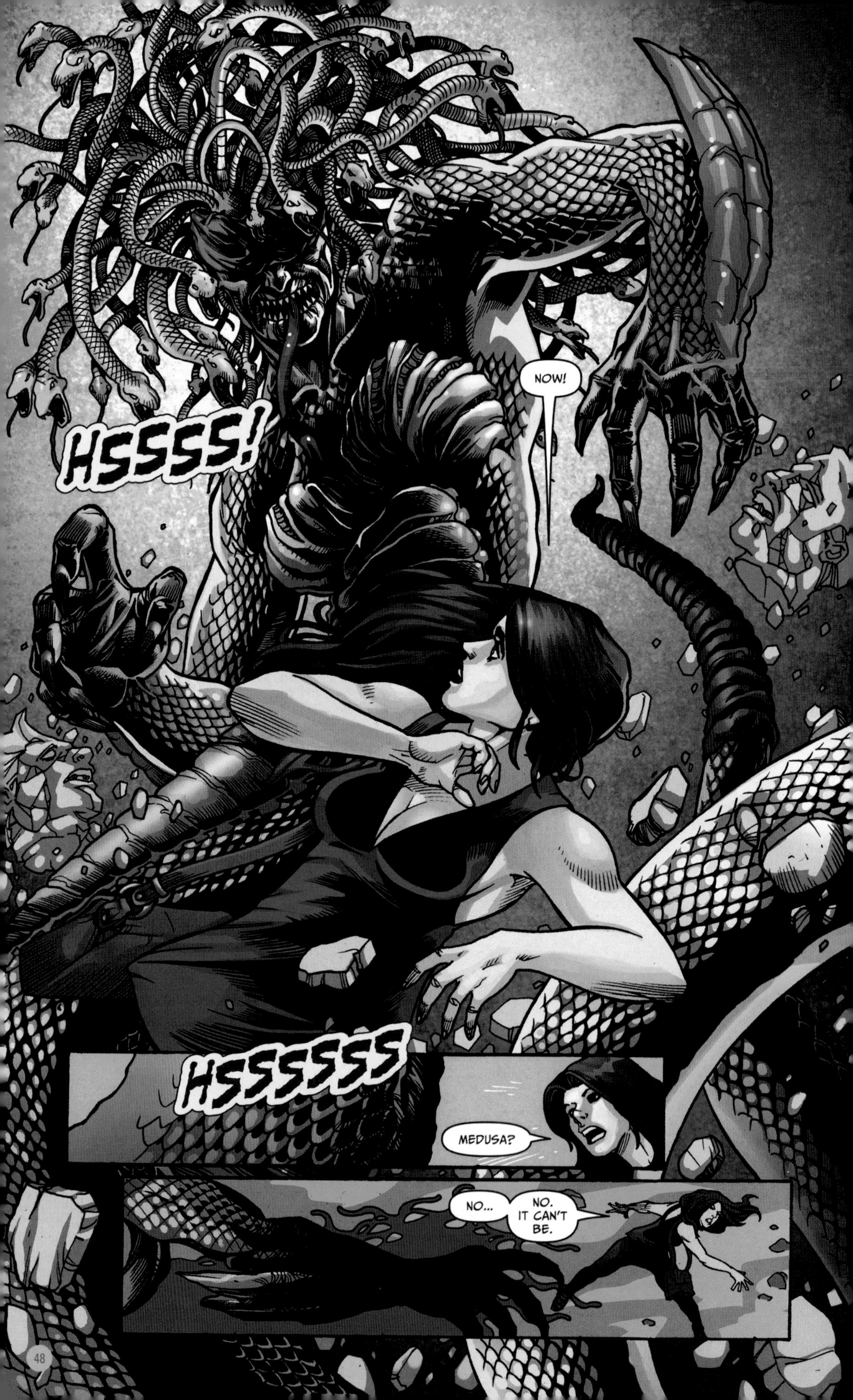
HSSSS!
NOW!
HSSSSSS
MEDUSA?
NO...
NO. IT CAN'T BE.

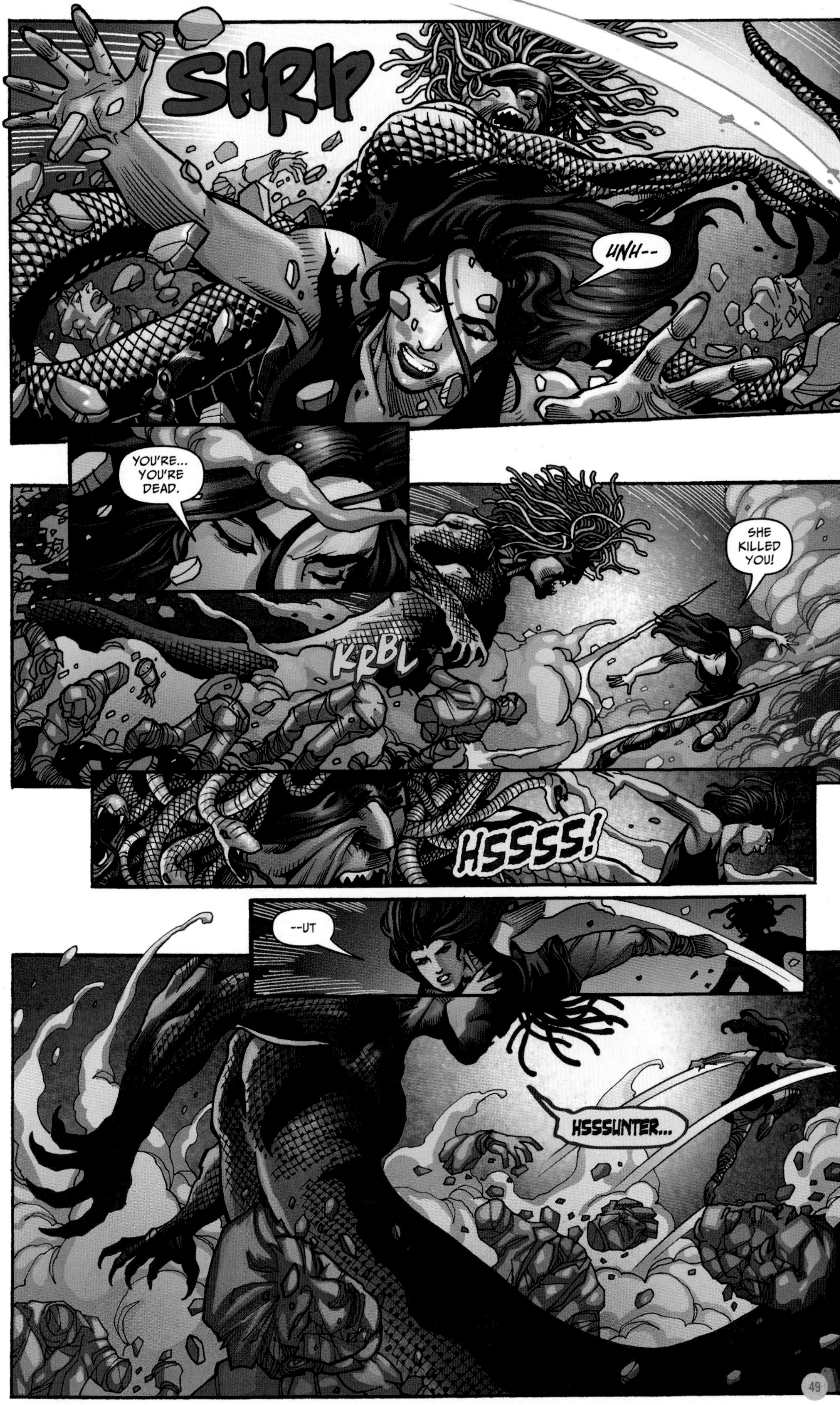
SHRIP
UNH--
YOU'RE... YOU'RE DEAD.
SHE KILLED YOU!
KRBL
HSSSS!
--UT
HSSSUNTER...

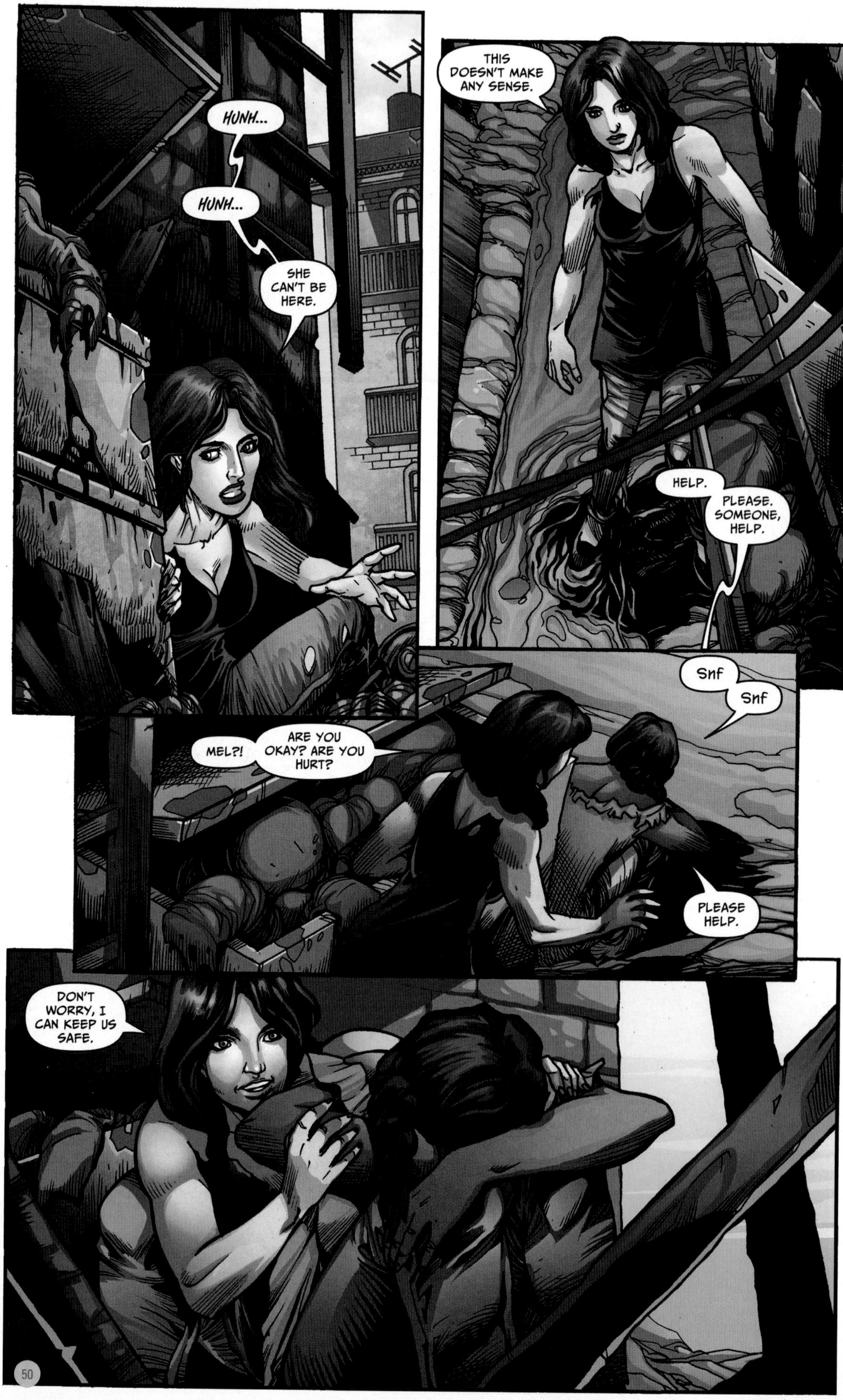
HUNH...
HUNH...
SHE CAN'T BE HERE.
THIS DOESN'T MAKE ANY SENSE.
HELP.
PLEASE. SOMEONE, HELP.
Snf
Snf
MEL?!
ARE YOU OKAY? ARE YOU HURT?
PLEASE HELP.
DON'T WORRY, I CAN KEEP US SAFE.

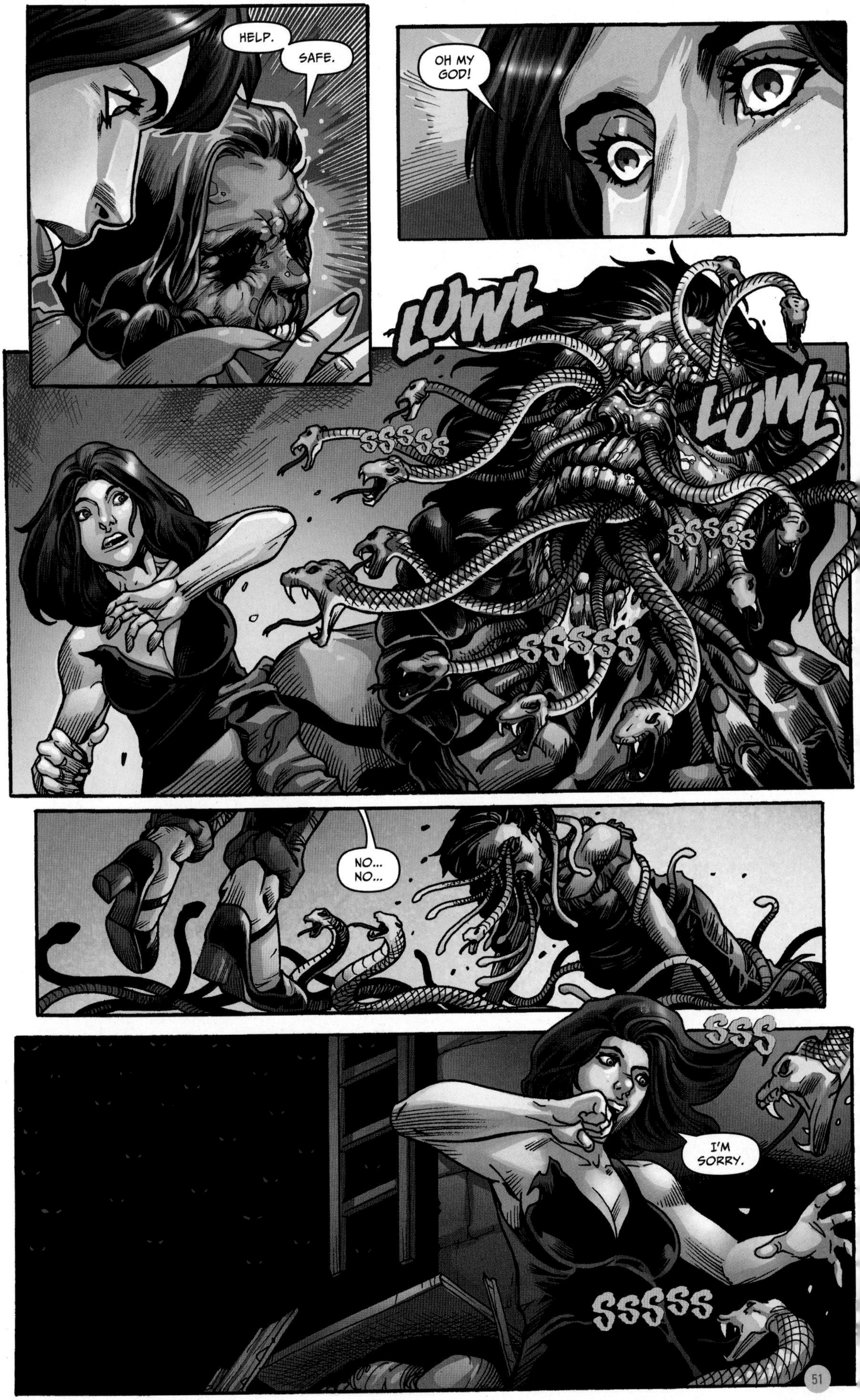
HELP.
SAFE.
OH MY GOD!
LUWL
LUWL
SSSSS
SSSSS
SSSSS
NO... NO...
SSS
I'M SORRY.
SSSSS

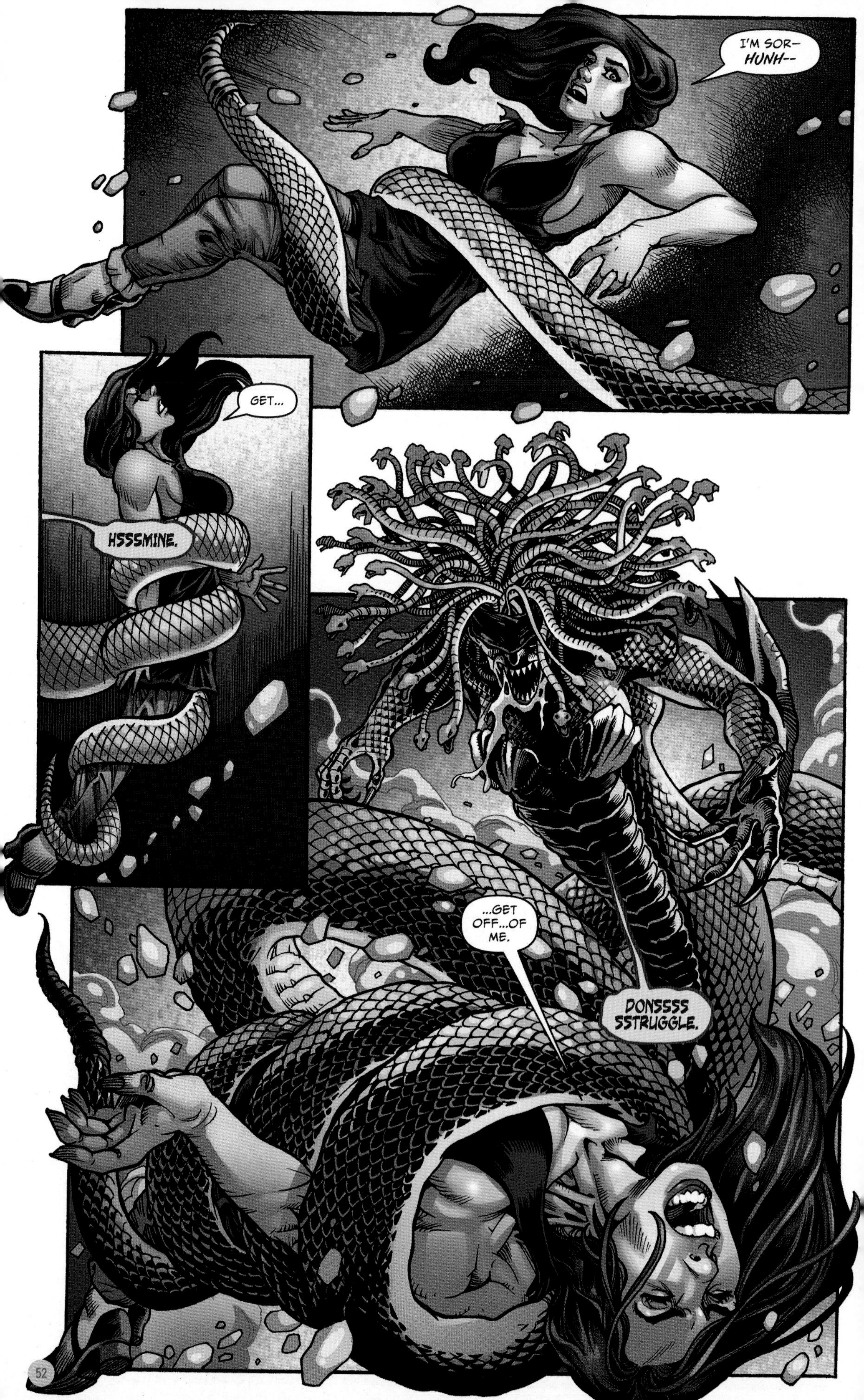
I'M SOR—
HUNH--
GET...
HSSSMINE.
...GET OFF...OF ME.
DONSSSS SSTRUGGLE.

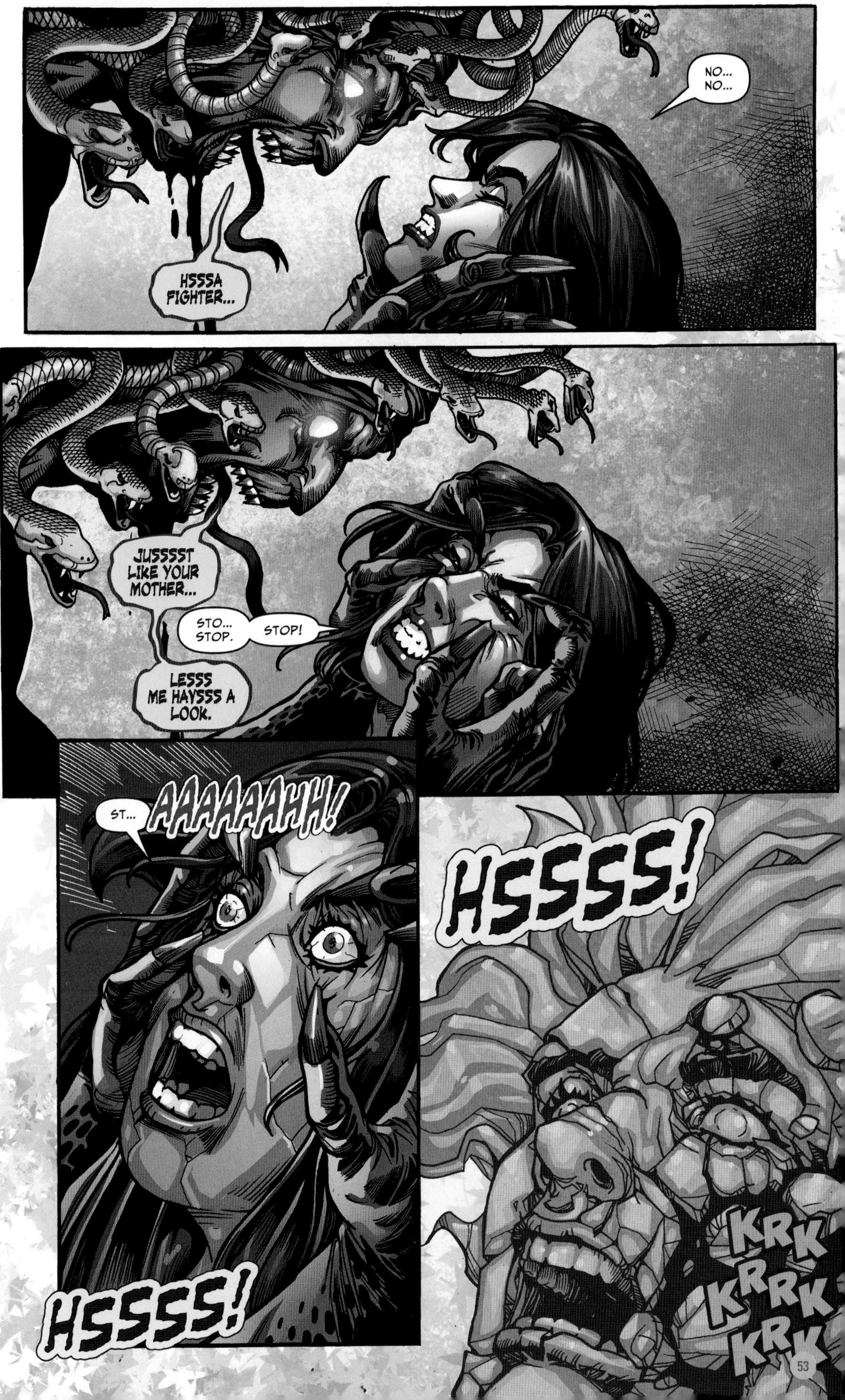
NO... NO...
HSSSA FIGHTER...
JUSSSST LIKE YOUR MOTHER...
STO... STOP.
STOP!
LESSS ME HAYSSS A LOOK.
ST...
AAAAAAHH!
HSSSS!
HSSSSS!
KRK KRRK KRK

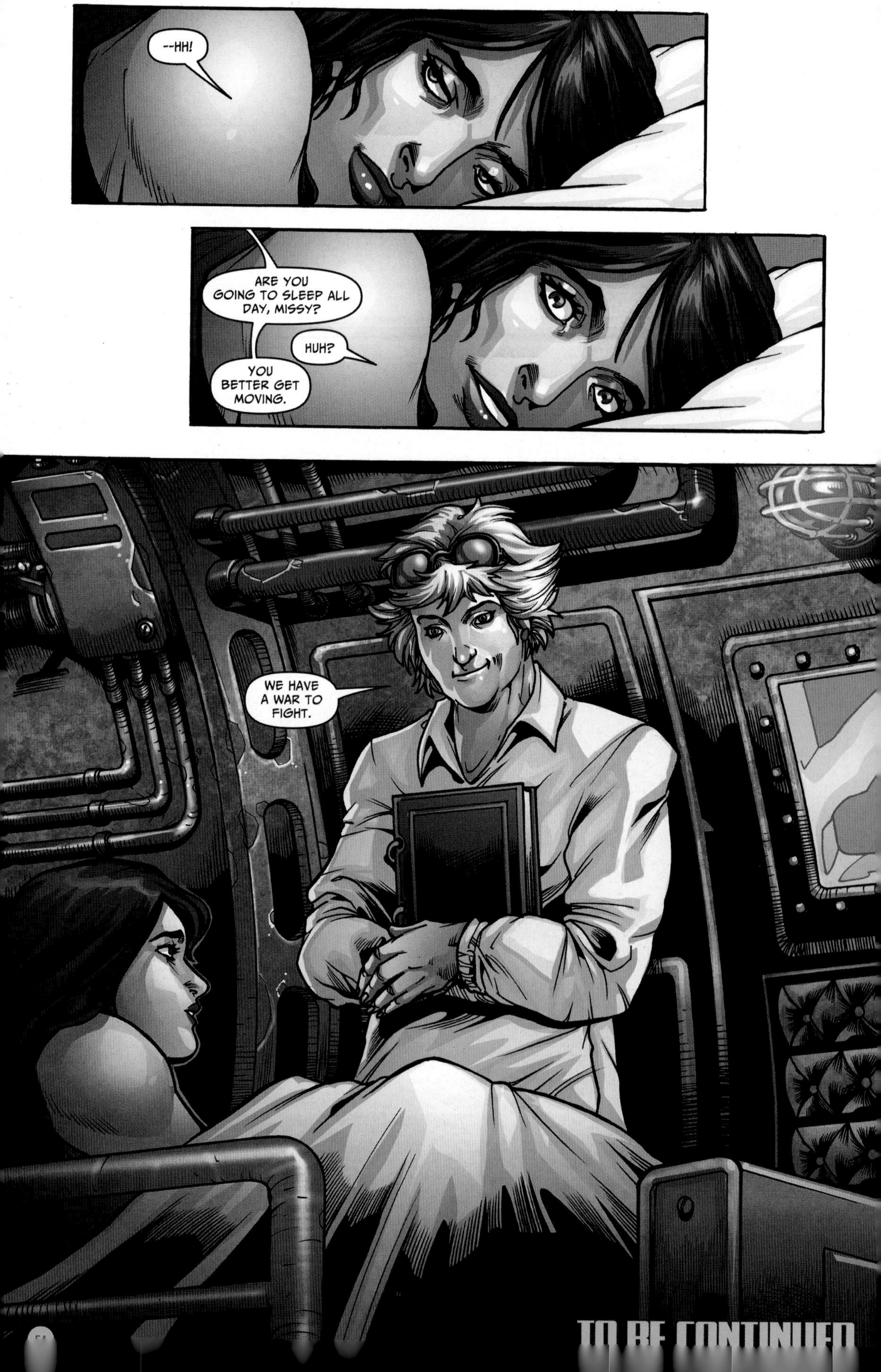
--HH!
ARE YOU GOING TO SLEEP ALL DAY, MISSY?
HUH?
YOU BETTER GET MOVING.
WE HAVE A WAR TO FIGHT.
TO BE CONTINUED

BELLE
BEAST HUNTER

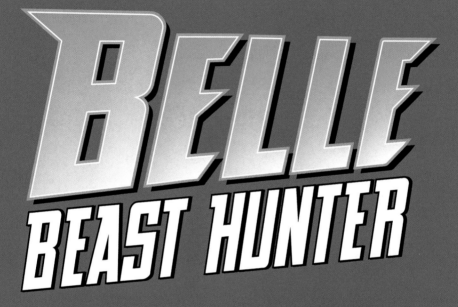

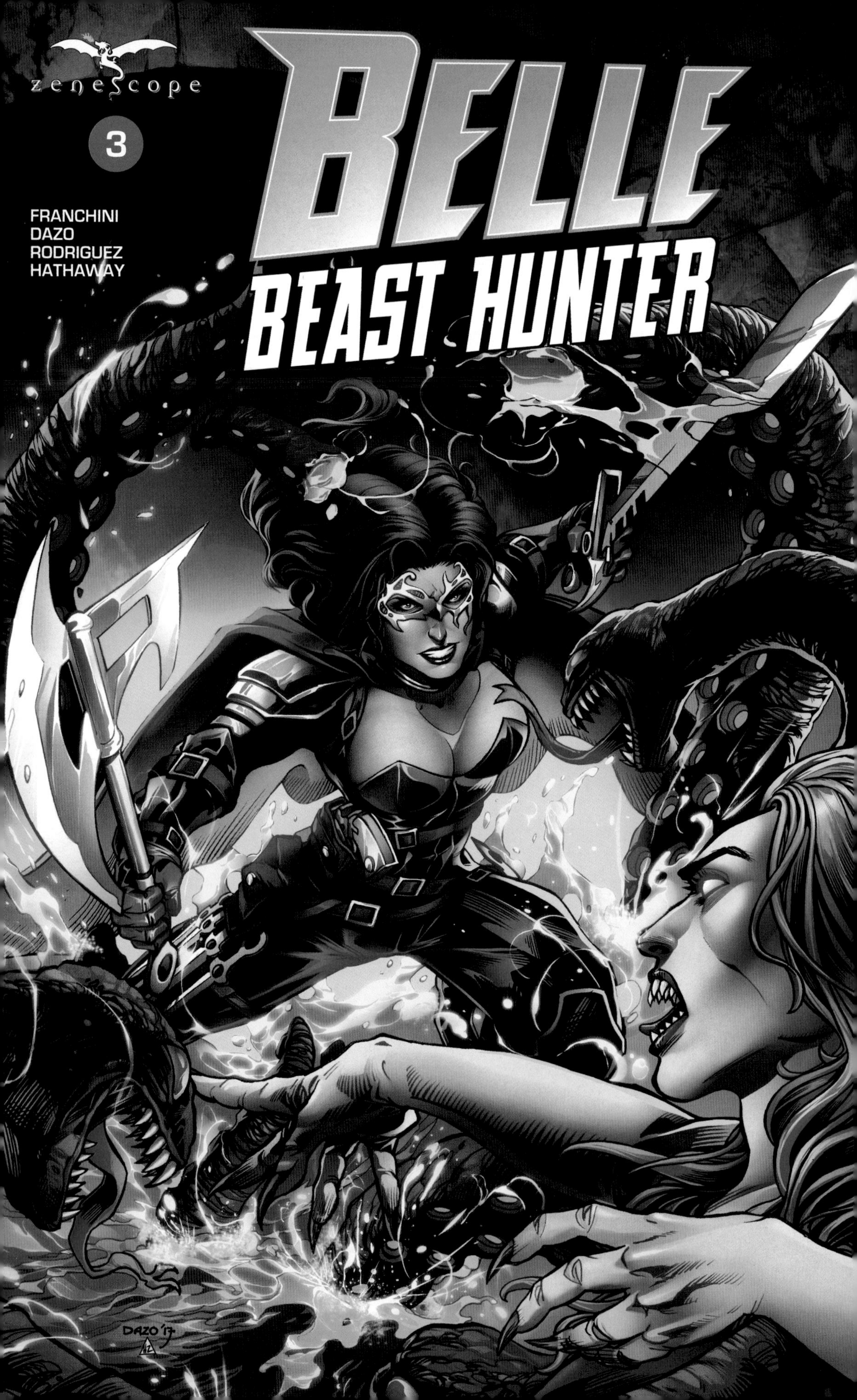
zenescope
3
FRANCHINI
DAZO
RODRIGUEZ
HATHAWAY
BELLE
BEAST HUNTER
DAZO '17

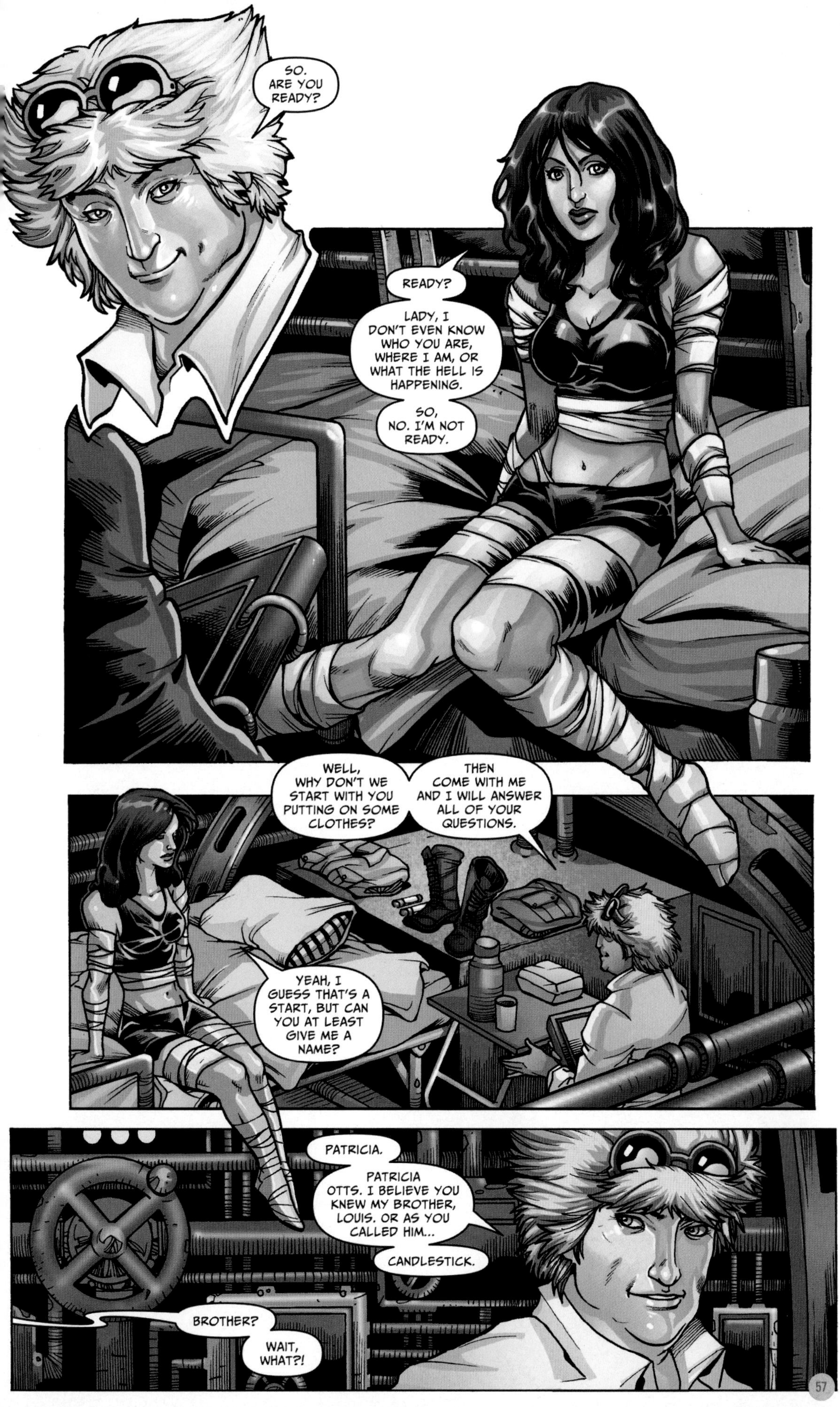
SO. ARE YOU READY?
READY?
LADY, I DON'T EVEN KNOW WHO YOU ARE, WHERE I AM, OR WHAT THE HELL IS HAPPENING.
SO, NO. I'M NOT READY.
WELL, WHY DON'T WE START WITH YOU PUTTING ON SOME CLOTHES?
THEN COME WITH ME AND I WILL ANSWER ALL OF YOUR QUESTIONS.
YEAH, I GUESS THAT'S A START, BUT CAN YOU AT LEAST GIVE ME A NAME?
PATRICIA.
PATRICIA OTTS. I BELIEVE YOU KNEW MY BROTHER, LOUIS. OR AS YOU CALLED HIM...
CANDLESTICK.
BROTHER?
WAIT, WHAT?!

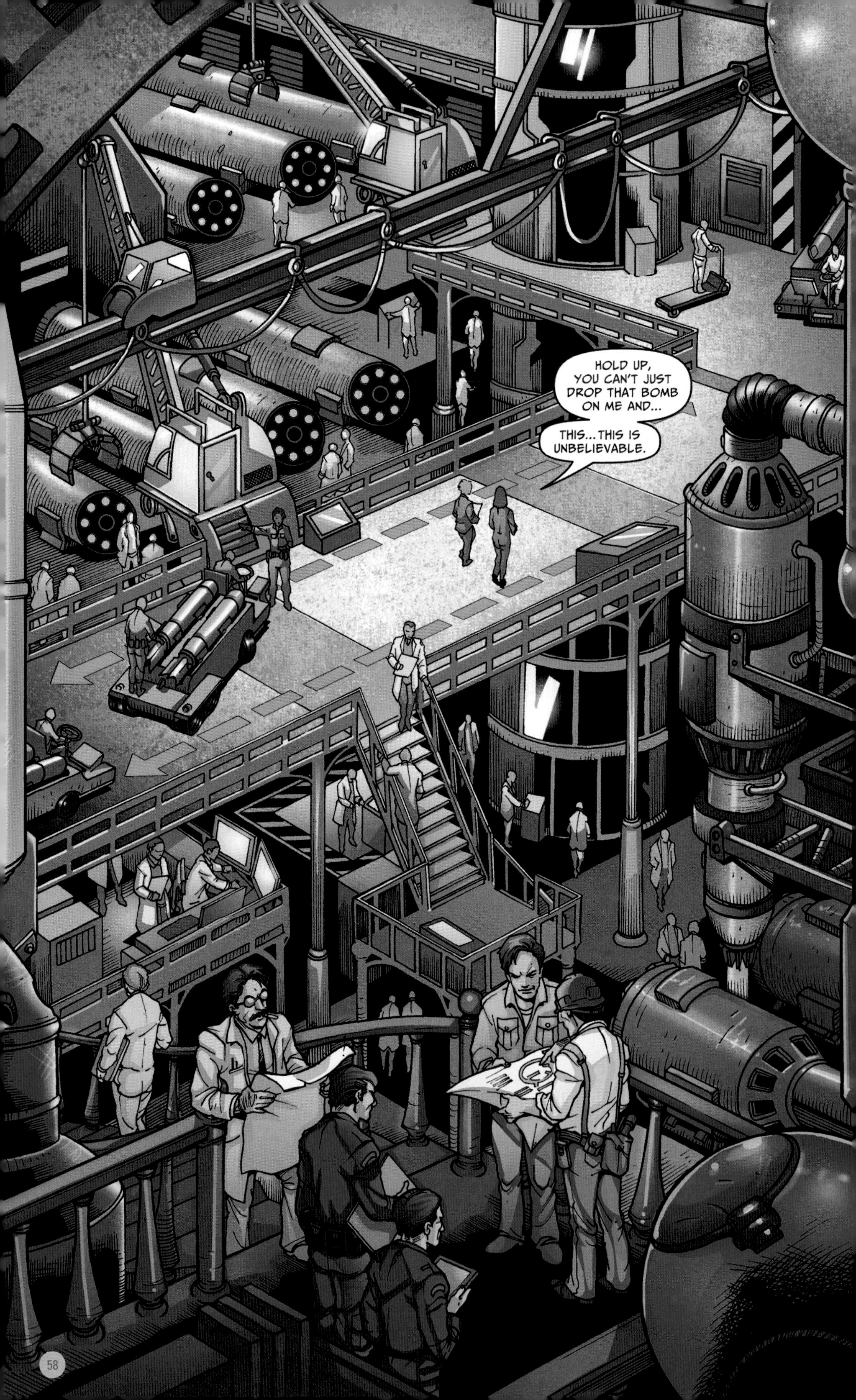
HOLD UP, YOU CAN'T JUST DROP THAT BOMB ON ME AND...
THIS... THIS IS UNBELIEVABLE.

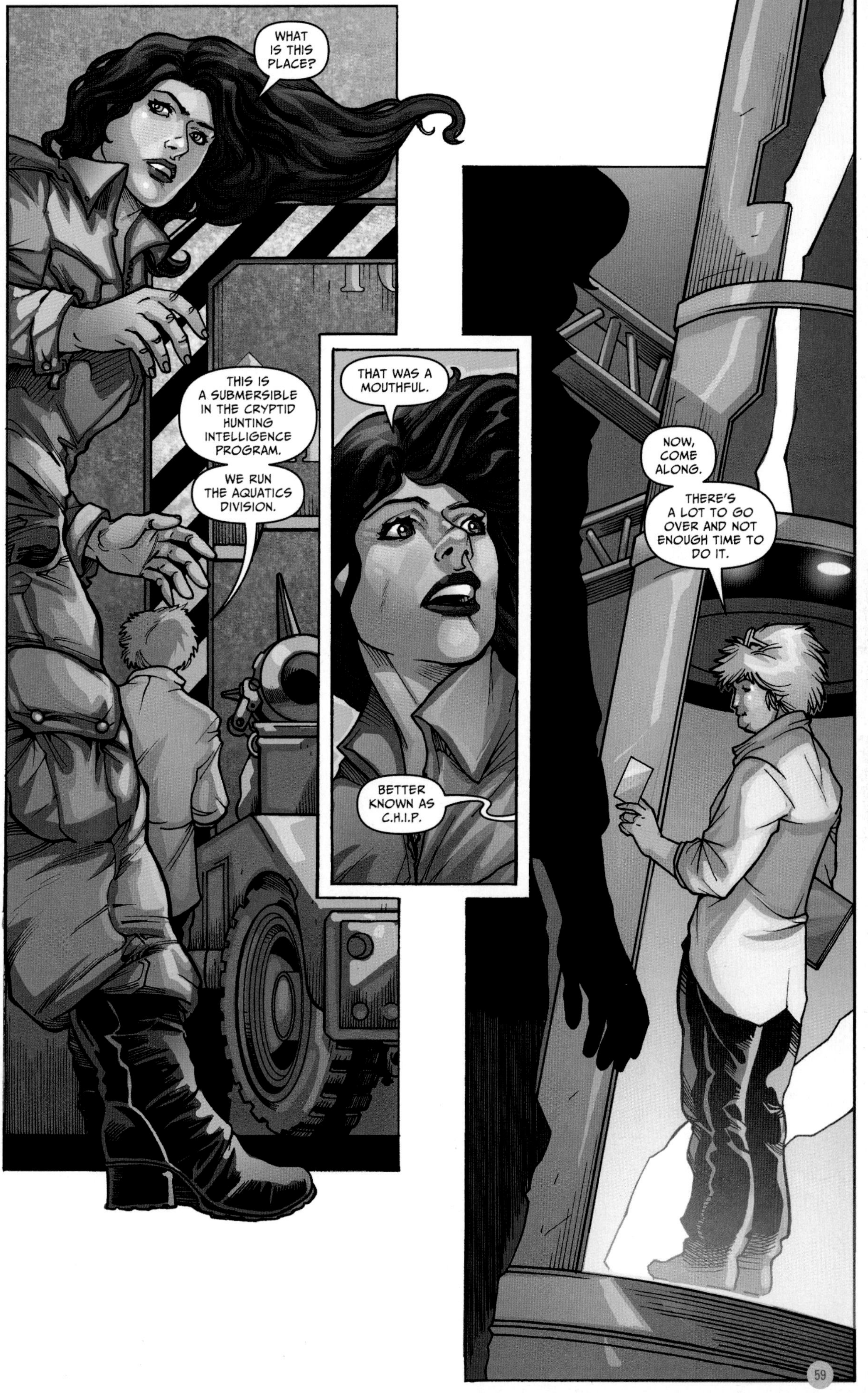
WHAT IS THIS PLACE?
THIS IS A SUBMERSIBLE IN THE CRYPTID HUNTING INTELLIGENCE PROGRAM.
WE RUN THE AQUATICS DIVISION.
THAT WAS A MOUTHFUL.
BETTER KNOWN AS C.H.I.P.
NOW, COME ALONG.
THERE'S A LOT TO GO OVER AND NOT ENOUGH TIME TO DO IT.

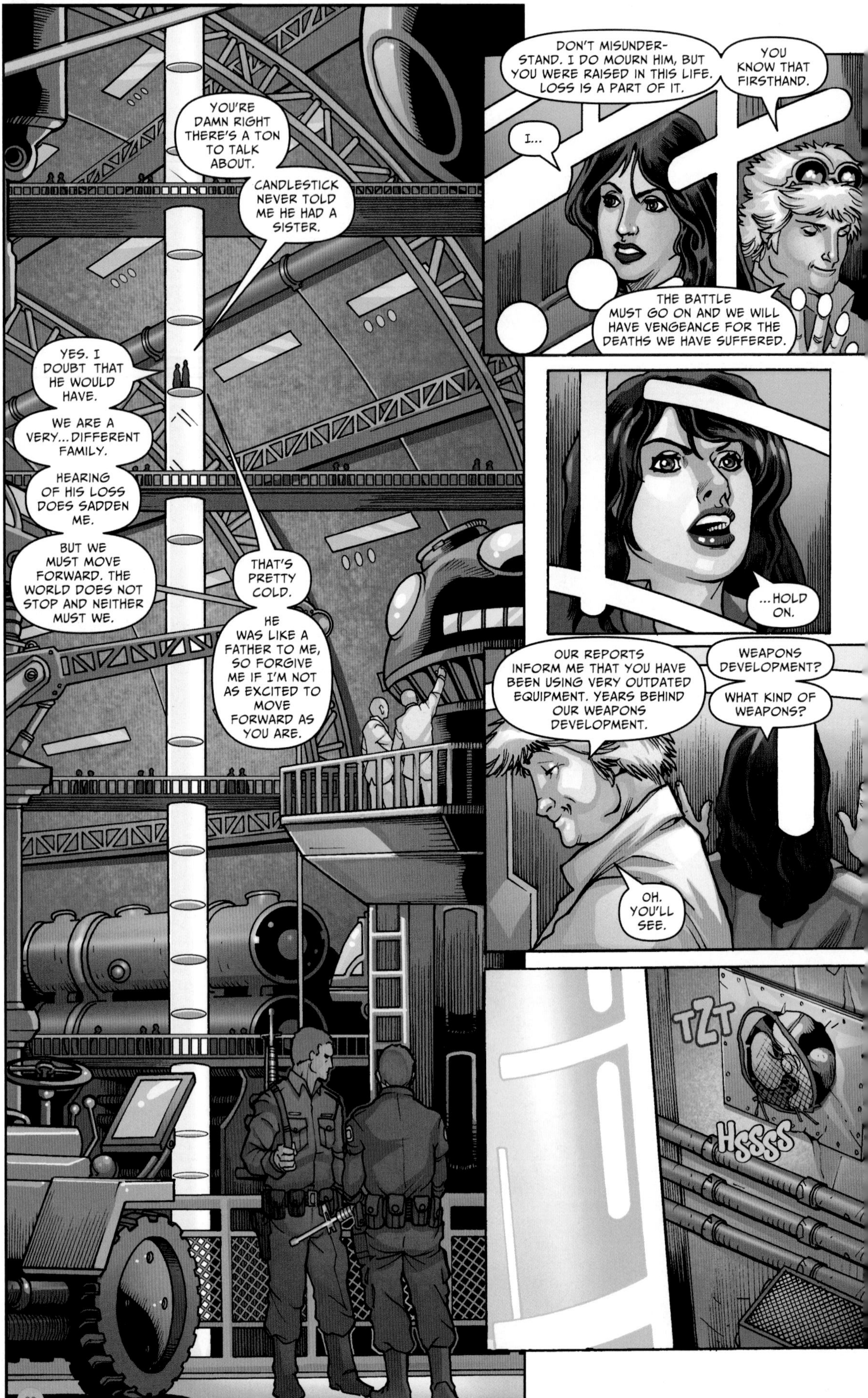
YOU'RE DAMN RIGHT THERE'S A TON TO TALK ABOUT.
CANDLESTICK NEVER TOLD ME HE HAD A SISTER.
YES. I DOUBT THAT HE WOULD HAVE.
WE ARE A VERY... DIFFERENT FAMILY.
HEARING OF HIS LOSS DOES SADDEN ME.
BUT WE MUST MOVE FORWARD. THE WORLD DOES NOT STOP AND NEITHER MUST WE.
THAT'S PRETTY COLD.
HE WAS LIKE A FATHER TO ME, SO FORGIVE ME IF I'M NOT AS EXCITED TO MOVE FORWARD AS YOU ARE.
DON'T MISUNDERSTAND. I DO MOURN HIM, BUT YOU WERE RAISED IN THIS LIFE. LOSS IS A PART OF IT.
YOU KNOW THAT FIRSTHAND.
I...
THE BATTLE MUST GO ON AND WE WILL HAVE VENGEANCE FOR THE DEATHS WE HAVE SUFFERED.
...HOLD ON.
OUR REPORTS INFORM ME THAT YOU HAVE BEEN USING VERY OUTDATED EQUIPMENT. YEARS BEHIND OUR WEAPONS DEVELOPMENT.
WEAPONS DEVELOPMENT?
WHAT KIND OF WEAPONS?
OH. YOU'LL SEE.
TZT
HSSSS

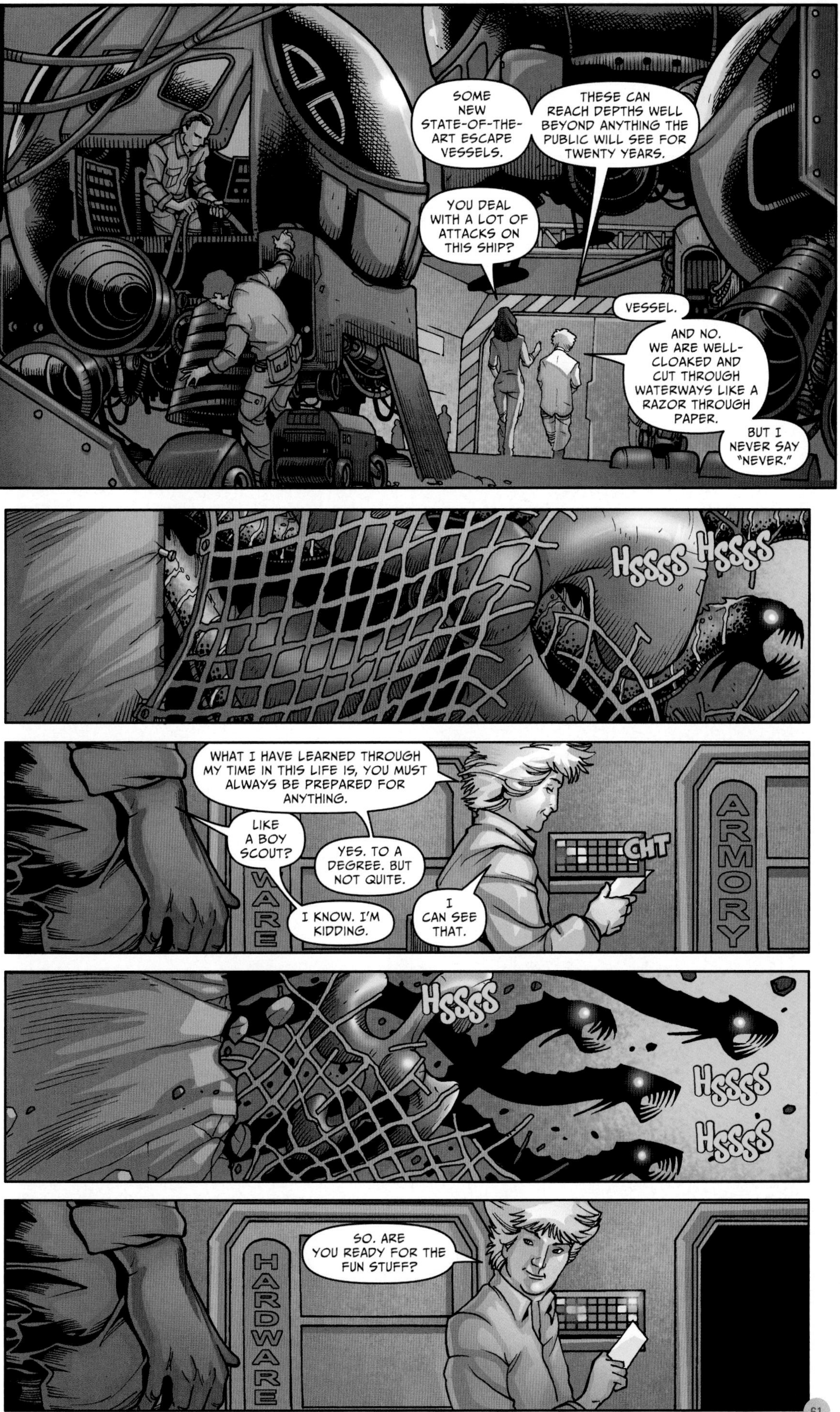

SOME NEW STATE-OF-THE-ART ESCAPE VESSELS.
THESE CAN REACH DEPTHS WELL BEYOND ANYTHING THE PUBLIC WILL SEE FOR TWENTY YEARS.
YOU DEAL WITH A LOT OF ATTACKS ON THIS SHIP?
VESSEL.
AND NO. WE ARE WELL-CLOAKED AND CUT THROUGH WATERWAYS LIKE A RAZOR THROUGH PAPER.
BUT I NEVER SAY "NEVER."
HSSSS HSSSS
WHAT I HAVE LEARNED THROUGH MY TIME IN THIS LIFE IS, YOU MUST ALWAYS BE PREPARED FOR ANYTHING.
LIKE A BOY SCOUT?
YES. TO A DEGREE. BUT NOT QUITE.
I KNOW. I'M KIDDING.
I CAN SEE THAT.
CHT
ARMORY
WARE
HSSSS
HSSSS
HSSSS
HARDWARE
SO. ARE YOU READY FOR THE FUN STUFF?

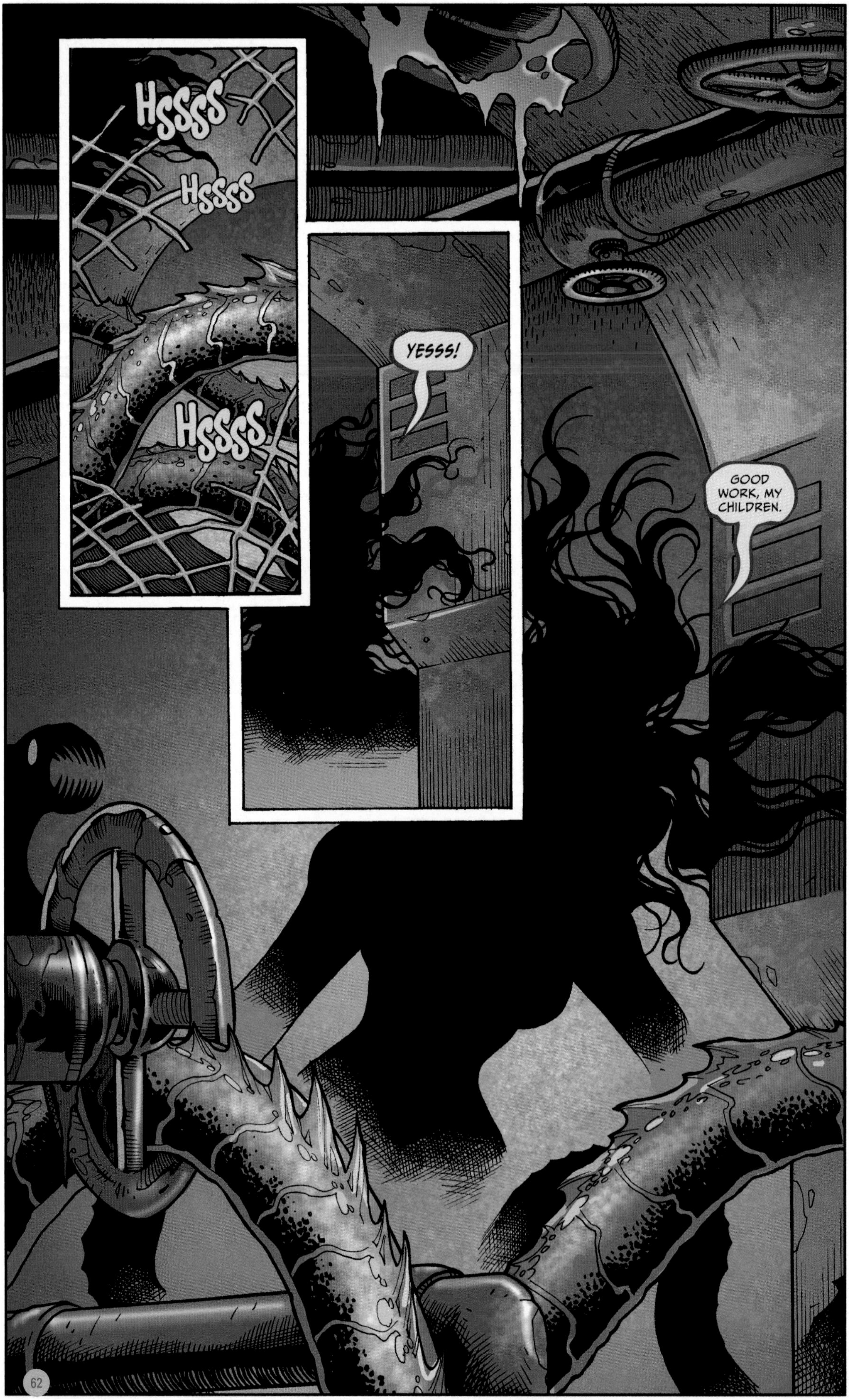
HSSSS
HSSSS
HSSSS
YESSS!
GOOD WORK, MY CHILDREN.

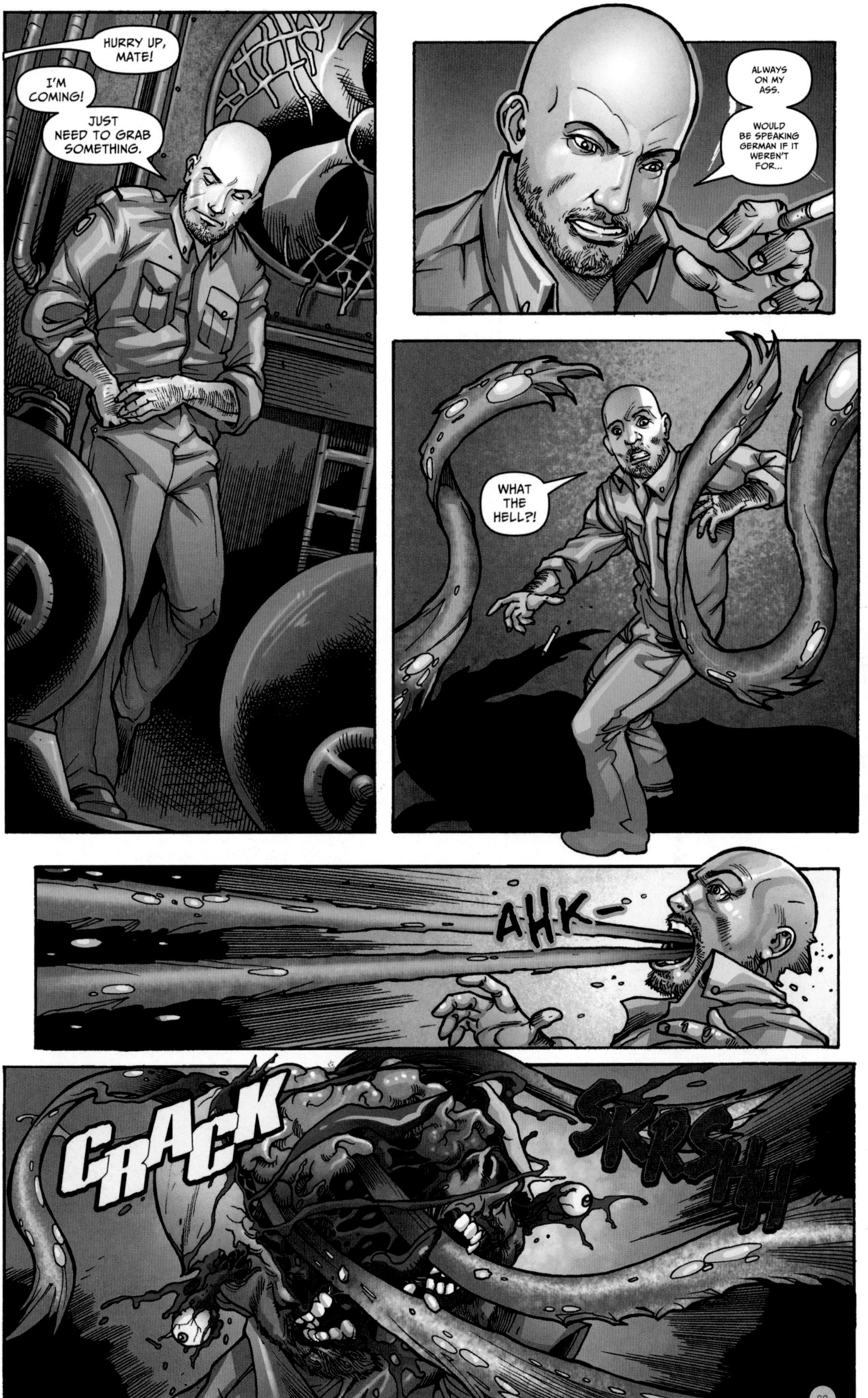
HURRY UP, MATE!
I'M COMING!
JUST NEED TO GRAB SOMETHING.
ALWAYS ON MY ASS.
WOULD BE SPEAKING GERMAN IF IT WEREN'T FOR...
WHAT THE HELL?!
AHK-
CRACK
SKRSHHH

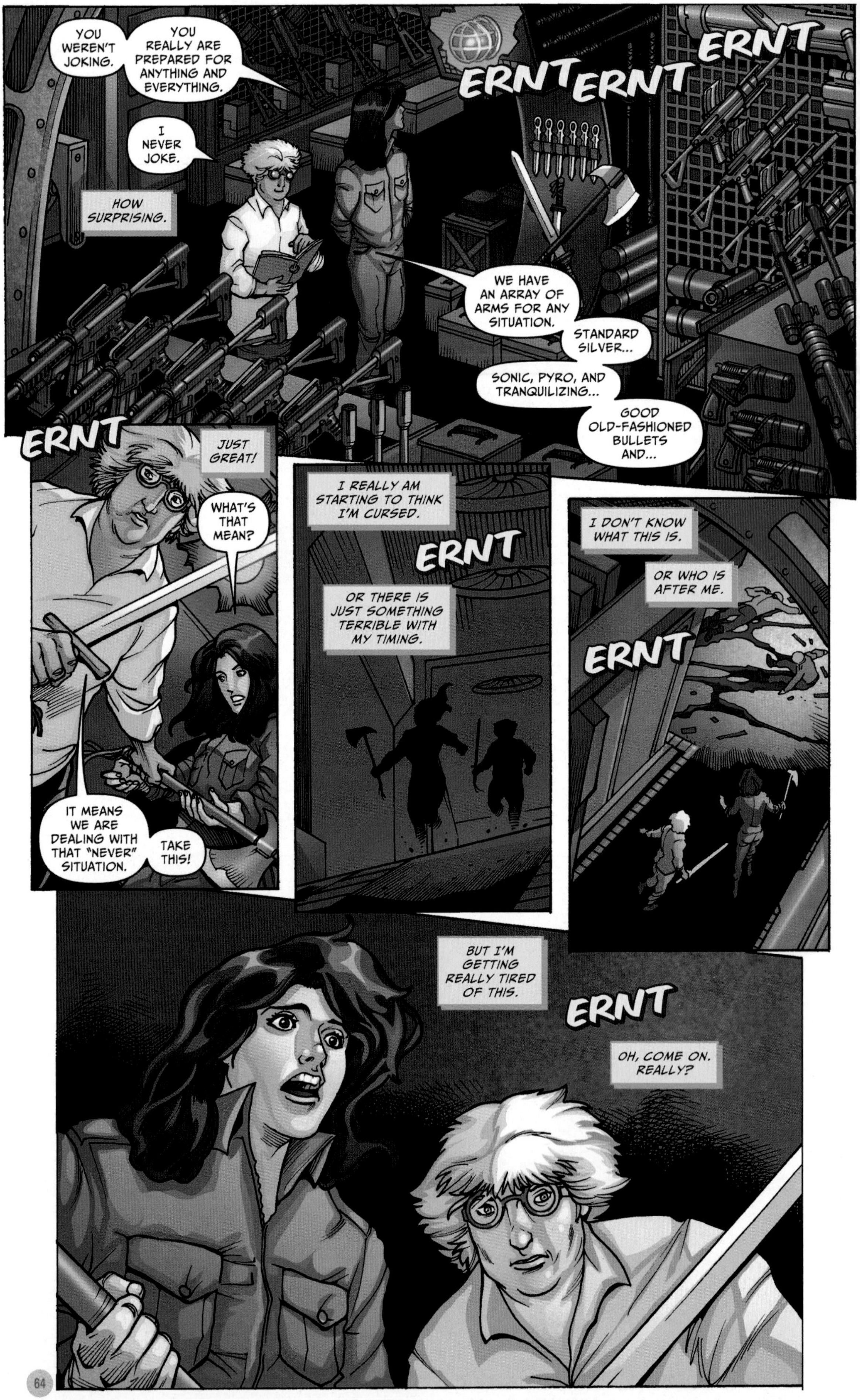
YOU WEREN'T JOKING.
YOU REALLY ARE PREPARED FOR ANYTHING AND EVERYTHING.
ERNT ERNT ERNT
I NEVER JOKE.
HOW SURPRISING.
WE HAVE AN ARRAY OF ARMS FOR ANY SITUATION.
STANDARD SILVER...
SONIC, PYRO, AND TRANQUILIZING...
GOOD OLD-FASHIONED BULLETS AND...
ERNT
JUST GREAT!
WHAT'S THAT MEAN?
IT MEANS WE ARE DEALING WITH THAT "NEVER" SITUATION.
TAKE THIS!
I REALLY AM STARTING TO THINK I'M CURSED.
ERNT
OR THERE IS JUST SOMETHING TERRIBLE WITH MY TIMING.
I DON'T KNOW WHAT THIS IS.
OR WHO IS AFTER ME.
ERNT
BUT I'M GETTING REALLY TIRED OF THIS.
ERNT
OH, COME ON. REALLY?

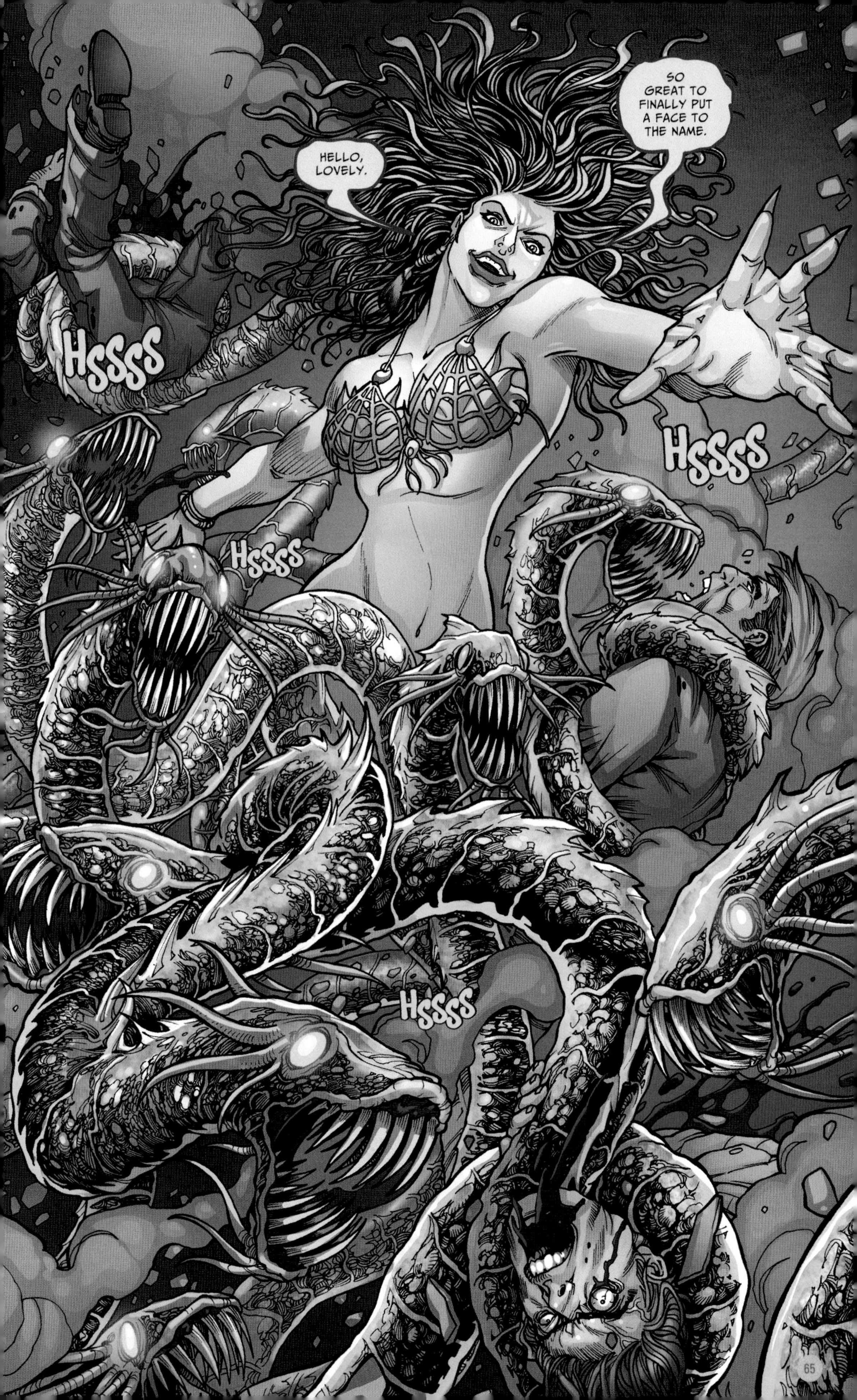
HELLO, LOVELY.
SO GREAT TO FINALLY PUT A FACE TO THE NAME.
HSSSS
HSSSS
HSSSS
HSSSS

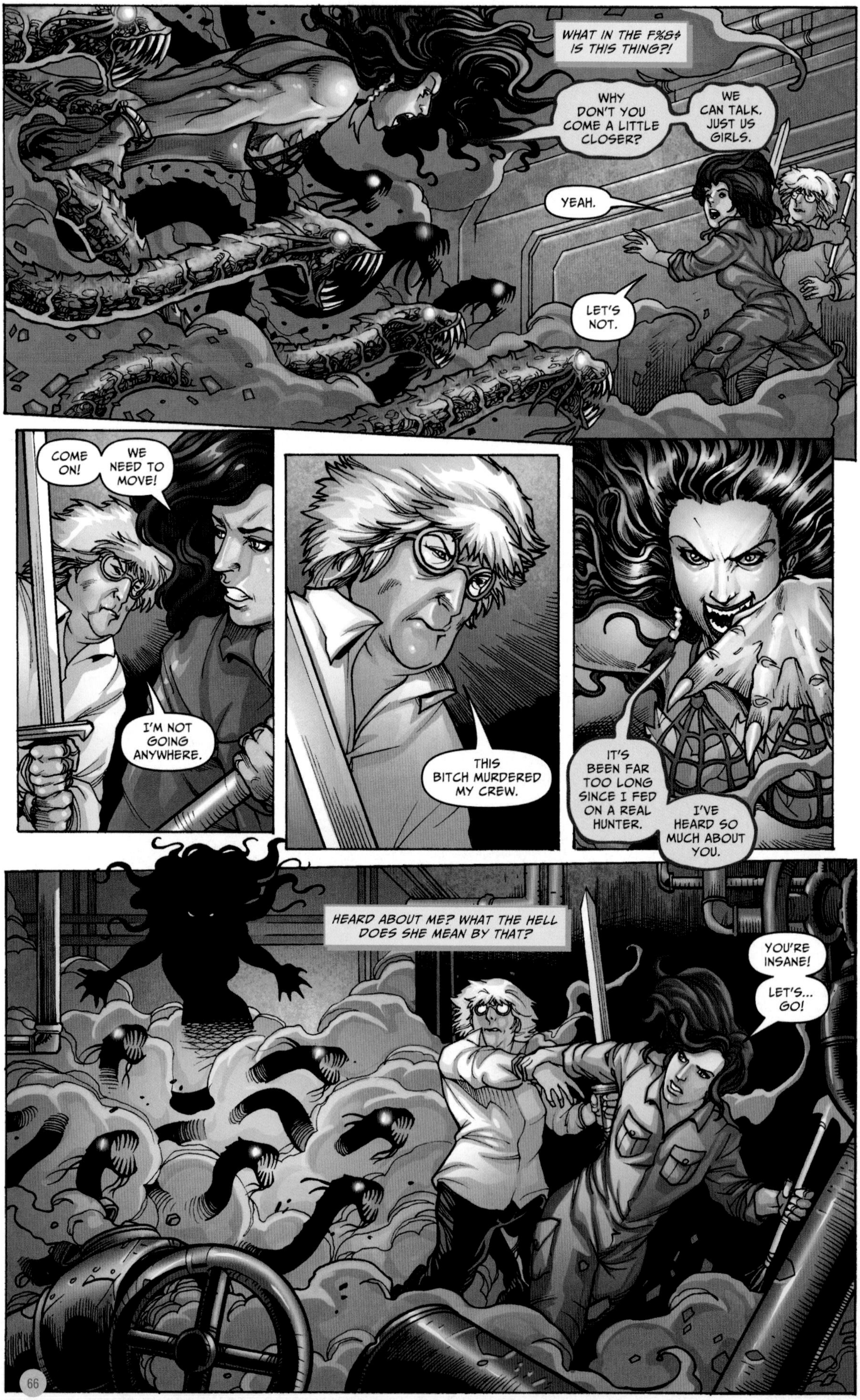
WHAT IN THE F%&$ IS THIS THING?!
WHY DON'T YOU COME A LITTLE CLOSER?
WE CAN TALK. JUST US GIRLS.
YEAH.
LET'S NOT.
COME ON!
WE NEED TO MOVE!
I'M NOT GOING ANYWHERE.
THIS BITCH MURDERED MY CREW.
IT'S BEEN FAR TOO LONG SINCE I FED ON A REAL HUNTER.
I'VE HEARD SO MUCH ABOUT YOU.
HEARD ABOUT ME? WHAT THE HELL DOES SHE MEAN BY THAT?
YOU'RE INSANE!
LET'S... GO!

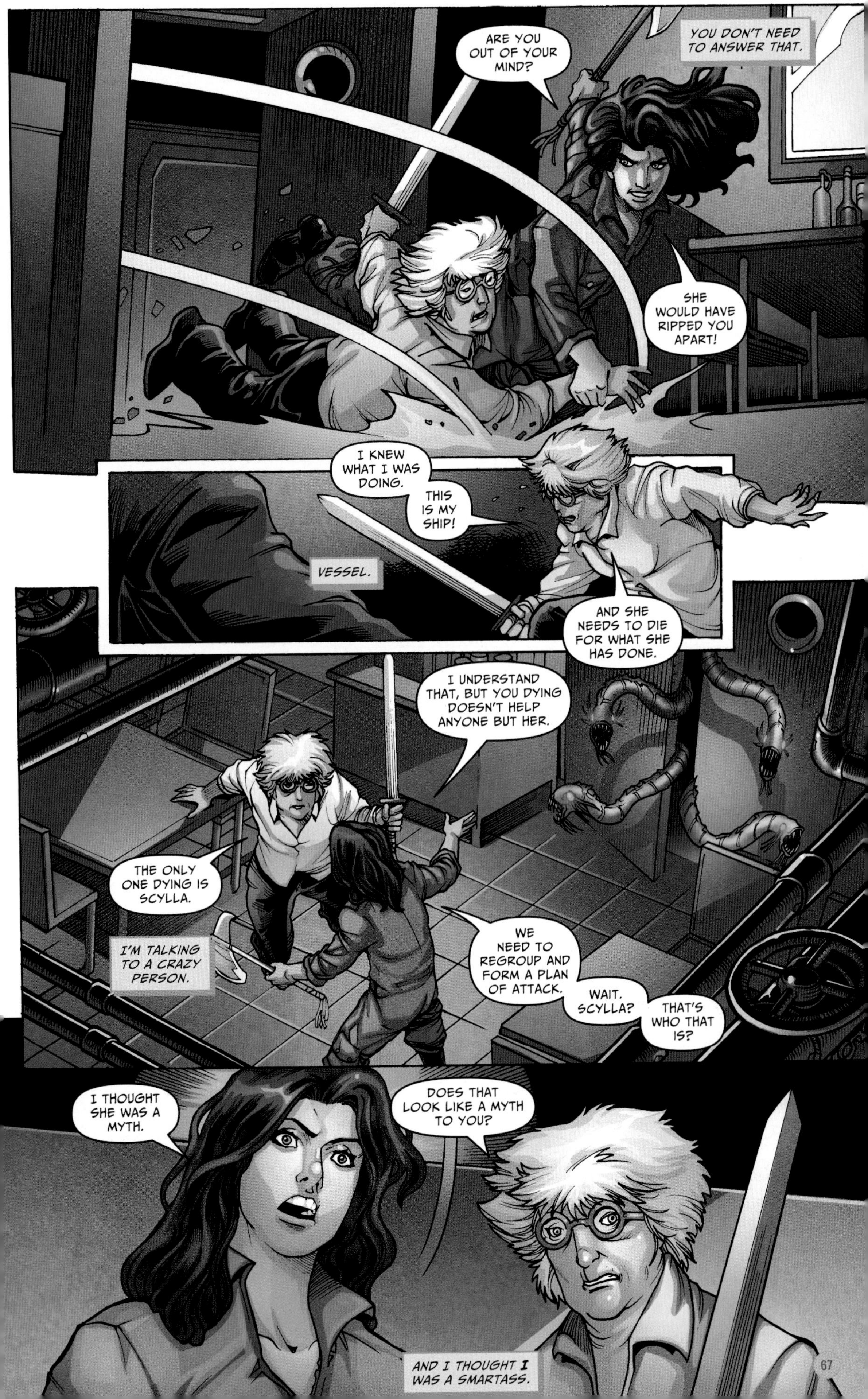
ARE YOU OUT OF YOUR MIND?
YOU DON'T NEED TO ANSWER THAT.
SHE WOULD HAVE RIPPED YOU APART!
I KNEW WHAT I WAS DOING.
THIS IS MY SHIP!
VESSEL.
AND SHE NEEDS TO DIE FOR WHAT SHE HAS DONE.
I UNDERSTAND THAT, BUT YOU DYING DOESN'T HELP ANYONE BUT HER.
THE ONLY ONE DYING IS SCYLLA.
I'M TALKING TO A CRAZY PERSON.
WE NEED TO REGROUP AND FORM A PLAN OF ATTACK.
WAIT. SCYLLA?
THAT'S WHO THAT IS?
I THOUGHT SHE WAS A MYTH.
DOES THAT LOOK LIKE A MYTH TO YOU?
AND I THOUGHT **I** WAS A SMARTASS.

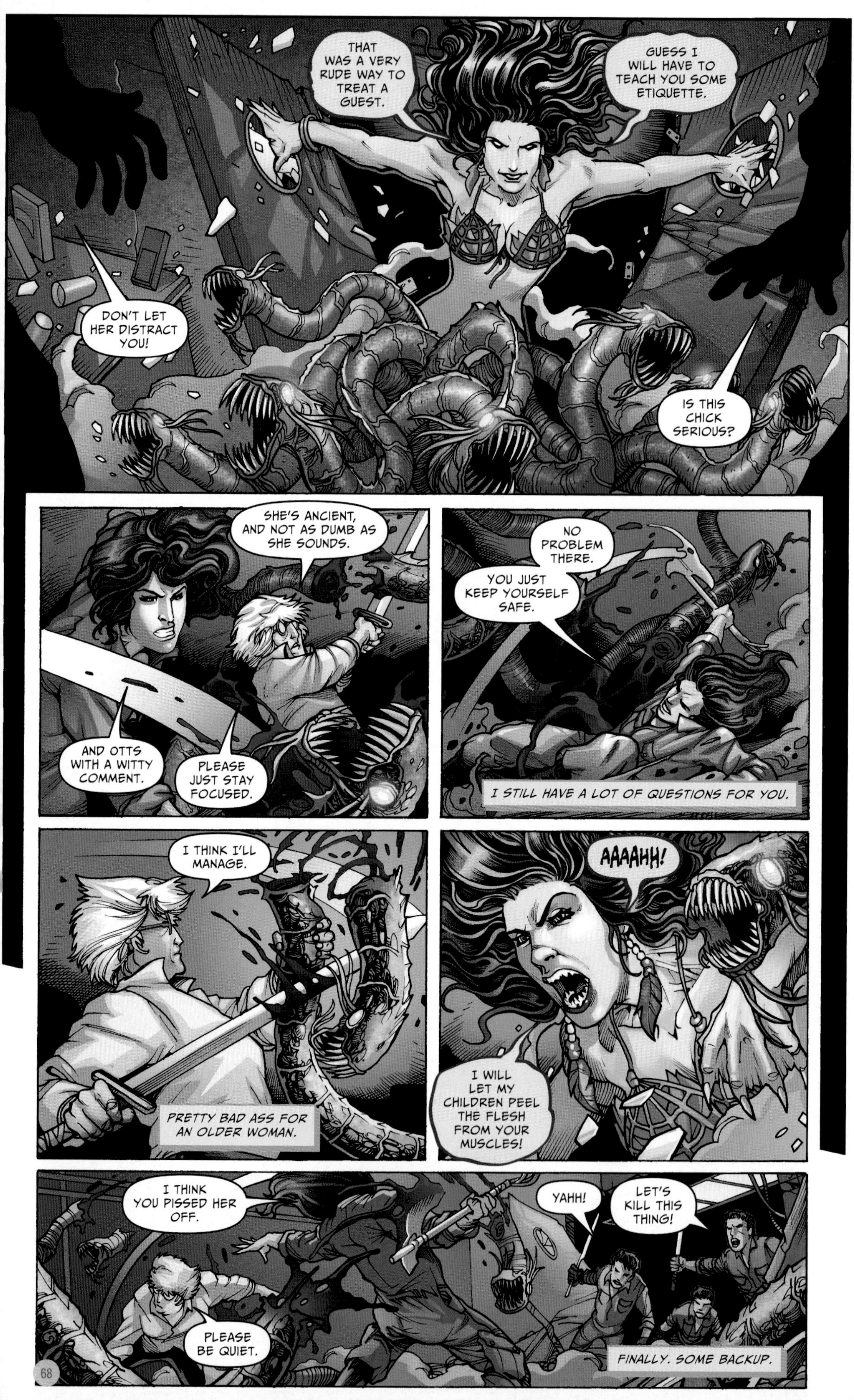

THAT WAS A VERY RUDE WAY TO TREAT A GUEST.
GUESS I WILL HAVE TO TEACH YOU SOME ETIQUETTE.
DON'T LET HER DISTRACT YOU!
IS THIS CHICK SERIOUS?
SHE'S ANCIENT, AND NOT AS DUMB AS SHE SOUNDS.
AND OTTS WITH A WITTY COMMENT.
PLEASE JUST STAY FOCUSED.
NO PROBLEM THERE.
YOU JUST KEEP YOURSELF SAFE.
I STILL HAVE A LOT OF QUESTIONS FOR YOU.
I THINK I'LL MANAGE.
PRETTY BAD ASS FOR AN OLDER WOMAN.
AAAAHH!
I WILL LET MY CHILDREN PEEL THE FLESH FROM YOUR MUSCLES!
I THINK YOU PISSED HER OFF.
PLEASE BE QUIET.
YAHH!
LET'S KILL THIS THING!
FINALLY. SOME BACKUP.

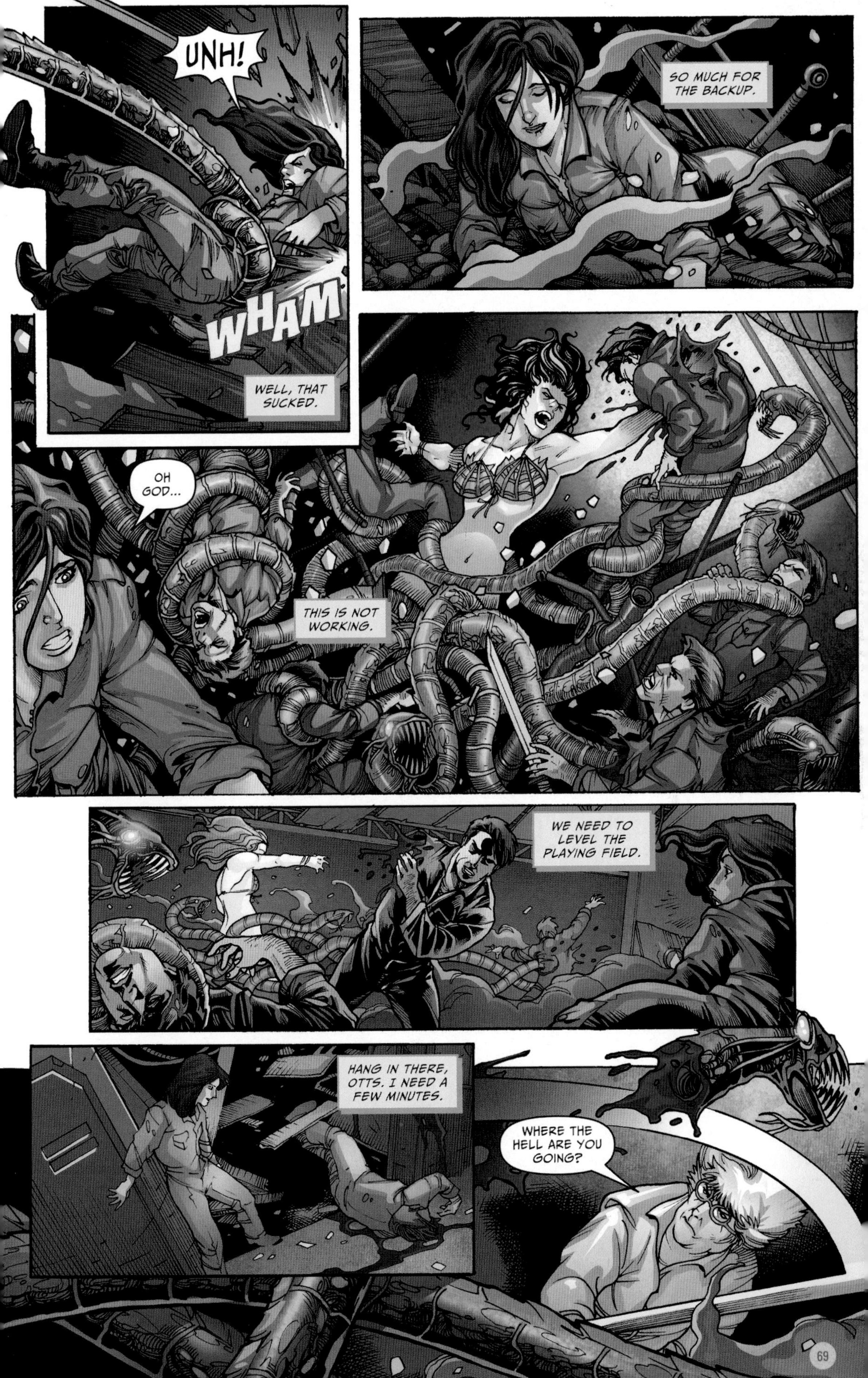
UNH!
WHAM
WELL, THAT SUCKED.
SO MUCH FOR THE BACKUP.
OH GOD...
THIS IS NOT WORKING.
WE NEED TO LEVEL THE PLAYING FIELD.
HANG IN THERE, OTTS. I NEED A FEW MINUTES.
WHERE THE HELL ARE YOU GOING?

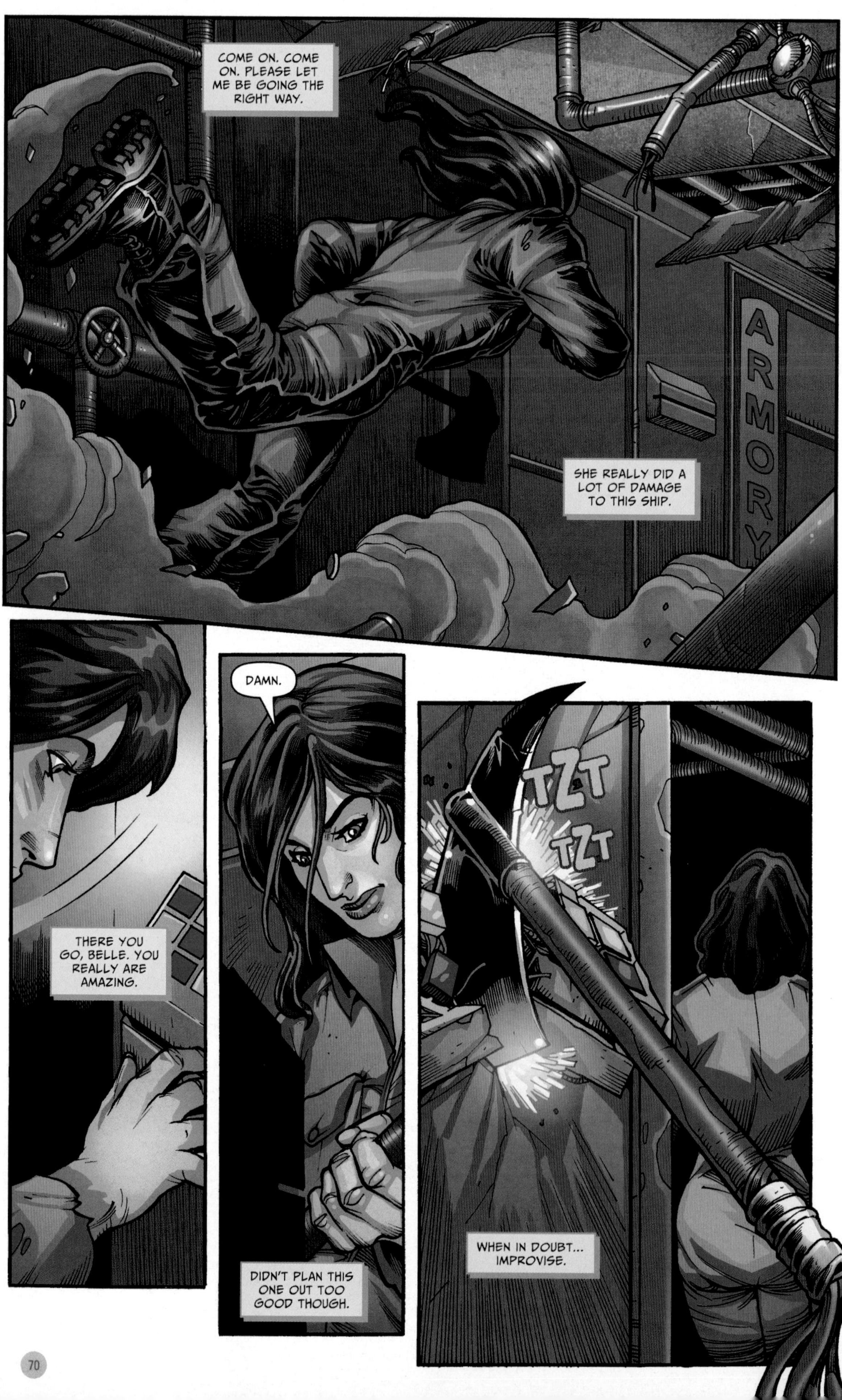
COME ON. COME ON. PLEASE LET ME BE GOING THE RIGHT WAY.
ARMORY
SHE REALLY DID A LOT OF DAMAGE TO THIS SHIP.
THERE YOU GO, BELLE. YOU REALLY ARE AMAZING.
DAMN.
DIDN'T PLAN THIS ONE OUT TOO GOOD THOUGH.
TZT
TZT
WHEN IN DOUBT... IMPROVISE.

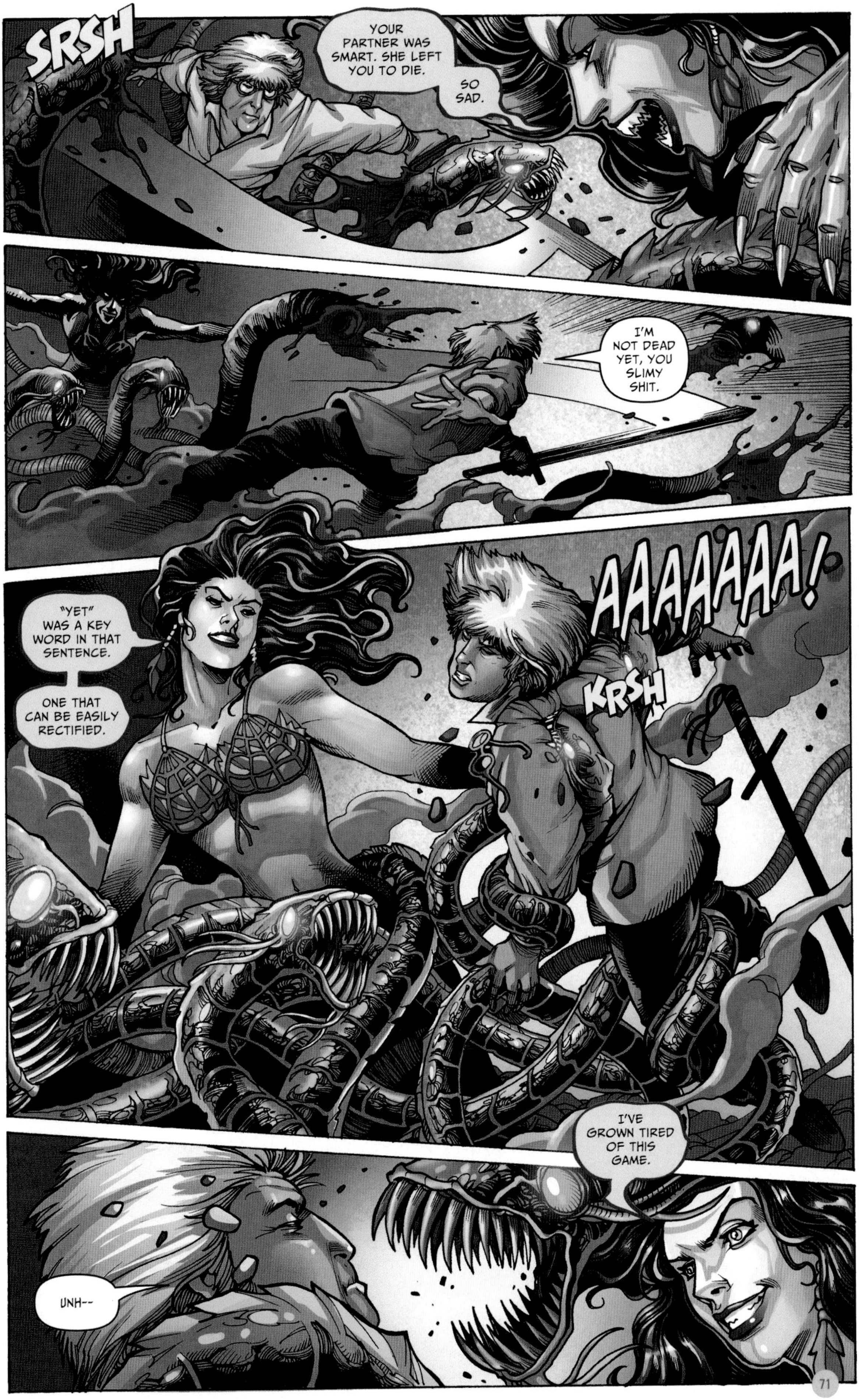

SRSH
YOUR PARTNER WAS SMART. SHE LEFT YOU TO DIE.
SO SAD.
I'M NOT DEAD YET, YOU SLIMY SHIT.
"YET" WAS A KEY WORD IN THAT SENTENCE.
ONE THAT CAN BE EASILY RECTIFIED.
AAAAAAA!
KRSH
I'VE GROWN TIRED OF THIS GAME.
UNH--

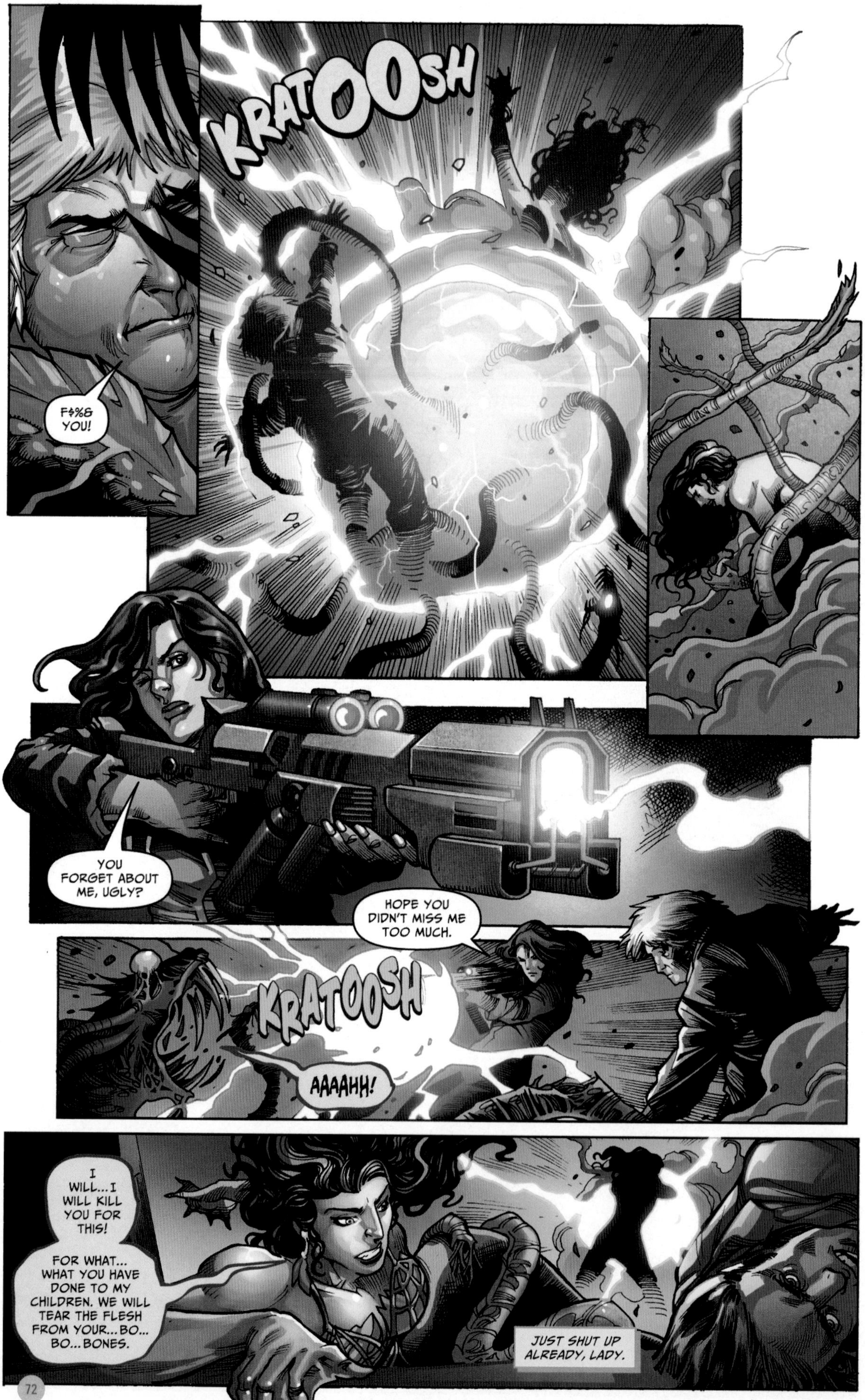
KRATOOSH
F$%& YOU!
YOU FORGET ABOUT ME, UGLY?
HOPE YOU DIDN'T MISS ME TOO MUCH.
KRATOOSH
AAAAHH!
I WILL...I WILL KILL YOU FOR THIS!
FOR WHAT... WHAT YOU HAVE DONE TO MY CHILDREN. WE WILL TEAR THE FLESH FROM YOUR...BO... BO...BONES.
JUST SHUT UP ALREADY, LADY.

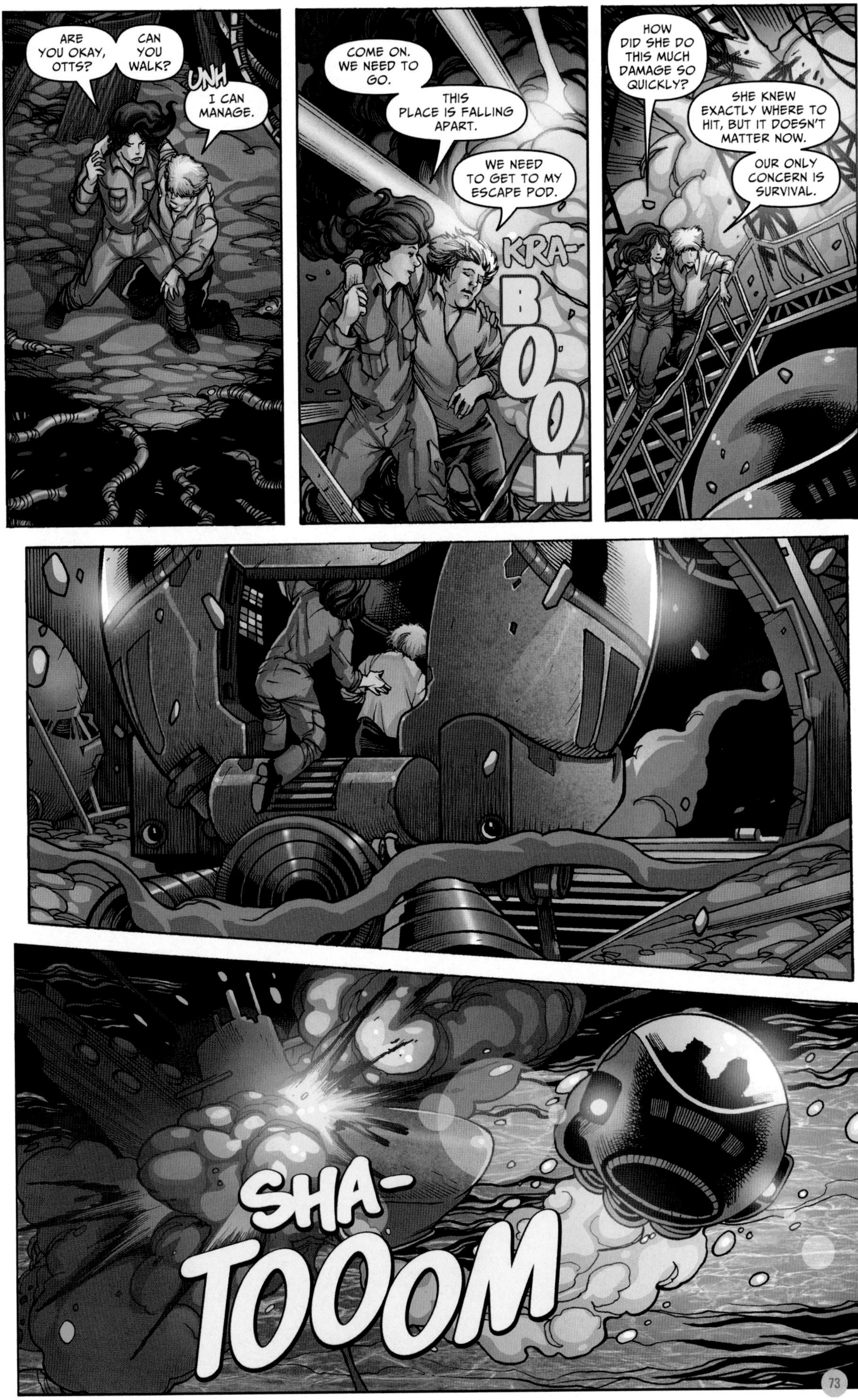
ARE YOU OKAY, OTTS?
CAN YOU WALK?
UNH
I CAN MANAGE.
COME ON. WE NEED TO GO.
THIS PLACE IS FALLING APART.
WE NEED TO GET TO MY ESCAPE POD.
KRA-BOOOM
HOW DID SHE DO THIS MUCH DAMAGE SO QUICKLY?
SHE KNEW EXACTLY WHERE TO HIT, BUT IT DOESN'T MATTER NOW.
OUR ONLY CONCERN IS SURVIVAL.
SHA-TOOOM

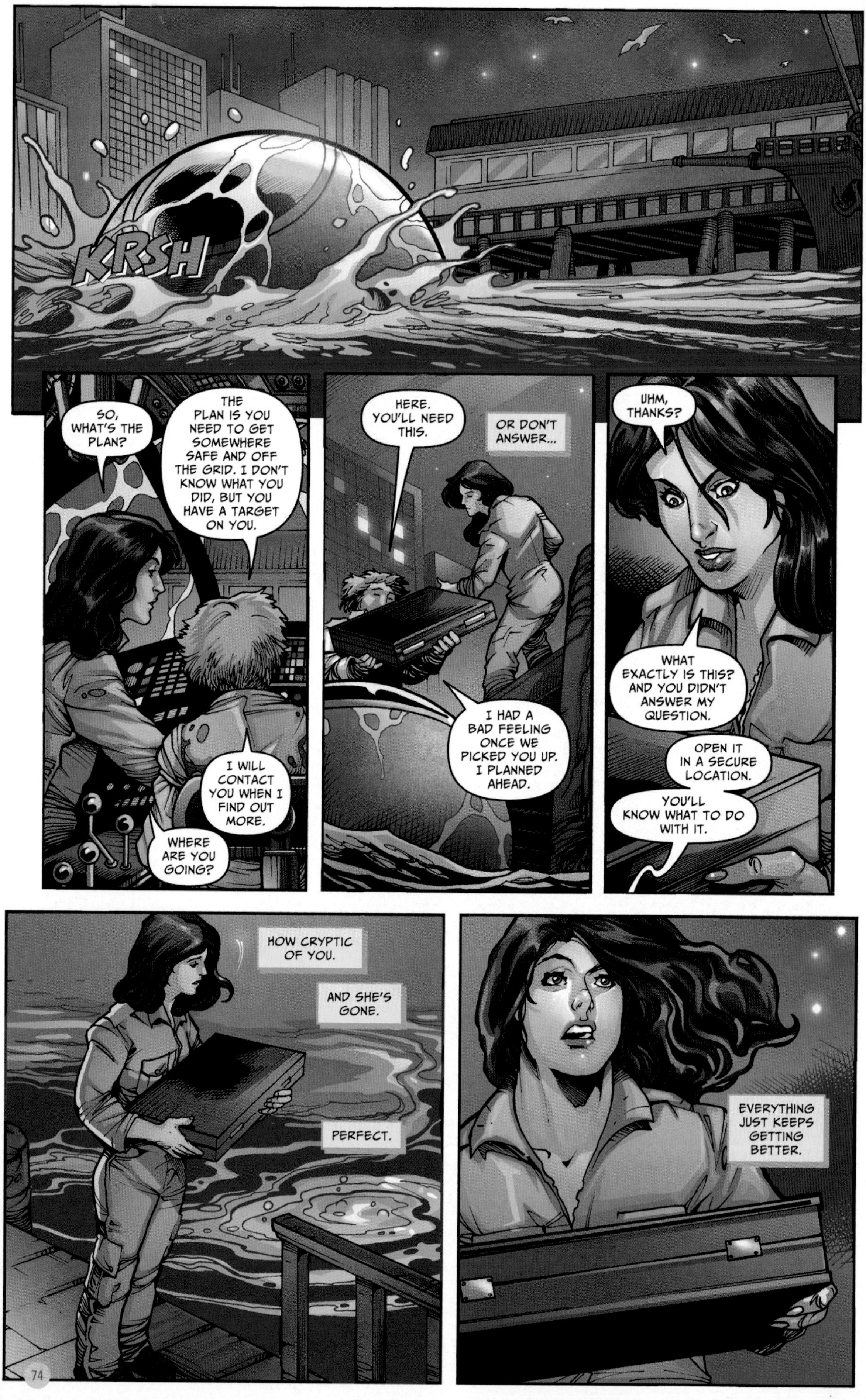
KRSH
SO, WHAT'S THE PLAN?
THE PLAN IS YOU NEED TO GET SOMEWHERE SAFE AND OFF THE GRID. I DON'T KNOW WHAT YOU DID, BUT YOU HAVE A TARGET ON YOU.
I WILL CONTACT YOU WHEN I FIND OUT MORE.
WHERE ARE YOU GOING?
HERE. YOU'LL NEED THIS.
OR DON'T ANSWER...
I HAD A BAD FEELING ONCE WE PICKED YOU UP. I PLANNED AHEAD.
UHM, THANKS?
WHAT EXACTLY IS THIS? AND YOU DIDN'T ANSWER MY QUESTION.
OPEN IT IN A SECURE LOCATION.
YOU'LL KNOW WHAT TO DO WITH IT.
HOW CRYPTIC OF YOU.
AND SHE'S GONE.
PERFECT.
EVERYTHING JUST KEEPS GETTING BETTER.

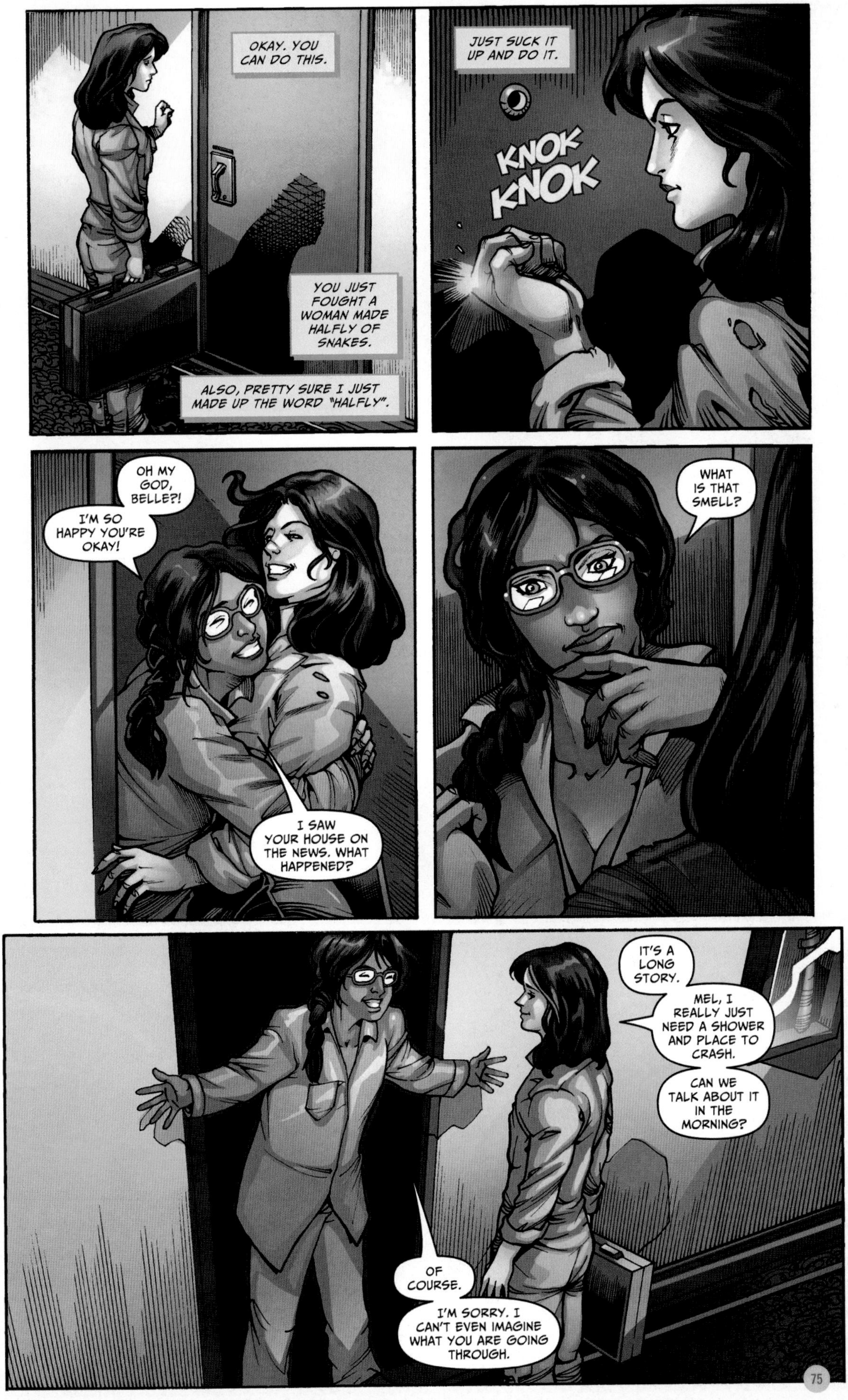
OKAY. YOU CAN DO THIS.
YOU JUST FOUGHT A WOMAN MADE HALFLY OF SNAKES.
ALSO, PRETTY SURE I JUST MADE UP THE WORD "HALFLY".
JUST SUCK IT UP AND DO IT.
KNOK KNOK
OH MY GOD, BELLE?!
I'M SO HAPPY YOU'RE OKAY!
I SAW YOUR HOUSE ON THE NEWS. WHAT HAPPENED?
WHAT IS THAT SMELL?
IT'S A LONG STORY.
MEL, I REALLY JUST NEED A SHOWER AND PLACE TO CRASH.
CAN WE TALK ABOUT IT IN THE MORNING?
OF COURSE.
I'M SORRY. I CAN'T EVEN IMAGINE WHAT YOU ARE GOING THROUGH.

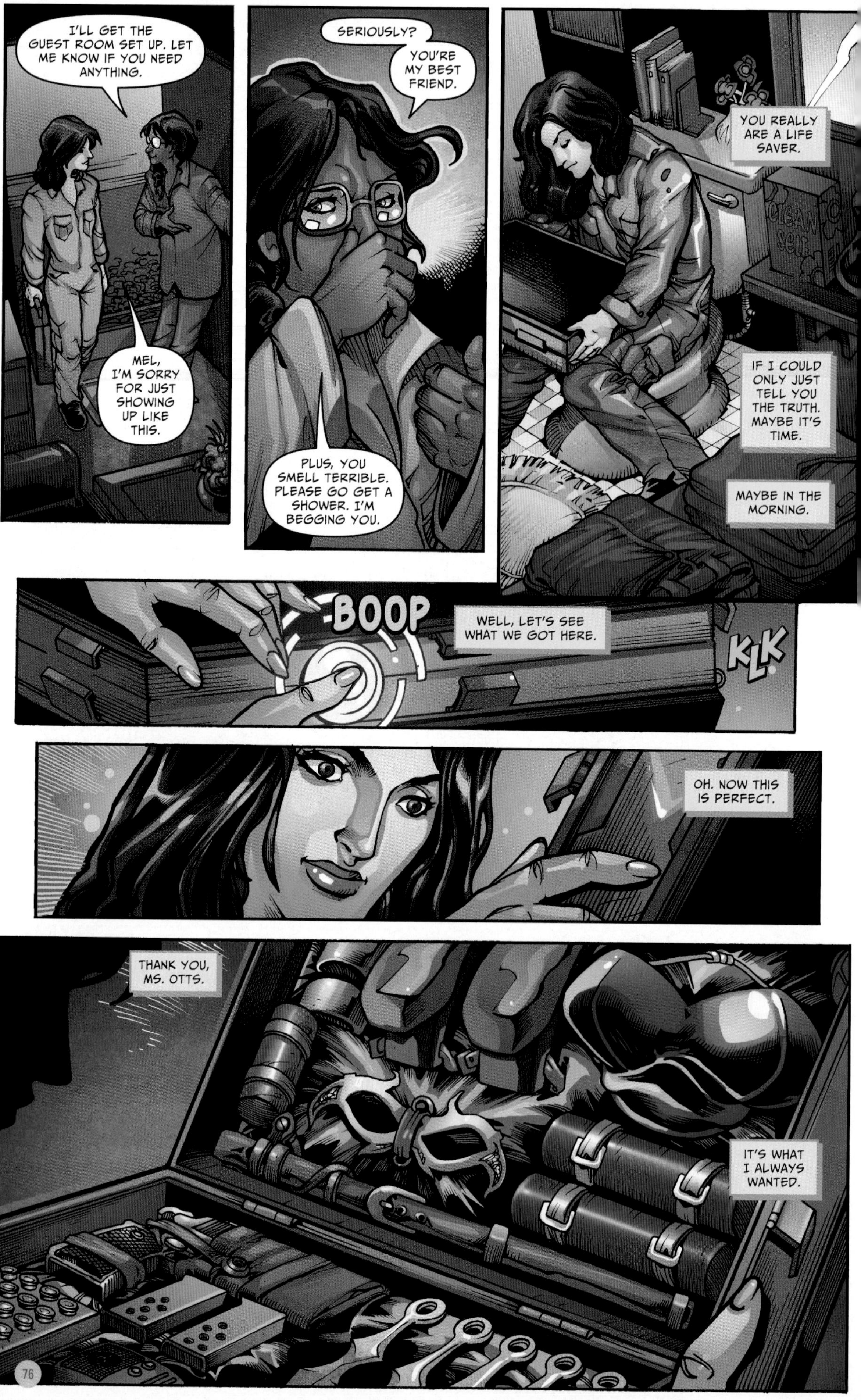
I'LL GET THE GUEST ROOM SET UP. LET ME KNOW IF YOU NEED ANYTHING.
MEL, I'M SORRY FOR JUST SHOWING UP LIKE THIS.
SERIOUSLY?
YOU'RE MY BEST FRIEND.
PLUS, YOU SMELL TERRIBLE. PLEASE GO GET A SHOWER. I'M BEGGING YOU.
YOU REALLY ARE A LIFE SAVER.
IF I COULD ONLY JUST TELL YOU THE TRUTH. MAYBE IT'S TIME.
MAYBE IN THE MORNING.
BOOP
WELL, LET'S SEE WHAT WE GOT HERE.
KLK
OH. NOW THIS IS PERFECT.
THANK YOU, MS. OTTS.
IT'S WHAT I ALWAYS WANTED.

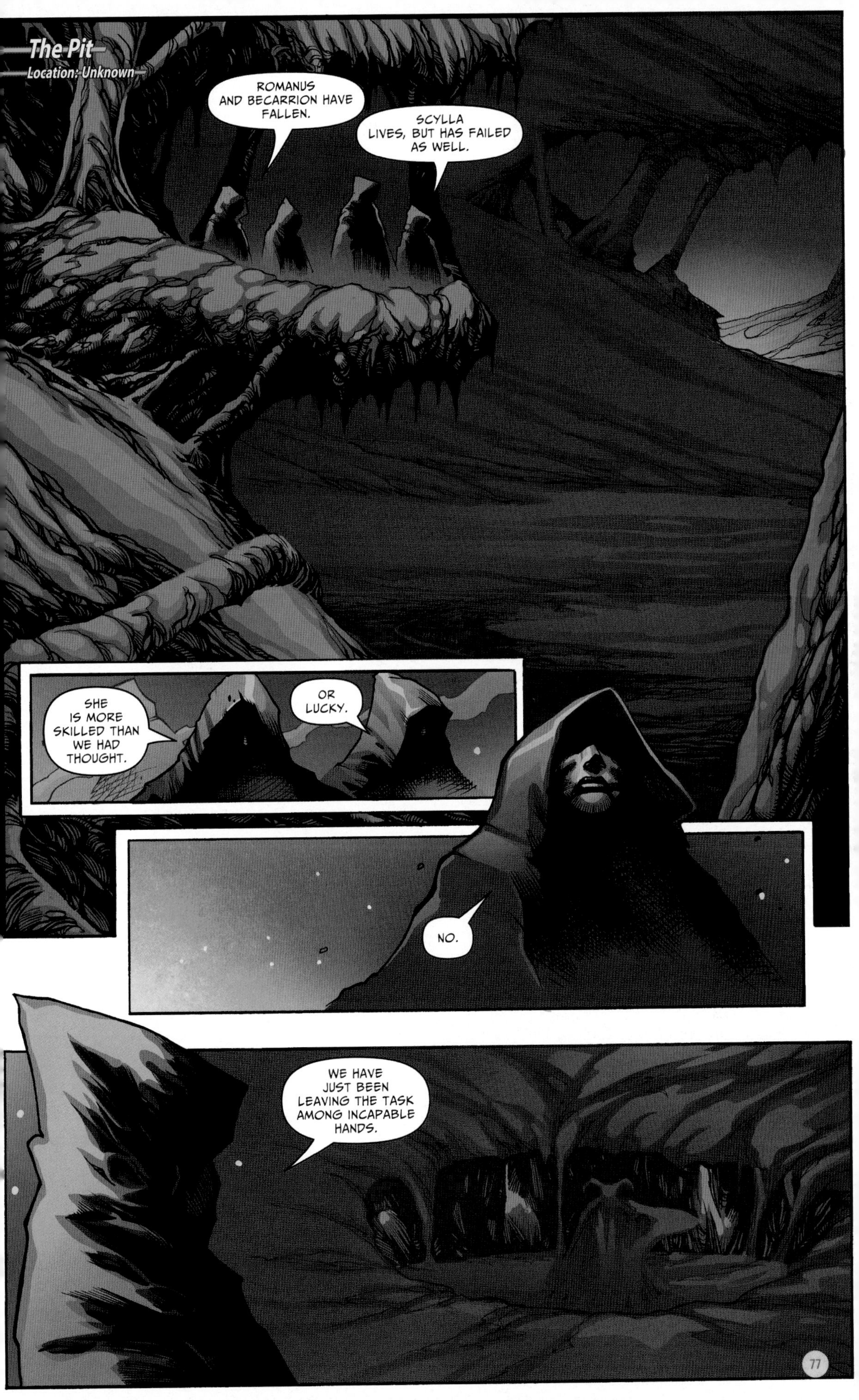
The Pit
Location: Unknown
ROMANUS AND BECARRION HAVE FALLEN.
SCYLLA LIVES, BUT HAS FAILED AS WELL.
SHE IS MORE SKILLED THAN WE HAD THOUGHT.
OR LUCKY.
NO.
WE HAVE JUST BEEN LEAVING THE TASK AMONG INCAPABLE HANDS.

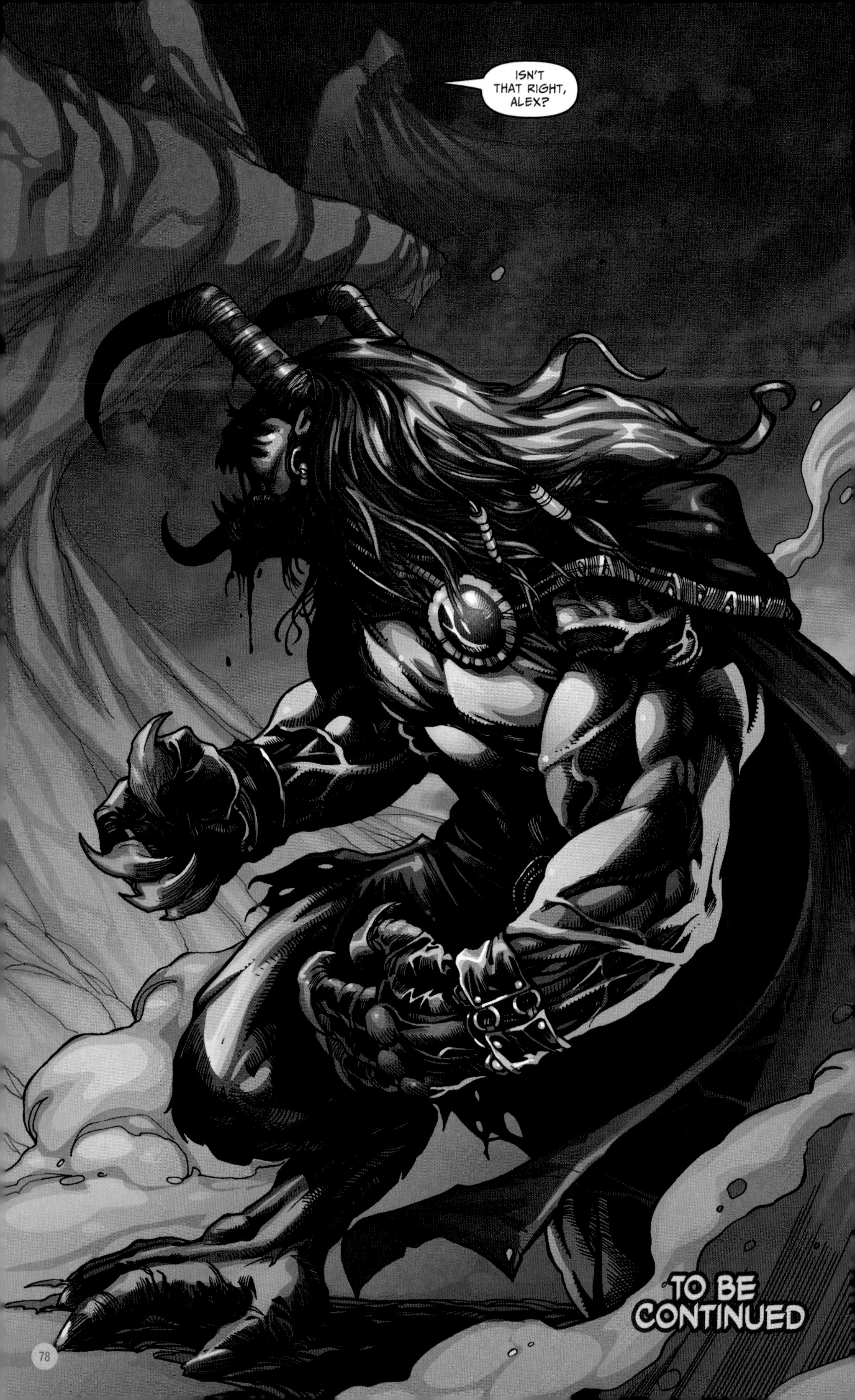
ISN'T THAT RIGHT, ALEX?
TO BE CONTINUED

BELLE
BEAST HUNTER

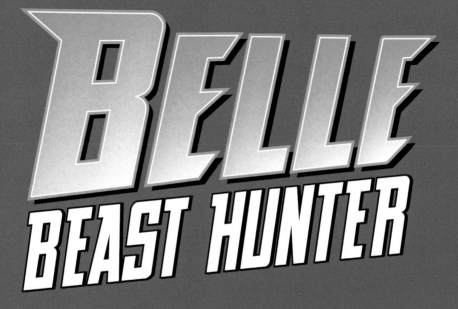

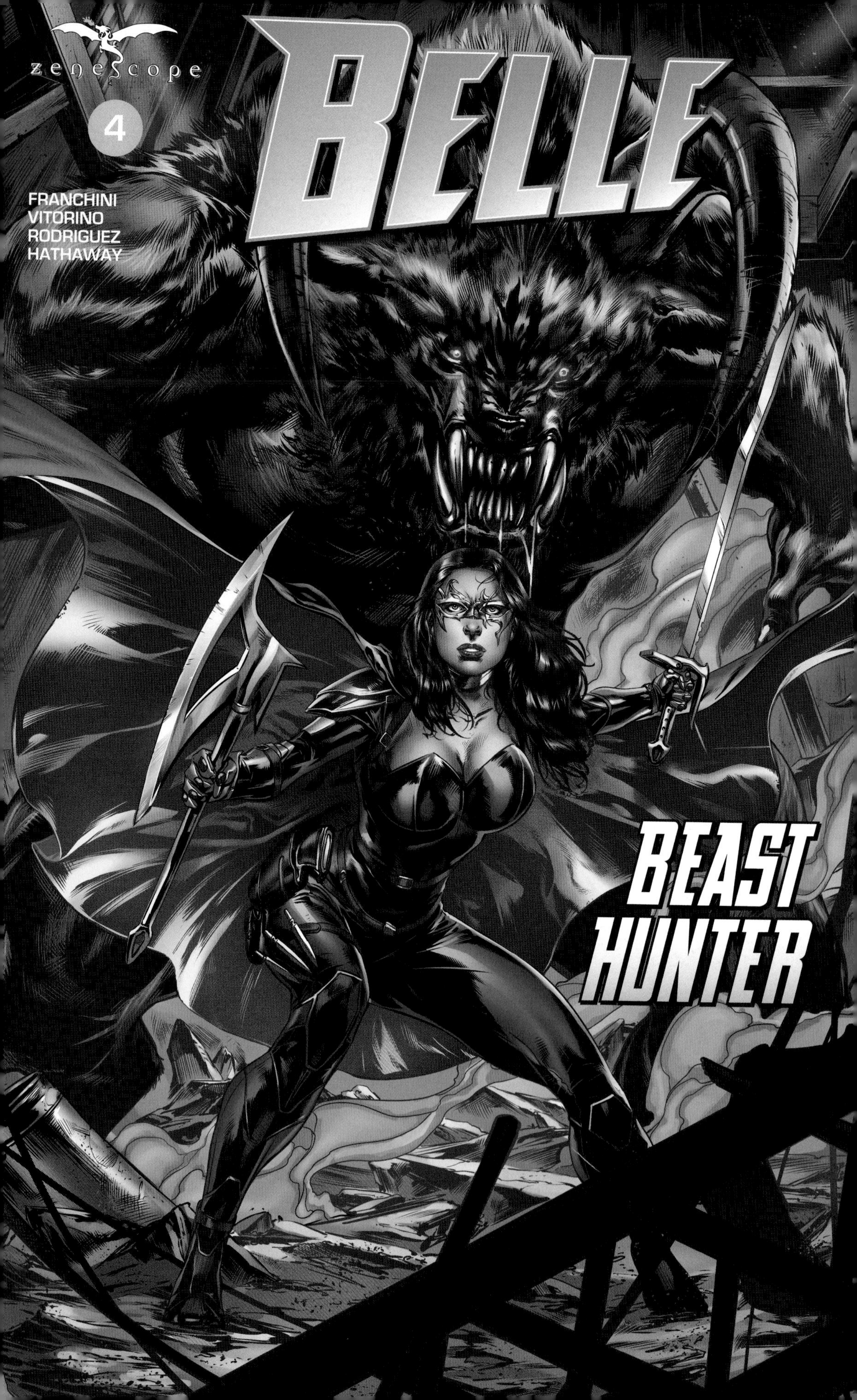
zenescope
4
BELLE
FRANCHINI
VITORINO
RODRIGUEZ
HATHAWAY
BEAST
HUNTER

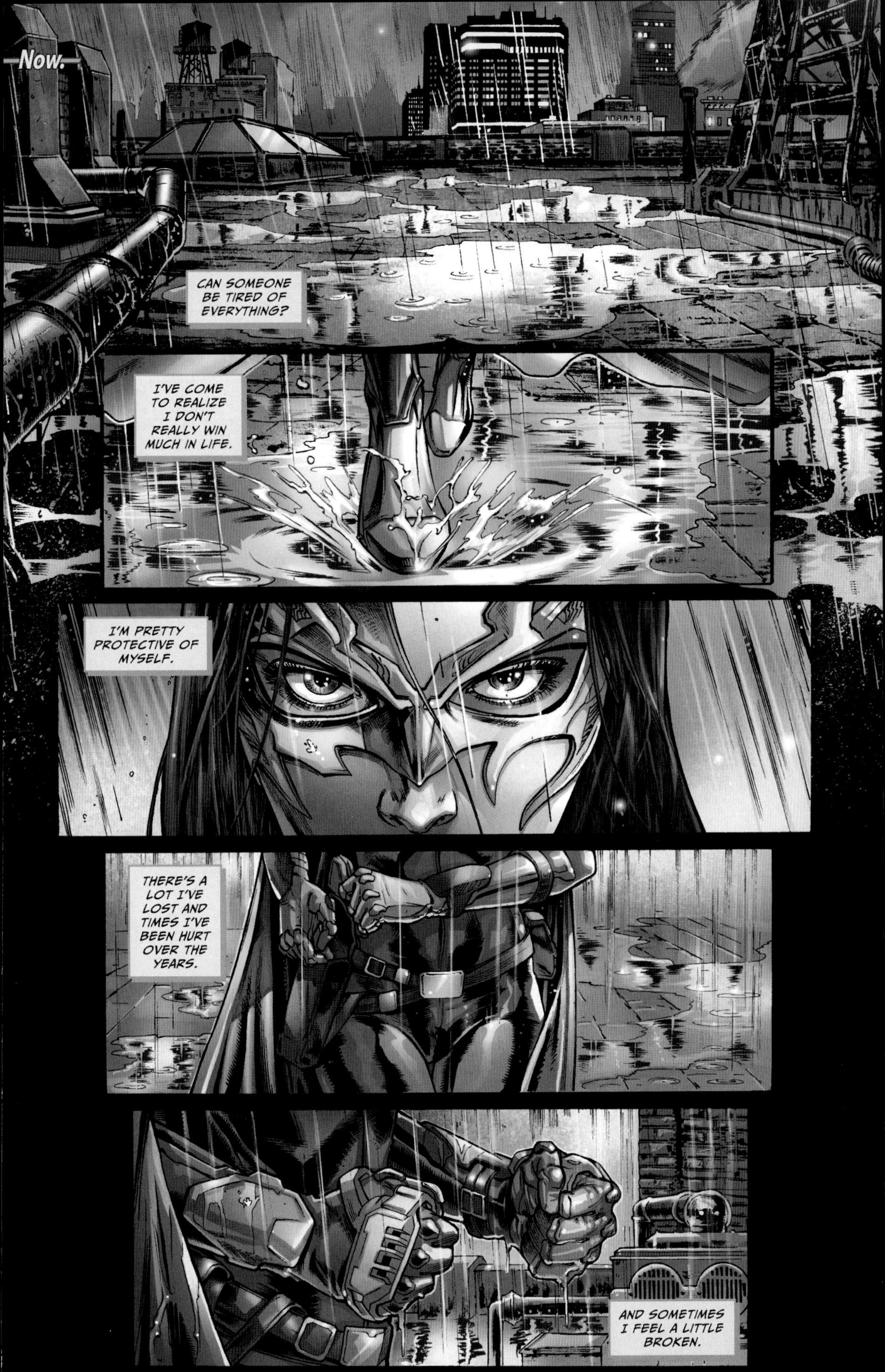
Now.
CAN SOMEONE BE TIRED OF EVERYTHING?
I'VE COME TO REALIZE I DON'T REALLY WIN MUCH IN LIFE.
I'M PRETTY PROTECTIVE OF MYSELF.
THERE'S A LOT I'VE LOST AND TIMES I'VE BEEN HURT OVER THE YEARS.
AND SOMETIMES I FEEL A LITTLE BROKEN.

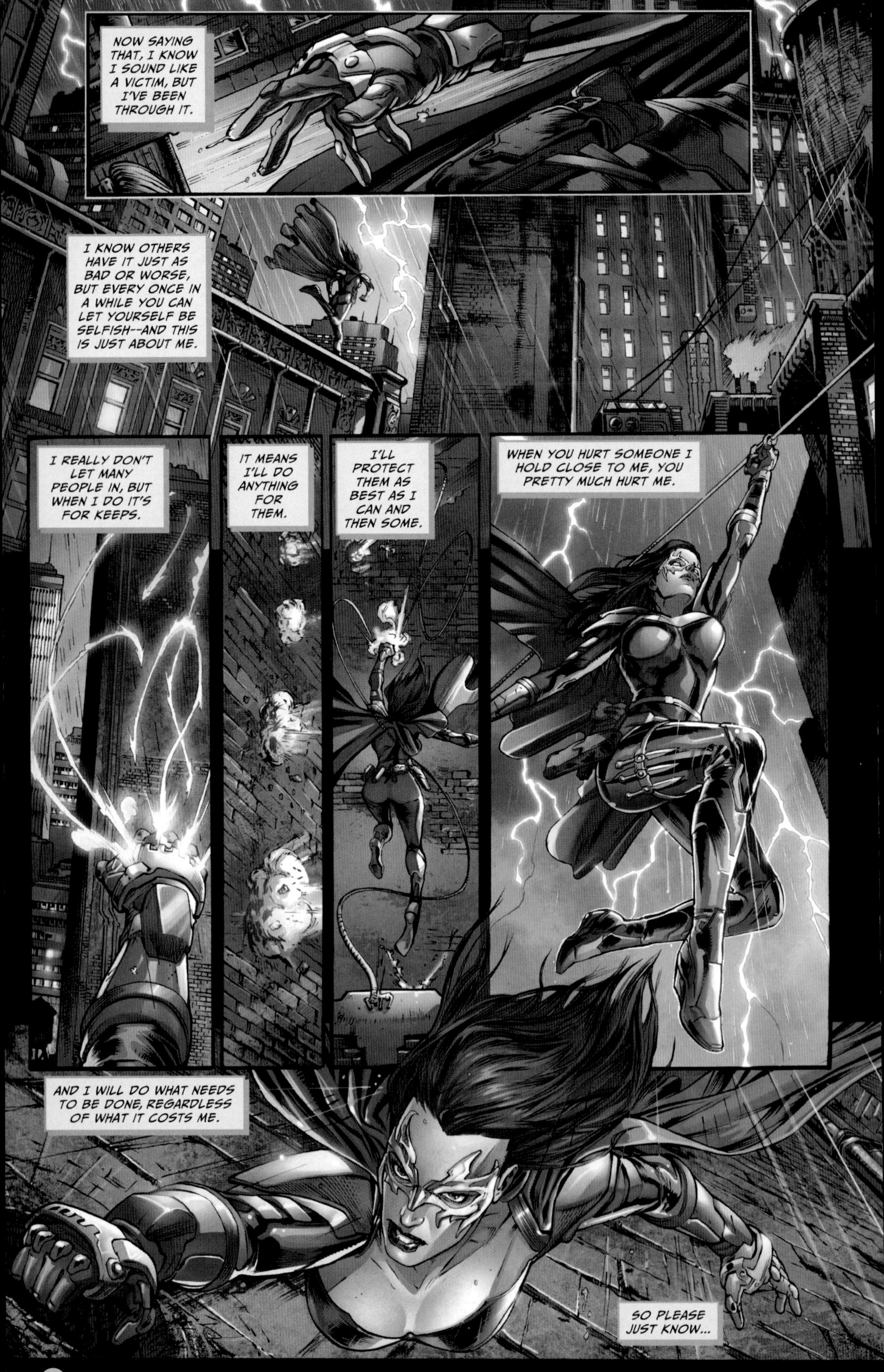
NOW SAYING THAT, I KNOW I SOUND LIKE A VICTIM, BUT I'VE BEEN THROUGH IT.
I KNOW OTHERS HAVE IT JUST AS BAD OR WORSE, BUT EVERY ONCE IN A WHILE YOU CAN LET YOURSELF BE SELFISH--AND THIS IS JUST ABOUT ME.
I REALLY DON'T LET MANY PEOPLE IN, BUT WHEN I DO IT'S FOR KEEPS.
IT MEANS I'LL DO ANYTHING FOR THEM.
I'LL PROTECT THEM AS BEST AS I CAN AND THEN SOME.
WHEN YOU HURT SOMEONE I HOLD CLOSE TO ME, YOU PRETTY MUCH HURT ME.
AND I WILL DO WHAT NEEDS TO BE DONE, REGARDLESS OF WHAT IT COSTS ME.
SO PLEASE JUST KNOW...

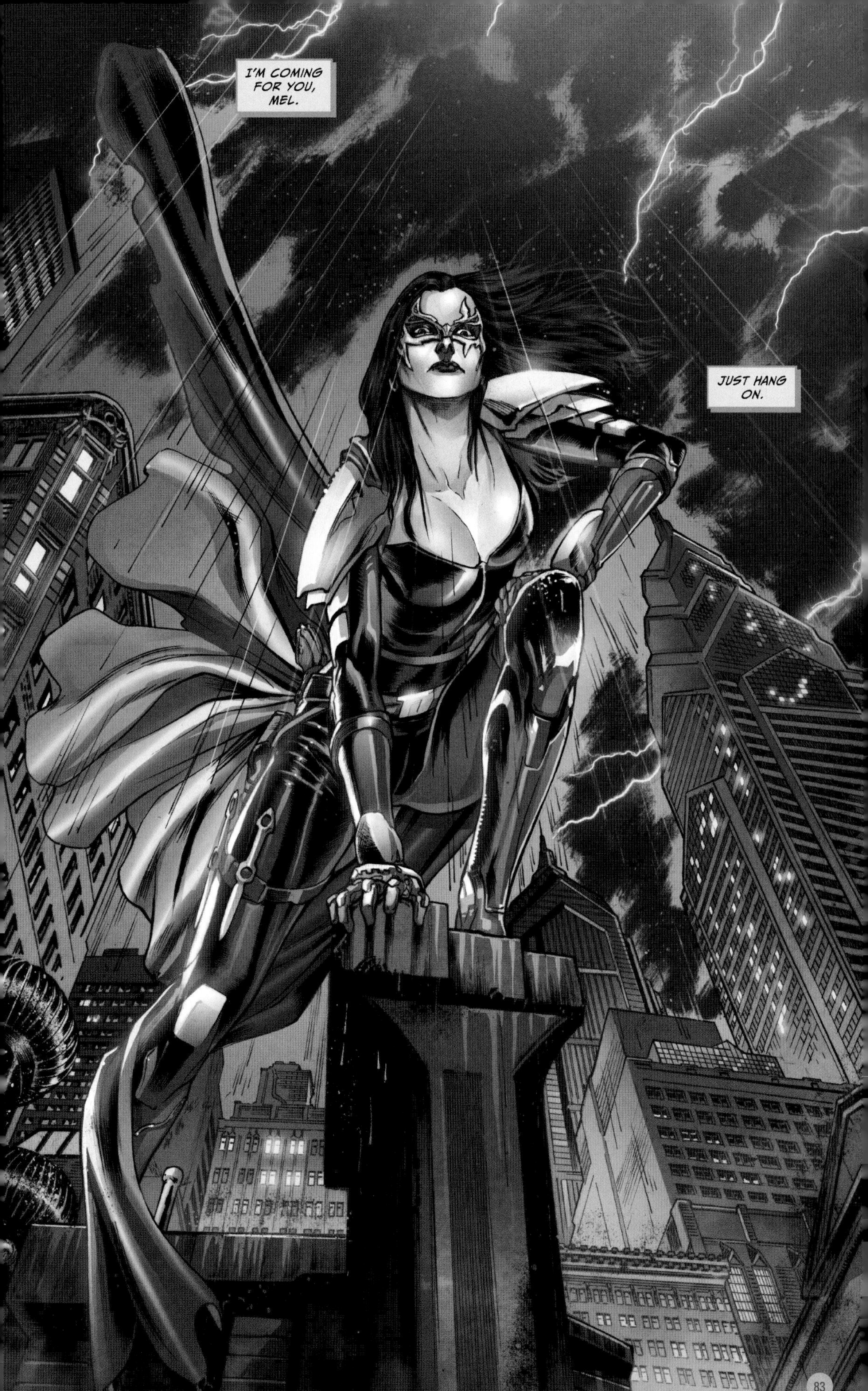
I'M COMING FOR YOU, MEL.
JUST HANG ON.

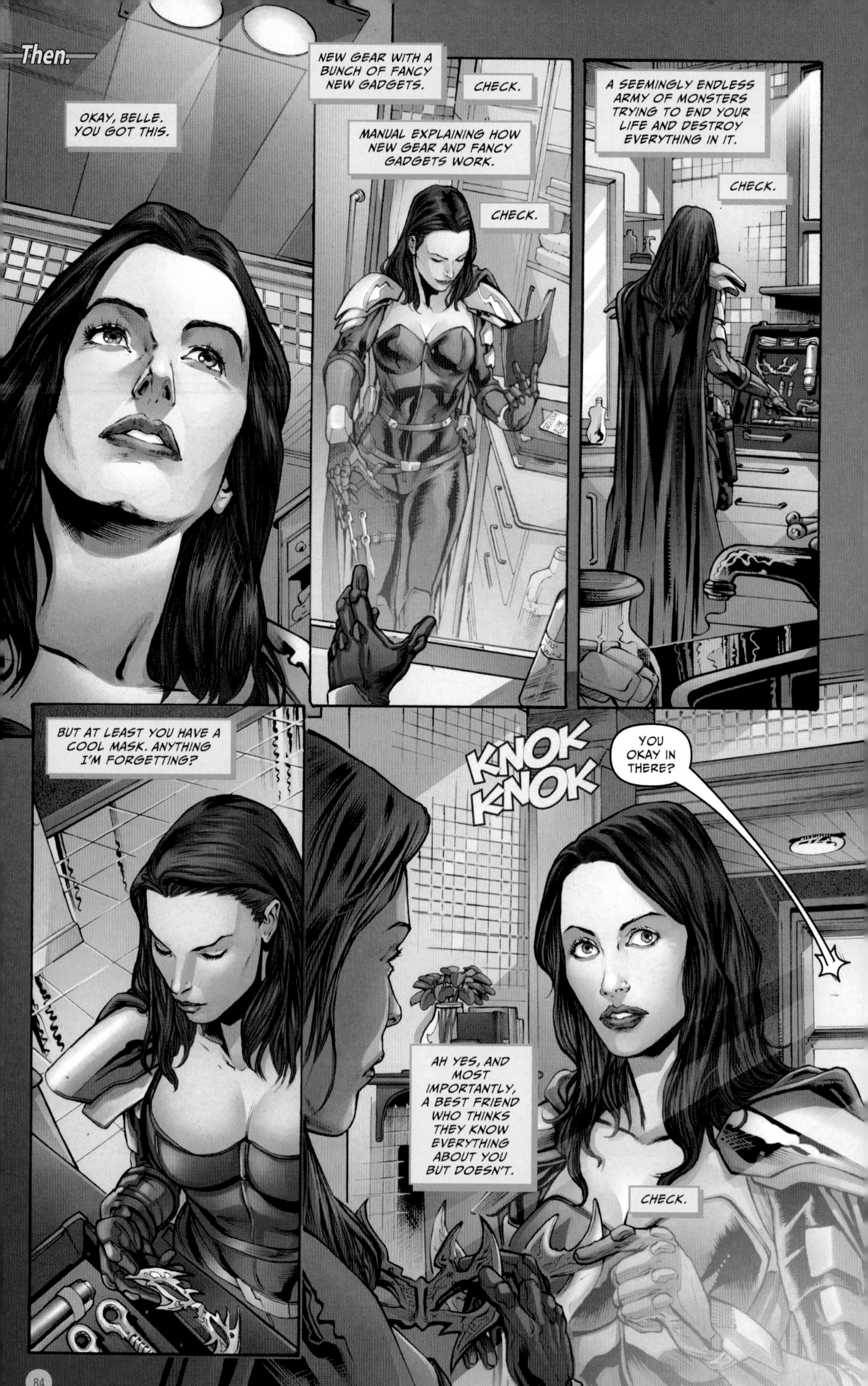
Then.
OKAY, BELLE. YOU GOT THIS.
NEW GEAR WITH A BUNCH OF FANCY NEW GADGETS.
CHECK.
MANUAL EXPLAINING HOW NEW GEAR AND FANCY GADGETS WORK.
CHECK.
A SEEMINGLY ENDLESS ARMY OF MONSTERS TRYING TO END YOUR LIFE AND DESTROY EVERYTHING IN IT.
CHECK.
BUT AT LEAST YOU HAVE A COOL MASK. ANYTHING I'M FORGETTING?
KNOK KNOK
YOU OKAY IN THERE?
AH YES, AND MOST IMPORTANTLY, A BEST FRIEND WHO THINKS THEY KNOW EVERYTHING ABOUT YOU BUT DOESN'T.
CHECK.

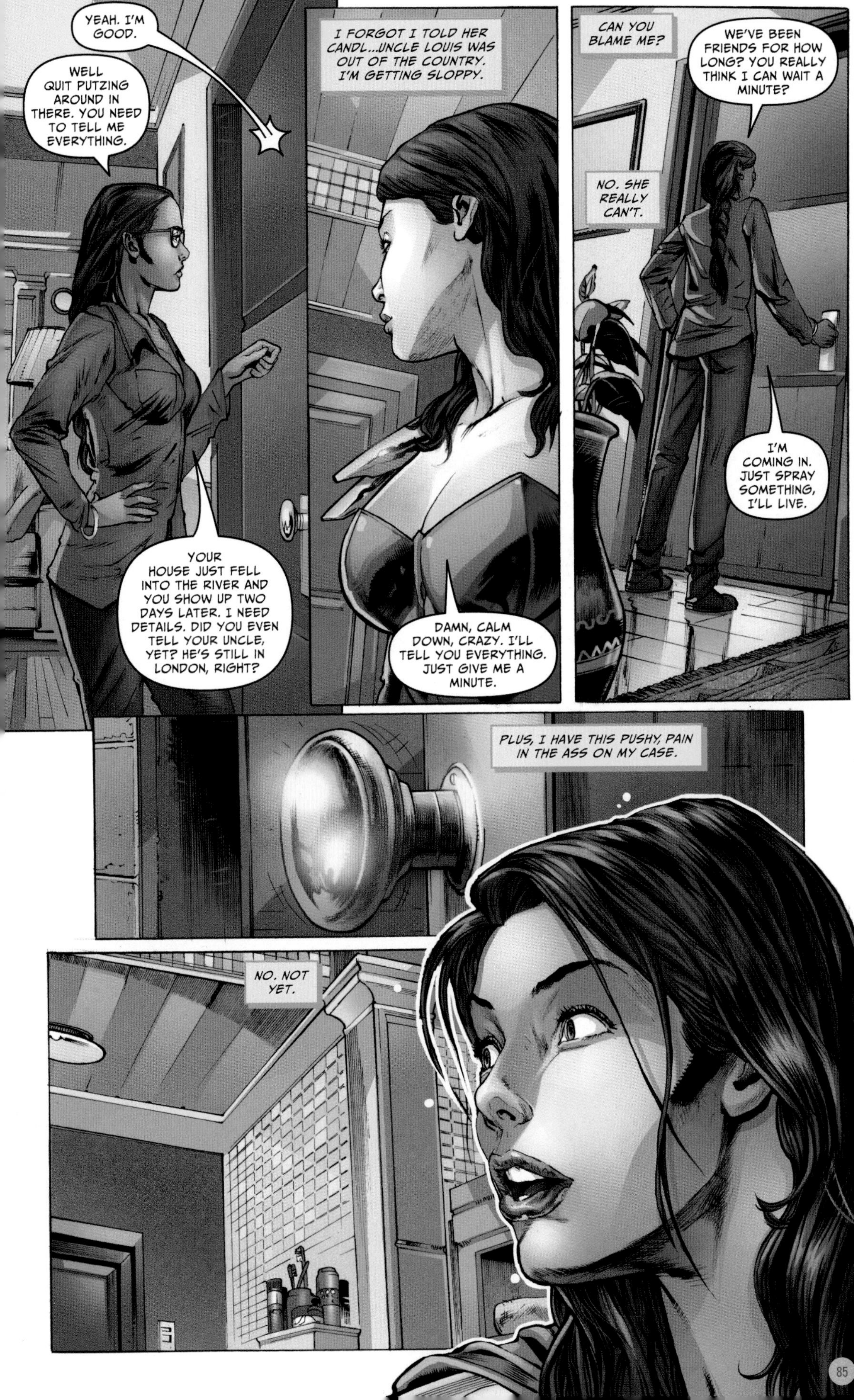

YEAH. I'M GOOD.
WELL QUIT PUTZING AROUND IN THERE. YOU NEED TO TELL ME EVERYTHING.
YOUR HOUSE JUST FELL INTO THE RIVER AND YOU SHOW UP TWO DAYS LATER. I NEED DETAILS. DID YOU EVEN TELL YOUR UNCLE, YET? HE'S STILL IN LONDON, RIGHT?
I FORGOT I TOLD HER CANDL...UNCLE LOUIS WAS OUT OF THE COUNTRY. I'M GETTING SLOPPY.
DAMN, CALM DOWN, CRAZY. I'LL TELL YOU EVERYTHING. JUST GIVE ME A MINUTE.
CAN YOU BLAME ME?
WE'VE BEEN FRIENDS FOR HOW LONG? YOU REALLY THINK I CAN WAIT A MINUTE?
NO. SHE REALLY CAN'T.
I'M COMING IN. JUST SPRAY SOMETHING, I'LL LIVE.
PLUS, I HAVE THIS PUSHY, PAIN IN THE ASS ON MY CASE.
NO. NOT YET.

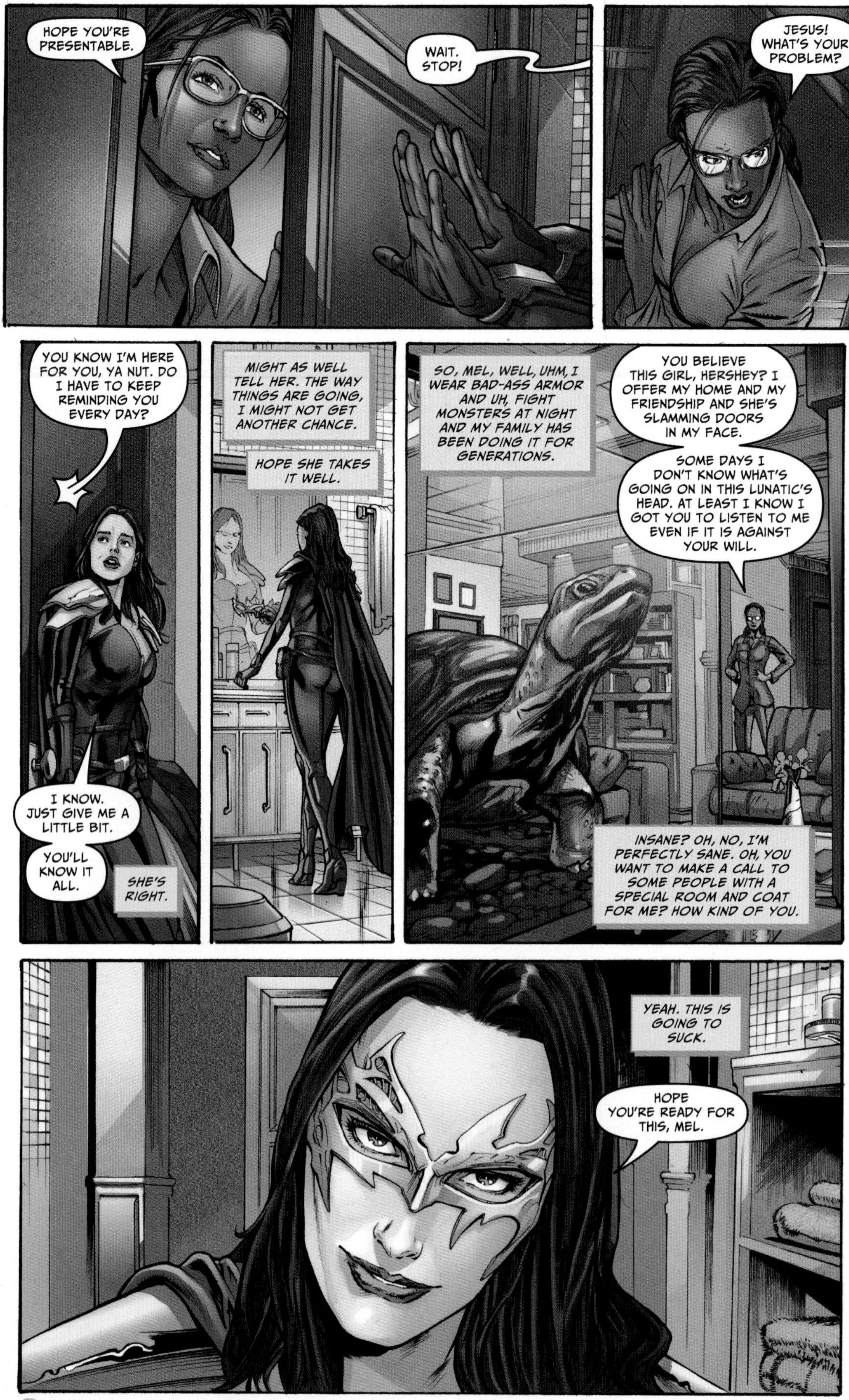

HOPE YOU'RE PRESENTABLE.
WAIT. STOP!
JESUS! WHAT'S YOUR PROBLEM?
YOU KNOW I'M HERE FOR YOU, YA NUT. DO I HAVE TO KEEP REMINDING YOU EVERY DAY?
I KNOW. JUST GIVE ME A LITTLE BIT.
YOU'LL KNOW IT ALL.
SHE'S RIGHT.
MIGHT AS WELL TELL HER. THE WAY THINGS ARE GOING, I MIGHT NOT GET ANOTHER CHANCE.
HOPE SHE TAKES IT WELL.
SO, MEL, WELL, UHM, I WEAR BAD-ASS ARMOR AND UH, FIGHT MONSTERS AT NIGHT AND MY FAMILY HAS BEEN DOING IT FOR GENERATIONS.
YOU BELIEVE THIS GIRL, HERSHEY? I OFFER MY HOME AND MY FRIENDSHIP AND SHE'S SLAMMING DOORS IN MY FACE.
SOME DAYS I DON'T KNOW WHAT'S GOING ON IN THIS LUNATIC'S HEAD. AT LEAST I KNOW I GOT YOU TO LISTEN TO ME EVEN IF IT IS AGAINST YOUR WILL.
INSANE? OH, NO, I'M PERFECTLY SANE. OH, YOU WANT TO MAKE A CALL TO SOME PEOPLE WITH A SPECIAL ROOM AND COAT FOR ME? HOW KIND OF YOU.
YEAH. THIS IS GOING TO SUCK.
HOPE YOU'RE READY FOR THIS, MEL.

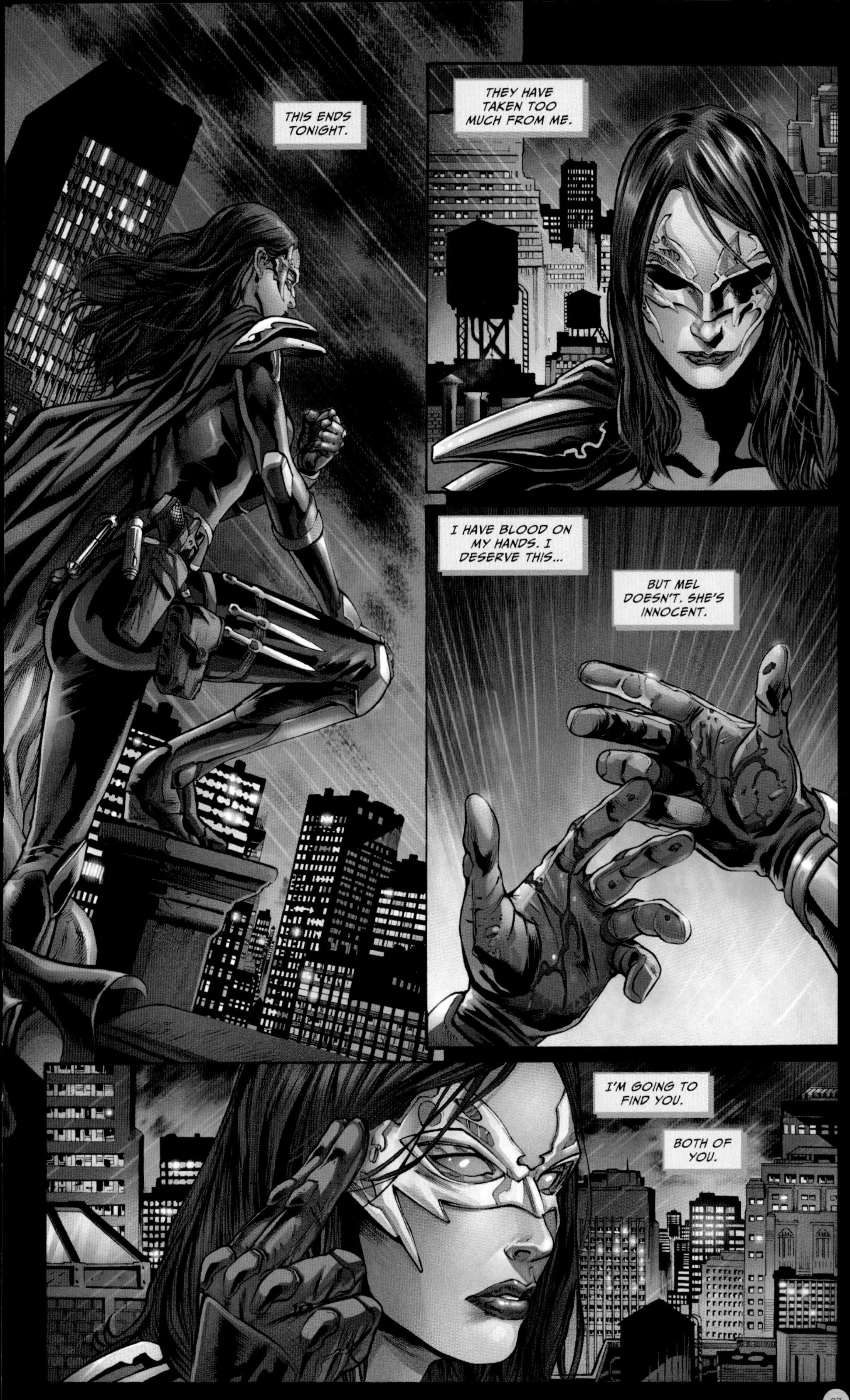
THIS ENDS TONIGHT.
THEY HAVE TAKEN TOO MUCH FROM ME.
I HAVE BLOOD ON MY HANDS. I DESERVE THIS...
BUT MEL DOESN'T. SHE'S INNOCENT.
I'M GOING TO FIND YOU.
BOTH OF YOU.

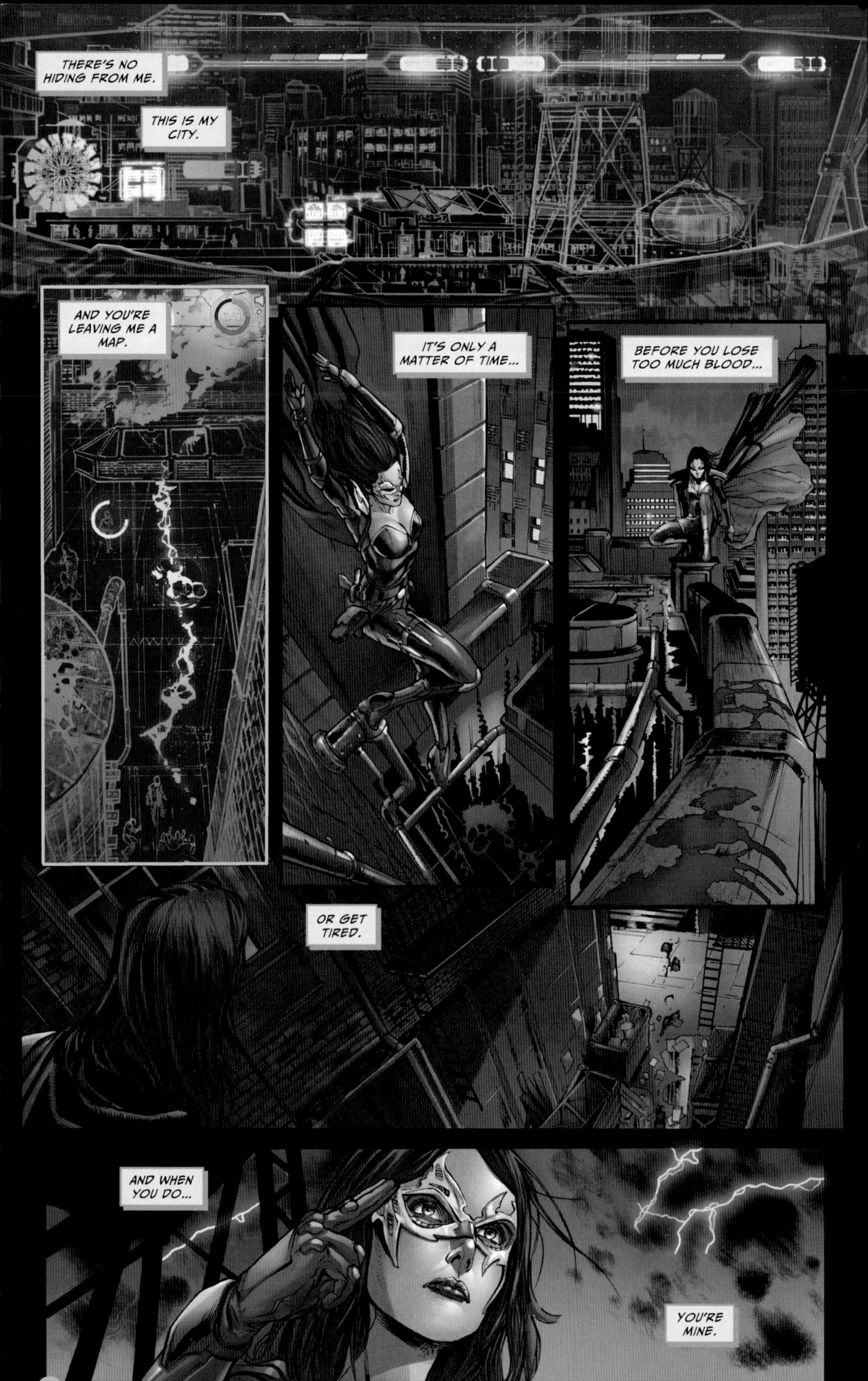
THERE'S NO HIDING FROM ME.
THIS IS MY CITY.
AND YOU'RE LEAVING ME A MAP.
IT'S ONLY A MATTER OF TIME...
BEFORE YOU LOSE TOO MUCH BLOOD...
OR GET TIRED.
AND WHEN YOU DO...
YOU'RE MINE.

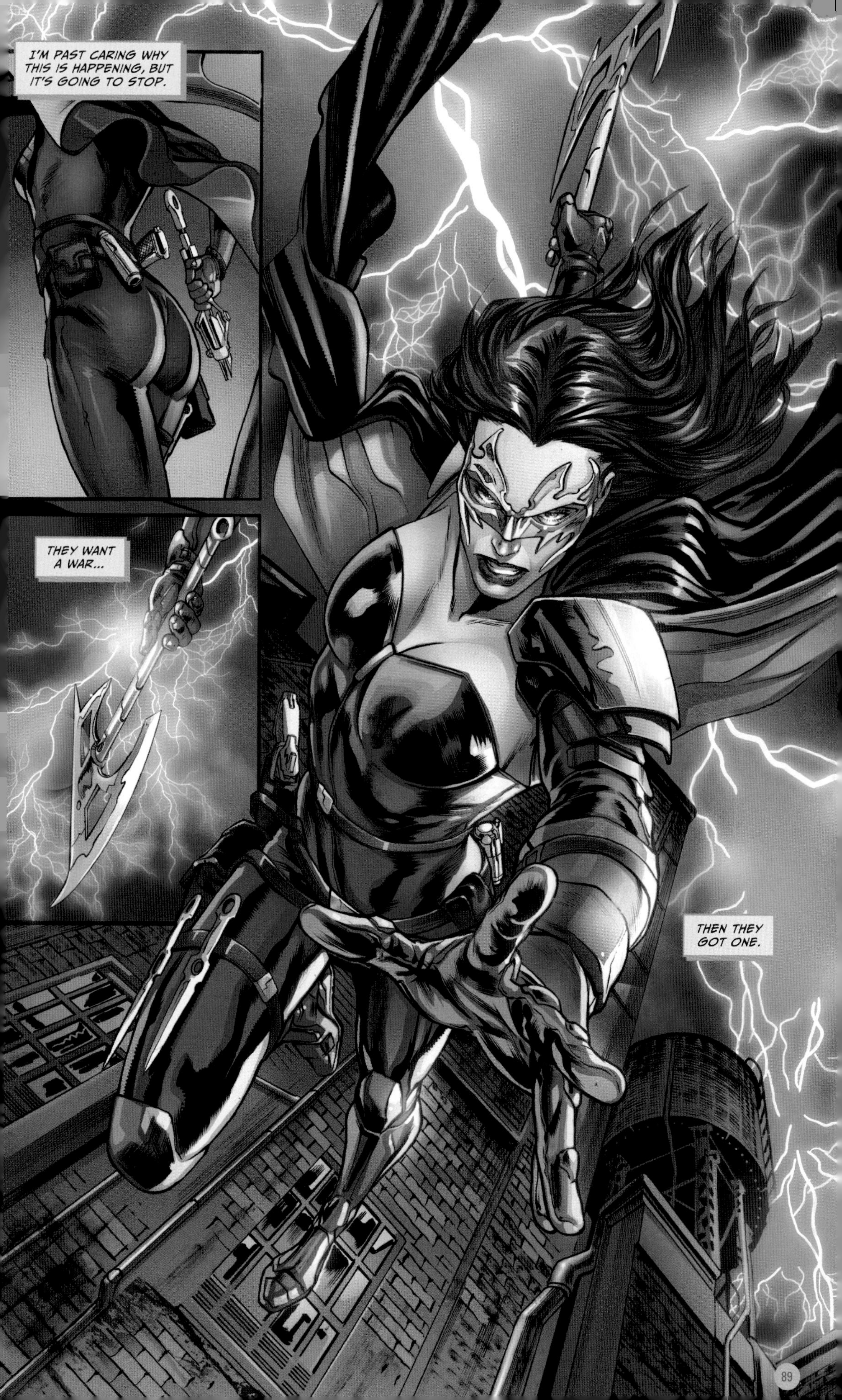
I'M PAST CARING WHY THIS IS HAPPENING, BUT IT'S GOING TO STOP.
THEY WANT A WAR...
THEN THEY GOT ONE.

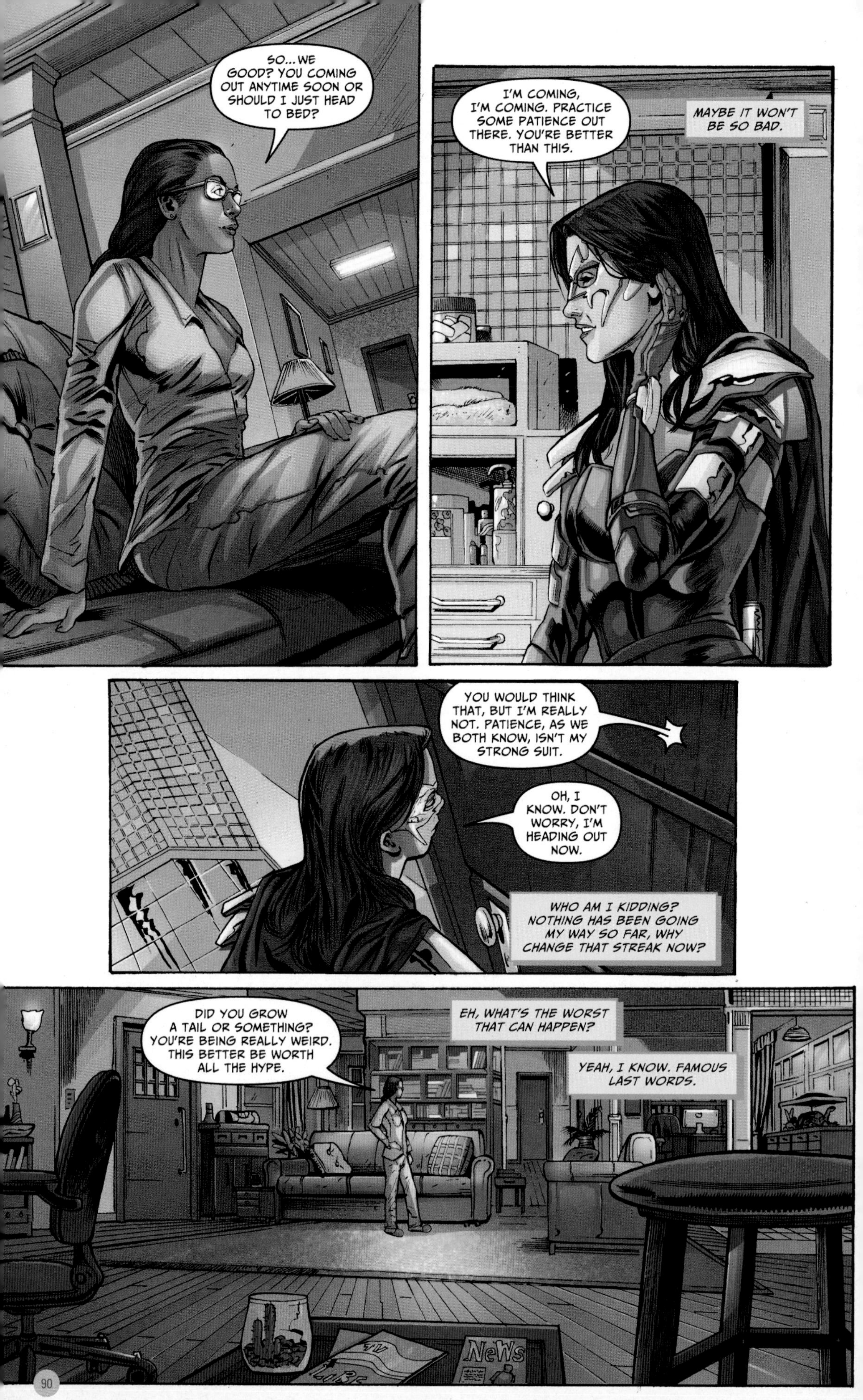

SO...WE GOOD? YOU COMING OUT ANYTIME SOON OR SHOULD I JUST HEAD TO BED?
I'M COMING, I'M COMING. PRACTICE SOME PATIENCE OUT THERE. YOU'RE BETTER THAN THIS.
MAYBE IT WON'T BE SO BAD.
YOU WOULD THINK THAT, BUT I'M REALLY NOT. PATIENCE, AS WE BOTH KNOW, ISN'T MY STRONG SUIT.
OH, I KNOW. DON'T WORRY, I'M HEADING OUT NOW.
WHO AM I KIDDING? NOTHING HAS BEEN GOING MY WAY SO FAR, WHY CHANGE THAT STREAK NOW?
DID YOU GROW A TAIL OR SOMETHING? YOU'RE BEING REALLY WEIRD. THIS BETTER BE WORTH ALL THE HYPE.
EH, WHAT'S THE WORST THAT CAN HAPPEN?
YEAH, I KNOW. FAMOUS LAST WORDS.
NeWs

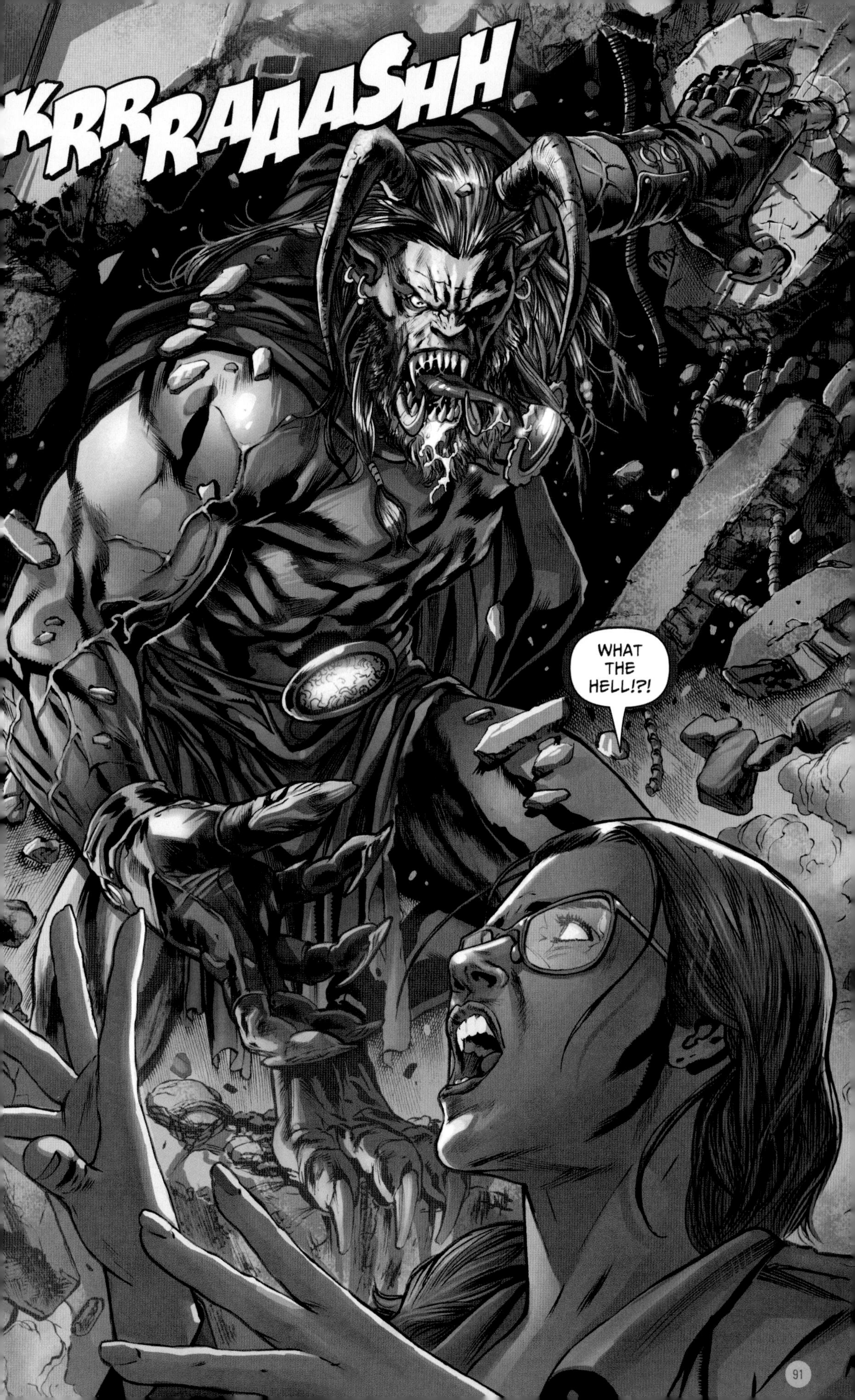
KRRRAAASHH
WHAT THE HELL!?!

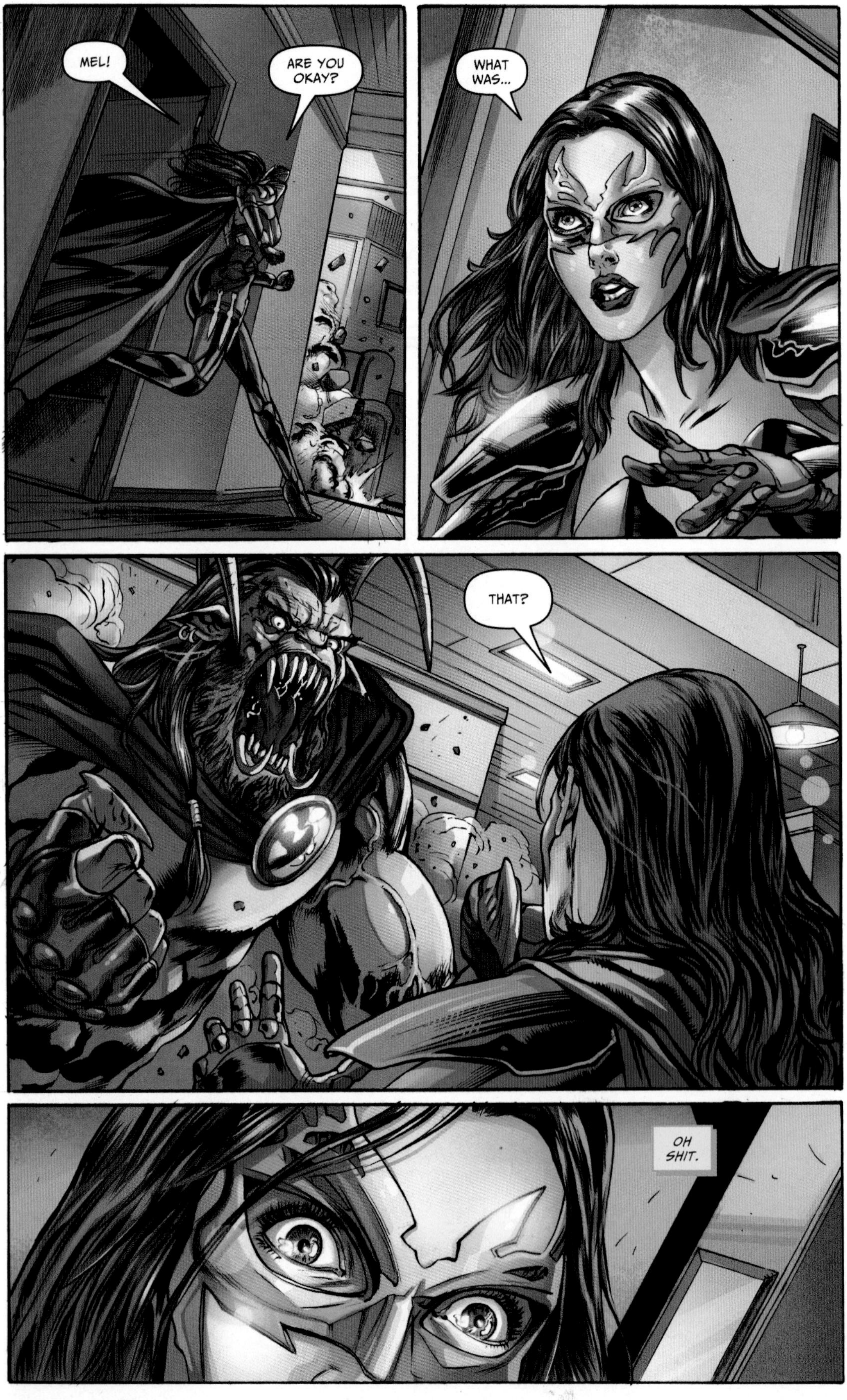
MEL!
ARE YOU OKAY?
WHAT WAS...
THAT?
OH SHIT.

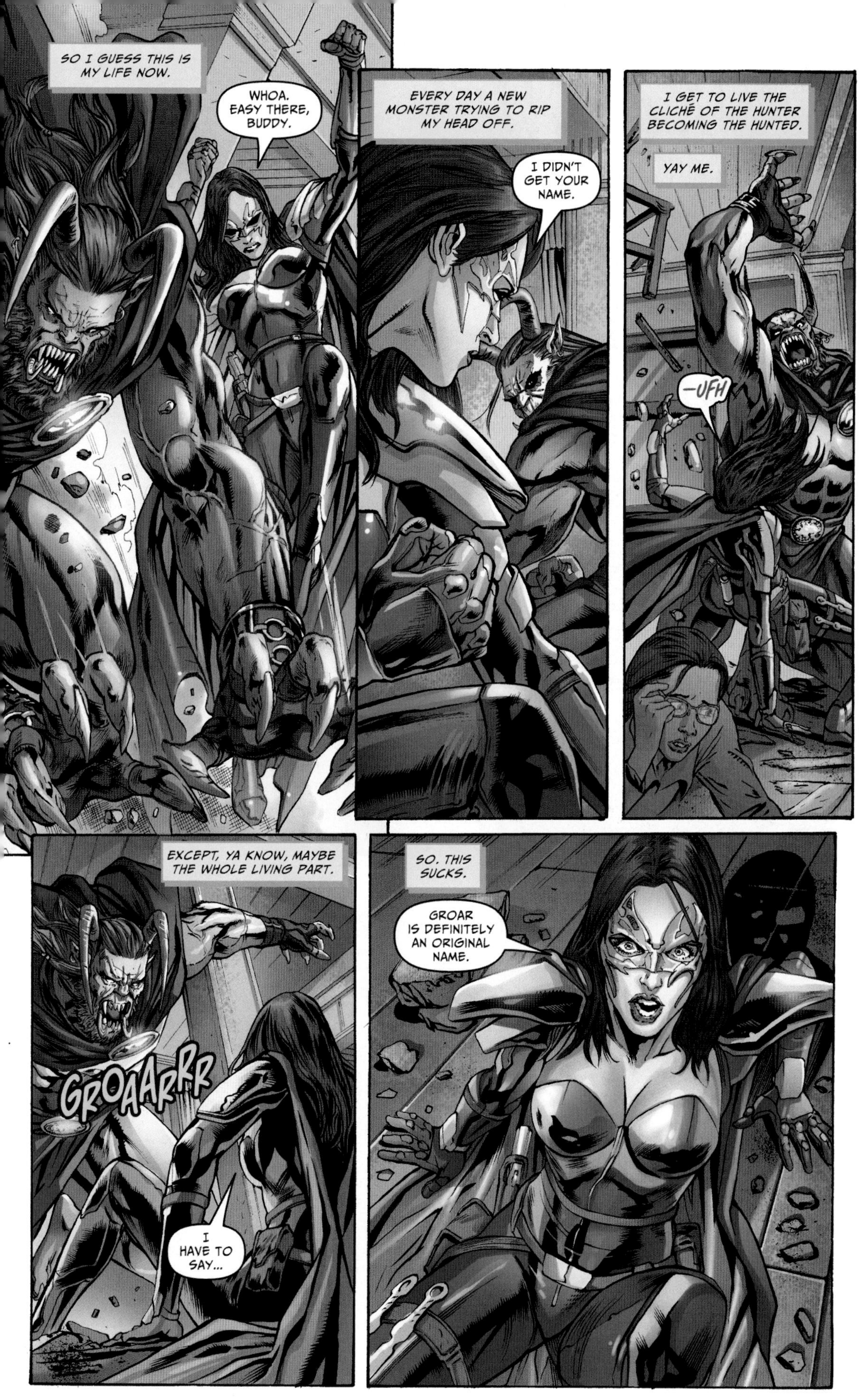
SO I GUESS THIS IS MY LIFE NOW.
WHOA. EASY THERE, BUDDY.
EVERY DAY A NEW MONSTER TRYING TO RIP MY HEAD OFF.
I DIDN'T GET YOUR NAME.
I GET TO LIVE THE CLICHÉ OF THE HUNTER BECOMING THE HUNTED.
YAY ME.
—UFH
EXCEPT, YA KNOW, MAYBE THE WHOLE LIVING PART.
GROAARRR
I HAVE TO SAY...
SO. THIS SUCKS.
GROAR IS DEFINITELY AN ORIGINAL NAME.

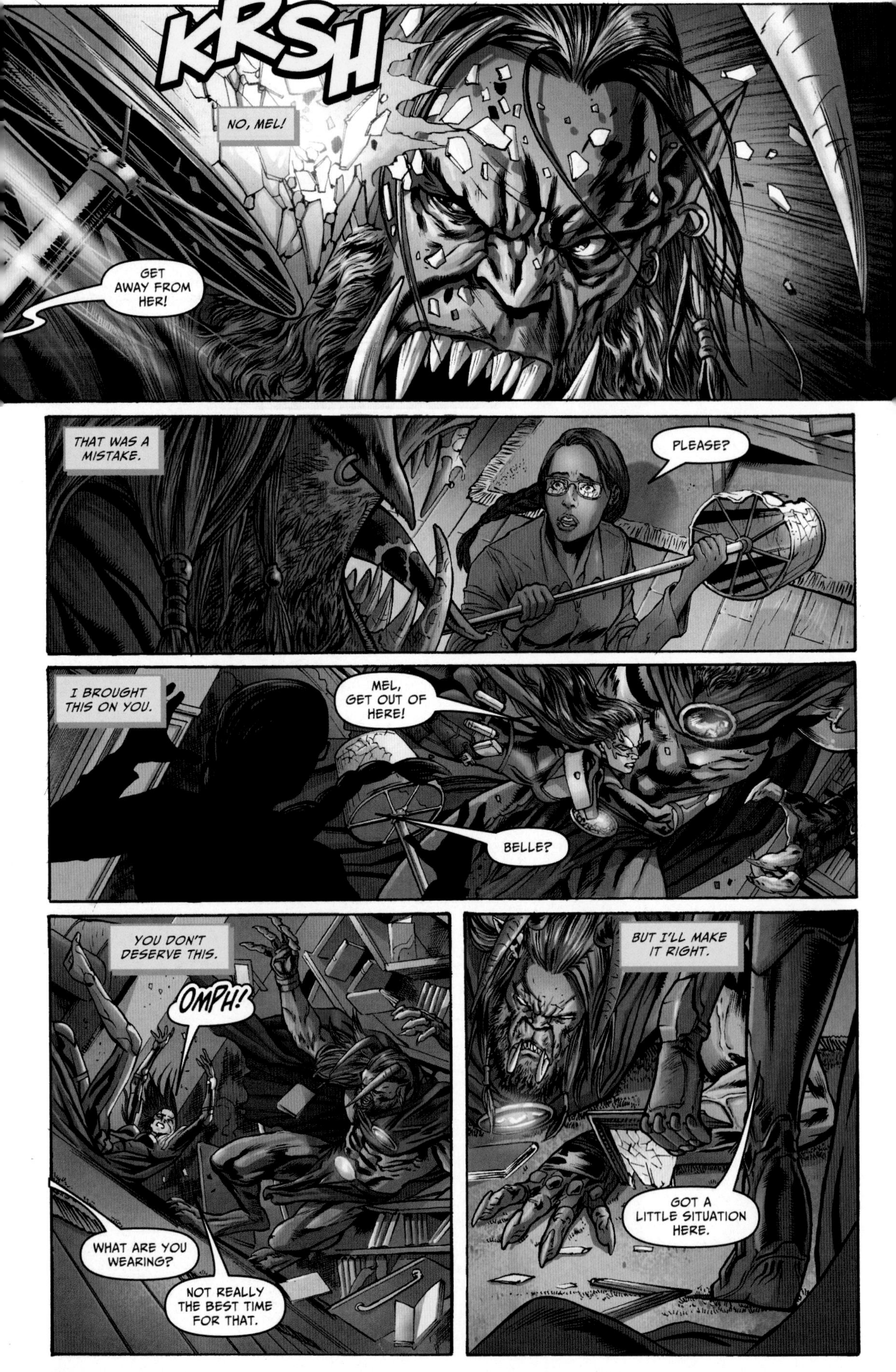
KRSH
NO, MEL!
GET AWAY FROM HER!
THAT WAS A MISTAKE.
PLEASE?
I BROUGHT THIS ON YOU.
MEL, GET OUT OF HERE!
BELLE?
YOU DON'T DESERVE THIS.
OMPH!
WHAT ARE YOU WEARING?
NOT REALLY THE BEST TIME FOR THAT.
BUT I'LL MAKE IT RIGHT.
GOT A LITTLE SITUATION HERE.

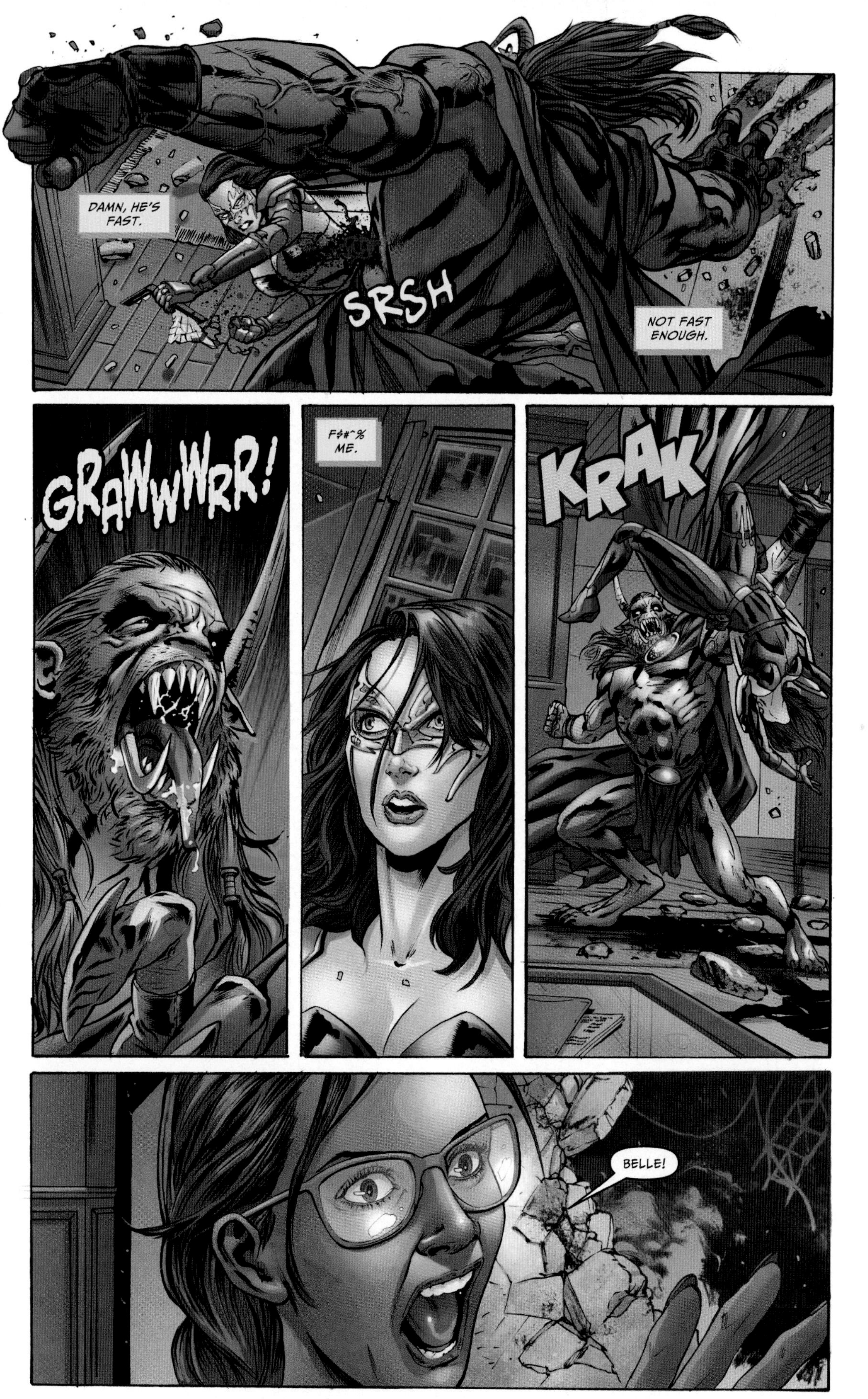
DAMN, HE'S FAST.
SRSH
NOT FAST ENOUGH.
GRAWWWRR!
F$#^% ME.
KRAK
BELLE!

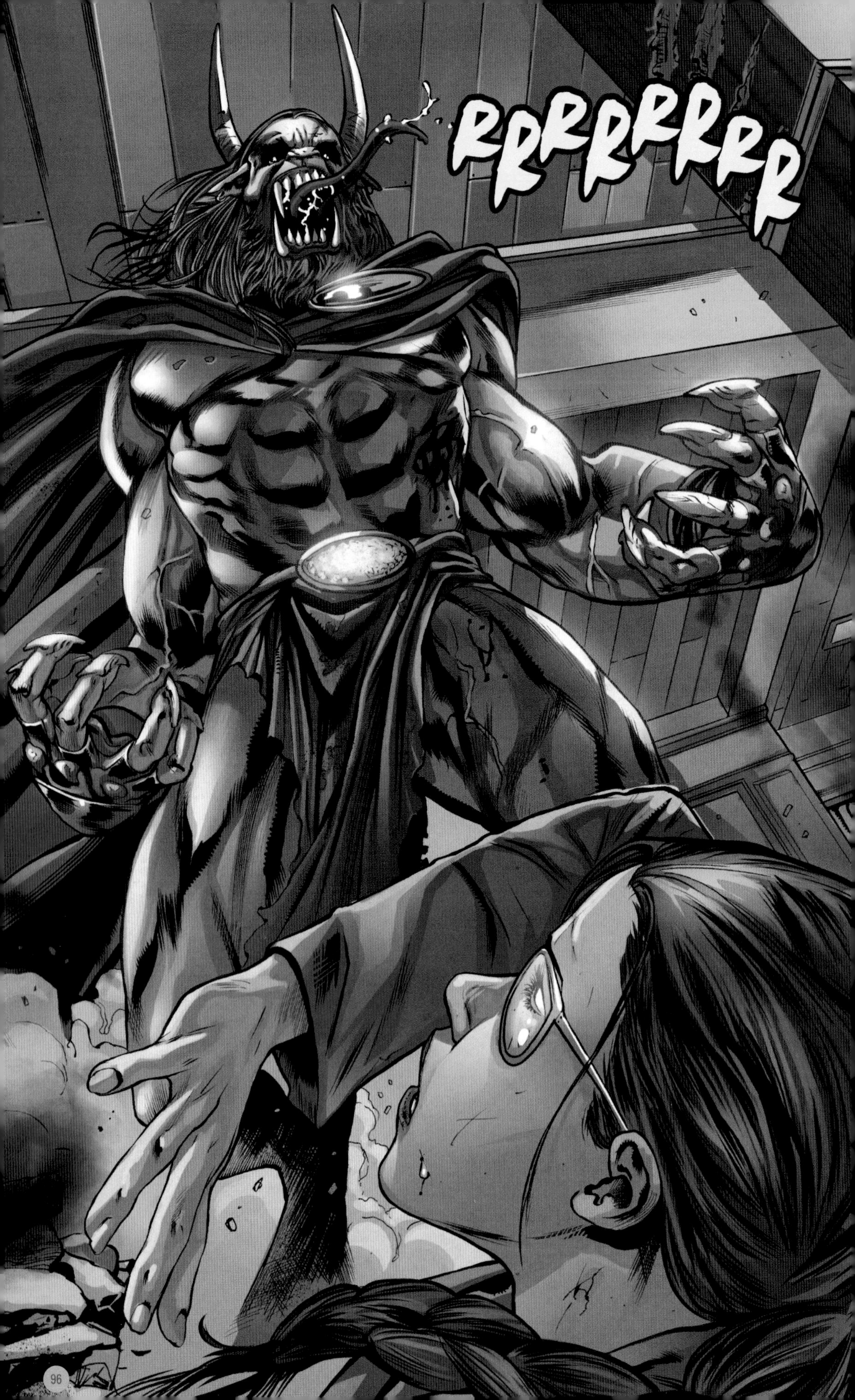
RRRRRRRRR

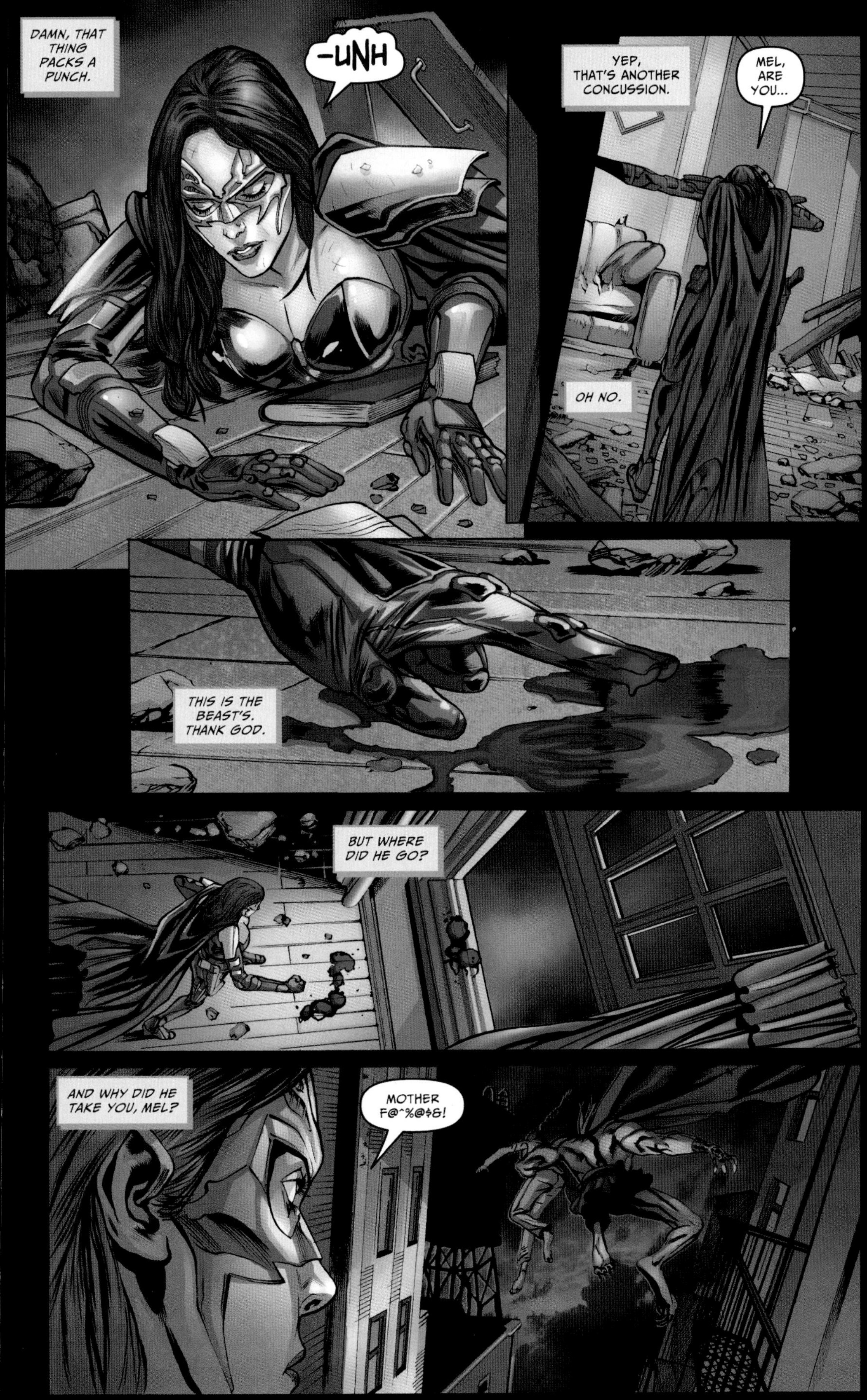

DAMN, THAT THING PACKS A PUNCH.
-UNH
YEP, THAT'S ANOTHER CONCUSSION.
MEL, ARE YOU...
OH NO.
THIS IS THE BEAST'S. THANK GOD.
BUT WHERE DID HE GO?
AND WHY DID HE TAKE YOU, MEL?
MOTHER F@^%@$&!

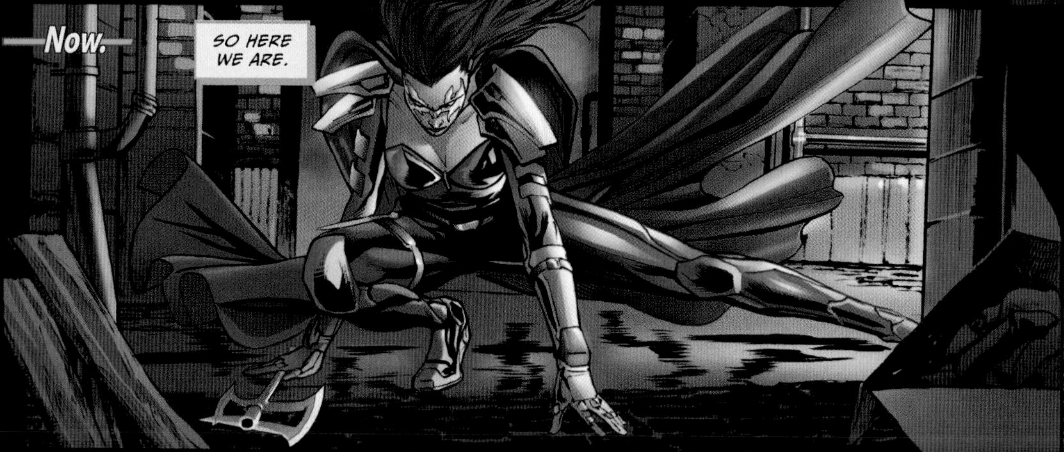
Now.
SO HERE WE ARE.

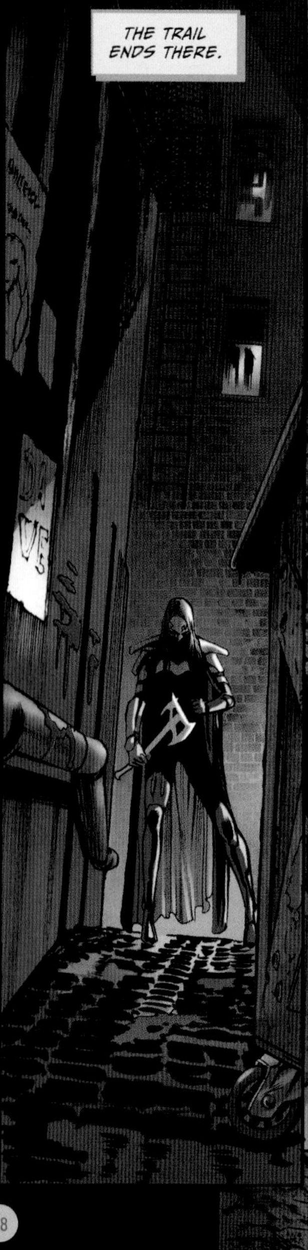
THE TRAIL ENDS THERE.

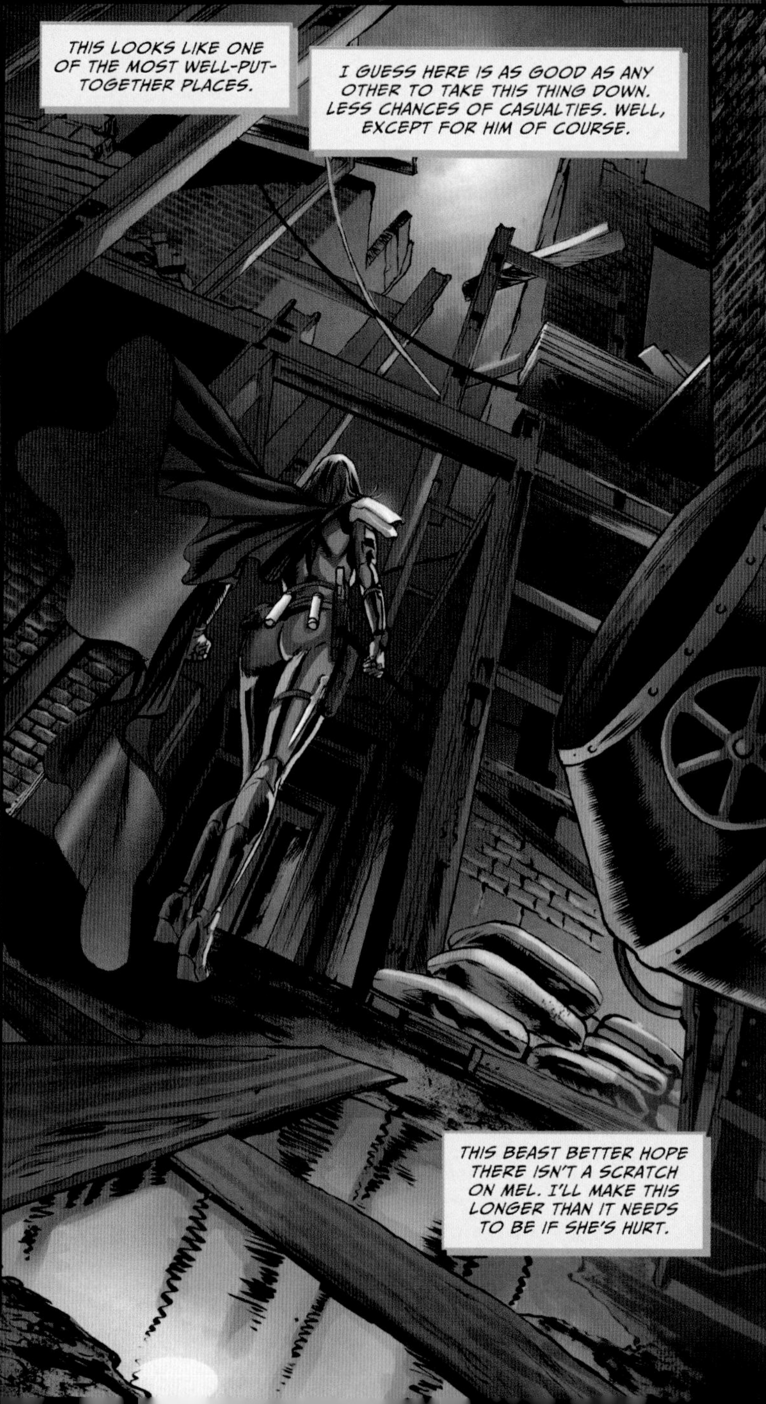
THIS LOOKS LIKE ONE OF THE MOST WELL-PUT-TOGETHER PLACES.
I GUESS HERE IS AS GOOD AS ANY OTHER TO TAKE THIS THING DOWN. LESS CHANCES OF CASUALTIES. WELL, EXCEPT FOR HIM OF COURSE.
THIS BEAST BETTER HOPE THERE ISN'T A SCRATCH ON MEL. I'LL MAKE THIS LONGER THAN IT NEEDS TO BE IF SHE'S HURT.

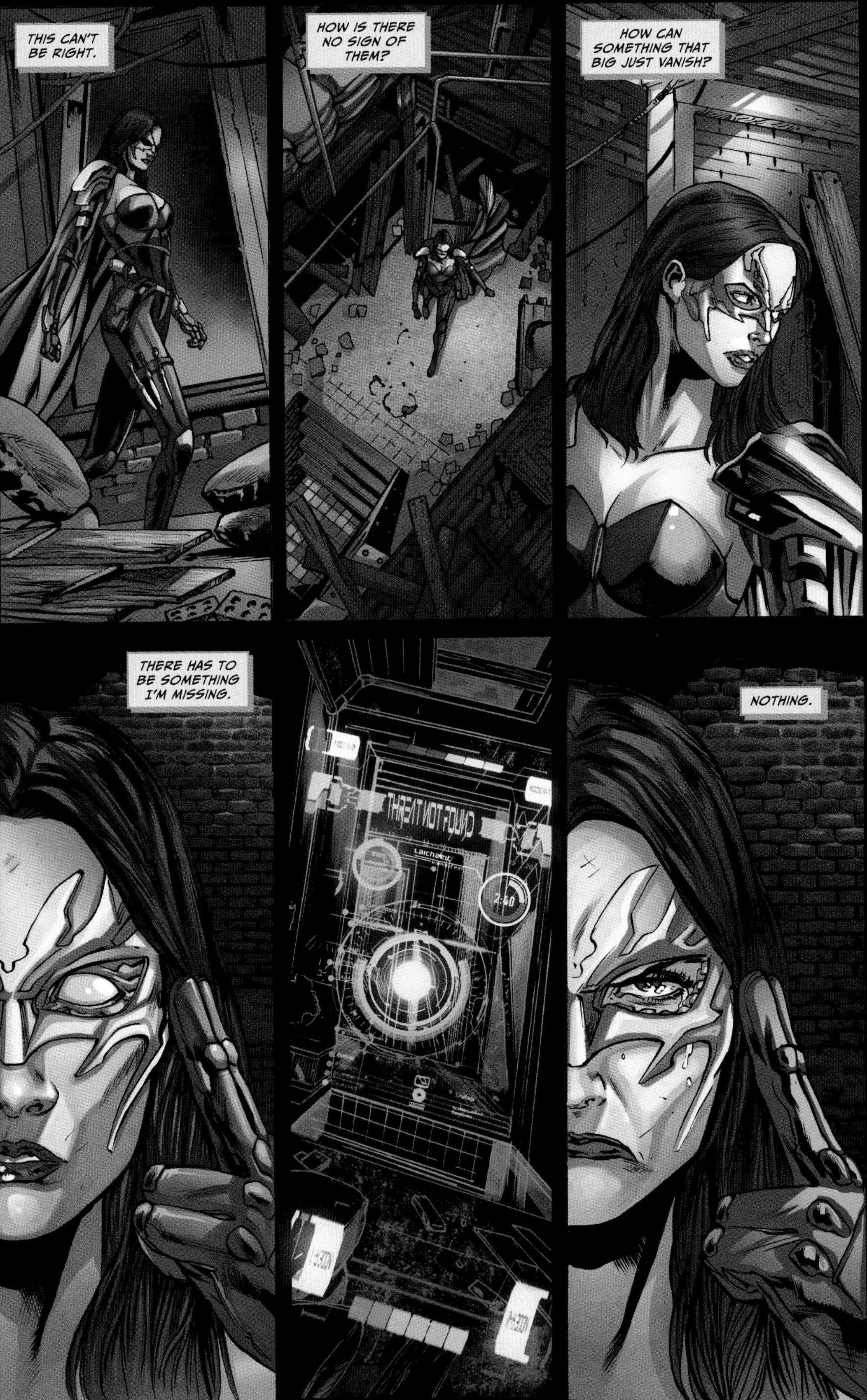
THIS CAN'T BE RIGHT.
HOW IS THERE NO SIGN OF THEM?
HOW CAN SOMETHING THAT BIG JUST VANISH?
THERE HAS TO BE SOMETHING I'M MISSING.
THREAT NOT FOUND
2:40
NOTHING.

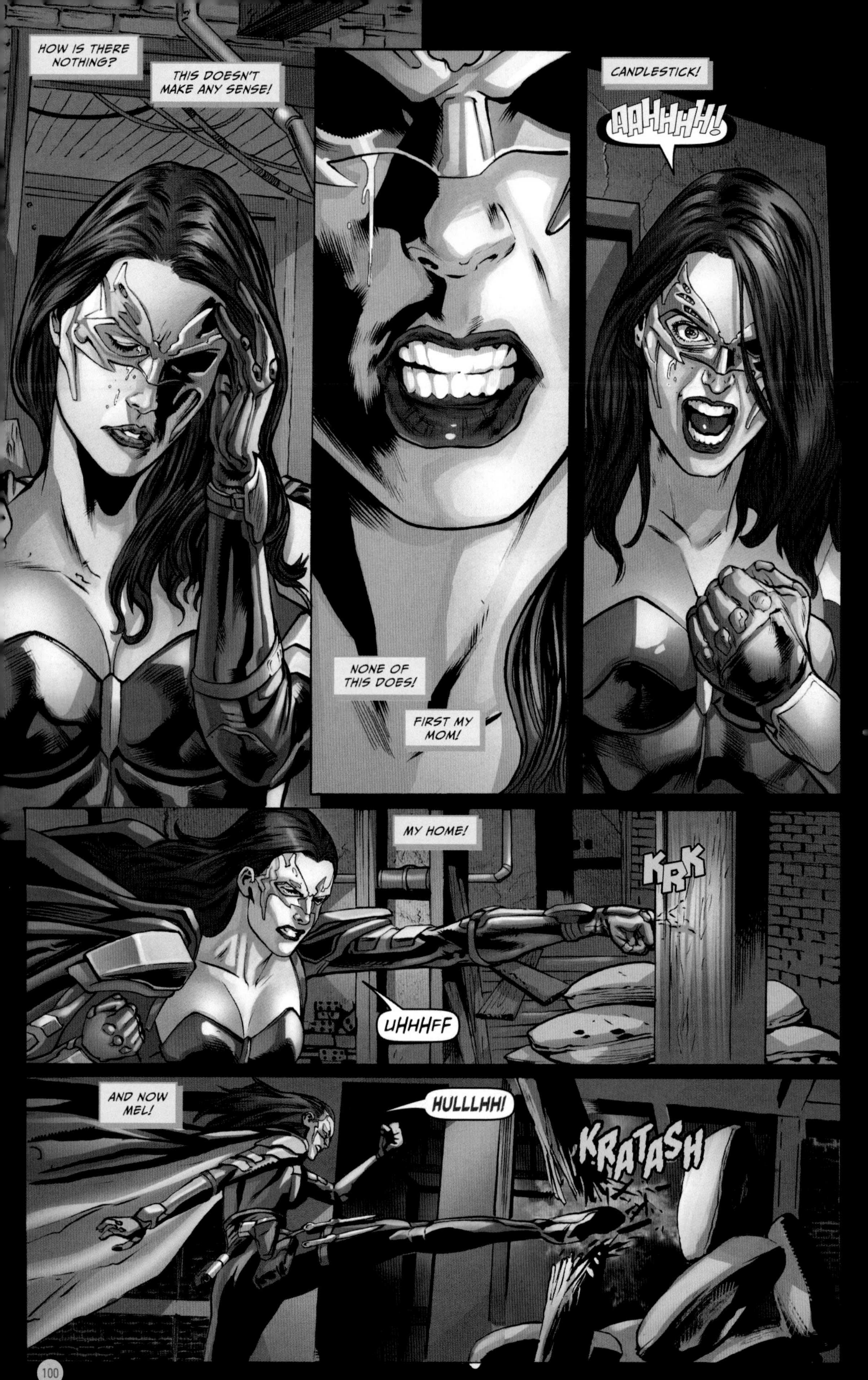

HOW IS THERE NOTHING?
THIS DOESN'T MAKE ANY SENSE!
NONE OF THIS DOES!
FIRST MY MOM!
CANDLESTICK!
AAHHHH!
MY HOME!
KRK
UHHHFF
AND NOW MEL!
HULLLHH!
KRATASH

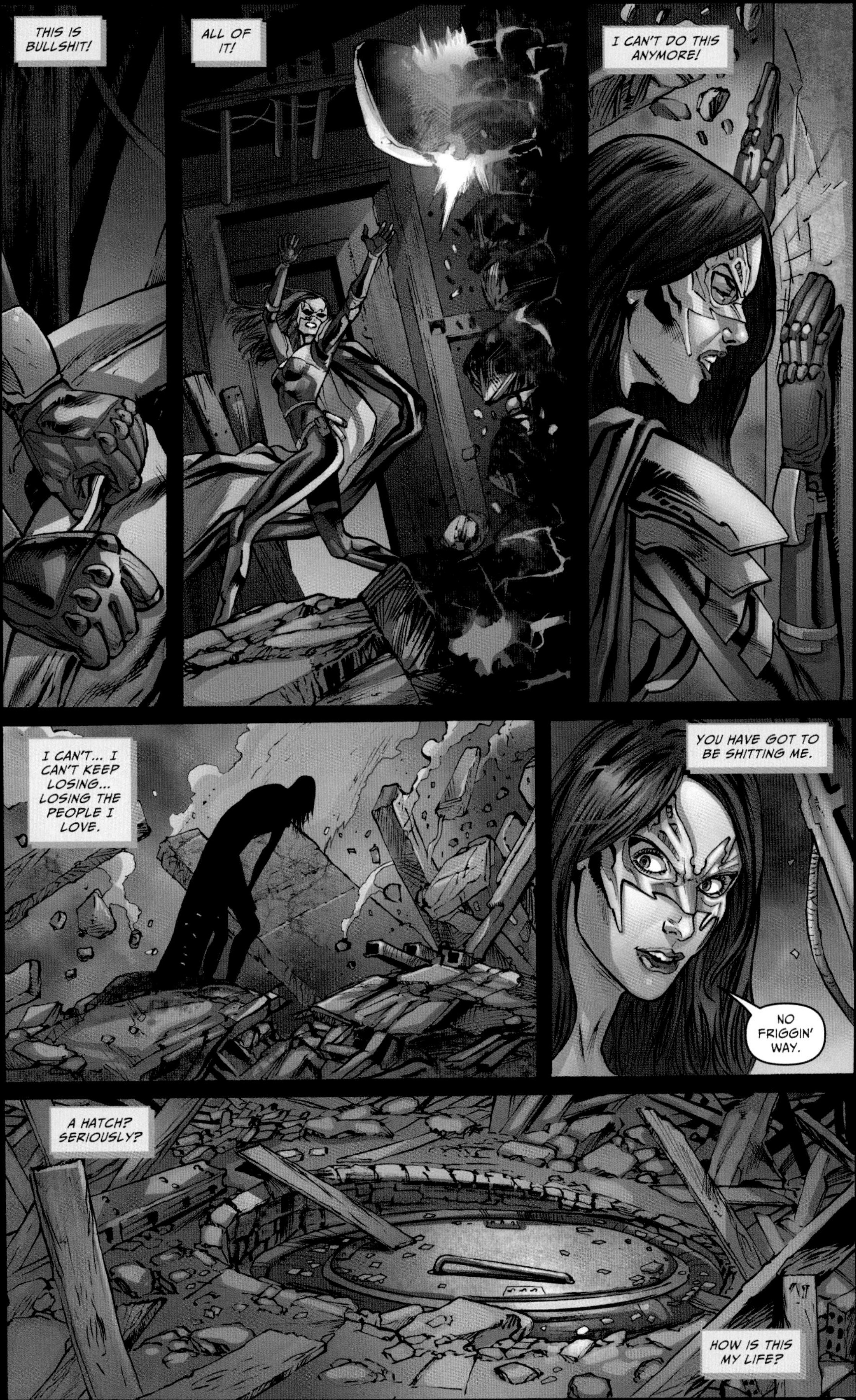
THIS IS BULLSHIT!
ALL OF IT!
I CAN'T DO THIS ANYMORE!
I CAN'T... I CAN'T KEEP LOSING... LOSING THE PEOPLE I LOVE.
YOU HAVE GOT TO BE SHITTING ME.
NO FRIGGIN' WAY.
A HATCH? SERIOUSLY?
HOW IS THIS MY LIFE?

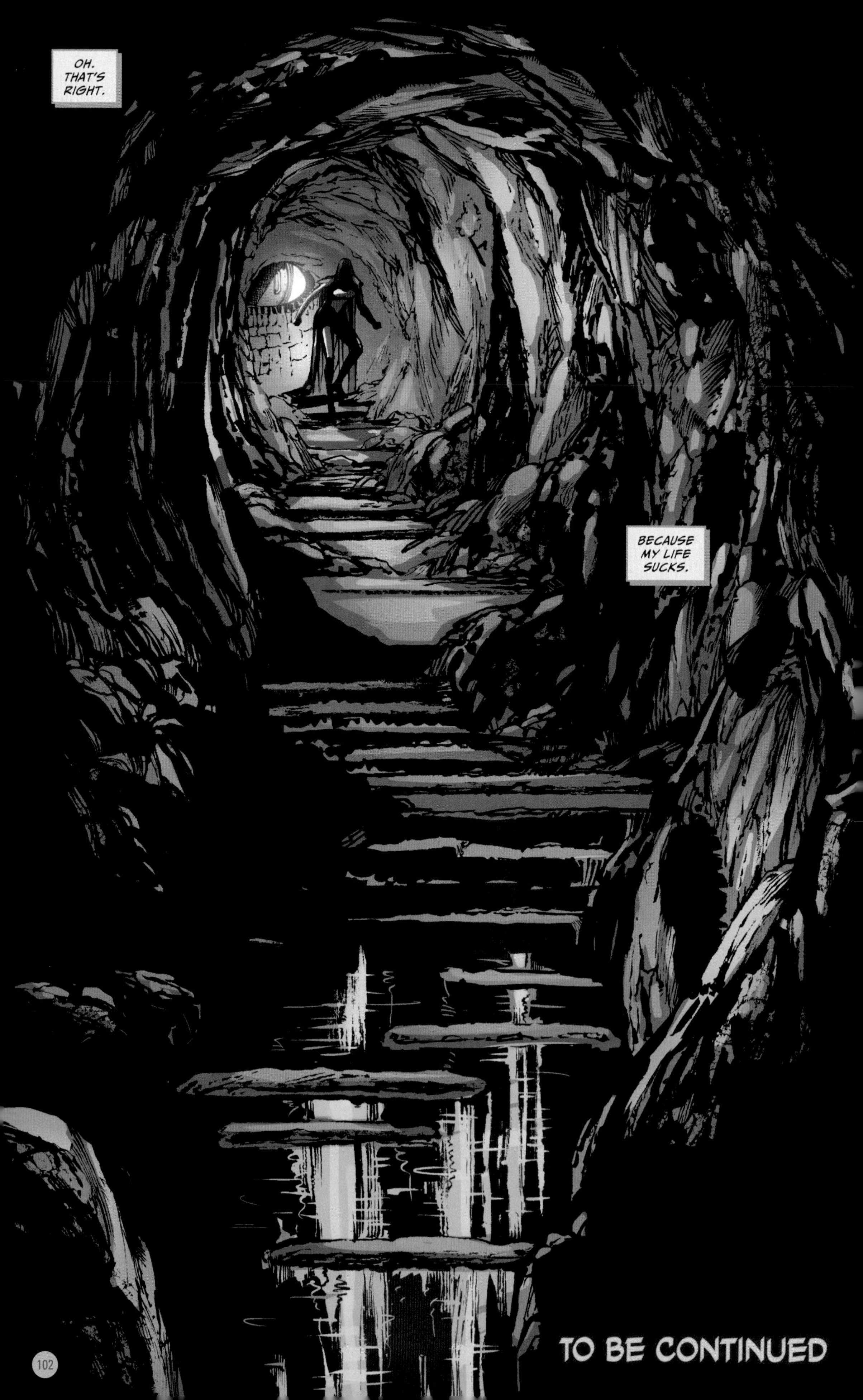
OH. THAT'S RIGHT.
BECAUSE MY LIFE SUCKS.
TO BE CONTINUED

BELLE
BEAST HUNTER

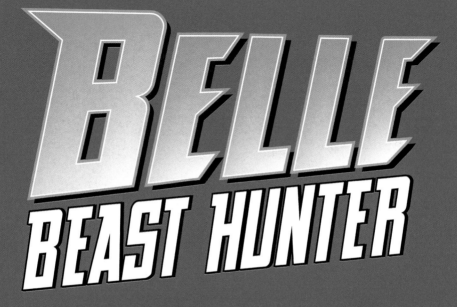

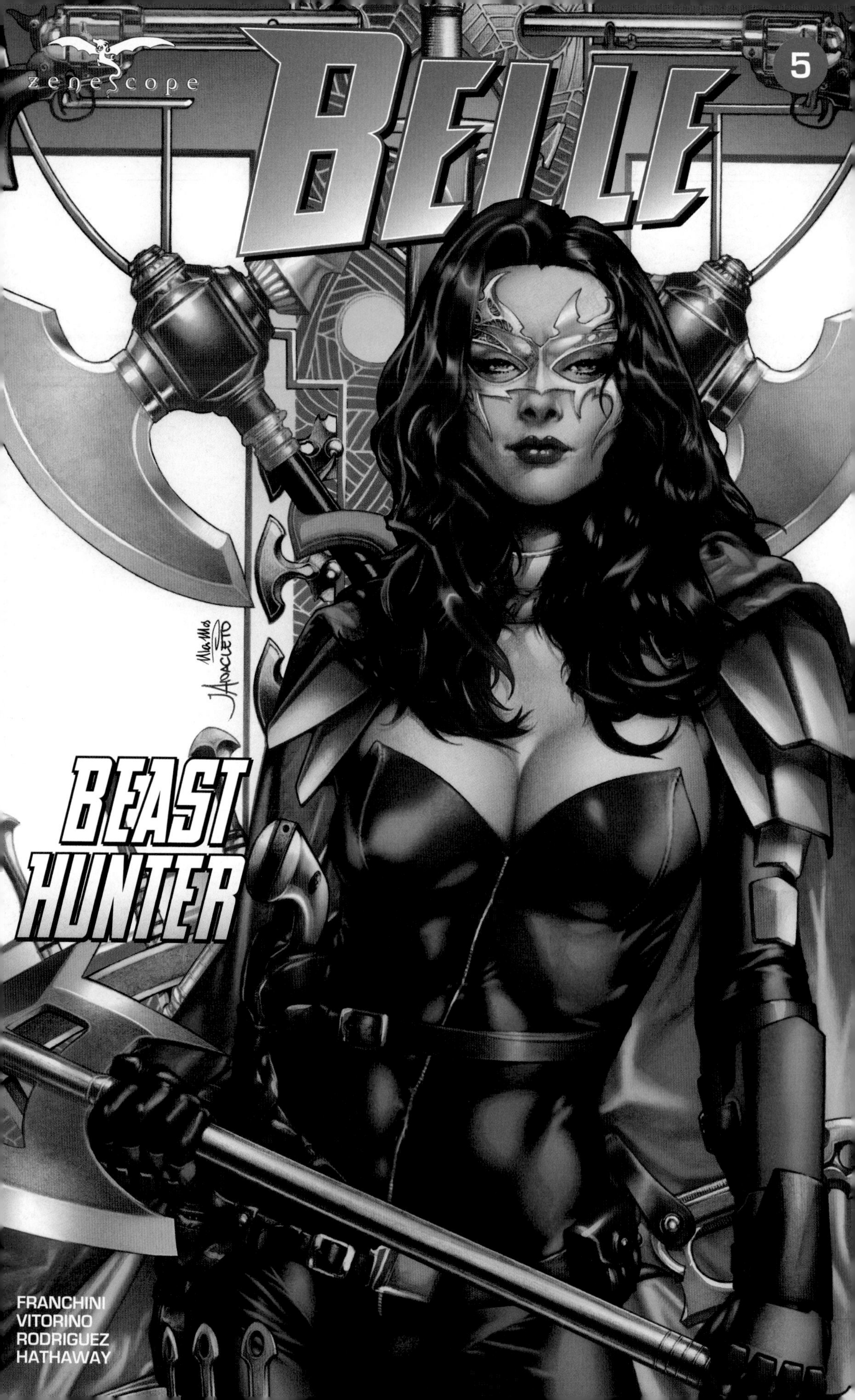
zenescope
5
BELLE
BEAST HUNTER
FRANCHINI
VITORINO
RODRIGUEZ
HATHAWAY

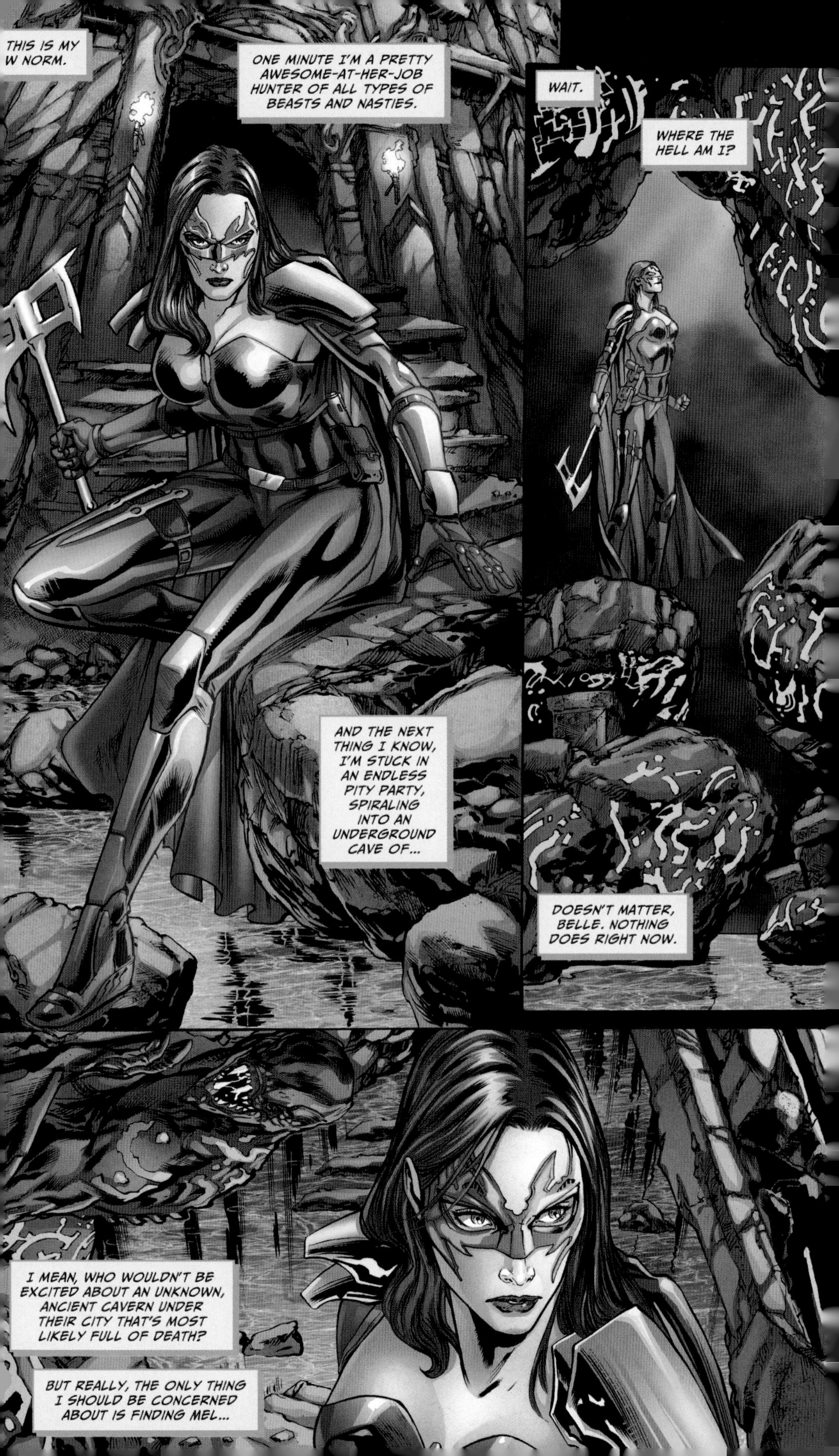
THIS IS MY
W NORM.
ONE MINUTE I'M A PRETTY AWESOME-AT-HER-JOB HUNTER OF ALL TYPES OF BEASTS AND NASTIES.
AND THE NEXT THING I KNOW, I'M STUCK IN AN ENDLESS PITY PARTY, SPIRALING INTO AN UNDERGROUND CAVE OF...
WAIT.
WHERE THE HELL AM I?
DOESN'T MATTER, BELLE. NOTHING DOES RIGHT NOW.
I MEAN, WHO WOULDN'T BE EXCITED ABOUT AN UNKNOWN, ANCIENT CAVERN UNDER THEIR CITY THAT'S MOST LIKELY FULL OF DEATH?
BUT REALLY, THE ONLY THING I SHOULD BE CONCERNED ABOUT IS FINDING MEL...

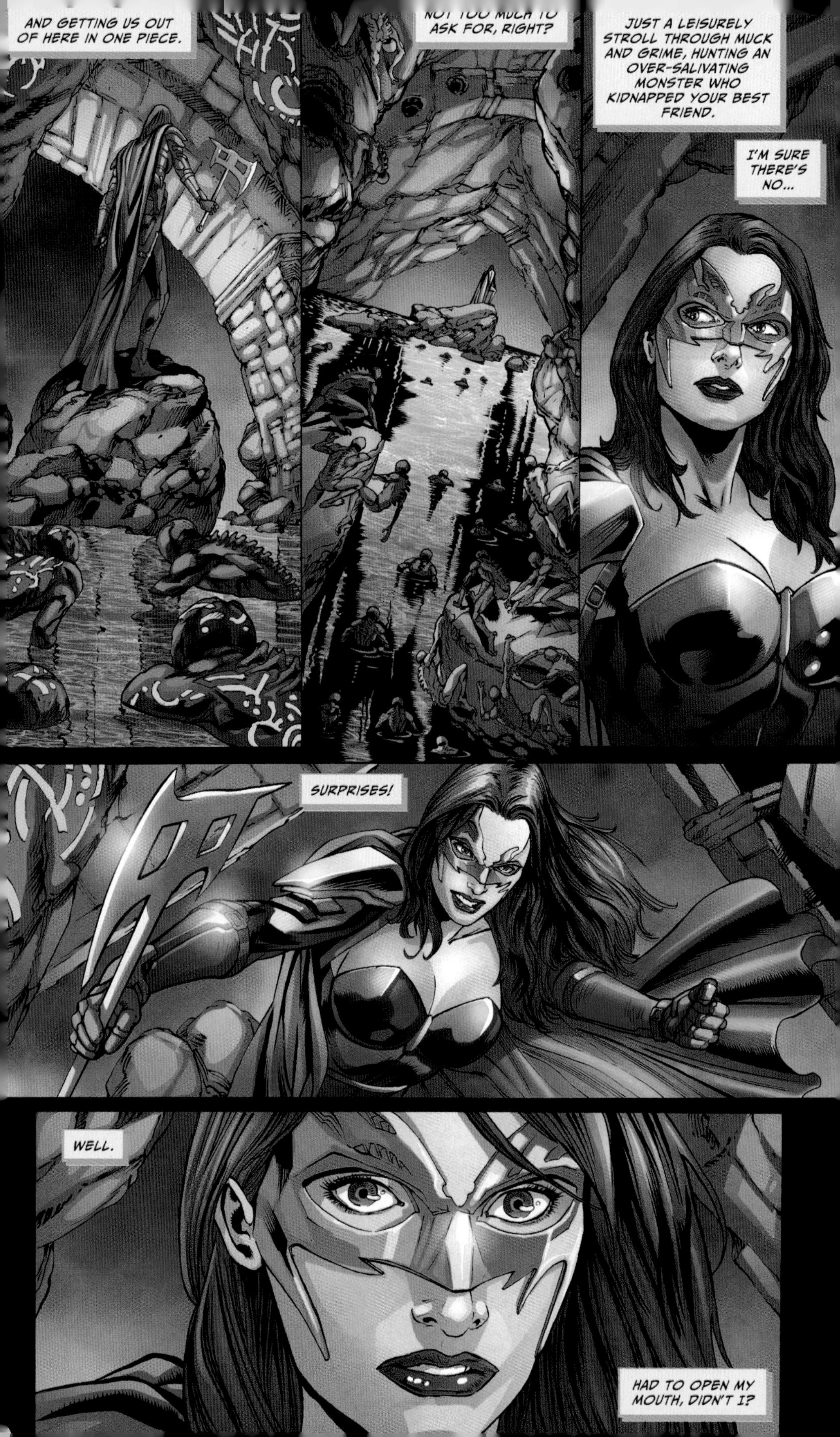
AND GETTING US OUT OF HERE IN ONE PIECE.
NOT TOO MUCH TO ASK FOR, RIGHT?
JUST A LEISURELY STROLL THROUGH MUCK AND GRIME, HUNTING AN OVER-SALIVATING MONSTER WHO KIDNAPPED YOUR BEST FRIEND.
I'M SURE THERE'S NO...
SURPRISES!
WELL.
HAD TO OPEN MY MOUTH, DIDN'T I?

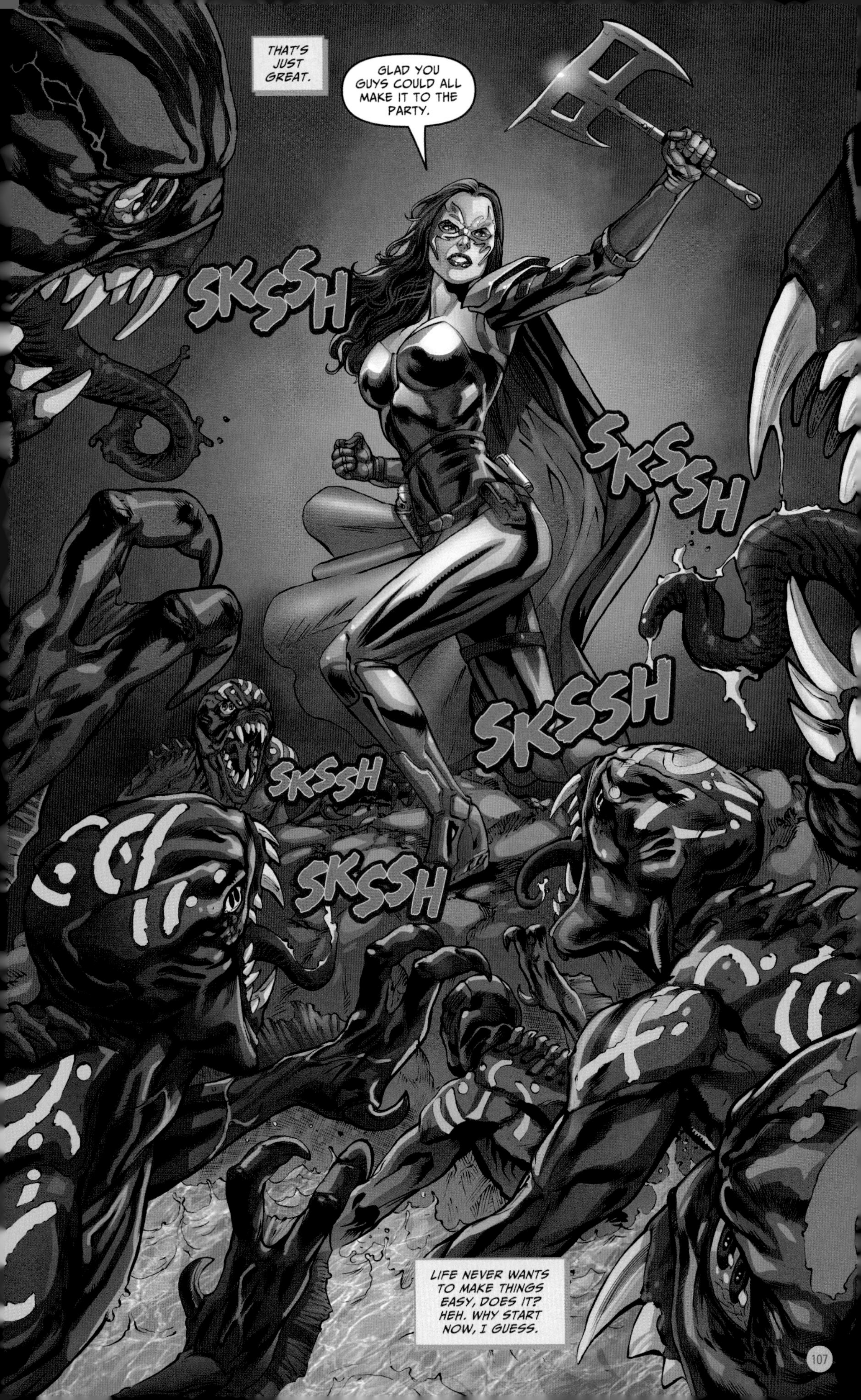
THAT'S JUST GREAT.
GLAD YOU GUYS COULD ALL MAKE IT TO THE PARTY.
SKSSH
SKSSSH
SKSSH
SKSSH
SKSSH
LIFE NEVER WANTS TO MAKE THINGS EASY, DOES IT? HEH. WHY START NOW, I GUESS.

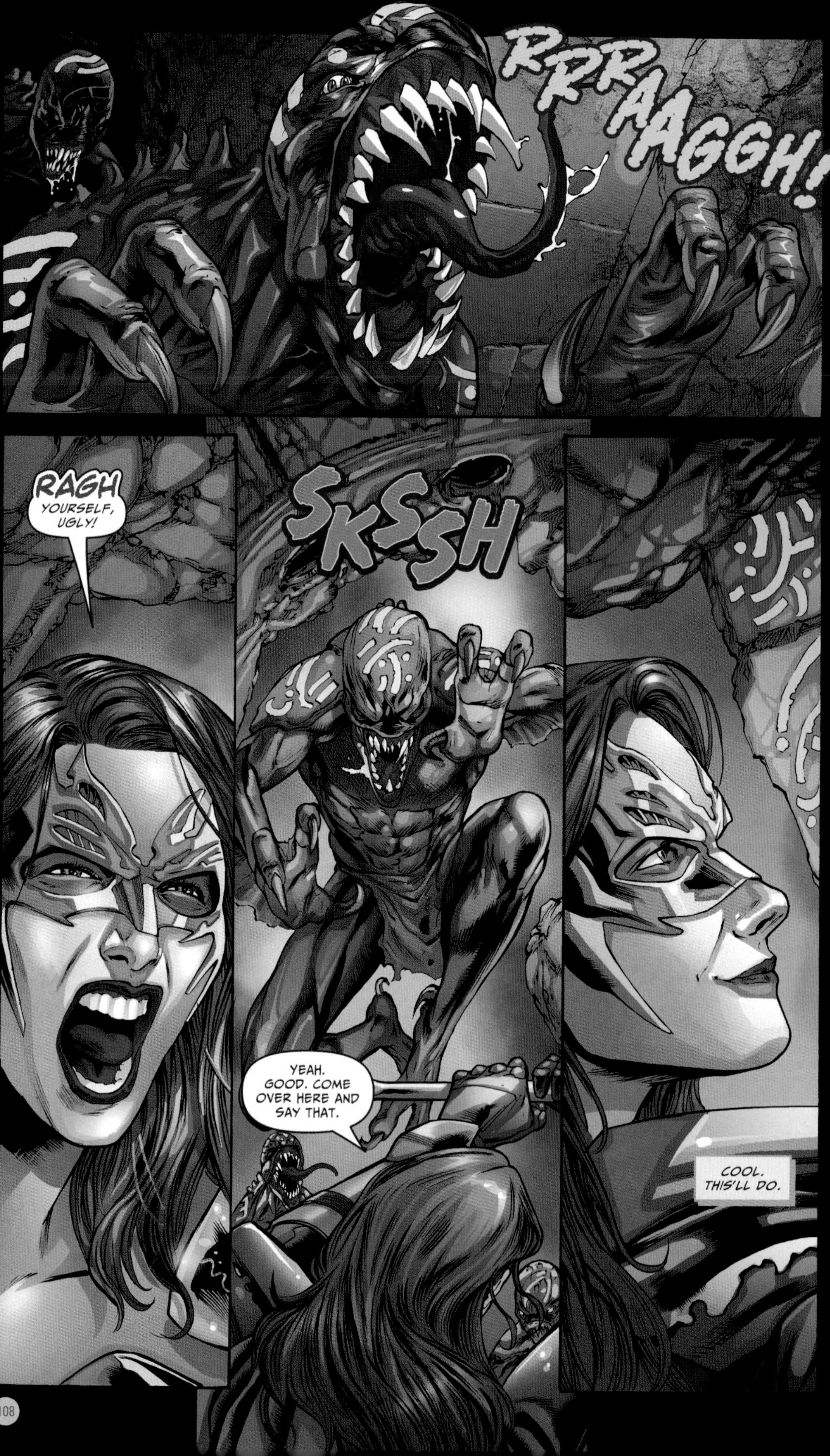
RRRAAGGH!
RAGH YOURSELF, UGLY!
SKSSH
YEAH. GOOD. COME OVER HERE AND SAY THAT.
COOL. THIS'LL DO.

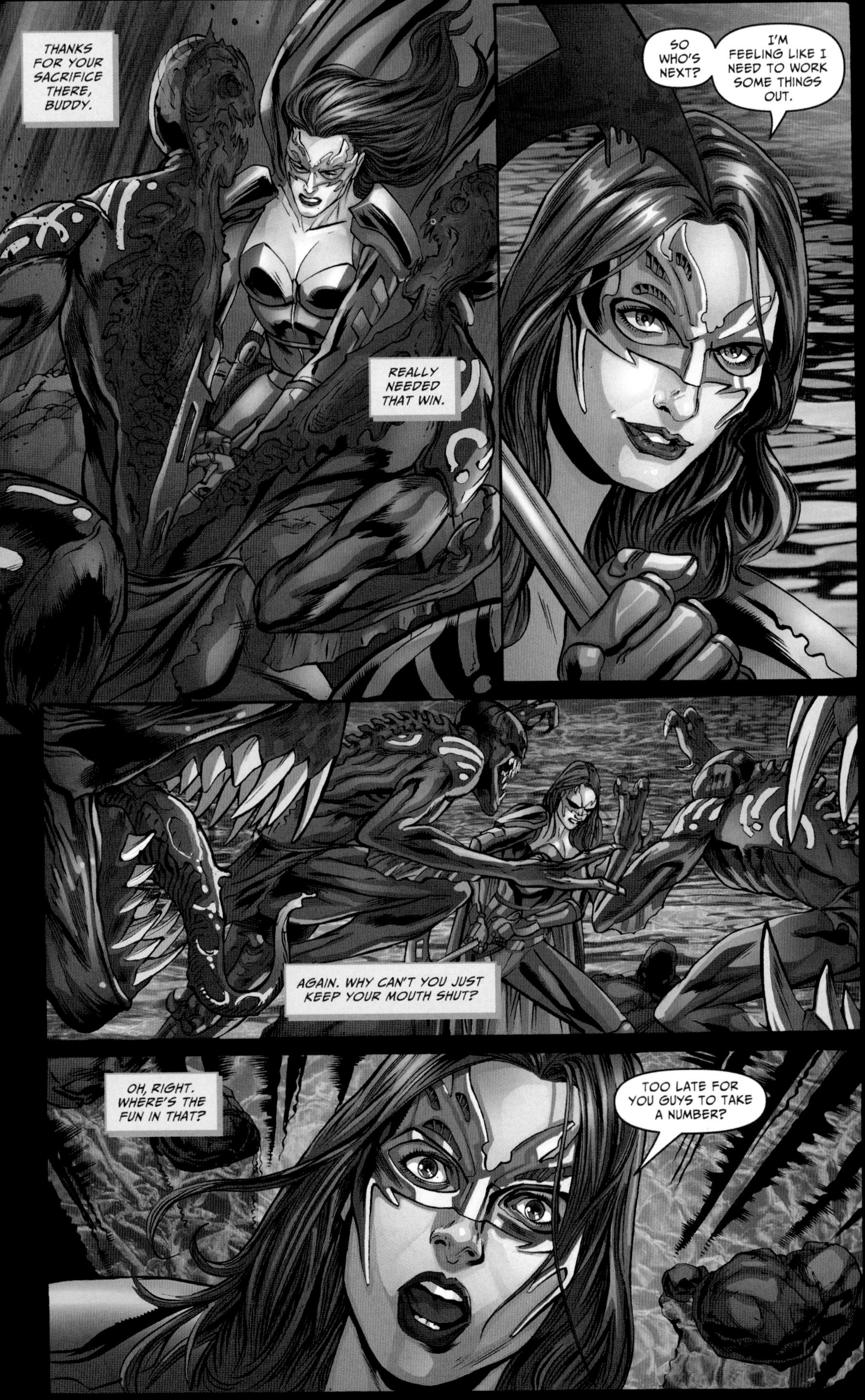

THANKS FOR YOUR SACRIFICE THERE, BUDDY.
REALLY NEEDED THAT WIN.
SO WHO'S NEXT?
I'M FEELING LIKE I NEED TO WORK SOME THINGS OUT.
AGAIN. WHY CAN'T YOU JUST KEEP YOUR MOUTH SHUT?
OH, RIGHT. WHERE'S THE FUN IN THAT?
TOO LATE FOR YOU GUYS TO TAKE A NUMBER?

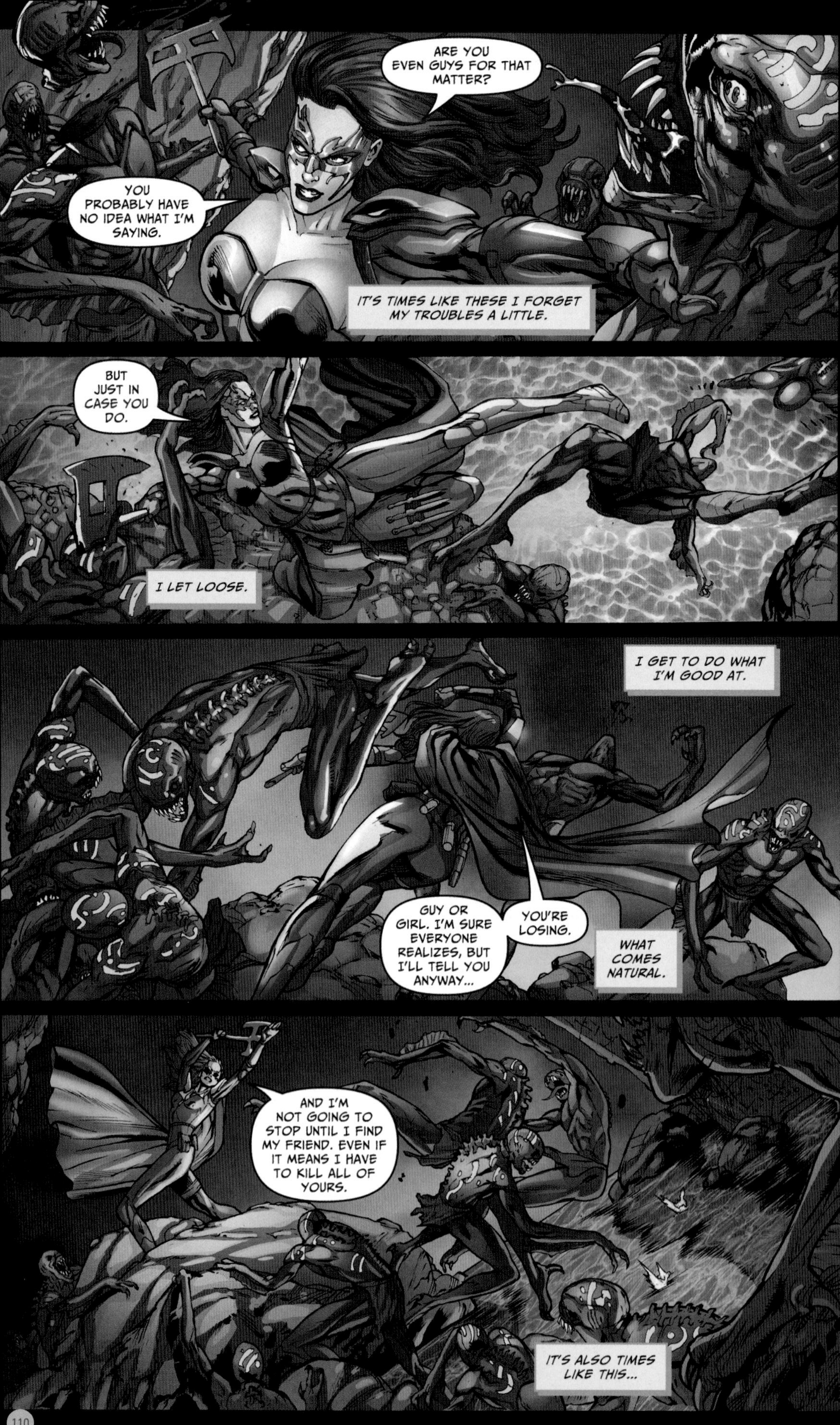
YOU PROBABLY HAVE NO IDEA WHAT I'M SAYING.
ARE YOU EVEN GUYS FOR THAT MATTER?
IT'S TIMES LIKE THESE I FORGET MY TROUBLES A LITTLE.
BUT JUST IN CASE YOU DO.
I LET LOOSE.
I GET TO DO WHAT I'M GOOD AT.
GUY OR GIRL. I'M SURE EVERYONE REALIZES, BUT I'LL TELL YOU ANYWAY...
YOU'RE LOSING.
WHAT COMES NATURAL.
AND I'M NOT GOING TO STOP UNTIL I FIND MY FRIEND. EVEN IF IT MEANS I HAVE TO KILL ALL OF YOURS.
IT'S ALSO TIMES LIKE THIS...

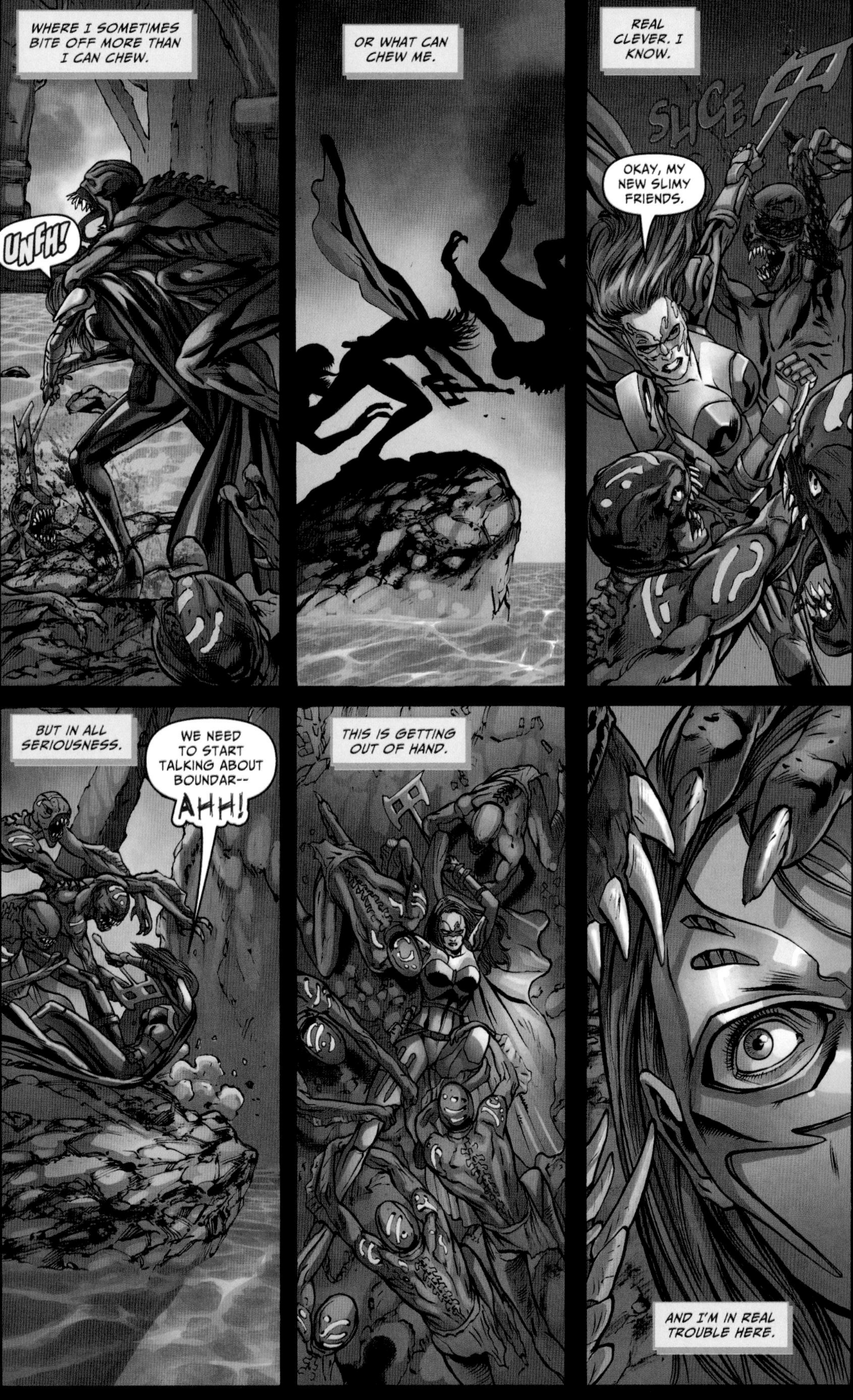
WHERE I SOMETIMES BITE OFF MORE THAN I CAN CHEW.
UNFH!
OR WHAT CAN CHEW ME.
REAL CLEVER. I KNOW.
SLICE
OKAY, MY NEW SLIMY FRIENDS.
BUT IN ALL SERIOUSNESS.
WE NEED TO START TALKING ABOUT BOUNDAR--
AHH!
THIS IS GETTING OUT OF HAND.
AND I'M IN REAL TROUBLE HERE.

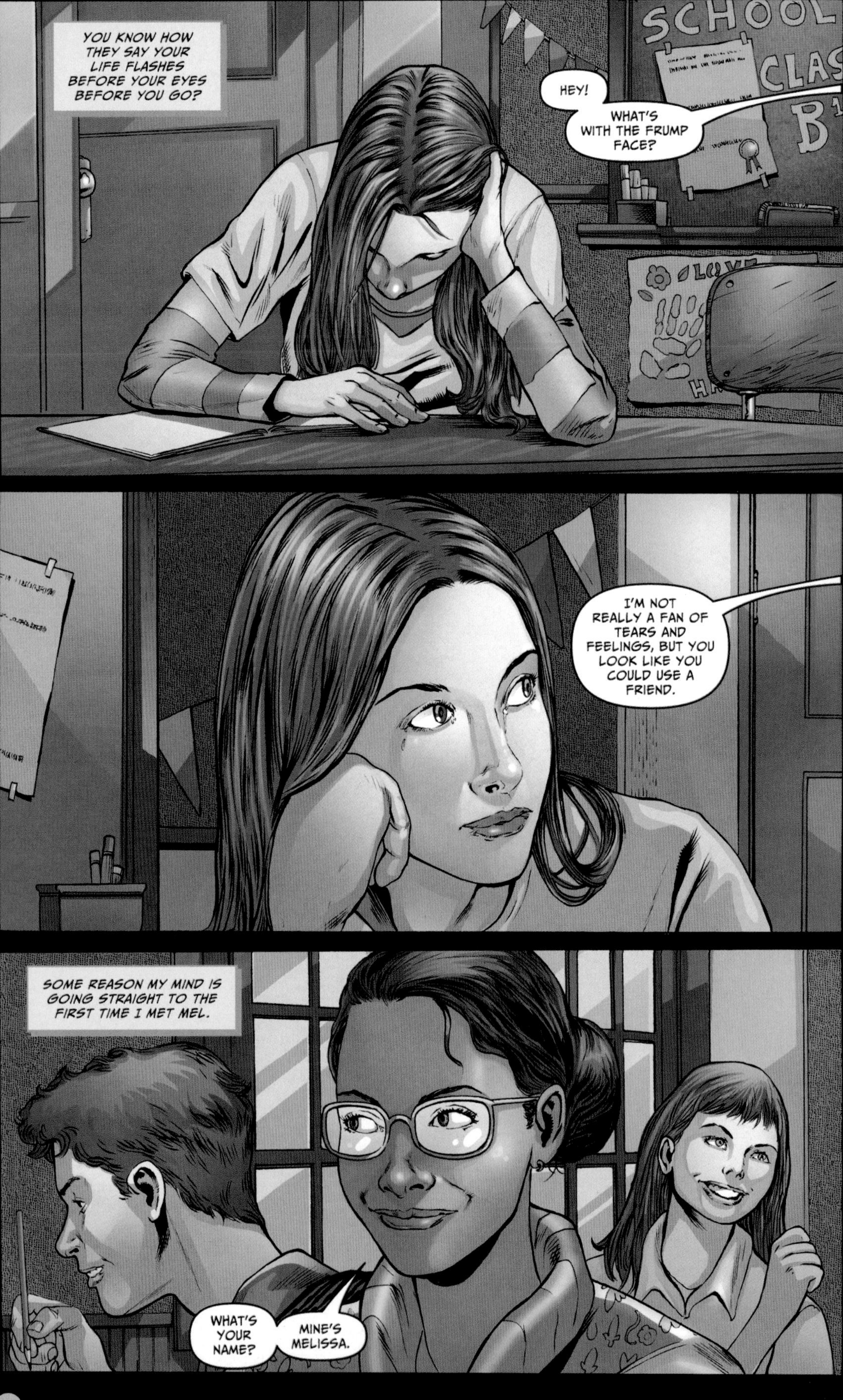
YOU KNOW HOW THEY SAY YOUR LIFE FLASHES BEFORE YOUR EYES BEFORE YOU GO?
SCHOOL
CLAS
HEY!
WHAT'S WITH THE FRUMP FACE?
I'M NOT REALLY A FAN OF TEARS AND FEELINGS, BUT YOU LOOK LIKE YOU COULD USE A FRIEND.
SOME REASON MY MIND IS GOING STRAIGHT TO THE FIRST TIME I MET MEL.
WHAT'S YOUR NAME?
MINE'S MELISSA.

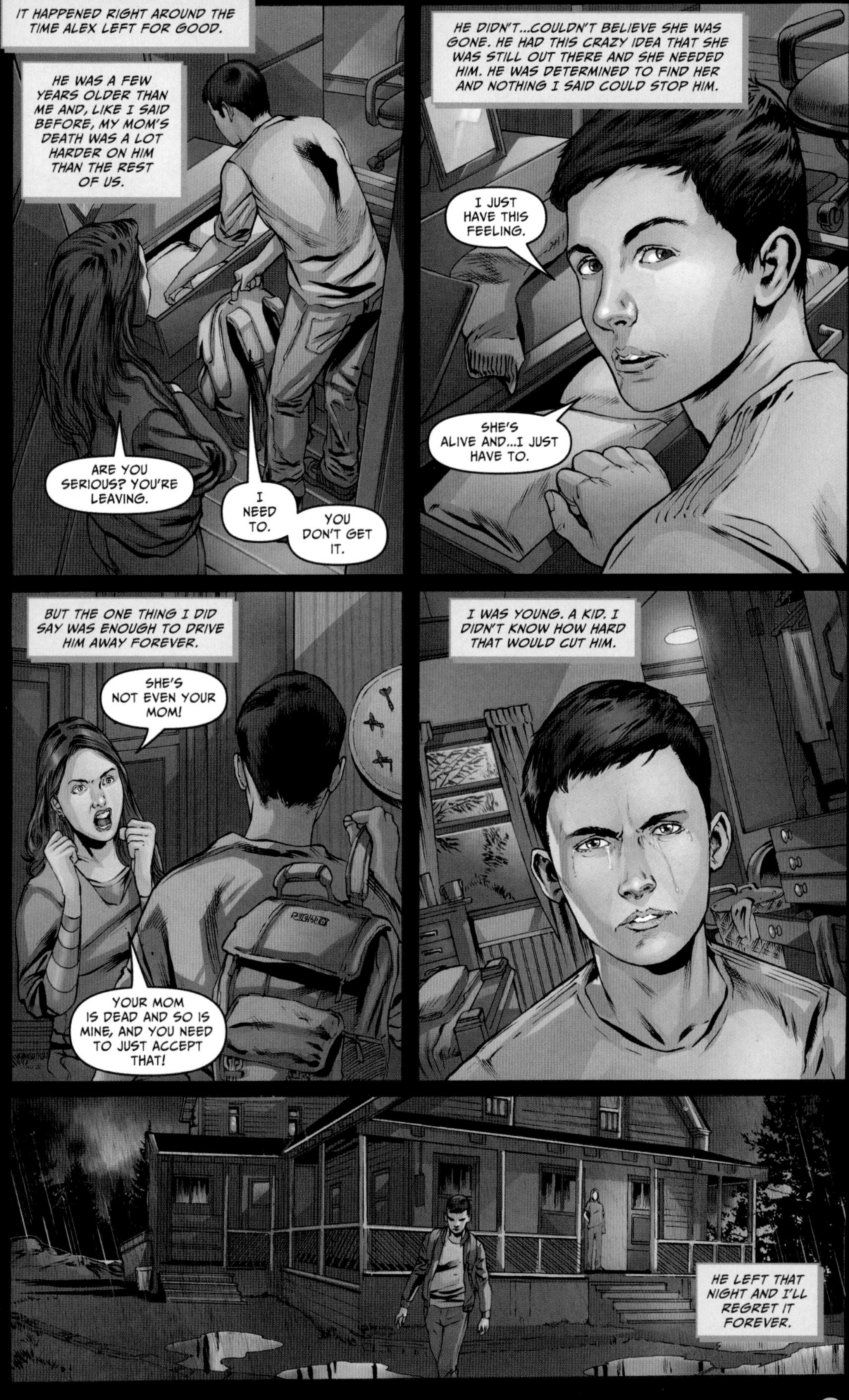
IT HAPPENED RIGHT AROUND THE TIME ALEX LEFT FOR GOOD.
HE WAS A FEW YEARS OLDER THAN ME AND, LIKE I SAID BEFORE, MY MOM'S DEATH WAS A LOT HARDER ON HIM THAN THE REST OF US.
ARE YOU SERIOUS? YOU'RE LEAVING.
I NEED TO.
YOU DON'T GET IT.
HE DIDN'T...COULDN'T BELIEVE SHE WAS GONE. HE HAD THIS CRAZY IDEA THAT SHE WAS STILL OUT THERE AND SHE NEEDED HIM. HE WAS DETERMINED TO FIND HER AND NOTHING I SAID COULD STOP HIM.
I JUST HAVE THIS FEELING.
SHE'S ALIVE AND...I JUST HAVE TO.
BUT THE ONE THING I DID SAY WAS ENOUGH TO DRIVE HIM AWAY FOREVER.
SHE'S NOT EVEN YOUR MOM!
YOUR MOM IS DEAD AND SO IS MINE, AND YOU NEED TO JUST ACCEPT THAT!
I WAS YOUNG. A KID. I DIDN'T KNOW HOW HARD THAT WOULD CUT HIM.
HE LEFT THAT NIGHT AND I'LL REGRET IT FOREVER.

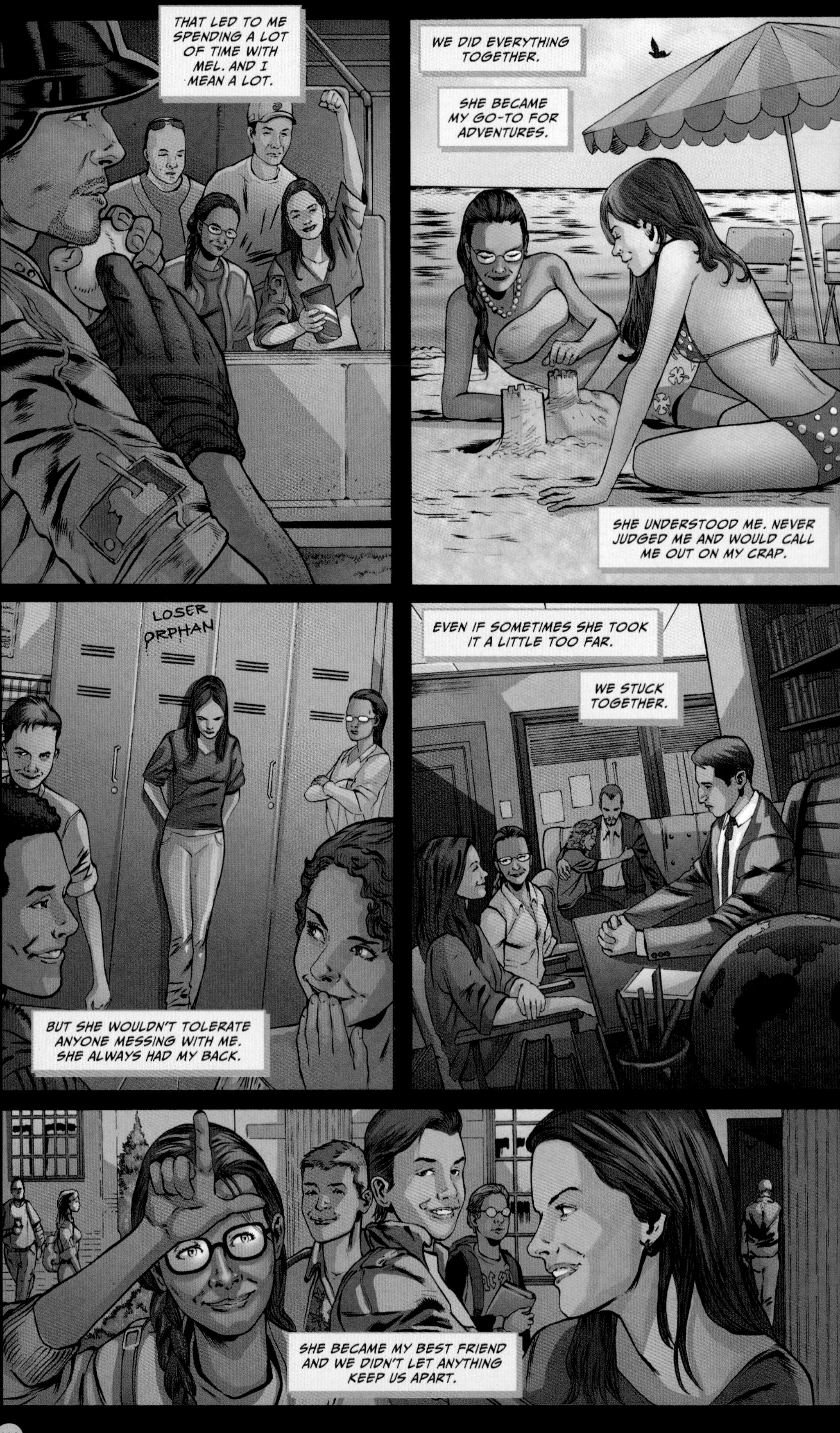
THAT LED TO ME SPENDING A LOT OF TIME WITH MEL. AND I MEAN A LOT.
WE DID EVERYTHING TOGETHER.
SHE BECAME MY GO-TO FOR ADVENTURES.
SHE UNDERSTOOD ME. NEVER JUDGED ME AND WOULD CALL ME OUT ON MY CRAP.
LOSER ORPHAN
BUT SHE WOULDN'T TOLERATE ANYONE MESSING WITH ME. SHE ALWAYS HAD MY BACK.
EVEN IF SOMETIMES SHE TOOK IT A LITTLE TOO FAR.
WE STUCK TOGETHER.
SHE BECAME MY BEST FRIEND AND WE DIDN'T LET ANYTHING KEEP US APART.

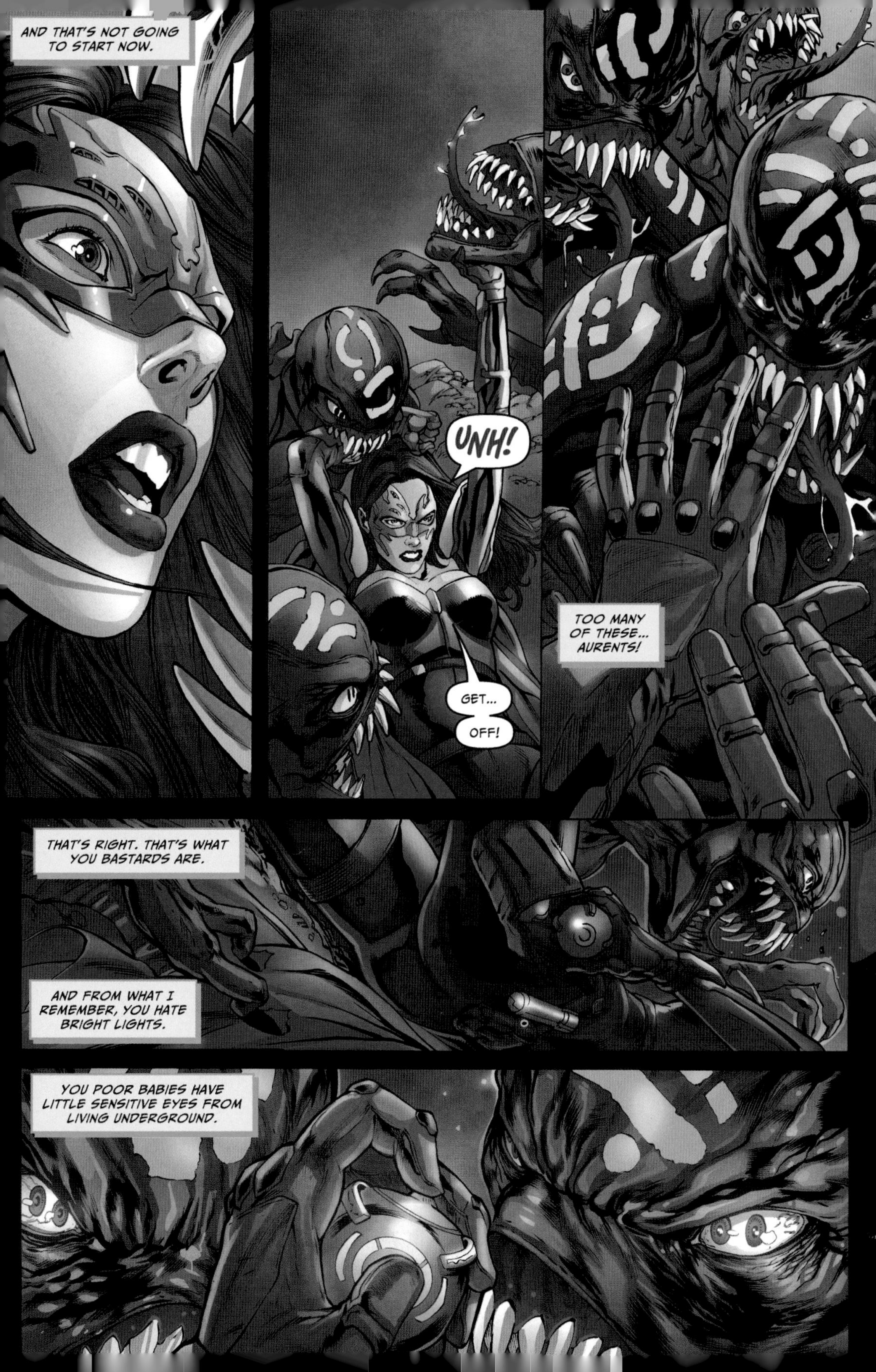
AND THAT'S NOT GOING TO START NOW.
UNH!
GET...
OFF!
TOO MANY OF THESE... AURENTS!
THAT'S RIGHT. THAT'S WHAT YOU BASTARDS ARE.
AND FROM WHAT I REMEMBER, YOU HATE BRIGHT LIGHTS.
YOU POOR BABIES HAVE LITTLE SENSITIVE EYES FROM LIVING UNDERGROUND.

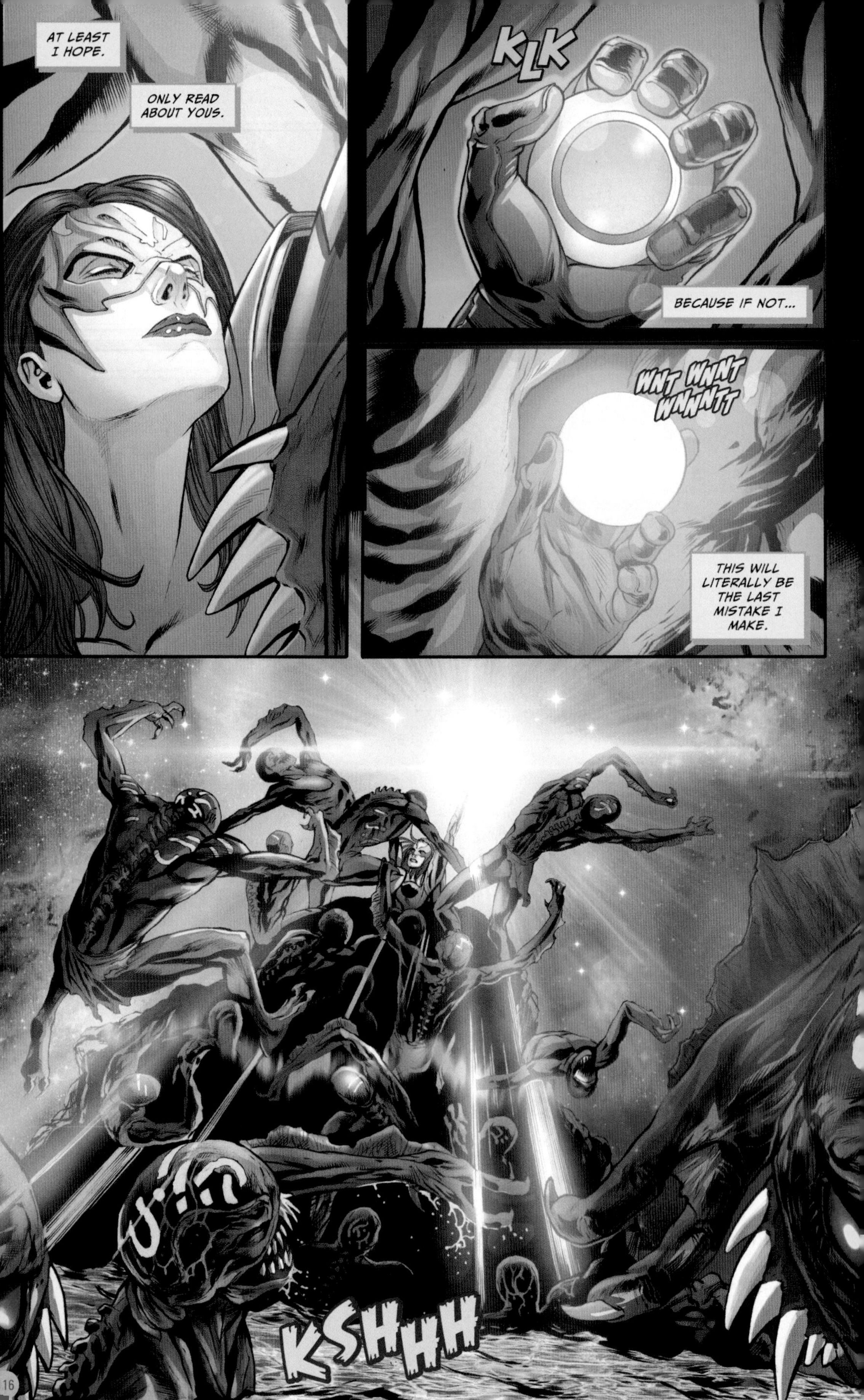

AT LEAST I HOPE.
ONLY READ ABOUT YOUS.
KLK
BECAUSE IF NOT...
WNT WNNT WNNNTT
THIS WILL LITERALLY BE THE LAST MISTAKE I MAKE.
KSHHH

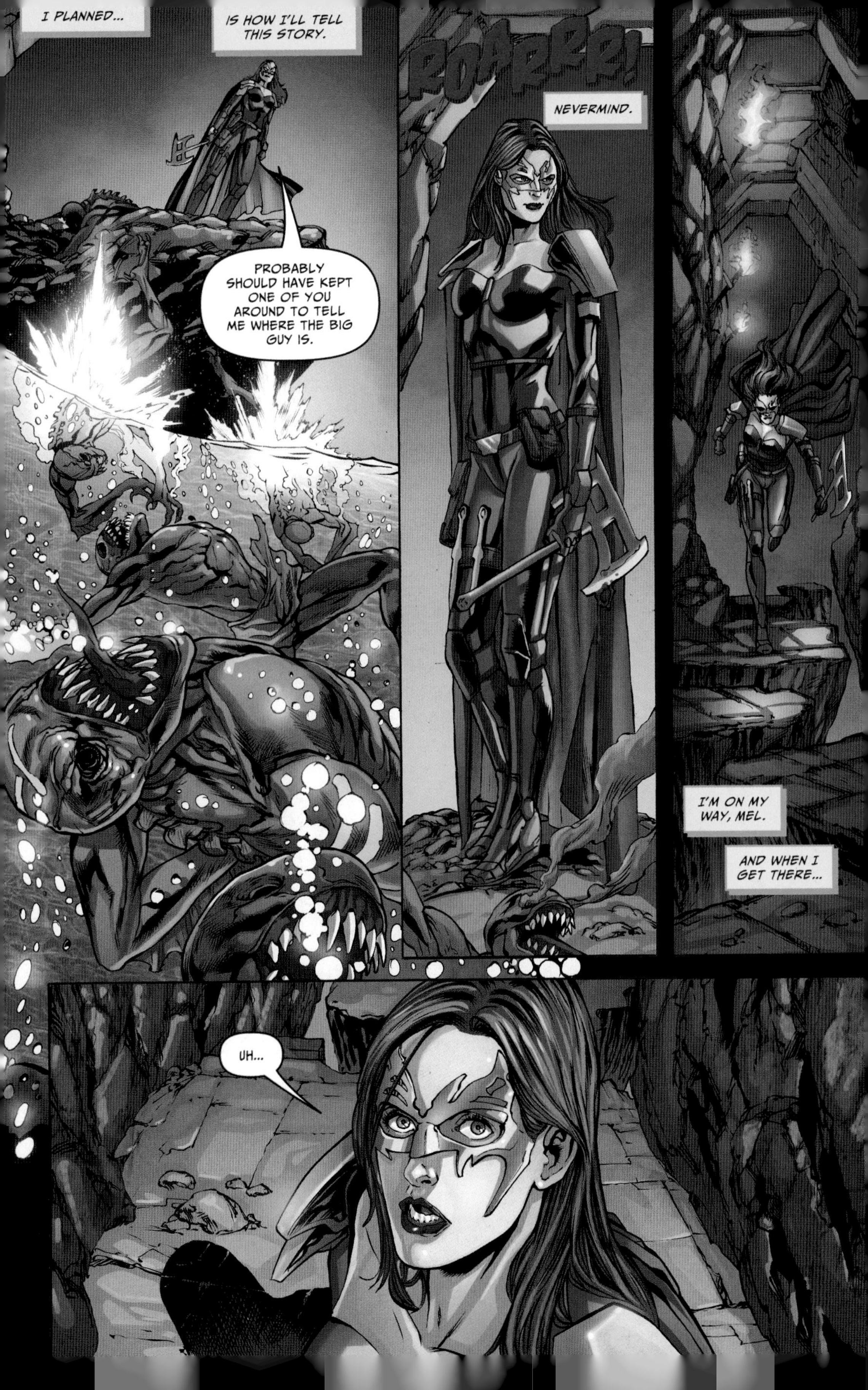
I PLANNED...
IS HOW I'LL TELL THIS STORY.
PROBABLY SHOULD HAVE KEPT ONE OF YOU AROUND TO TELL ME WHERE THE BIG GUY IS.
ROARRR!
NEVERMIND.
I'M ON MY WAY, MEL.
AND WHEN I GET THERE...
UH...

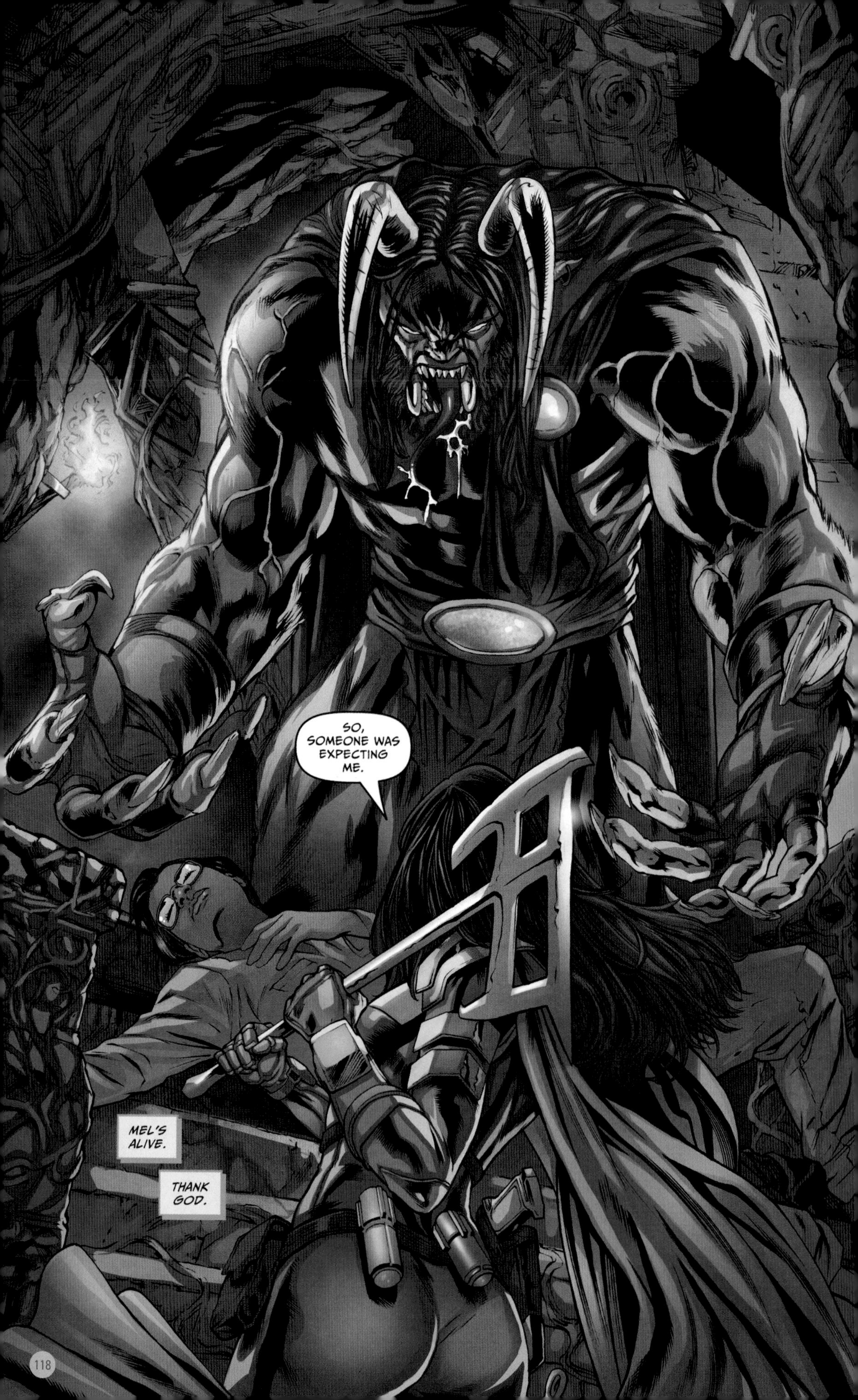
SO, SOMEONE WAS EXPECTING ME.
MEL'S ALIVE.
THANK GOD.

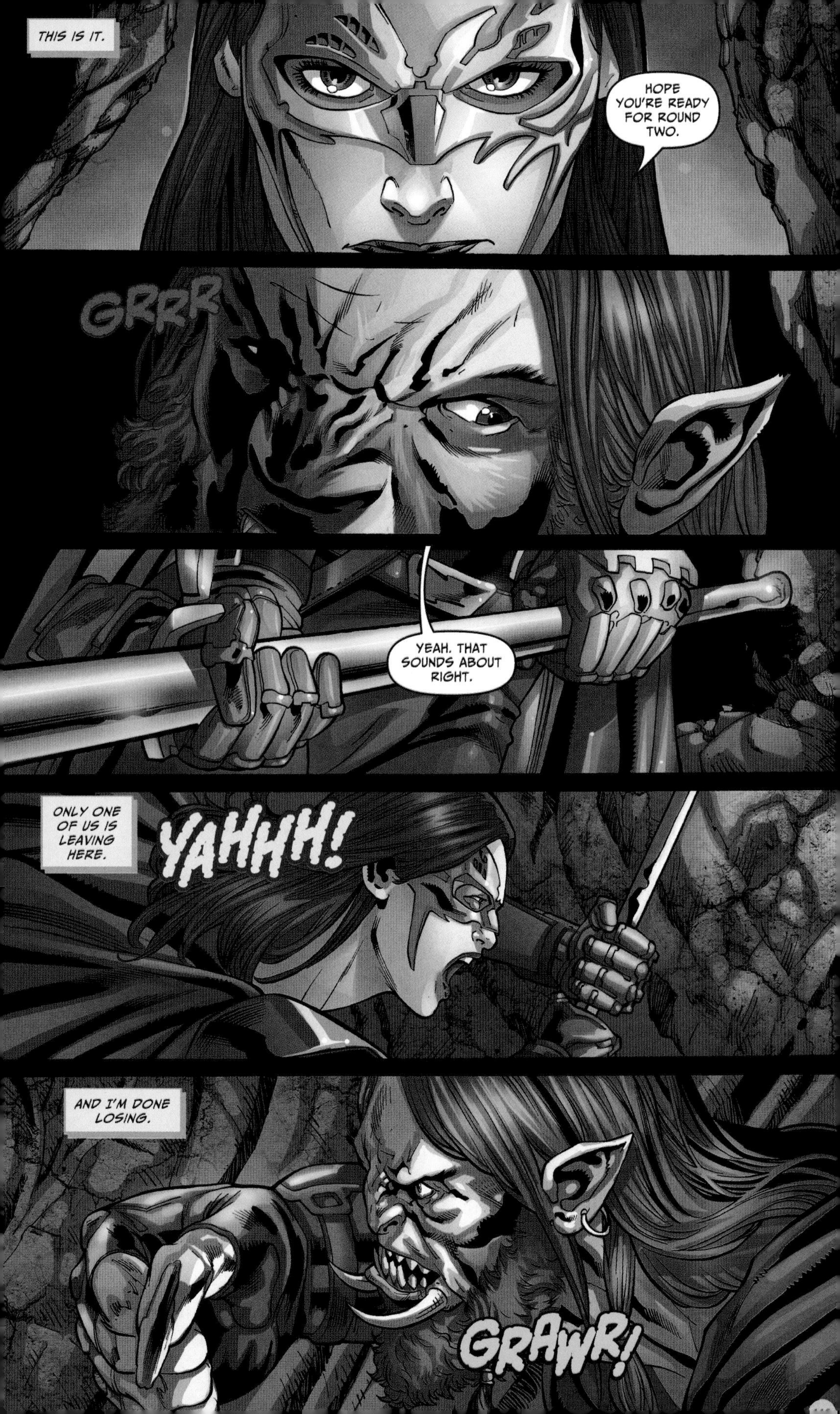

THIS IS IT.
HOPE YOU'RE READY FOR ROUND TWO.
GRRR
YEAH. THAT SOUNDS ABOUT RIGHT.
ONLY ONE OF US IS LEAVING HERE.
YAHHH!
AND I'M DONE LOSING.
GRAWR!

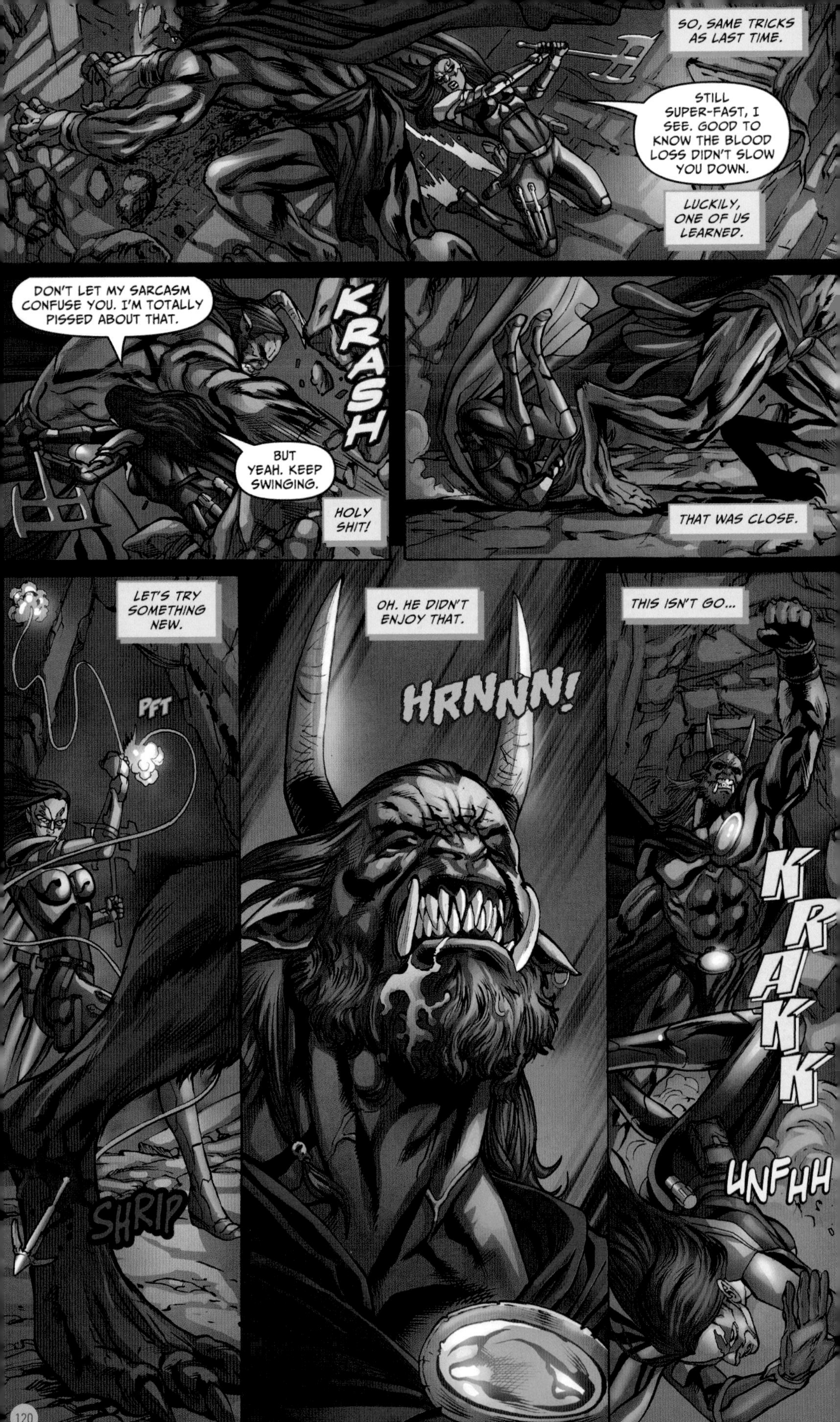

SO, SAME TRICKS AS LAST TIME.
STILL SUPER-FAST, I SEE. GOOD TO KNOW THE BLOOD LOSS DIDN'T SLOW YOU DOWN.
LUCKILY, ONE OF US LEARNED.
DON'T LET MY SARCASM CONFUSE YOU. I'M TOTALLY PISSED ABOUT THAT.
KRASH
BUT YEAH. KEEP SWINGING.
HOLY SHIT!
THAT WAS CLOSE.
LET'S TRY SOMETHING NEW.
PFT
SHRIP
OH. HE DIDN'T ENJOY THAT.
HRNNN!
THIS ISN'T GO...
KRAKK
UNFHH

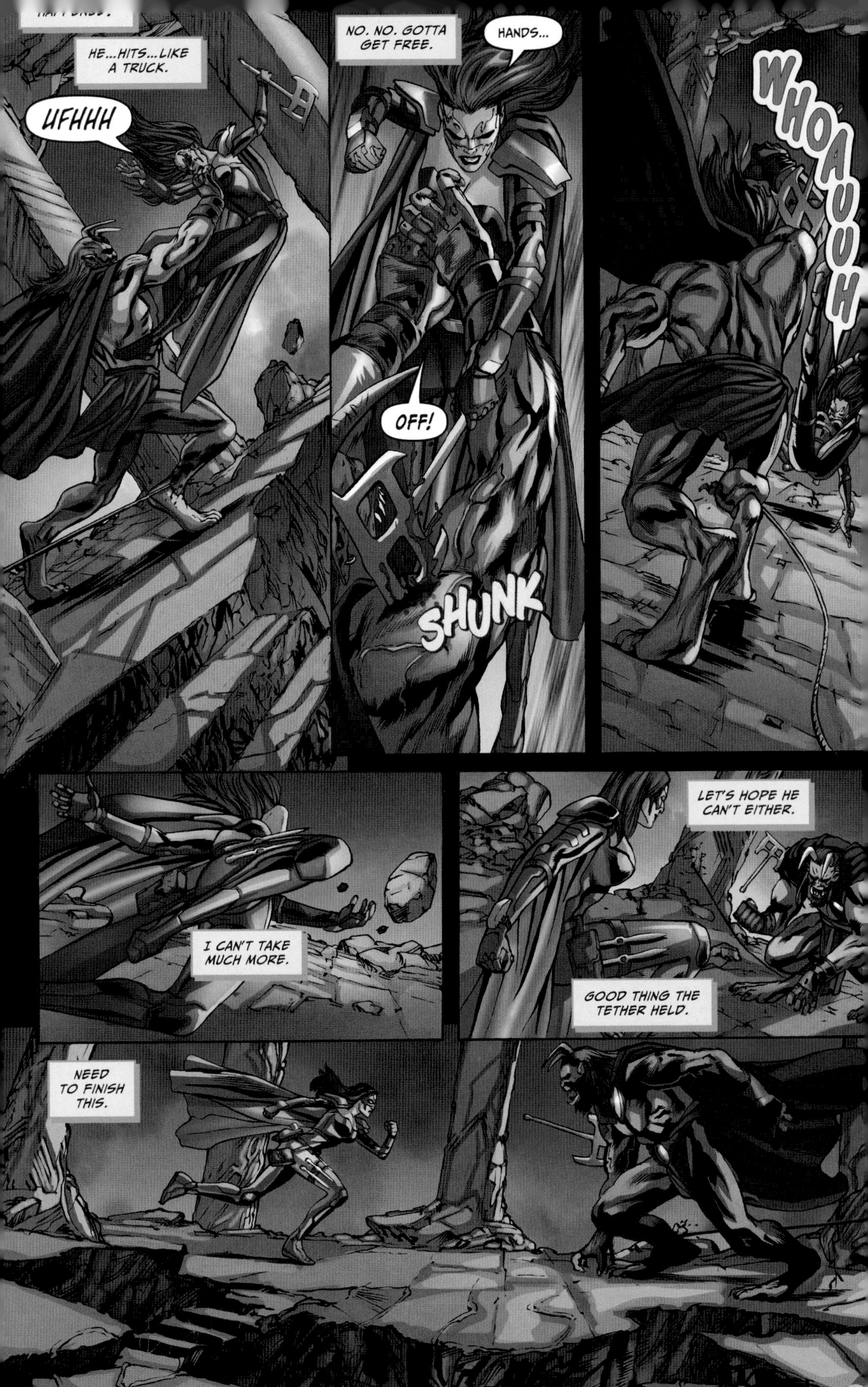
HE...HITS...LIKE A TRUCK.
UFHHH
NO. NO. GOTTA GET FREE.
HANDS...
OFF!
SHUNK
WHOAAUUH
I CAN'T TAKE MUCH MORE.
LET'S HOPE HE CAN'T EITHER.
GOOD THING THE TETHER HELD.
NEED TO FINISH THIS.

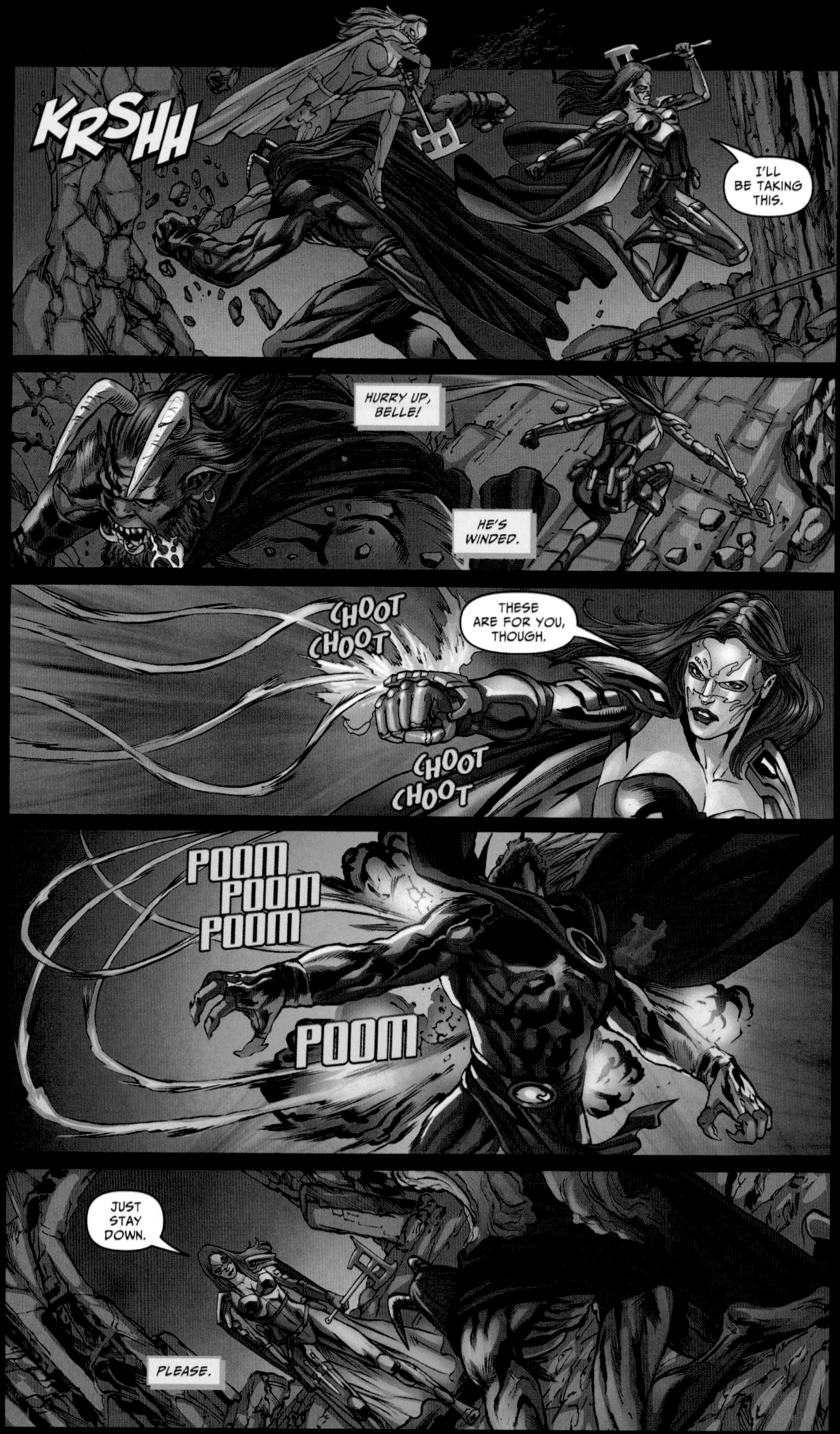
KRSHH
I'LL BE TAKING THIS.
HURRY UP, BELLE!
HE'S WINDED.
CHOOT CHOOT
THESE ARE FOR YOU, THOUGH.
CHOOT CHOOT
POOM POOM POOM
POOM
JUST STAY DOWN.
PLEASE.

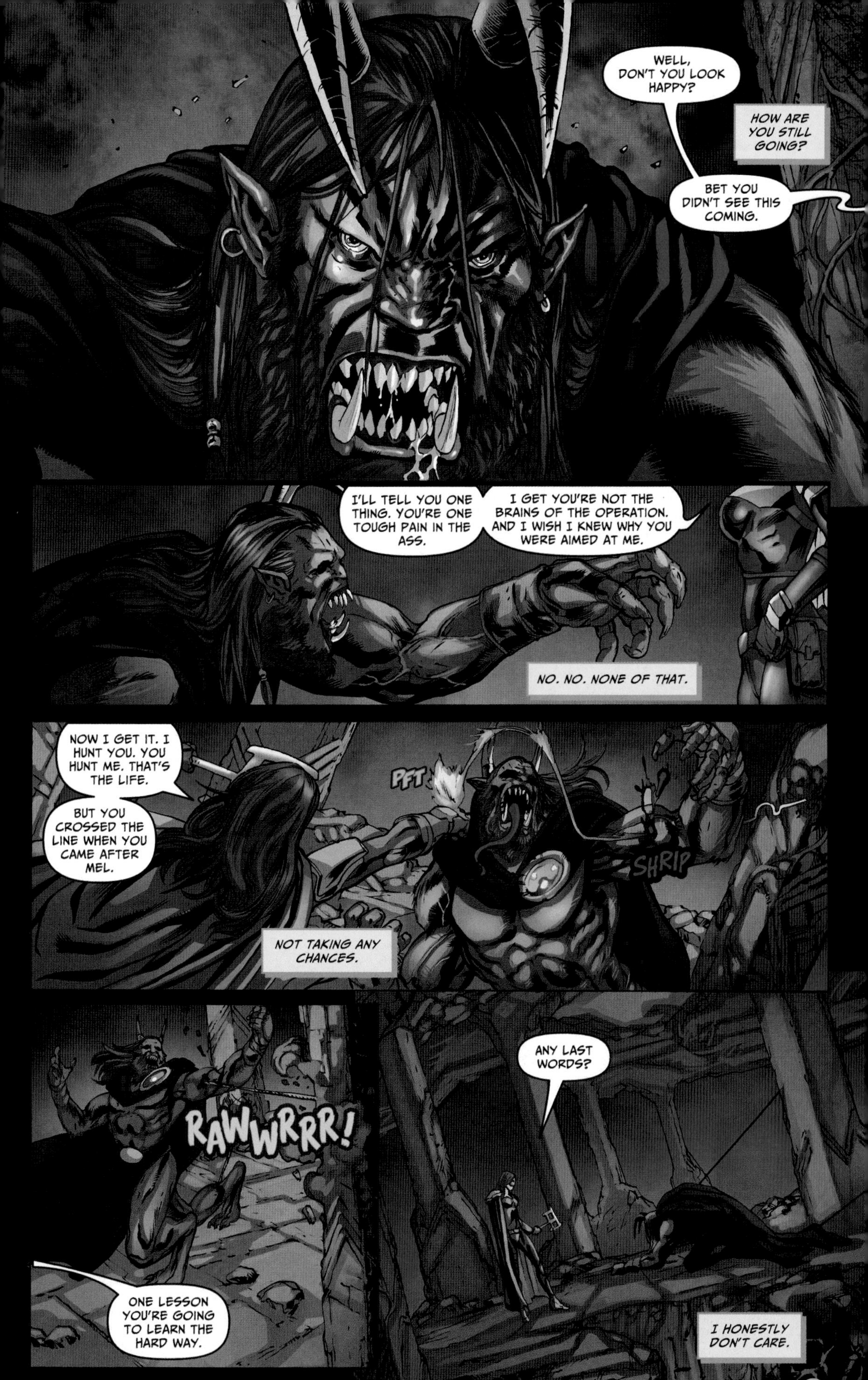
WELL, DON'T YOU LOOK HAPPY?
HOW ARE YOU STILL GOING?
BET YOU DIDN'T SEE THIS COMING.
I'LL TELL YOU ONE THING. YOU'RE ONE TOUGH PAIN IN THE ASS.
I GET YOU'RE NOT THE BRAINS OF THE OPERATION. AND I WISH I KNEW WHY YOU WERE AIMED AT ME.
NO. NO. NONE OF THAT.
NOW I GET IT. I HUNT YOU. YOU HUNT ME. THAT'S THE LIFE.
BUT YOU CROSSED THE LINE WHEN YOU CAME AFTER MEL.
PFT
SHRIP
NOT TAKING ANY CHANCES.
RAWWRRR!
ONE LESSON YOU'RE GOING TO LEARN THE HARD WAY.
ANY LAST WORDS?
I HONESTLY DON'T CARE.

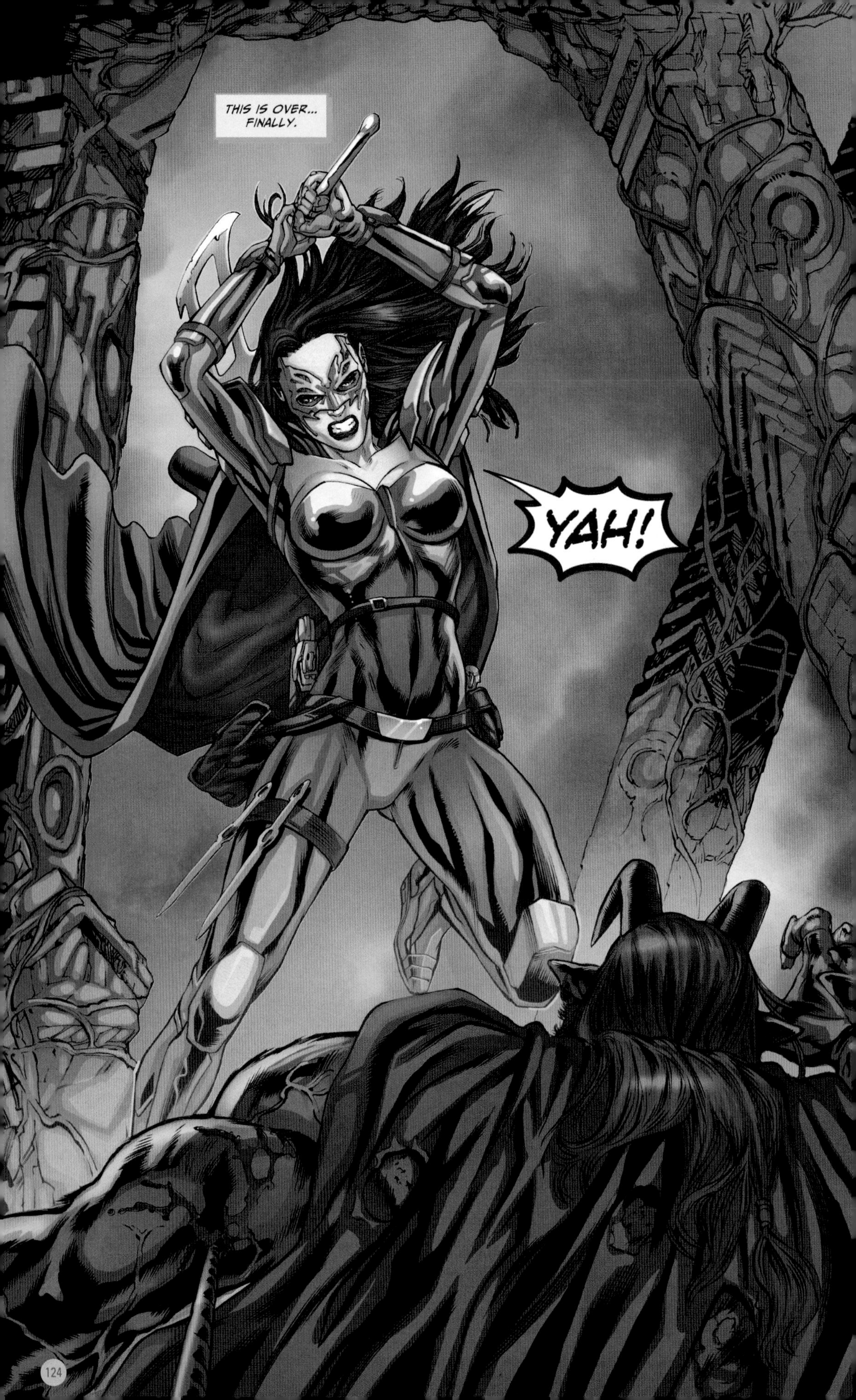
THIS IS OVER... FINALLY.
YAH!

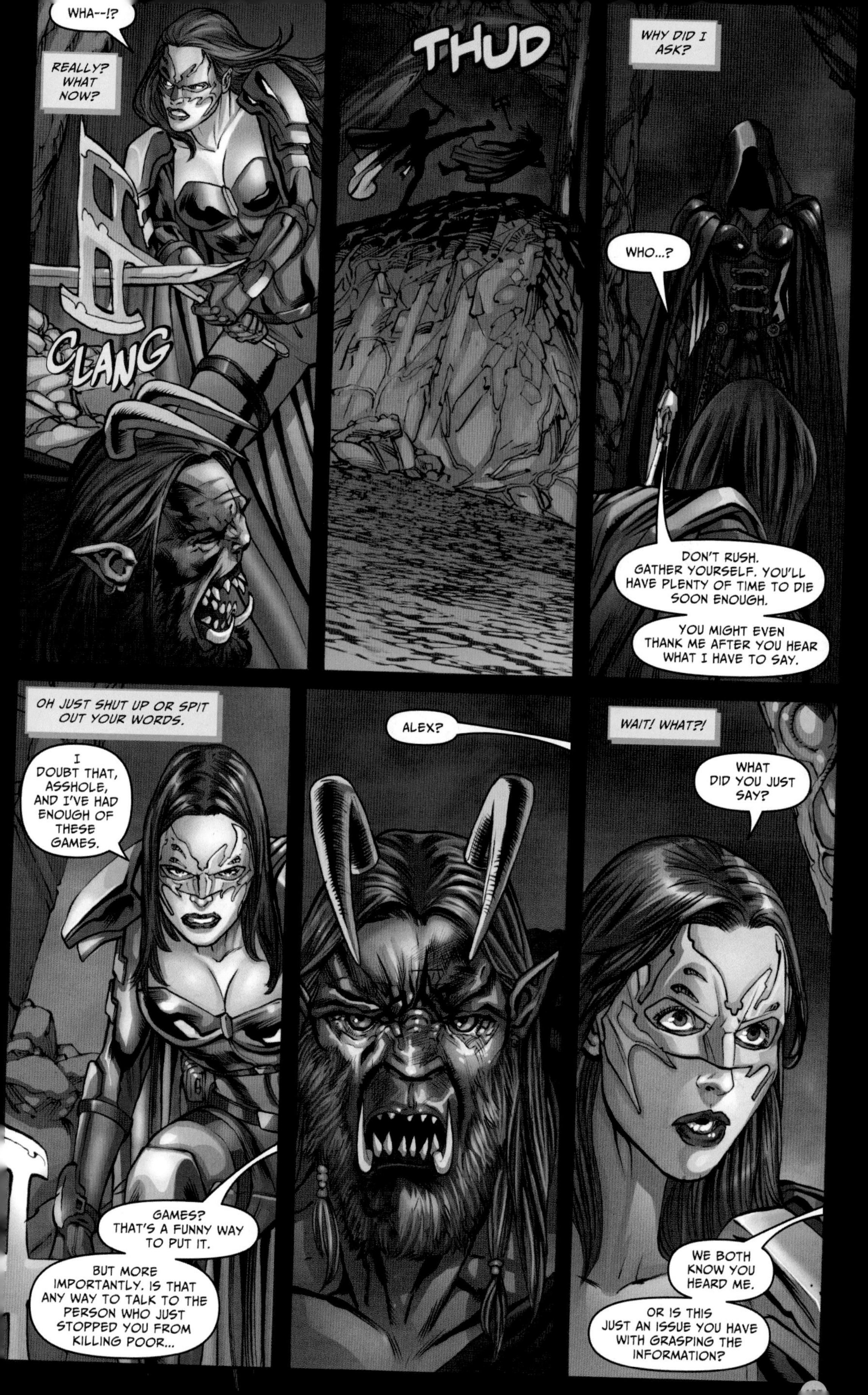
WHA--!?
REALLY? WHAT NOW?
CLANG
THUD
WHY DID I ASK?
WHO...?
DON'T RUSH. GATHER YOURSELF. YOU'LL HAVE PLENTY OF TIME TO DIE SOON ENOUGH.
YOU MIGHT EVEN THANK ME AFTER YOU HEAR WHAT I HAVE TO SAY.
OH JUST SHUT UP OR SPIT OUT YOUR WORDS.
I DOUBT THAT, ASSHOLE, AND I'VE HAD ENOUGH OF THESE GAMES.
GAMES? THAT'S A FUNNY WAY TO PUT IT.
BUT MORE IMPORTANTLY. IS THAT ANY WAY TO TALK TO THE PERSON WHO JUST STOPPED YOU FROM KILLING POOR...
ALEX?
WAIT! WHAT?!
WHAT DID YOU JUST SAY?
WE BOTH KNOW YOU HEARD ME.
OR IS THIS JUST AN ISSUE YOU HAVE WITH GRASPING THE INFORMATION?

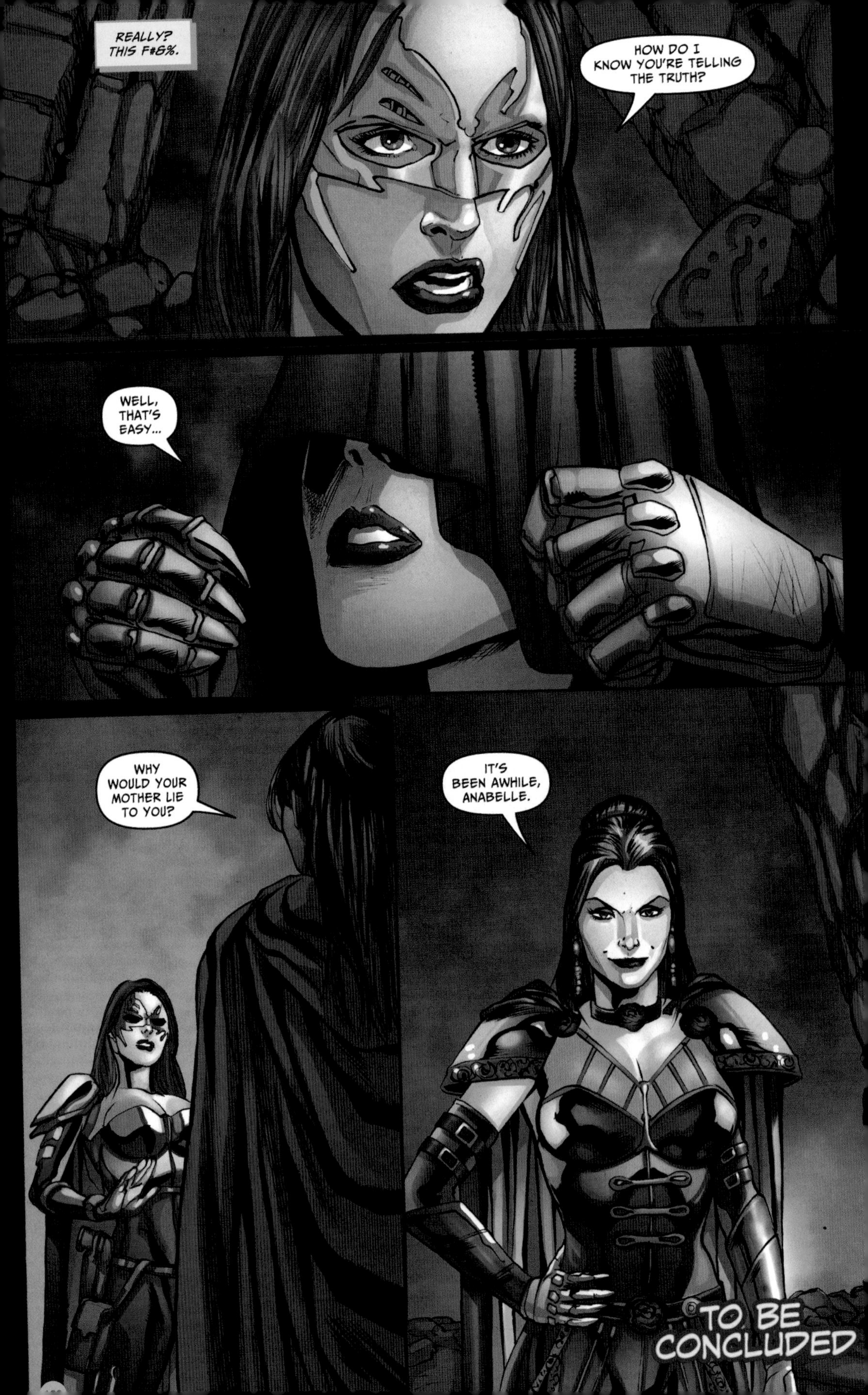
REALLY? THIS F#&%.
HOW DO I KNOW YOU'RE TELLING THE TRUTH?
WELL, THAT'S EASY...
WHY WOULD YOUR MOTHER LIE TO YOU?
IT'S BEEN AWHILE, ANABELLE.
TO BE CONCLUDED

BELLE BEAST HUNTER

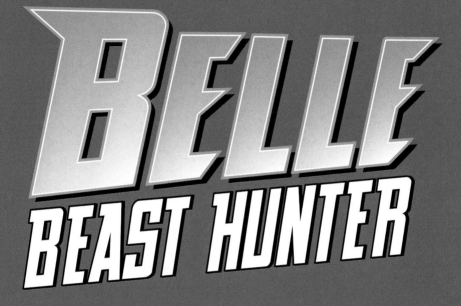

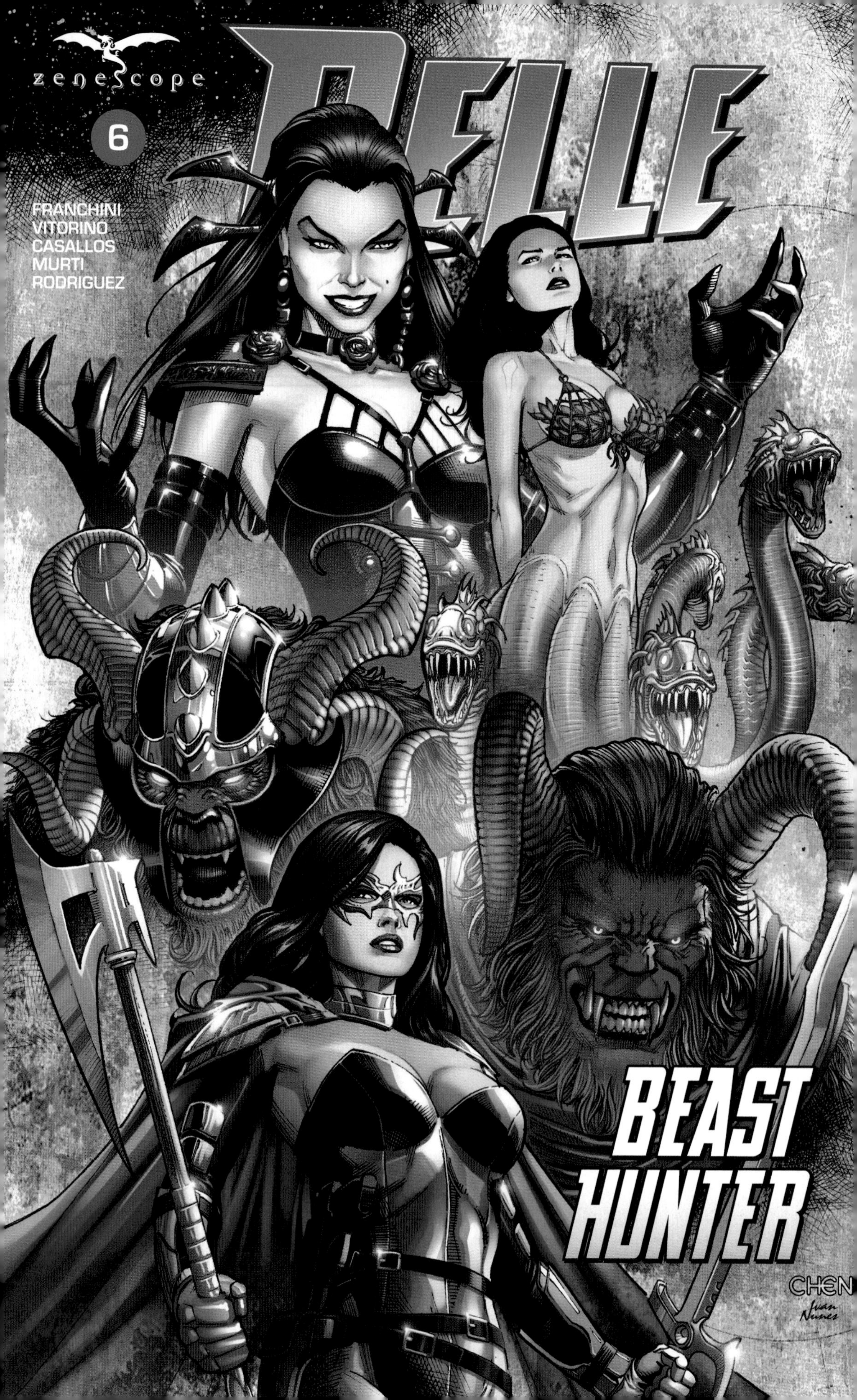
zenescope
6
BELLE
FRANCHINI
VITORINO
CASALLOS
MURTI
RODRIGUEZ
BEAST
HUNTER
CHEN
Juan Nunes

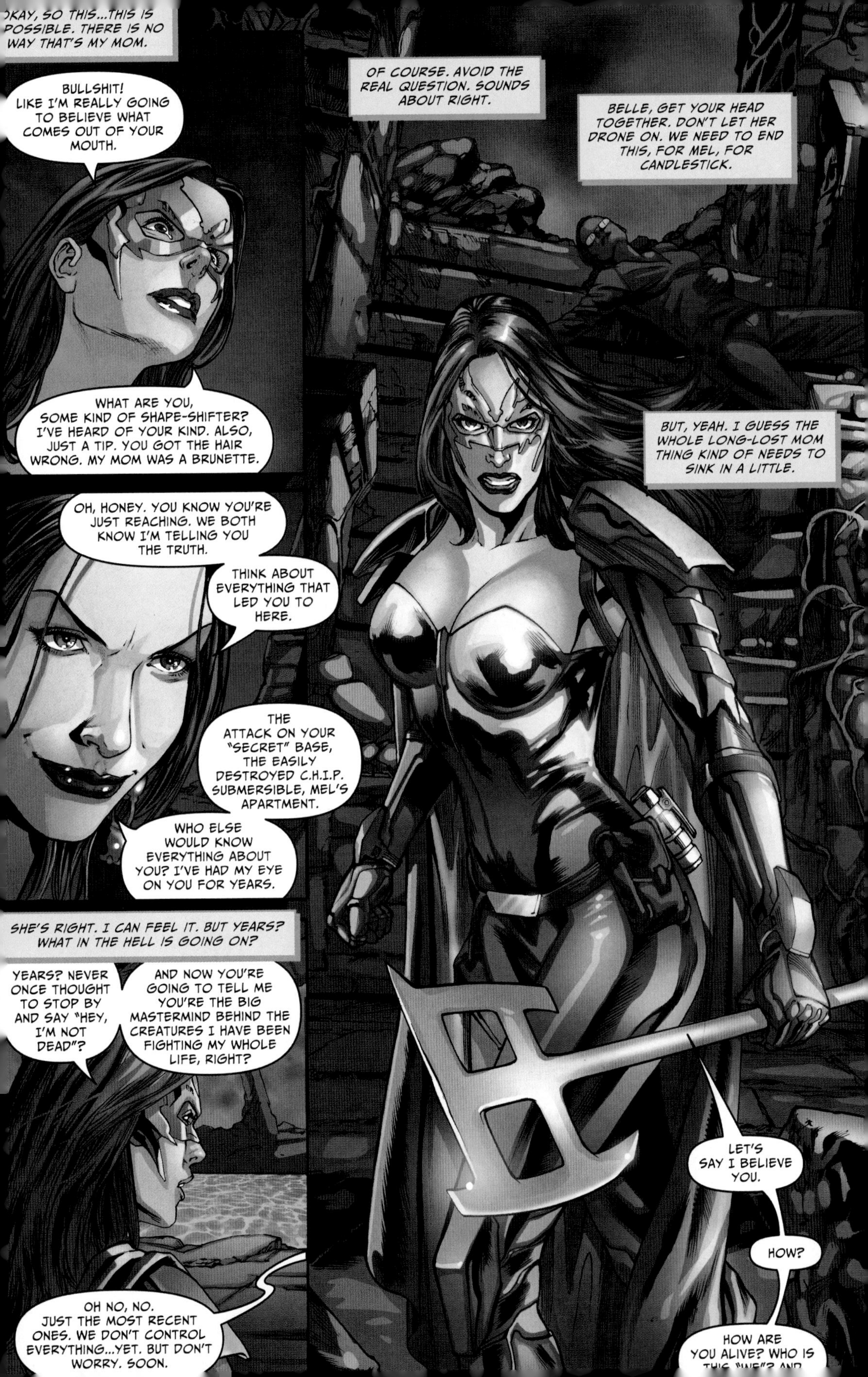

OKAY, SO THIS...THIS IS POSSIBLE. THERE IS NO WAY THAT'S MY MOM.
BULLSHIT! LIKE I'M REALLY GOING TO BELIEVE WHAT COMES OUT OF YOUR MOUTH.
WHAT ARE YOU, SOME KIND OF SHAPE-SHIFTER? I'VE HEARD OF YOUR KIND. ALSO, JUST A TIP. YOU GOT THE HAIR WRONG. MY MOM WAS A BRUNETTE.
OH, HONEY. YOU KNOW YOU'RE JUST REACHING. WE BOTH KNOW I'M TELLING YOU THE TRUTH.
THINK ABOUT EVERYTHING THAT LED YOU TO HERE.
THE ATTACK ON YOUR "SECRET" BASE, THE EASILY DESTROYED C.H.I.P. SUBMERSIBLE, MEL'S APARTMENT.
WHO ELSE WOULD KNOW EVERYTHING ABOUT YOU? I'VE HAD MY EYE ON YOU FOR YEARS.
SHE'S RIGHT. I CAN FEEL IT. BUT YEARS? WHAT IN THE HELL IS GOING ON?
YEARS? NEVER ONCE THOUGHT TO STOP BY AND SAY "HEY, I'M NOT DEAD"?
AND NOW YOU'RE GOING TO TELL ME YOU'RE THE BIG MASTERMIND BEHIND THE CREATURES I HAVE BEEN FIGHTING MY WHOLE LIFE, RIGHT?
OH NO, NO. JUST THE MOST RECENT ONES. WE DON'T CONTROL EVERYTHING...YET. BUT DON'T WORRY. SOON.
OF COURSE. AVOID THE REAL QUESTION. SOUNDS ABOUT RIGHT.
BELLE, GET YOUR HEAD TOGETHER. DON'T LET HER DRONE ON. WE NEED TO END THIS, FOR MEL, FOR CANDLESTICK.
BUT, YEAH. I GUESS THE WHOLE LONG-LOST MOM THING KIND OF NEEDS TO SINK IN A LITTLE.
LET'S SAY I BELIEVE YOU.
HOW?
HOW ARE YOU ALIVE? WHO IS

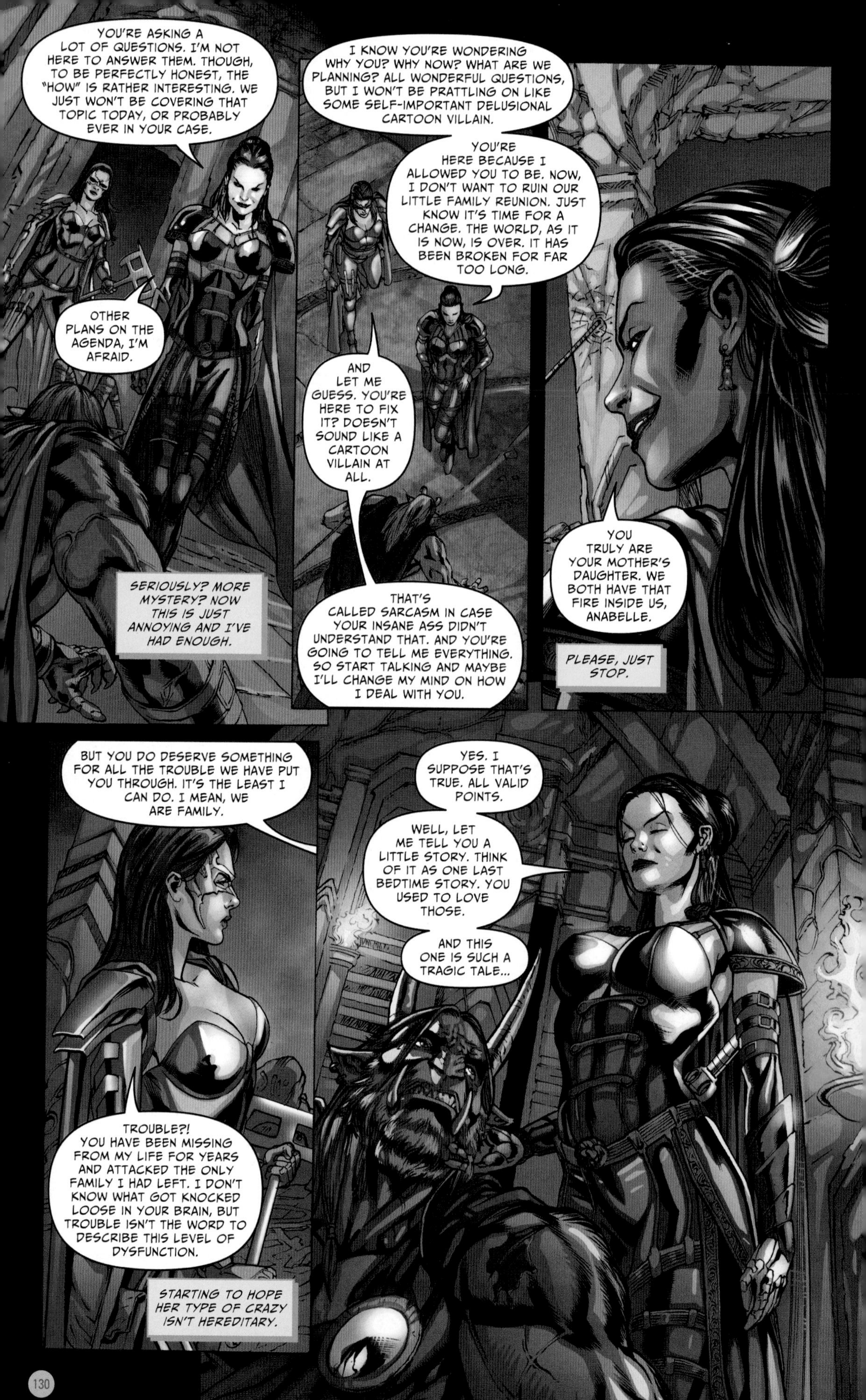
YOU'RE ASKING A LOT OF QUESTIONS. I'M NOT HERE TO ANSWER THEM. THOUGH, TO BE PERFECTLY HONEST, THE "HOW" IS RATHER INTERESTING. WE JUST WON'T BE COVERING THAT TOPIC TODAY, OR PROBABLY EVER IN YOUR CASE.
OTHER PLANS ON THE AGENDA, I'M AFRAID.
SERIOUSLY? MORE MYSTERY? NOW THIS IS JUST ANNOYING AND I'VE HAD ENOUGH.
I KNOW YOU'RE WONDERING WHY YOU? WHY NOW? WHAT ARE WE PLANNING? ALL WONDERFUL QUESTIONS, BUT I WON'T BE PRATTLING ON LIKE SOME SELF-IMPORTANT DELUSIONAL CARTOON VILLAIN.
YOU'RE HERE BECAUSE I ALLOWED YOU TO BE. NOW, I DON'T WANT TO RUIN OUR LITTLE FAMILY REUNION. JUST KNOW IT'S TIME FOR A CHANGE. THE WORLD, AS IT IS NOW, IS OVER. IT HAS BEEN BROKEN FOR FAR TOO LONG.
AND LET ME GUESS. YOU'RE HERE TO FIX IT? DOESN'T SOUND LIKE A CARTOON VILLAIN AT ALL.
THAT'S CALLED SARCASM IN CASE YOUR INSANE ASS DIDN'T UNDERSTAND THAT. AND YOU'RE GOING TO TELL ME EVERYTHING. SO START TALKING AND MAYBE I'LL CHANGE MY MIND ON HOW I DEAL WITH YOU.
YOU TRULY ARE YOUR MOTHER'S DAUGHTER. WE BOTH HAVE THAT FIRE INSIDE US, ANABELLE.
PLEASE, JUST STOP.
BUT YOU DO DESERVE SOMETHING FOR ALL THE TROUBLE WE HAVE PUT YOU THROUGH. IT'S THE LEAST I CAN DO. I MEAN, WE ARE FAMILY.
TROUBLE?! YOU HAVE BEEN MISSING FROM MY LIFE FOR YEARS AND ATTACKED THE ONLY FAMILY I HAD LEFT. I DON'T KNOW WHAT GOT KNOCKED LOOSE IN YOUR BRAIN, BUT TROUBLE ISN'T THE WORD TO DESCRIBE THIS LEVEL OF DYSFUNCTION.
STARTING TO HOPE HER TYPE OF CRAZY ISN'T HEREDITARY.
YES. I SUPPOSE THAT'S TRUE. ALL VALID POINTS.
WELL, LET ME TELL YOU A LITTLE STORY. THINK OF IT AS ONE LAST BEDTIME STORY. YOU USED TO LOVE THOSE.
AND THIS ONE IS SUCH A TRAGIC TALE...

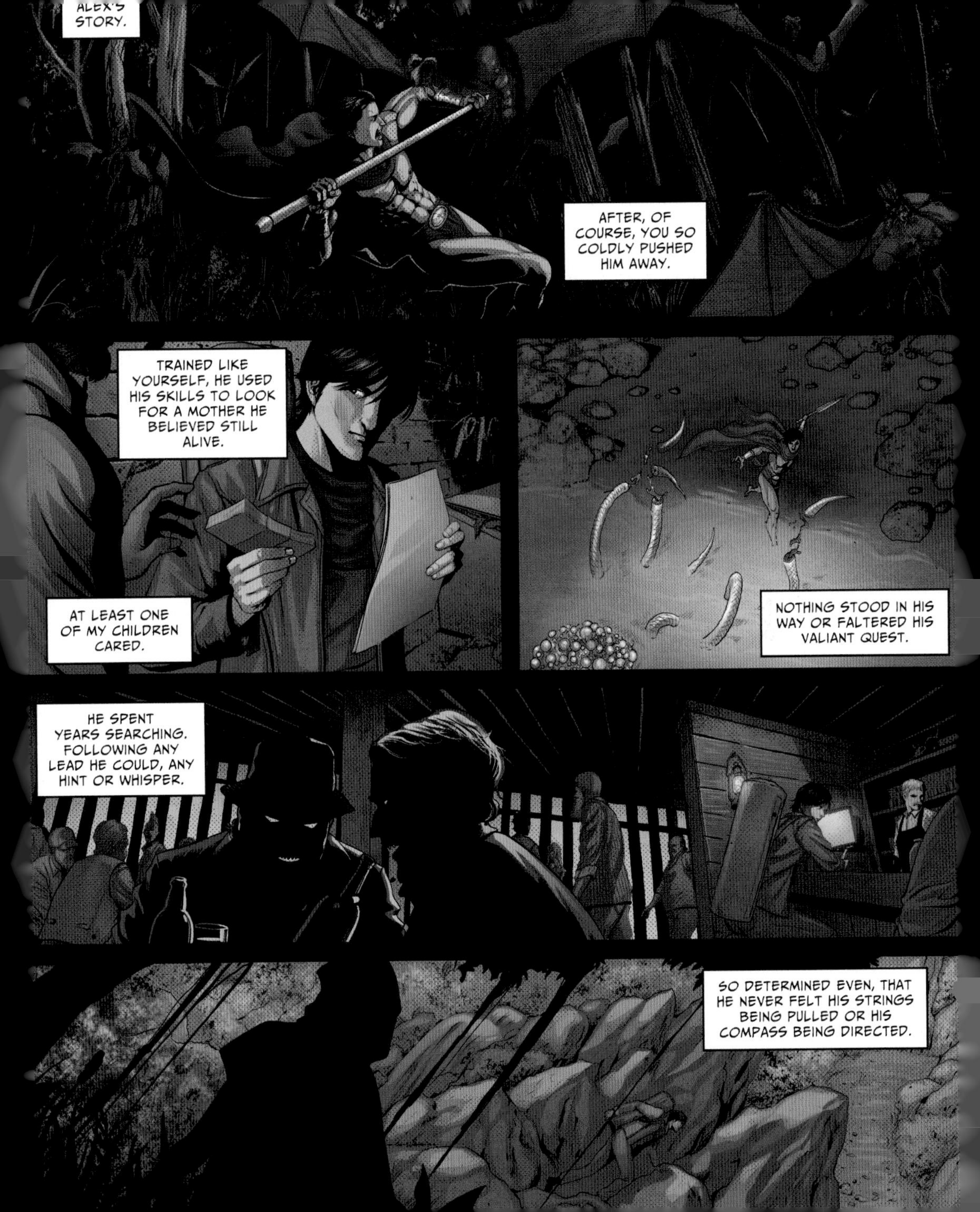

ALEX'S STORY.
AFTER, OF COURSE, YOU SO COLDLY PUSHED HIM AWAY.
TRAINED LIKE YOURSELF, HE USED HIS SKILLS TO LOOK FOR A MOTHER HE BELIEVED STILL ALIVE.
AT LEAST ONE OF MY CHILDREN CARED.
NOTHING STOOD IN HIS WAY OR FALTERED HIS VALIANT QUEST.
HE SPENT YEARS SEARCHING. FOLLOWING ANY LEAD HE COULD, ANY HINT OR WHISPER.
SO DETERMINED EVEN, THAT HE NEVER FELT HIS STRINGS BEING PULLED OR HIS COMPASS BEING DIRECTED.

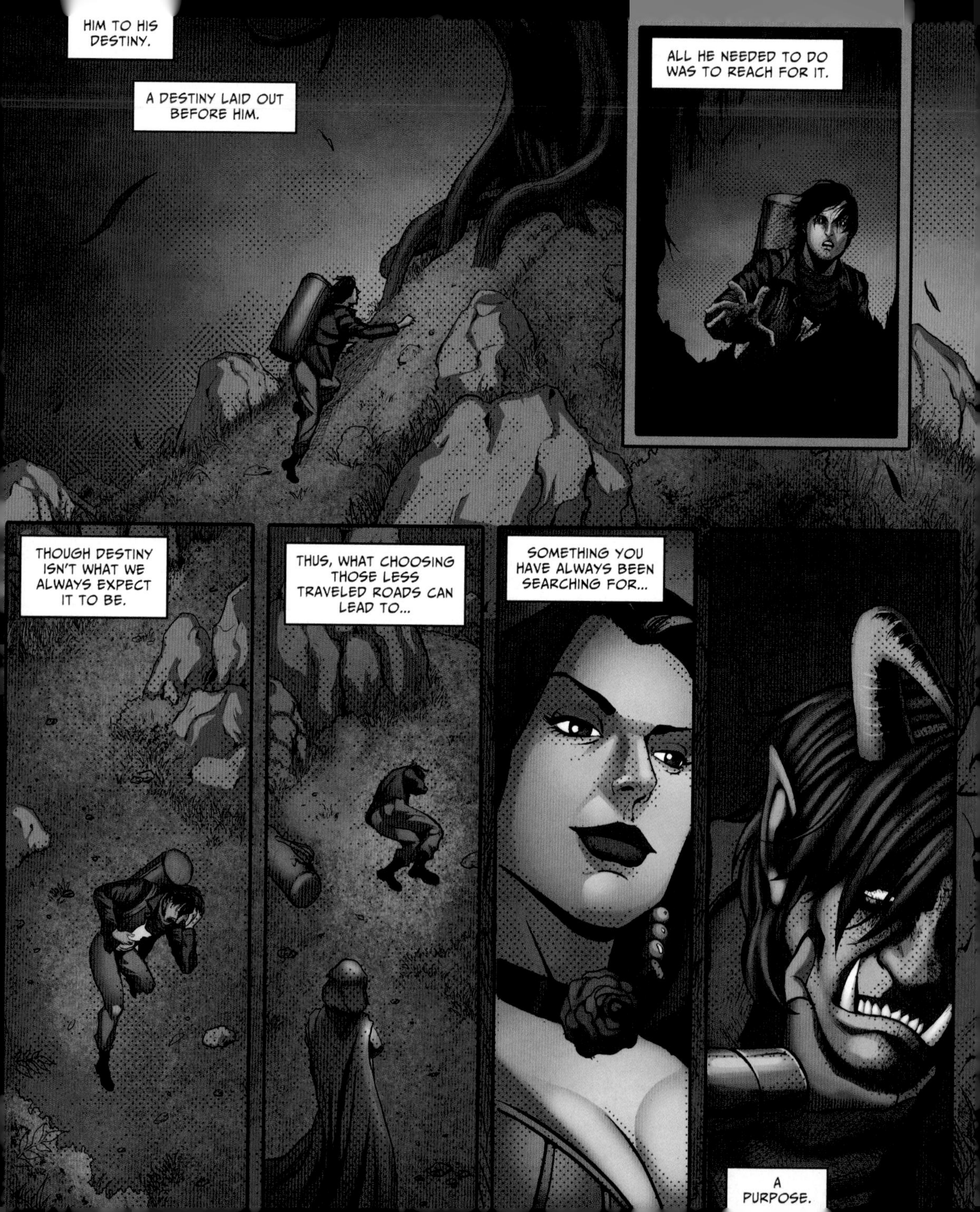
HIM TO HIS DESTINY.
A DESTINY LAID OUT BEFORE HIM.
ALL HE NEEDED TO DO WAS TO REACH FOR IT.
THOUGH DESTINY ISN'T WHAT WE ALWAYS EXPECT IT TO BE.
THUS, WHAT CHOOSING THOSE LESS TRAVELED ROADS CAN LEAD TO...
SOMETHING YOU HAVE ALWAYS BEEN SEARCHING FOR...
A PURPOSE.

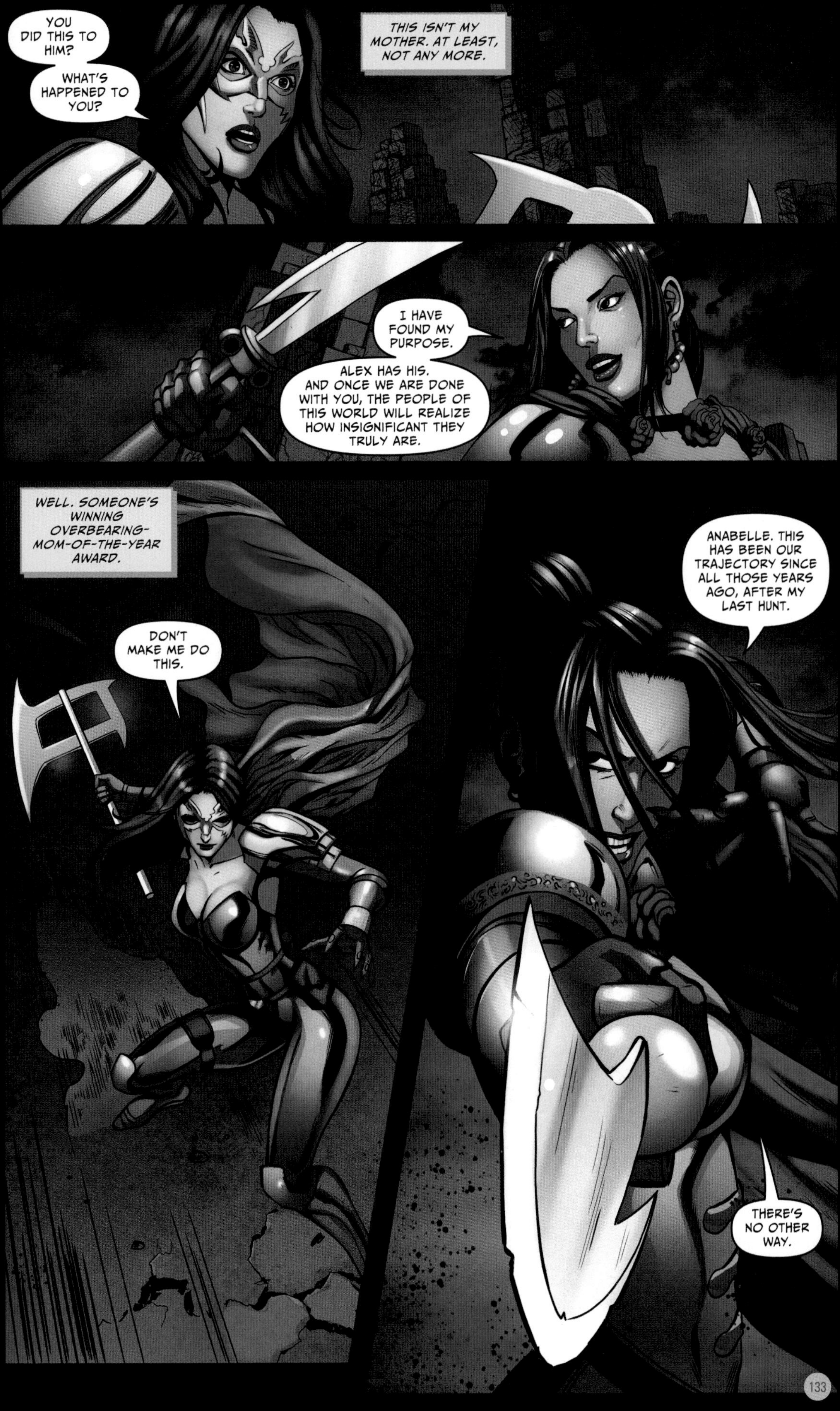

YOU DID THIS TO HIM?
WHAT'S HAPPENED TO YOU?
THIS ISN'T MY MOTHER. AT LEAST, NOT ANY MORE.
I HAVE FOUND MY PURPOSE.
ALEX HAS HIS. AND ONCE WE ARE DONE WITH YOU, THE PEOPLE OF THIS WORLD WILL REALIZE HOW INSIGNIFICANT THEY TRULY ARE.
WELL. SOMEONE'S WINNING OVERBEARING-MOM-OF-THE-YEAR AWARD.
DON'T MAKE ME DO THIS.
ANABELLE. THIS HAS BEEN OUR TRAJECTORY SINCE ALL THOSE YEARS AGO, AFTER MY LAST HUNT.
THERE'S NO OTHER WAY.

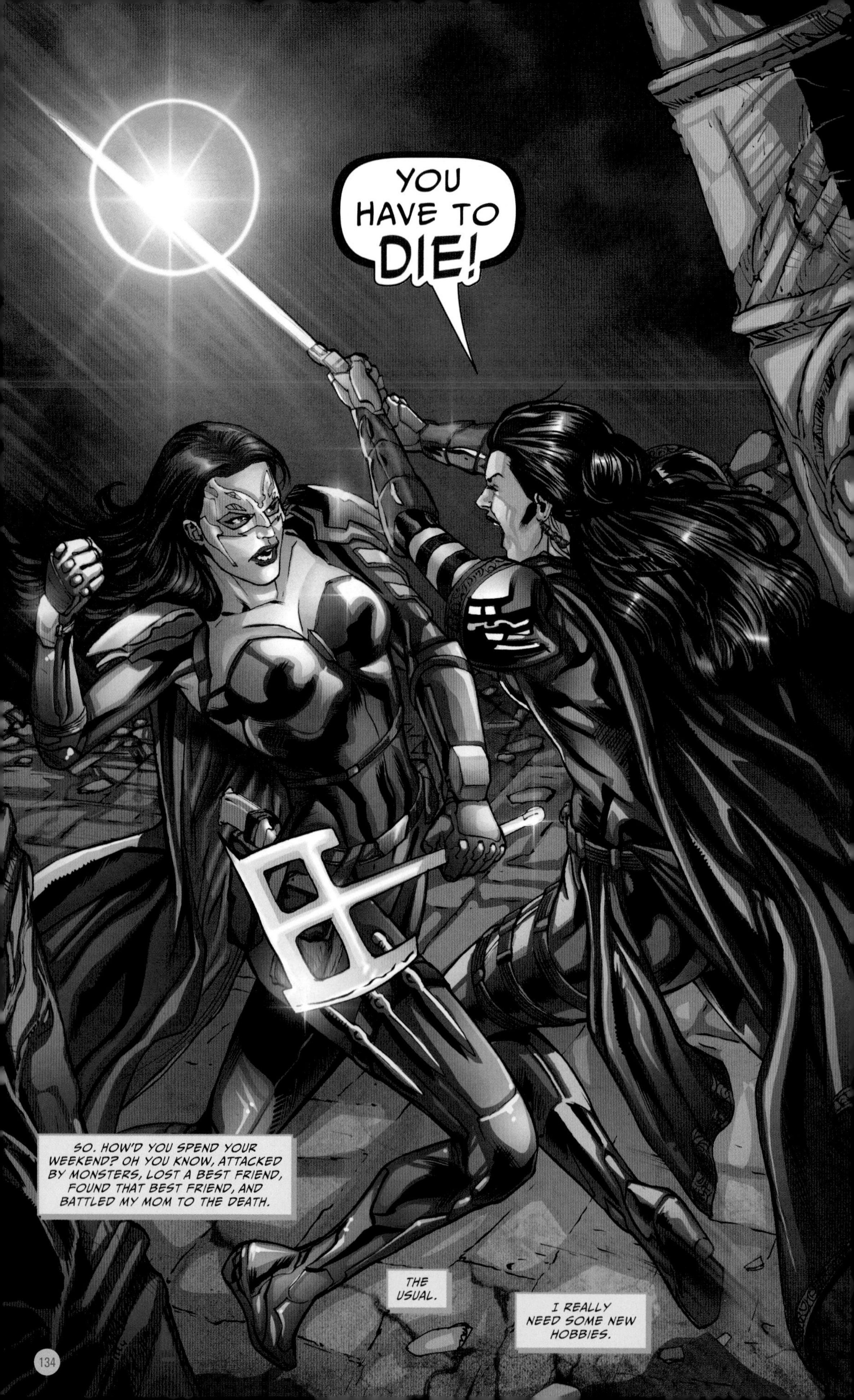
YOU HAVE TO DIE!
SO. HOW'D YOU SPEND YOUR WEEKEND? OH YOU KNOW, ATTACKED BY MONSTERS, LOST A BEST FRIEND, FOUND THAT BEST FRIEND, AND BATTLED MY MOM TO THE DEATH.
THE USUAL.
I REALLY NEED SOME NEW HOBBIES.

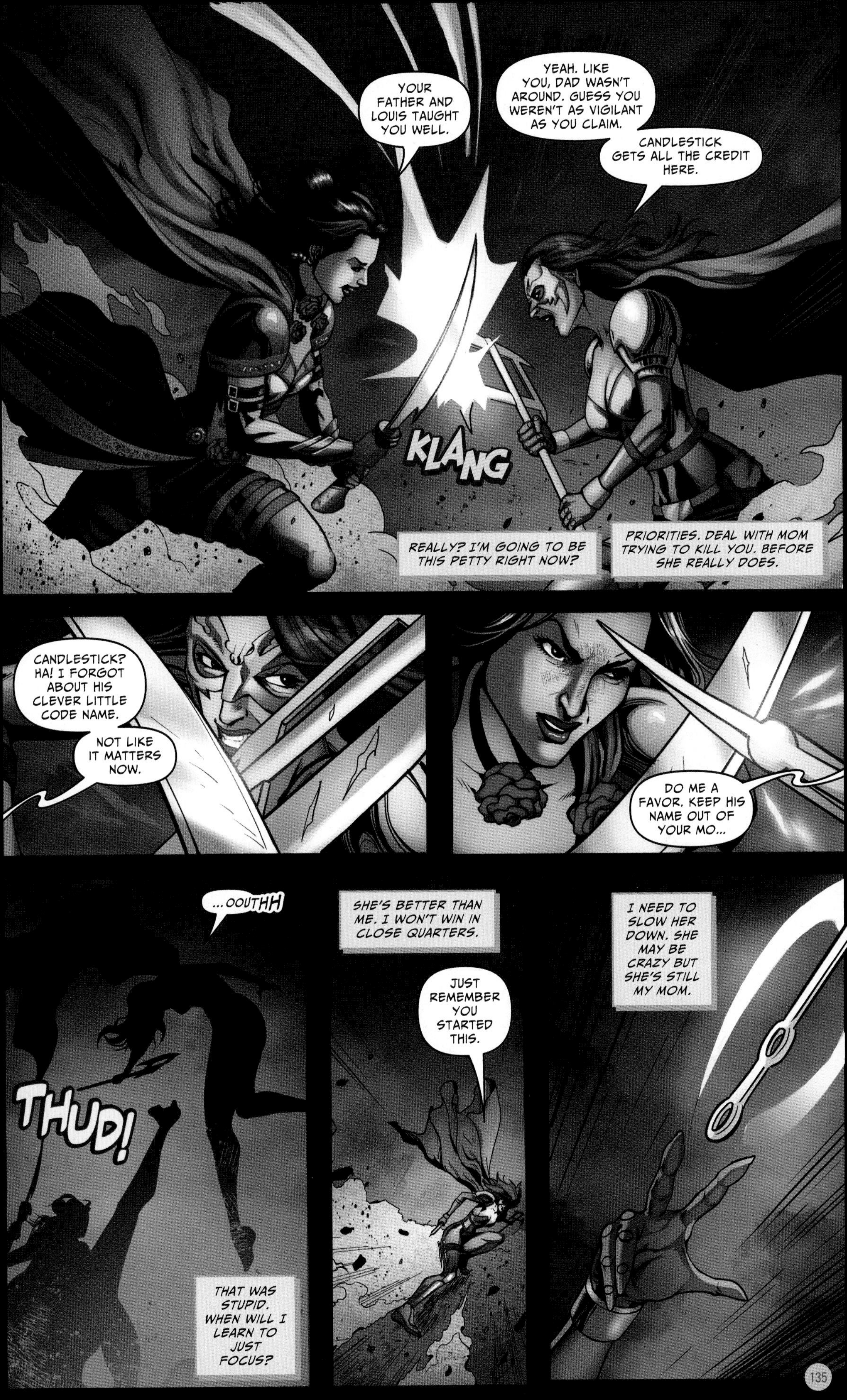

YOUR FATHER AND LOUIS TAUGHT YOU WELL.
YEAH. LIKE YOU, DAD WASN'T AROUND. GUESS YOU WEREN'T AS VIGILANT AS YOU CLAIM.
CANDLESTICK GETS ALL THE CREDIT HERE.
KLANG
REALLY? I'M GOING TO BE THIS PETTY RIGHT NOW?
PRIORITIES. DEAL WITH MOM TRYING TO KILL YOU. BEFORE SHE REALLY DOES.
CANDLESTICK? HA! I FORGOT ABOUT HIS CLEVER LITTLE CODE NAME.
NOT LIKE IT MATTERS NOW.
DO ME A FAVOR. KEEP HIS NAME OUT OF YOUR MO...
...OOUTHH
THUD!
THAT WAS STUPID. WHEN WILL I LEARN TO JUST FOCUS?
SHE'S BETTER THAN ME. I WON'T WIN IN CLOSE QUARTERS.
JUST REMEMBER YOU STARTED THIS.
I NEED TO SLOW HER DOWN. SHE MAY BE CRAZY BUT SHE'S STILL MY MOM.

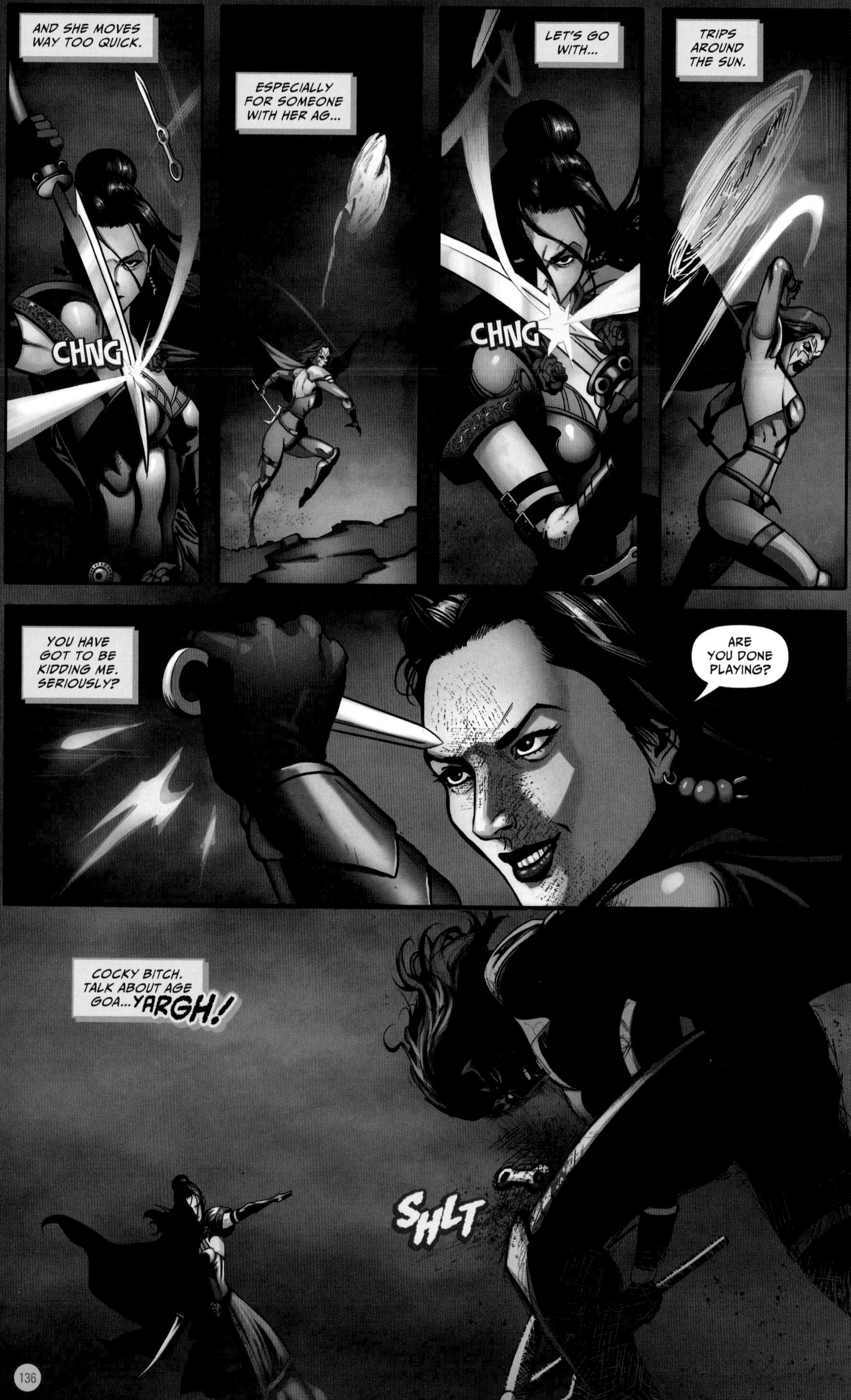
AND SHE MOVES WAY TOO QUICK.
CHNG
ESPECIALLY FOR SOMEONE WITH HER AG...
LET'S GO WITH...
CHNG
TRIPS AROUND THE SUN.
YOU HAVE GOT TO BE KIDDING ME. SERIOUSLY?
ARE YOU DONE PLAYING?
COCKY BITCH. TALK ABOUT AGE GOA...YARGH!
SHLT

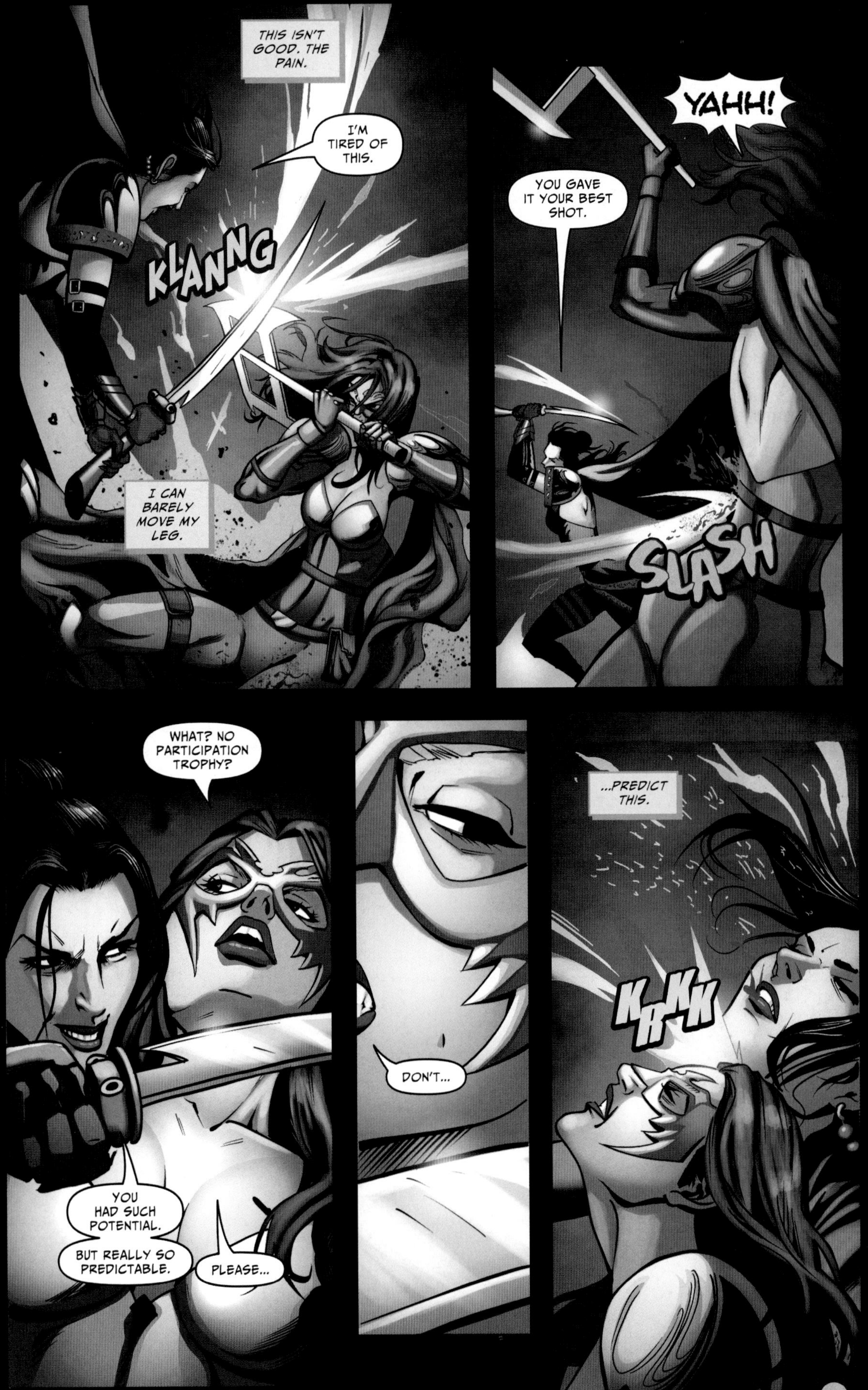
THIS ISN'T GOOD. THE PAIN.
I'M TIRED OF THIS.
KLANNG
I CAN BARELY MOVE MY LEG.
YAHH!
YOU GAVE IT YOUR BEST SHOT.
SLASH
WHAT? NO PARTICIPATION TROPHY?
YOU HAD SUCH POTENTIAL.
BUT REALLY SO PREDICTABLE.
PLEASE...
DON'T...
...PREDICT THIS.
KKRKK

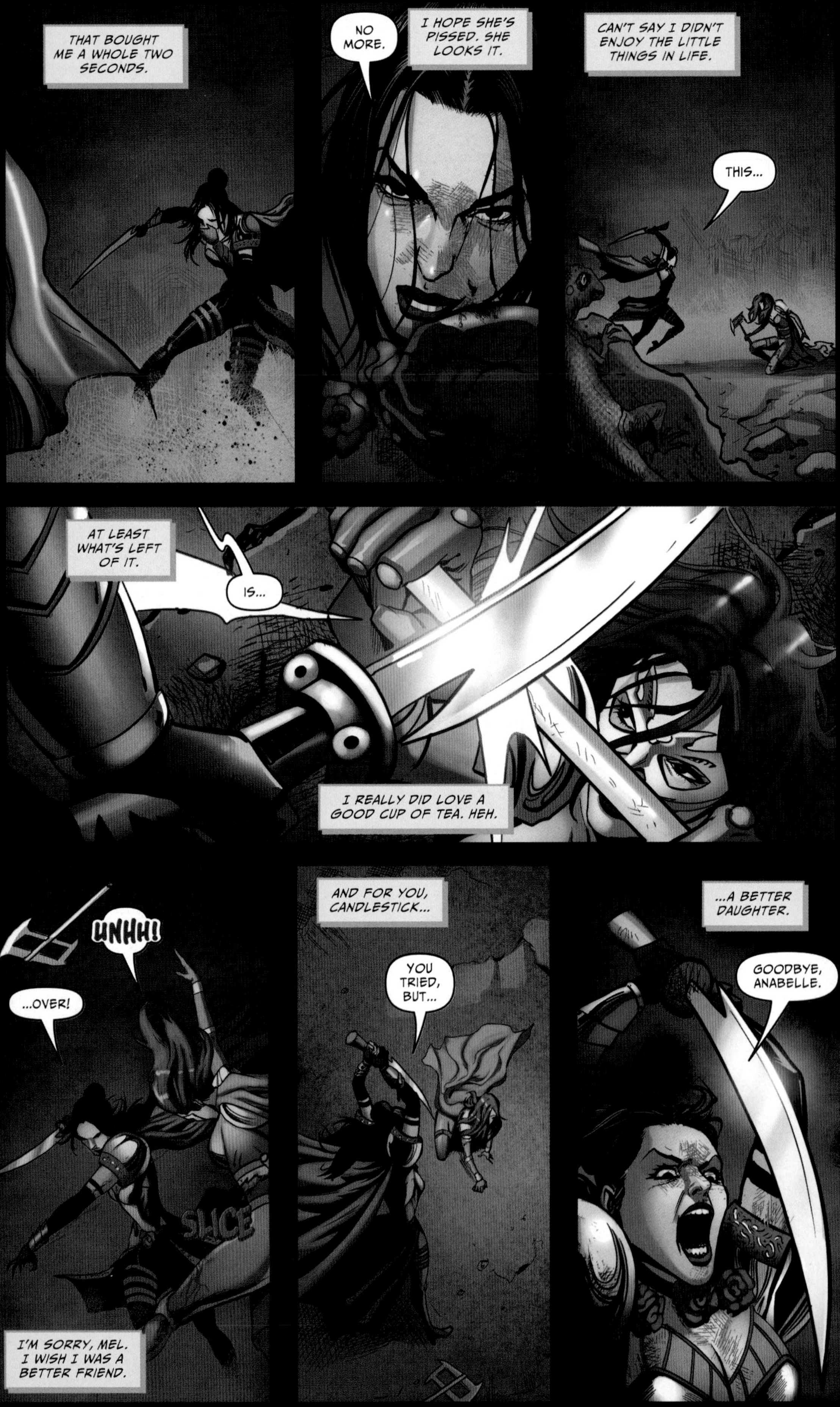
THAT BOUGHT ME A WHOLE TWO SECONDS.
NO MORE.
I HOPE SHE'S PISSED. SHE LOOKS IT.
CAN'T SAY I DIDN'T ENJOY THE LITTLE THINGS IN LIFE.
THIS...
AT LEAST WHAT'S LEFT OF IT.
IS...
I REALLY DID LOVE A GOOD CUP OF TEA. HEH.
UNHH!
...OVER!
SLICE
I'M SORRY, MEL. I WISH I WAS A BETTER FRIEND.
AND FOR YOU, CANDLESTICK...
YOU TRIED, BUT...
...A BETTER DAUGHTER.
GOODBYE, ANABELLE.

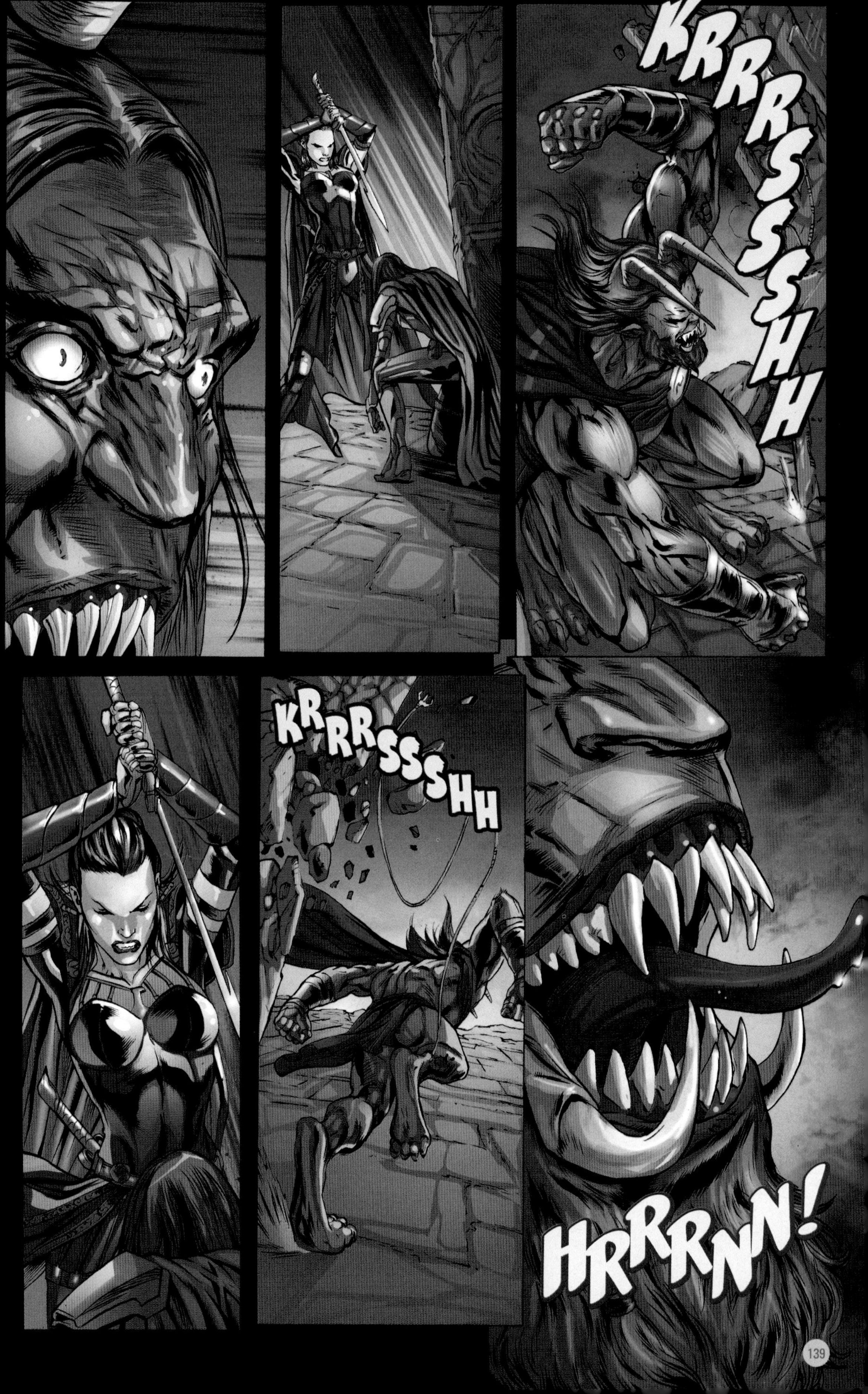
KRRRSSSHH
KRRRSSSHH
HRRRNN!

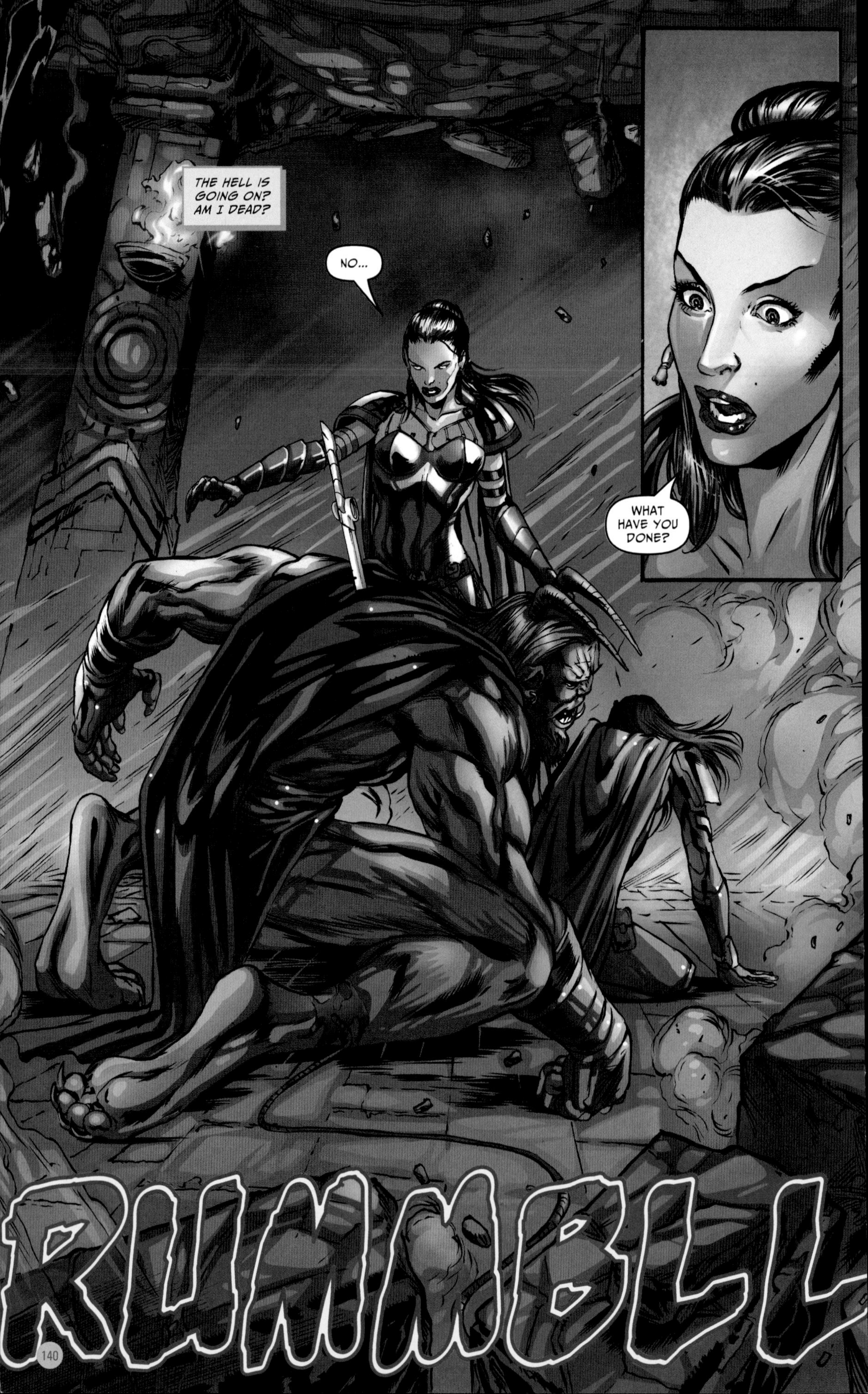
THE HELL IS GOING ON? AM I DEAD?
NO...
WHAT HAVE YOU DONE?
RUMMBLL

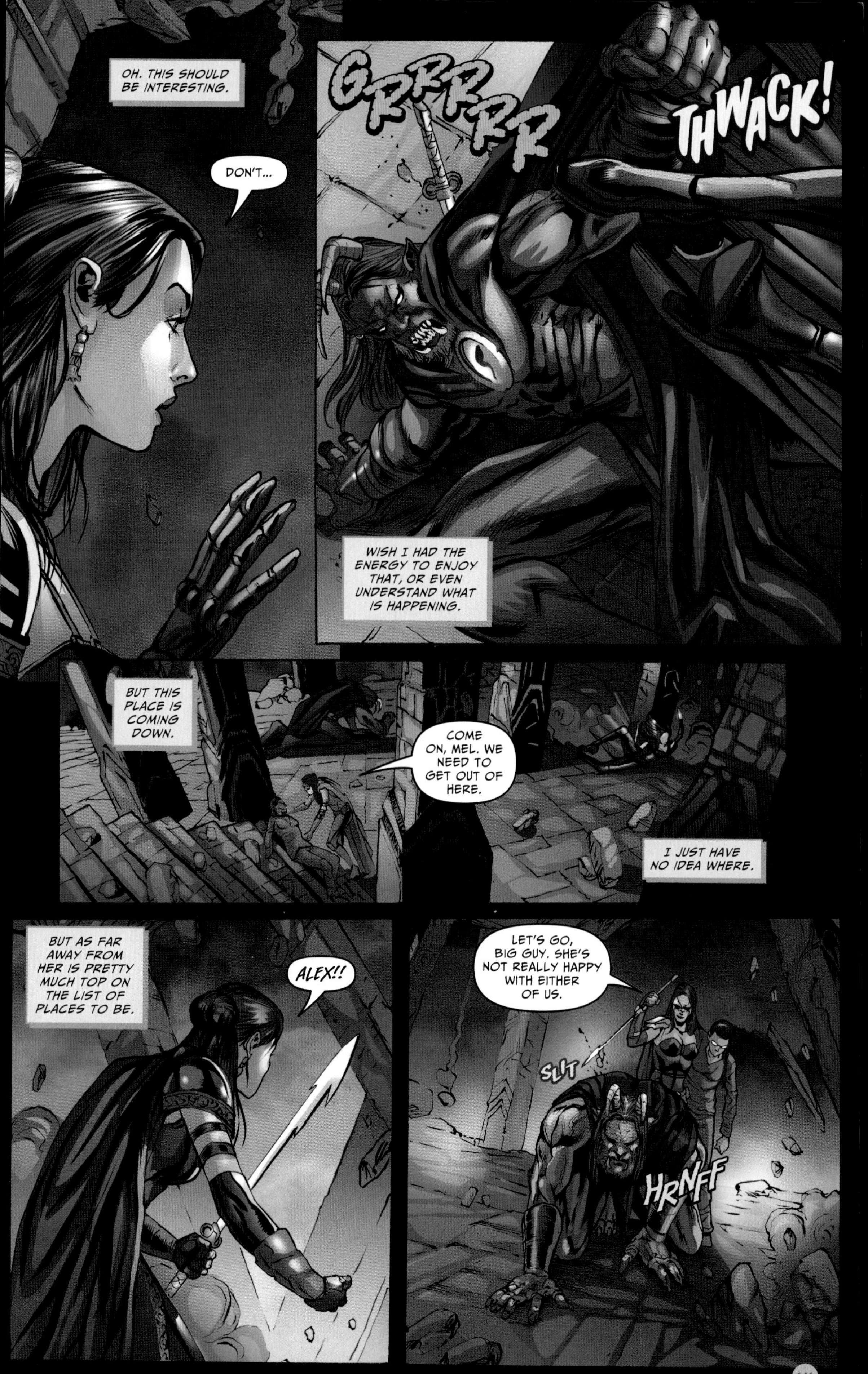
OH. THIS SHOULD BE INTERESTING.
DON'T...
GRRRRR
THWACK!
WISH I HAD THE ENERGY TO ENJOY THAT, OR EVEN UNDERSTAND WHAT IS HAPPENING.
BUT THIS PLACE IS COMING DOWN.
COME ON, MEL. WE NEED TO GET OUT OF HERE.
I JUST HAVE NO IDEA WHERE.
BUT AS FAR AWAY FROM HER IS PRETTY MUCH TOP ON THE LIST OF PLACES TO BE.
ALEX!!
LET'S GO, BIG GUY. SHE'S NOT REALLY HAPPY WITH EITHER OF US.
SLIT
HRNFF

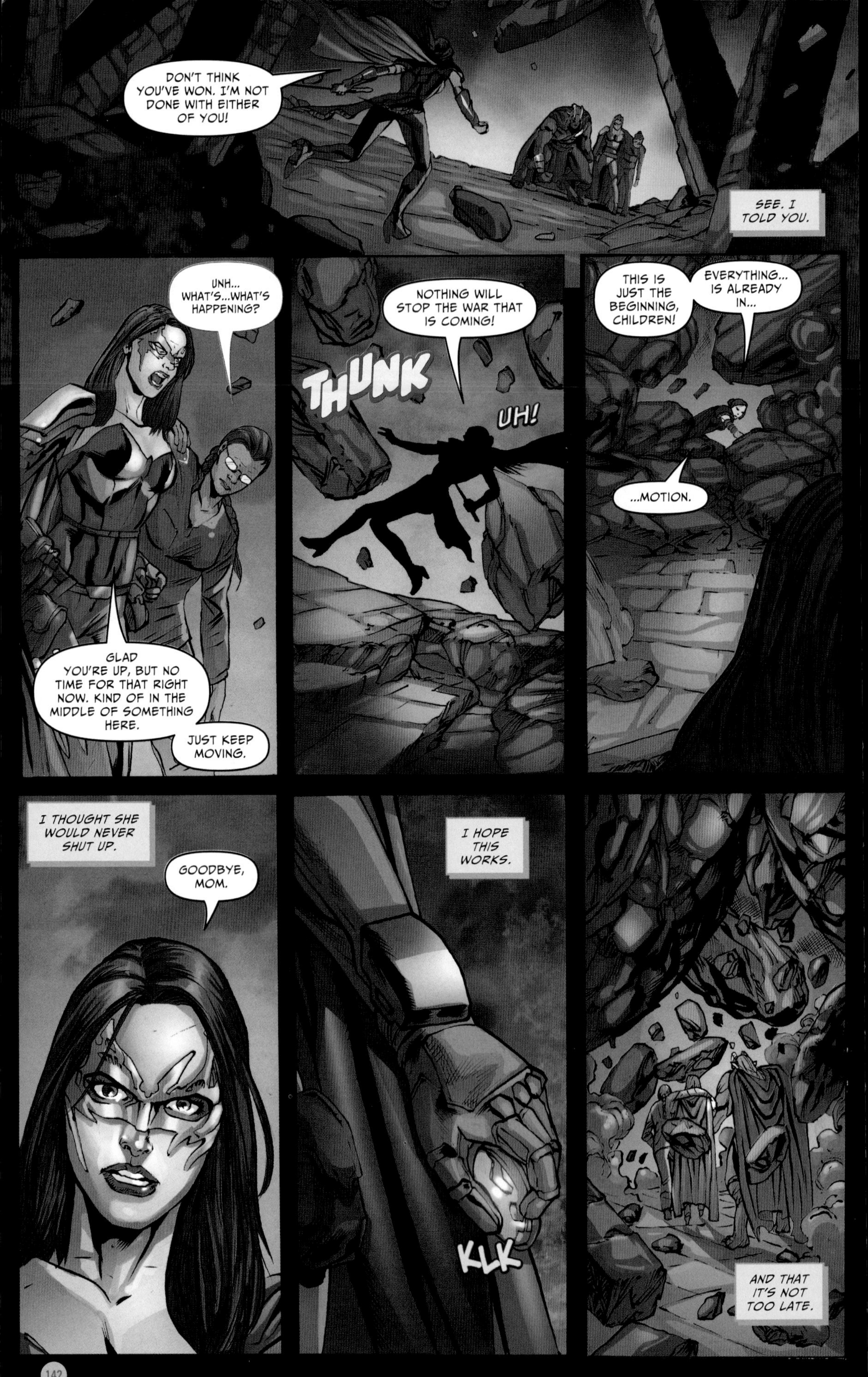
DON'T THINK YOU'VE WON. I'M NOT DONE WITH EITHER OF YOU!
SEE. I TOLD YOU.
UNH... WHAT'S...WHAT'S HAPPENING?
GLAD YOU'RE UP, BUT NO TIME FOR THAT RIGHT NOW. KIND OF IN THE MIDDLE OF SOMETHING HERE.
JUST KEEP MOVING.
NOTHING WILL STOP THE WAR THAT IS COMING!
THUNK
UH!
THIS IS JUST THE BEGINNING, CHILDREN!
EVERYTHING... IS ALREADY IN...
...MOTION.
I THOUGHT SHE WOULD NEVER SHUT UP.
GOODBYE, MOM.
I HOPE THIS WORKS.
KLK
AND THAT IT'S NOT TOO LATE.

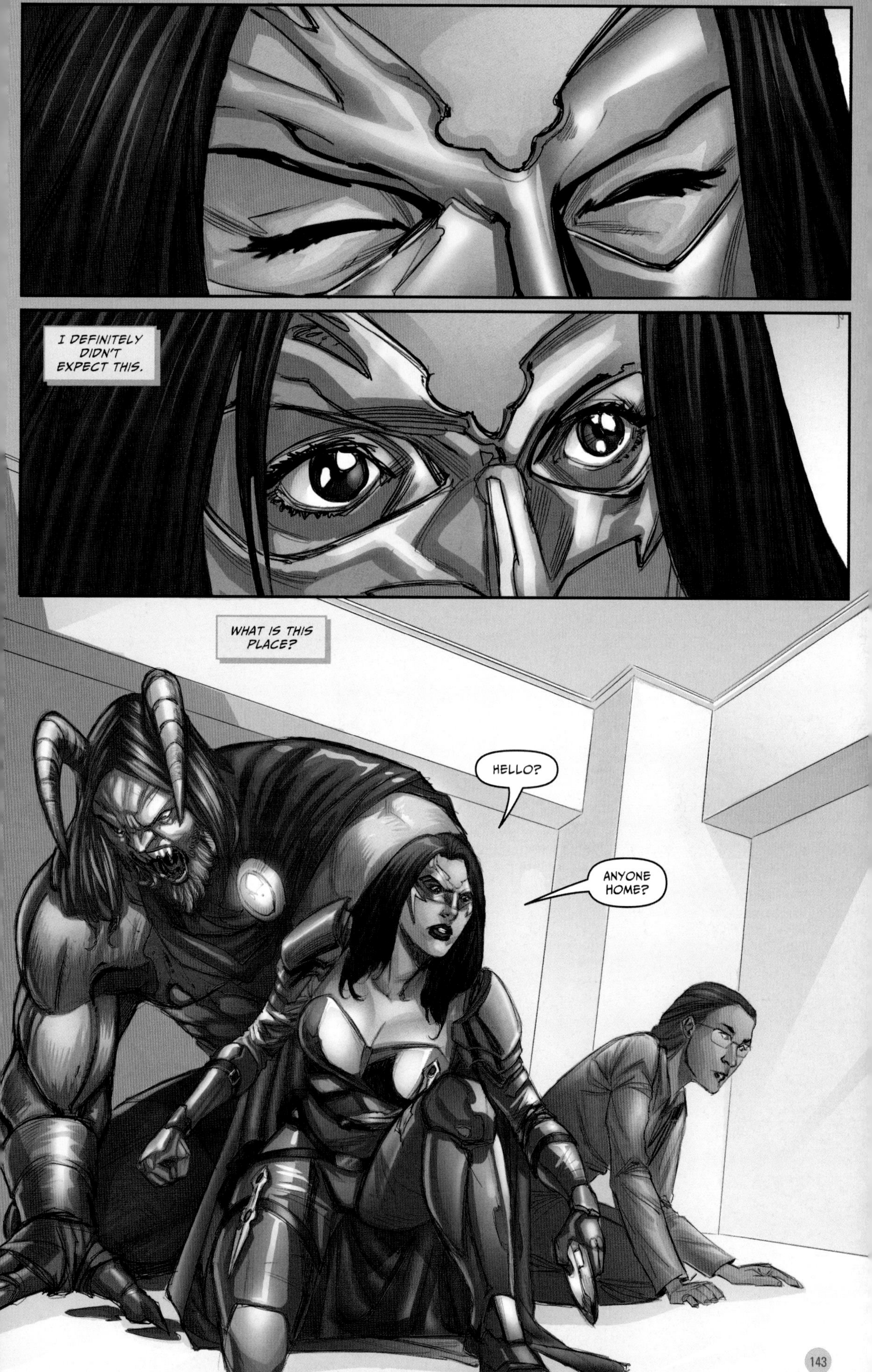
I DEFINITELY DIDN'T EXPECT THIS.
WHAT IS THIS PLACE?
HELLO?
ANYONE HOME?

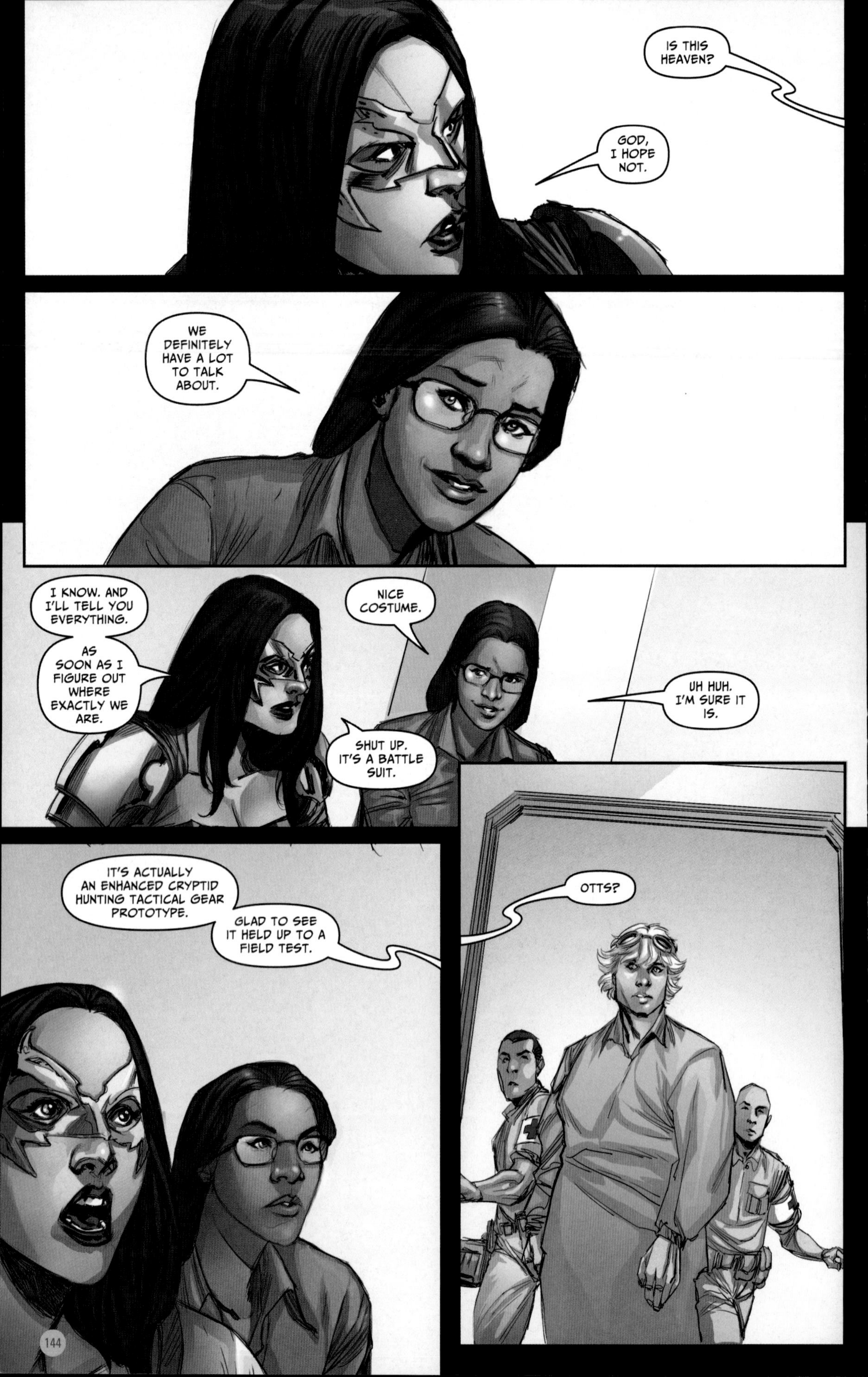
IS THIS HEAVEN?
GOD, I HOPE NOT.
WE DEFINITELY HAVE A LOT TO TALK ABOUT.
I KNOW. AND I'LL TELL YOU EVERYTHING.
AS SOON AS I FIGURE OUT WHERE EXACTLY WE ARE.
NICE COSTUME.
SHUT UP. IT'S A BATTLE SUIT.
UH HUH. I'M SURE IT IS.
IT'S ACTUALLY AN ENHANCED CRYPTID HUNTING TACTICAL GEAR PROTOTYPE.
GLAD TO SEE IT HELD UP TO A FIELD TEST.
OTTS?

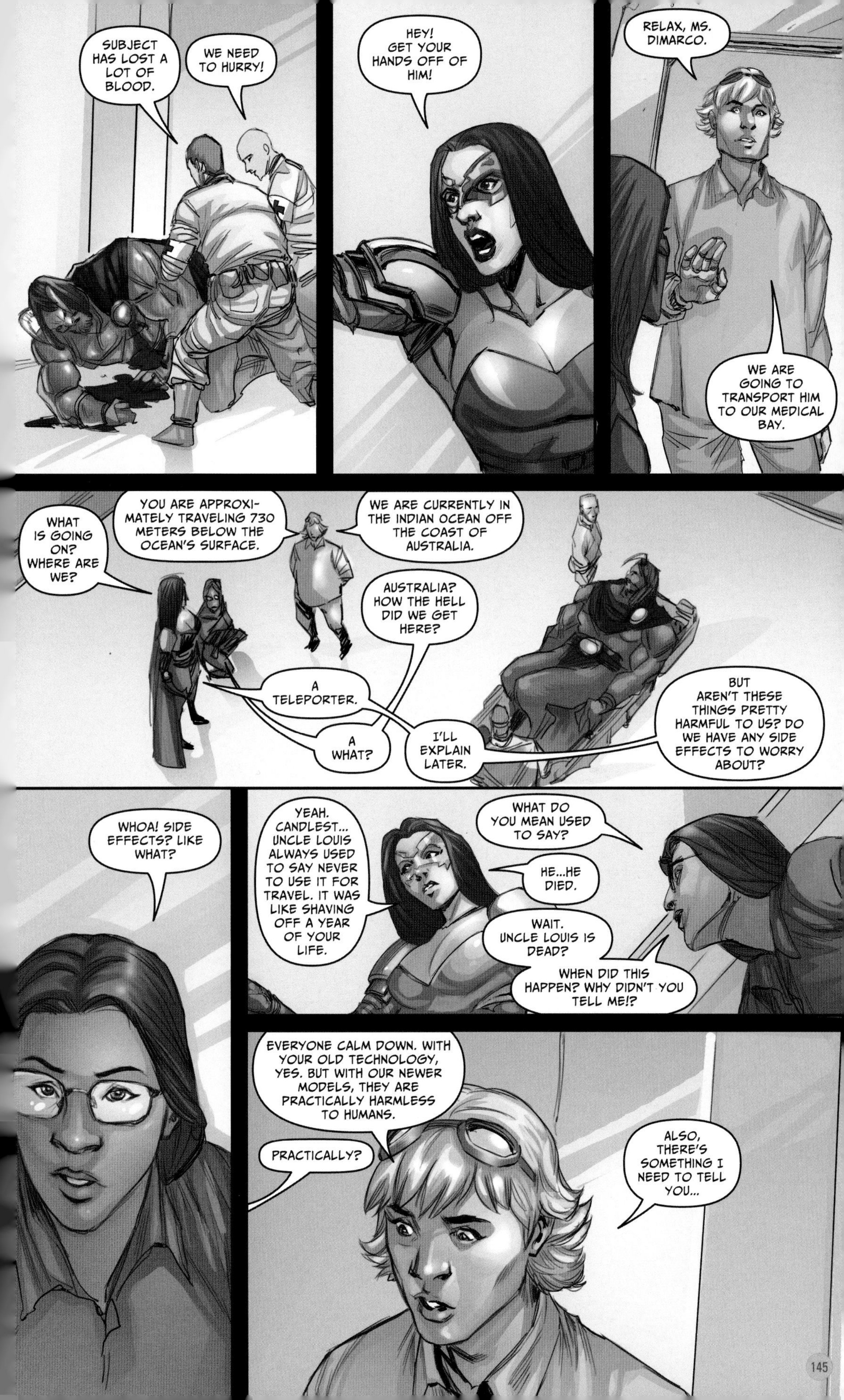
SUBJECT HAS LOST A LOT OF BLOOD.
WE NEED TO HURRY!
HEY! GET YOUR HANDS OFF OF HIM!
RELAX, MS. DIMARCO.
WE ARE GOING TO TRANSPORT HIM TO OUR MEDICAL BAY.
WHAT IS GOING ON? WHERE ARE WE?
YOU ARE APPROXIMATELY TRAVELING 730 METERS BELOW THE OCEAN'S SURFACE.
WE ARE CURRENTLY IN THE INDIAN OCEAN OFF THE COAST OF AUSTRALIA.
AUSTRALIA? HOW THE HELL DID WE GET HERE?
A TELEPORTER.
A WHAT?
I'LL EXPLAIN LATER.
BUT AREN'T THESE THINGS PRETTY HARMFUL TO US? DO WE HAVE ANY SIDE EFFECTS TO WORRY ABOUT?
WHOA! SIDE EFFECTS? LIKE WHAT?
YEAH. CANDLEST... UNCLE LOUIS ALWAYS USED TO SAY NEVER TO USE IT FOR TRAVEL. IT WAS LIKE SHAVING OFF A YEAR OF YOUR LIFE.
WHAT DO YOU MEAN USED TO SAY?
HE...HE DIED.
WAIT. UNCLE LOUIS IS DEAD?
WHEN DID THIS HAPPEN? WHY DIDN'T YOU TELL ME!?
EVERYONE CALM DOWN. WITH YOUR OLD TECHNOLOGY, YES. BUT WITH OUR NEWER MODELS, THEY ARE PRACTICALLY HARMLESS TO HUMANS.
PRACTICALLY?
ALSO, THERE'S SOMETHING I NEED TO TELL YOU...

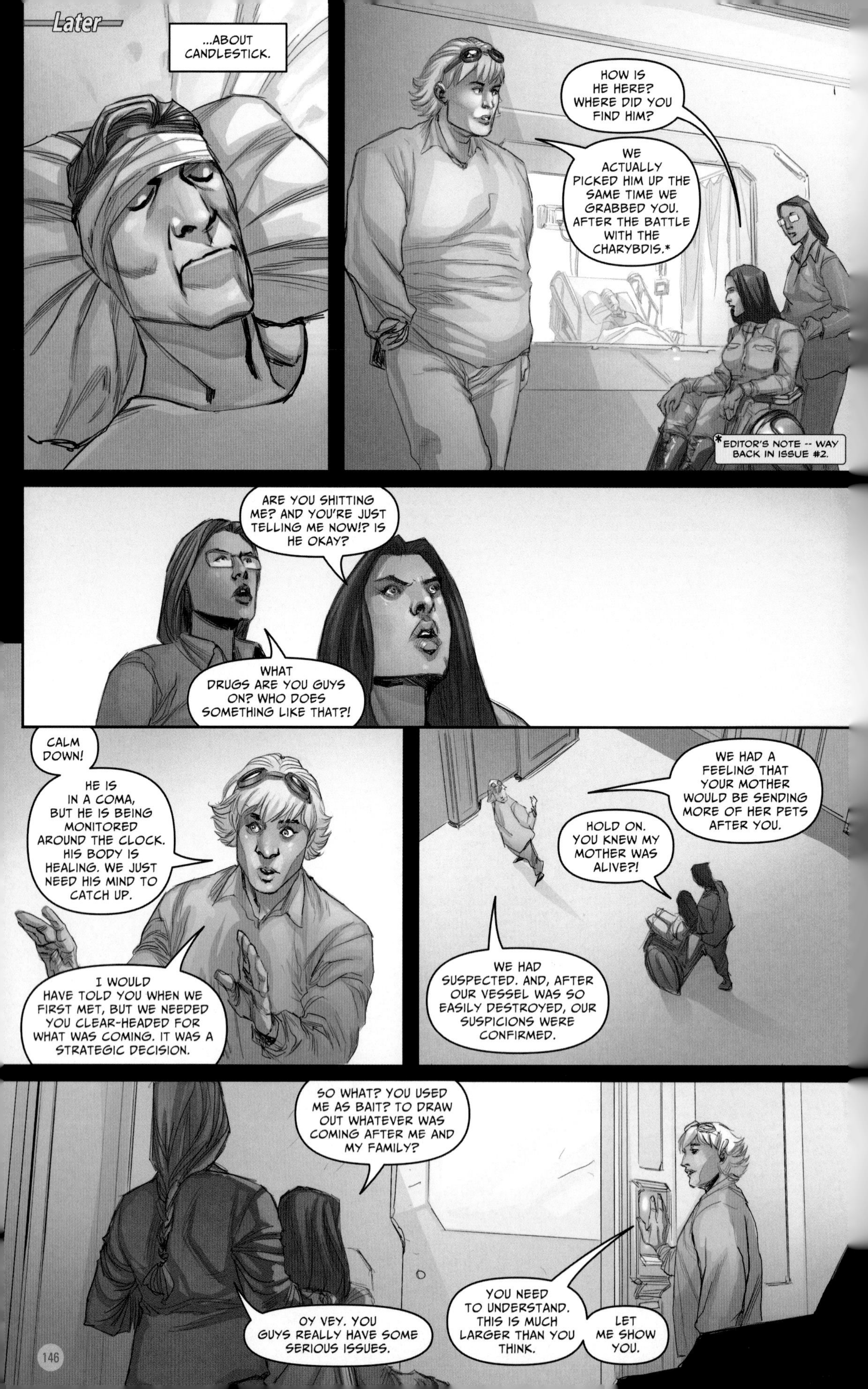
Later
...ABOUT CANDLESTICK.
HOW IS HE HERE? WHERE DID YOU FIND HIM?
WE ACTUALLY PICKED HIM UP THE SAME TIME WE GRABBED YOU. AFTER THE BATTLE WITH THE CHARYBDIS.*
*EDITOR'S NOTE -- WAY BACK IN ISSUE #2.
ARE YOU SHITTING ME? AND YOU'RE JUST TELLING ME NOW!? IS HE OKAY?
WHAT DRUGS ARE YOU GUYS ON? WHO DOES SOMETHING LIKE THAT?!
CALM DOWN!
HE IS IN A COMA, BUT HE IS BEING MONITORED AROUND THE CLOCK. HIS BODY IS HEALING. WE JUST NEED HIS MIND TO CATCH UP.
I WOULD HAVE TOLD YOU WHEN WE FIRST MET, BUT WE NEEDED YOU CLEAR-HEADED FOR WHAT WAS COMING. IT WAS A STRATEGIC DECISION.
WE HAD A FEELING THAT YOUR MOTHER WOULD BE SENDING MORE OF HER PETS AFTER YOU.
HOLD ON. YOU KNEW MY MOTHER WAS ALIVE?!
WE HAD SUSPECTED. AND, AFTER OUR VESSEL WAS SO EASILY DESTROYED, OUR SUSPICIONS WERE CONFIRMED.
SO WHAT? YOU USED ME AS BAIT? TO DRAW OUT WHATEVER WAS COMING AFTER ME AND MY FAMILY?
OY VEY. YOU GUYS REALLY HAVE SOME SERIOUS ISSUES.
YOU NEED TO UNDERSTAND. THIS IS MUCH LARGER THAN YOU THINK.
LET ME SHOW YOU.

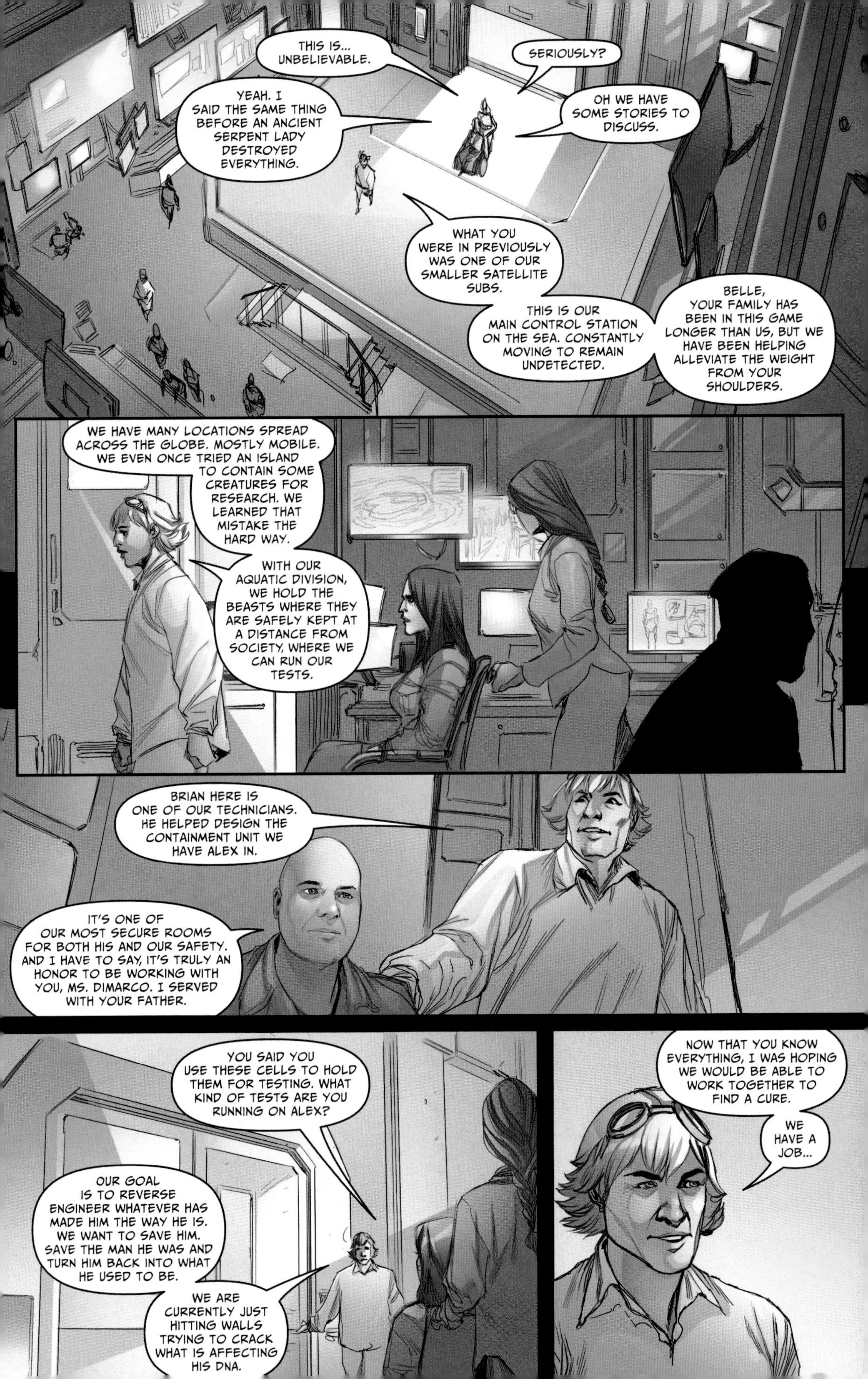

THIS IS... UNBELIEVABLE.
SERIOUSLY?
YEAH. I SAID THE SAME THING BEFORE AN ANCIENT SERPENT LADY DESTROYED EVERYTHING.
OH WE HAVE SOME STORIES TO DISCUSS.
WHAT YOU WERE IN PREVIOUSLY WAS ONE OF OUR SMALLER SATELLITE SUBS.
THIS IS OUR MAIN CONTROL STATION ON THE SEA. CONSTANTLY MOVING TO REMAIN UNDETECTED.
BELLE, YOUR FAMILY HAS BEEN IN THIS GAME LONGER THAN US, BUT WE HAVE BEEN HELPING ALLEVIATE THE WEIGHT FROM YOUR SHOULDERS.
WE HAVE MANY LOCATIONS SPREAD ACROSS THE GLOBE. MOSTLY MOBILE. WE EVEN ONCE TRIED AN ISLAND TO CONTAIN SOME CREATURES FOR RESEARCH. WE LEARNED THAT MISTAKE THE HARD WAY.
WITH OUR AQUATIC DIVISION, WE HOLD THE BEASTS WHERE THEY ARE SAFELY KEPT AT A DISTANCE FROM SOCIETY, WHERE WE CAN RUN OUR TESTS.
BRIAN HERE IS ONE OF OUR TECHNICIANS. HE HELPED DESIGN THE CONTAINMENT UNIT WE HAVE ALEX IN.
IT'S ONE OF OUR MOST SECURE ROOMS FOR BOTH HIS AND OUR SAFETY. AND I HAVE TO SAY, IT'S TRULY AN HONOR TO BE WORKING WITH YOU, MS. DIMARCO. I SERVED WITH YOUR FATHER.
YOU SAID YOU USE THESE CELLS TO HOLD THEM FOR TESTING. WHAT KIND OF TESTS ARE YOU RUNNING ON ALEX?
OUR GOAL IS TO REVERSE ENGINEER WHATEVER HAS MADE HIM THE WAY HE IS. WE WANT TO SAVE HIM. SAVE THE MAN HE WAS AND TURN HIM BACK INTO WHAT HE USED TO BE.
WE ARE CURRENTLY JUST HITTING WALLS TRYING TO CRACK WHAT IS AFFECTING HIS DNA.
NOW THAT YOU KNOW EVERYTHING, I WAS HOPING WE WOULD BE ABLE TO WORK TOGETHER TO FIND A CURE.
WE HAVE A JOB...

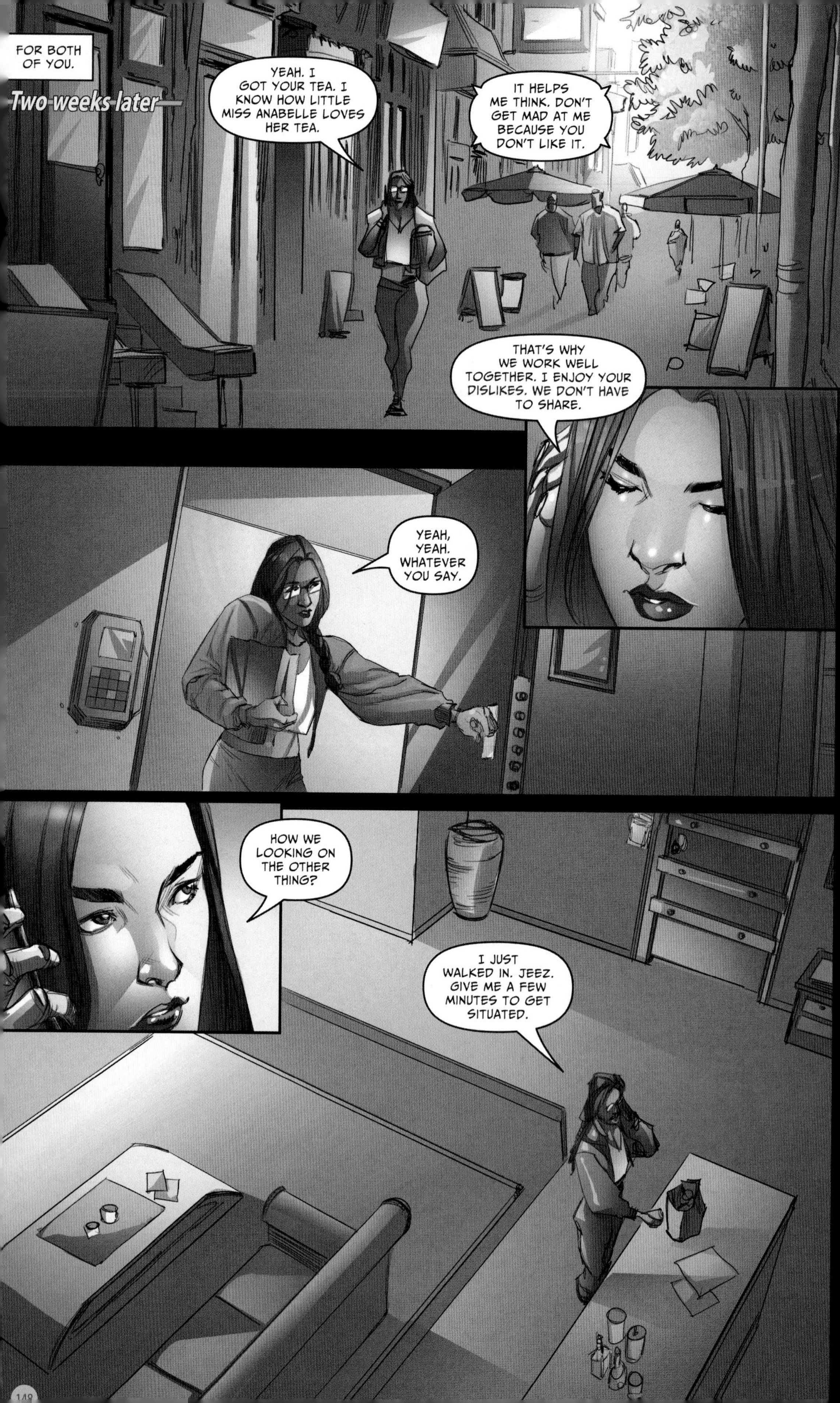
FOR BOTH OF YOU.
Two weeks later
YEAH. I GOT YOUR TEA. I KNOW HOW LITTLE MISS ANABELLE LOVES HER TEA.
IT HELPS ME THINK. DON'T GET MAD AT ME BECAUSE YOU DON'T LIKE IT.
THAT'S WHY WE WORK WELL TOGETHER. I ENJOY YOUR DISLIKES. WE DON'T HAVE TO SHARE.
YEAH, YEAH. WHATEVER YOU SAY.
HOW WE LOOKING ON THE OTHER THING?
I JUST WALKED IN. JEEZ. GIVE ME A FEW MINUTES TO GET SITUATED.

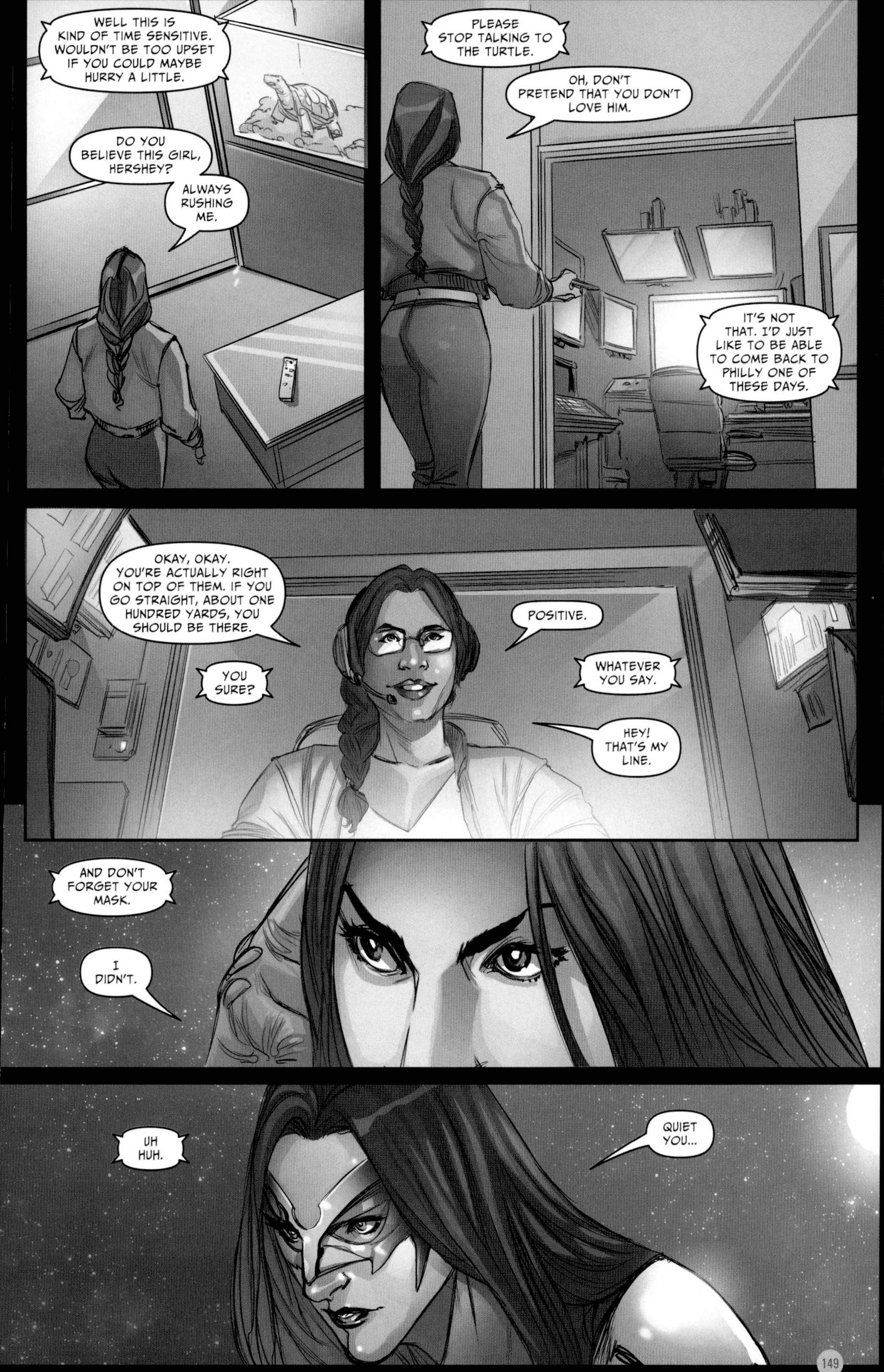
WELL THIS IS KIND OF TIME SENSITIVE. WOULDN'T BE TOO UPSET IF YOU COULD MAYBE HURRY A LITTLE.
DO YOU BELIEVE THIS GIRL, HERSHEY?
ALWAYS RUSHING ME.
PLEASE STOP TALKING TO THE TURTLE.
OH, DON'T PRETEND THAT YOU DON'T LOVE HIM.
IT'S NOT THAT. I'D JUST LIKE TO BE ABLE TO COME BACK TO PHILLY ONE OF THESE DAYS.
OKAY, OKAY. YOU'RE ACTUALLY RIGHT ON TOP OF THEM. IF YOU GO STRAIGHT, ABOUT ONE HUNDRED YARDS, YOU SHOULD BE THERE.
YOU SURE?
POSITIVE.
WHATEVER YOU SAY.
HEY! THAT'S MY LINE.
AND DON'T FORGET YOUR MASK.
I DIDN'T.
UH HUH.
QUIET YOU...

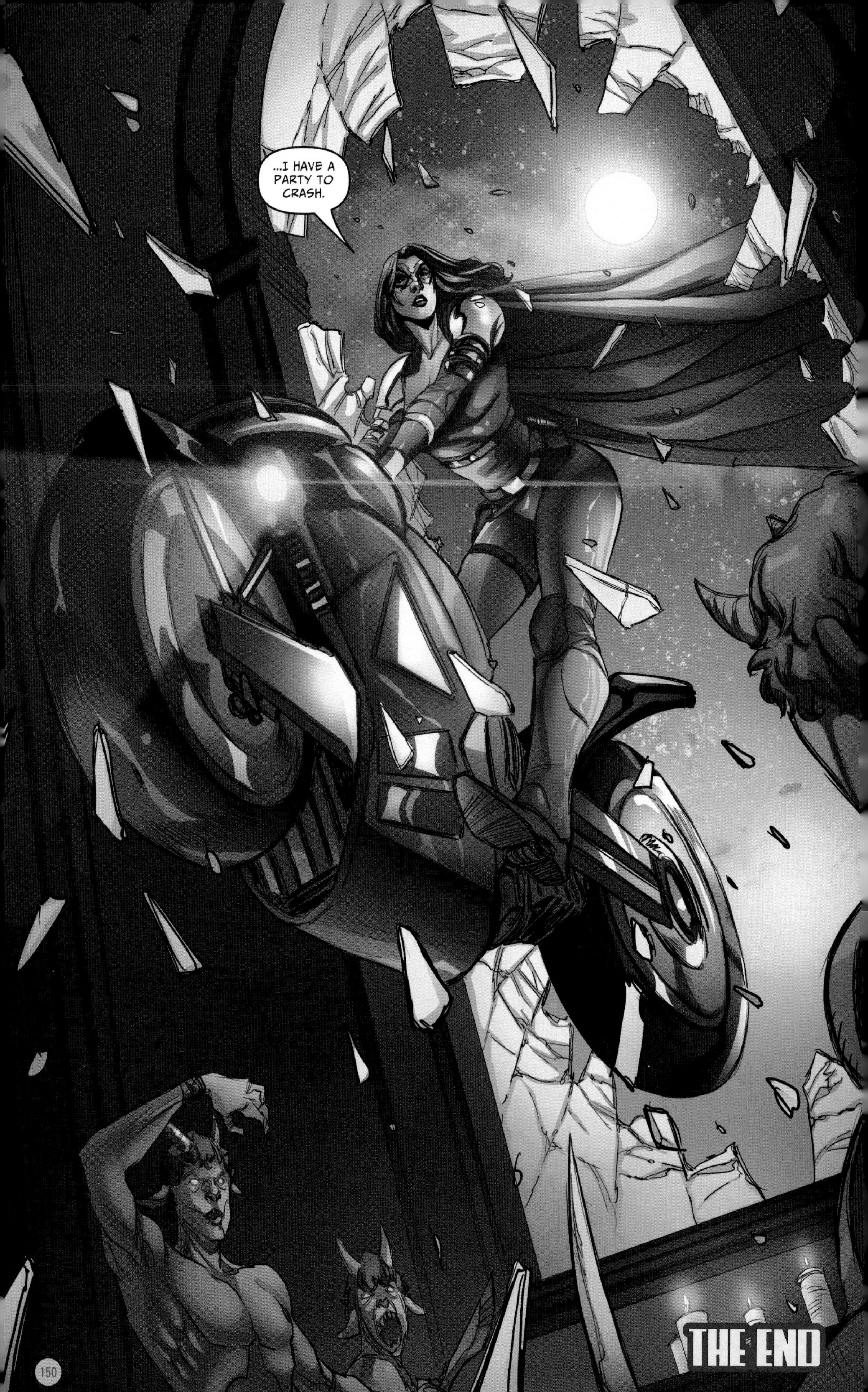
...I HAVE A PARTY TO CRASH.
THE END

BELLE
BEAST HUNTER

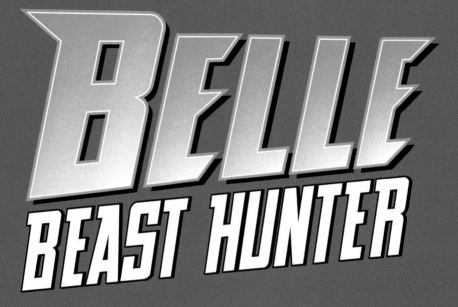

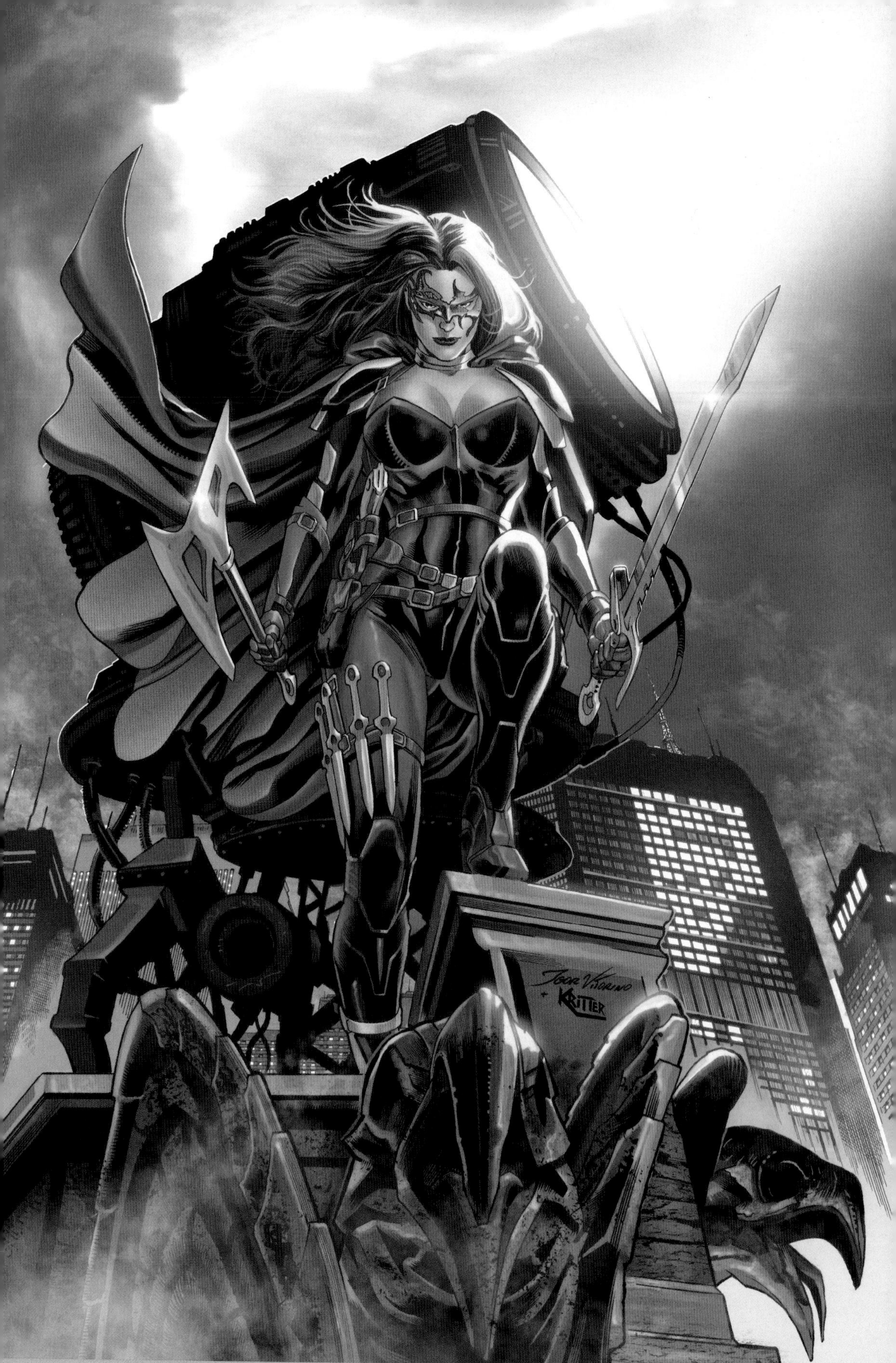
Igor Vitorino
+ Kritter

BELLE: BEAST HUNTER 1 • COVER A

Artwork by Igor Vitorino • Colors by Kyle Ritter

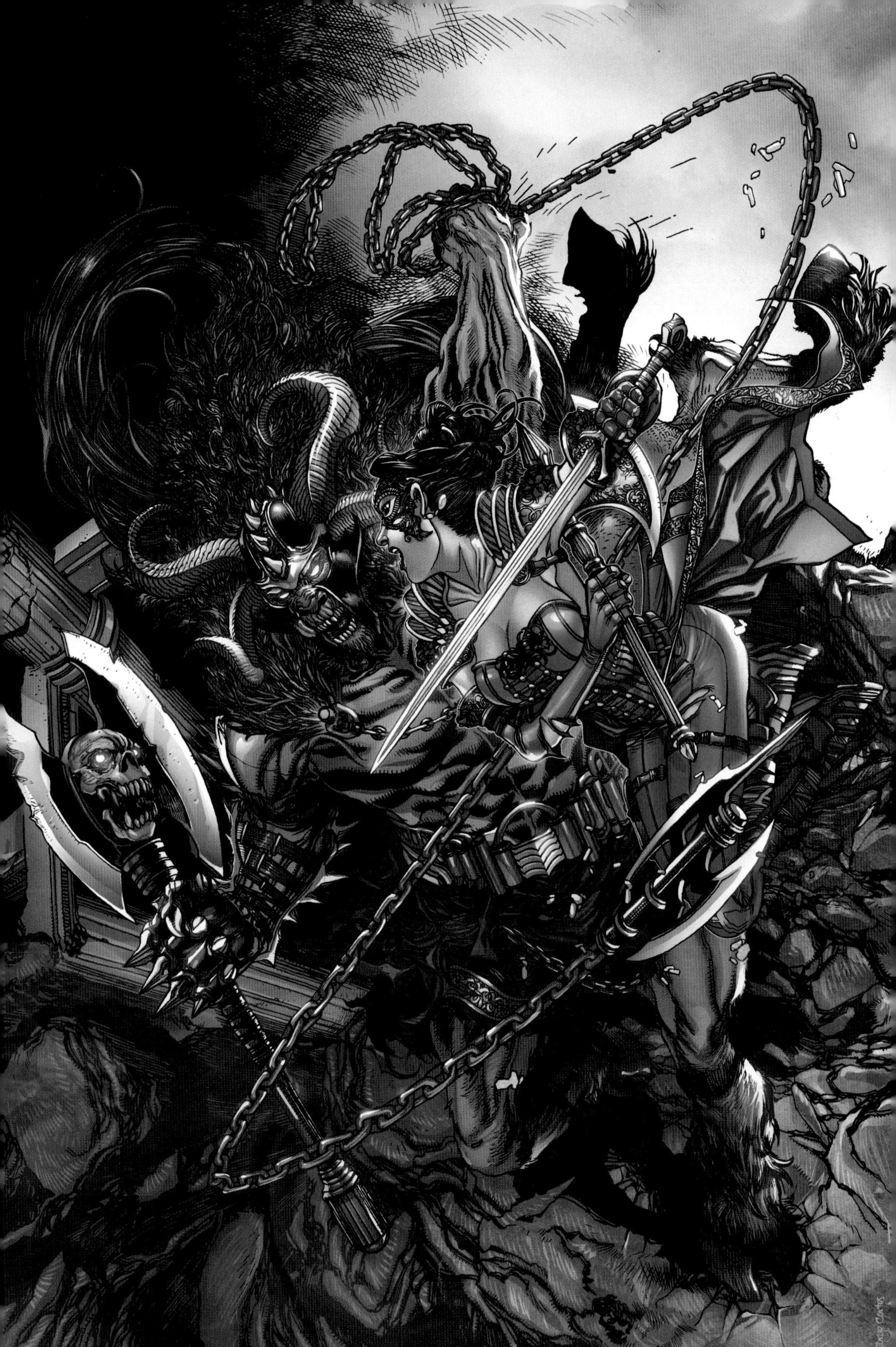

BELLE: BEAST HUNTER 1 • COVER B

Artwork by Harvey Tolibao • Colors by Jorge Cortes

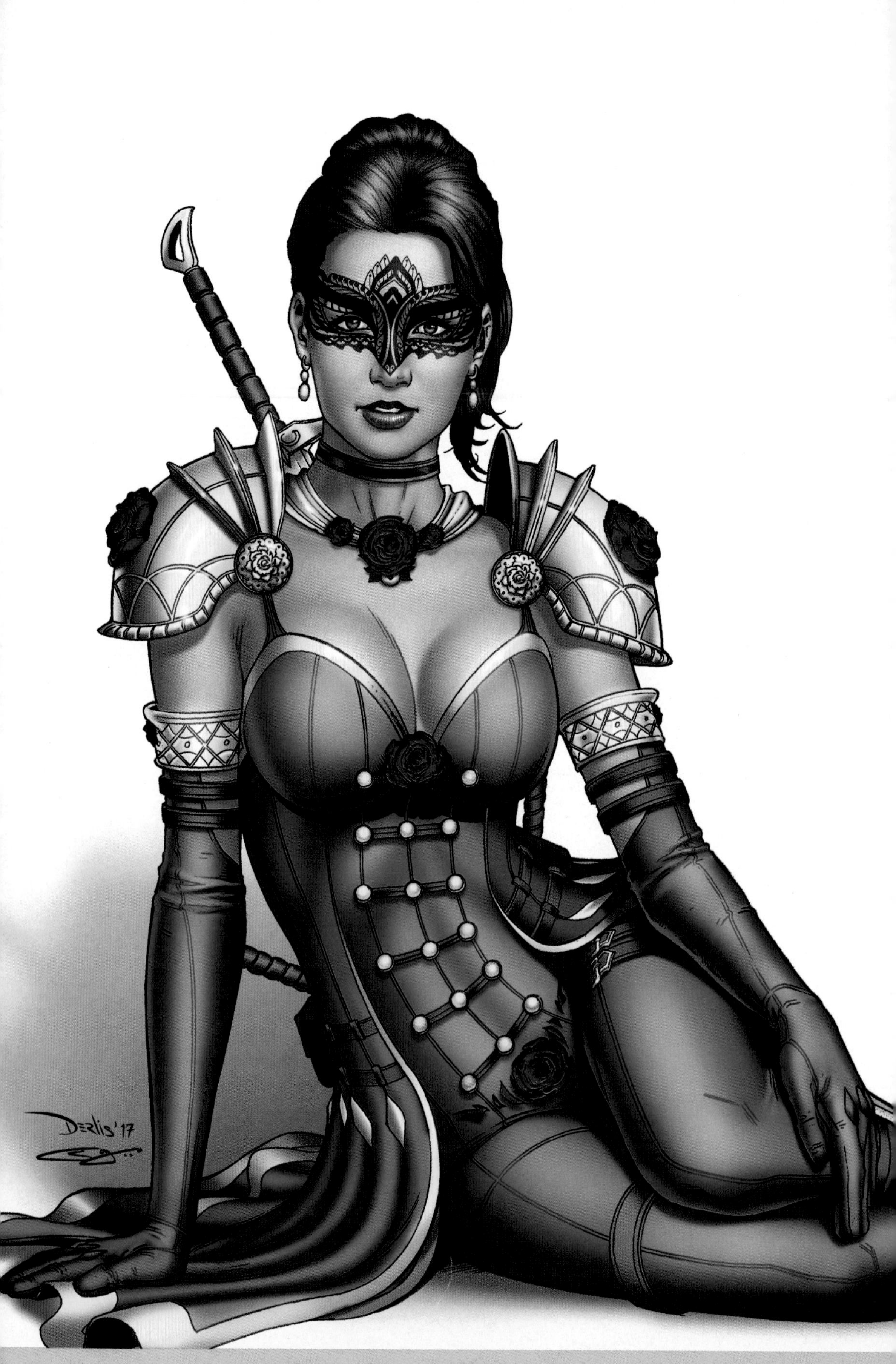
Derlis '17

BELLE: BEAST HUNTER 1 • COVER C

Artwork by Derlis Santacruz • Colors by Sanju Nivangune

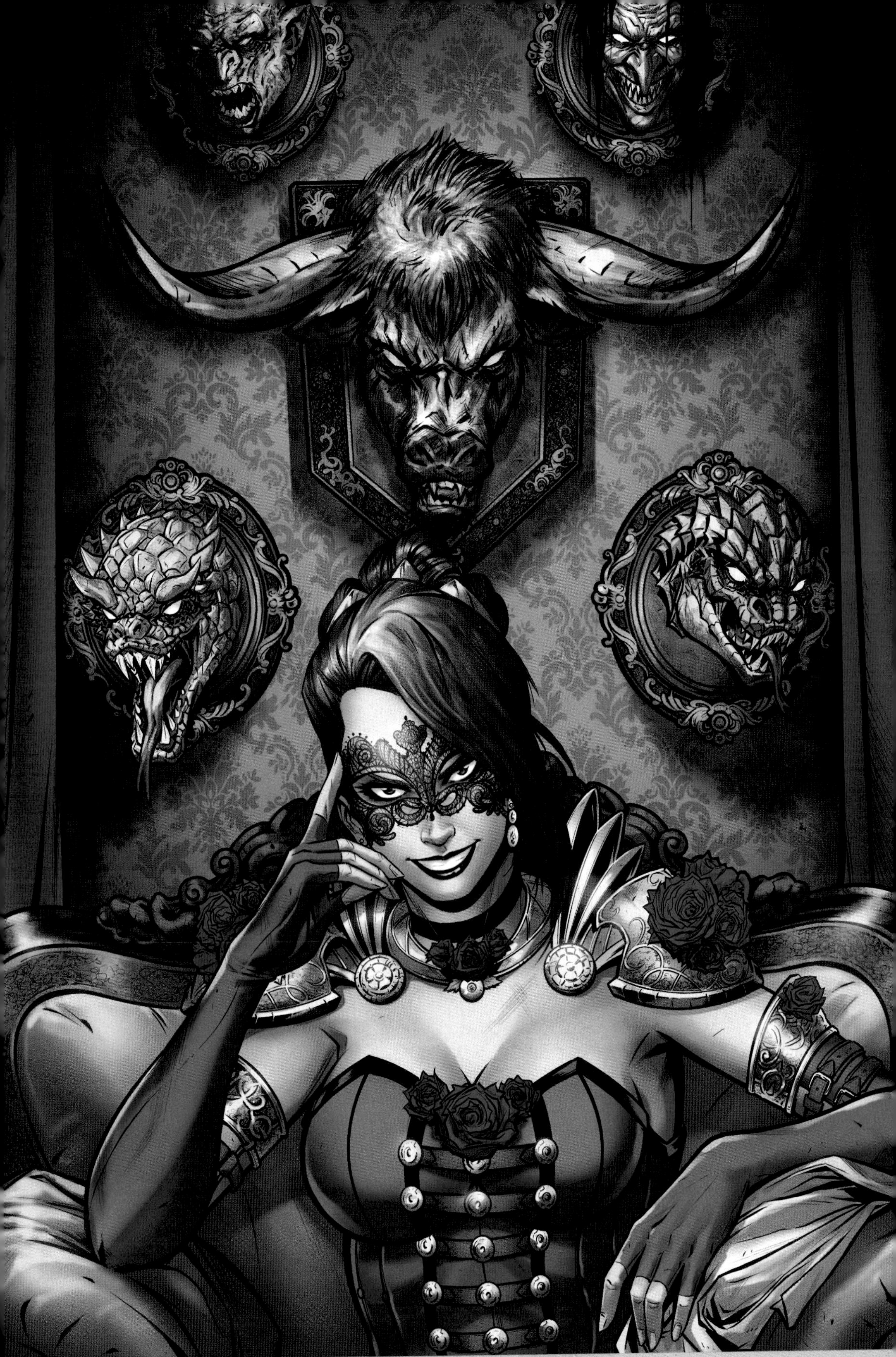

BELLE: BEAST HUNTER 1 • COVER D

Artwork by Riveiro • Colors by Mohan Sivakami

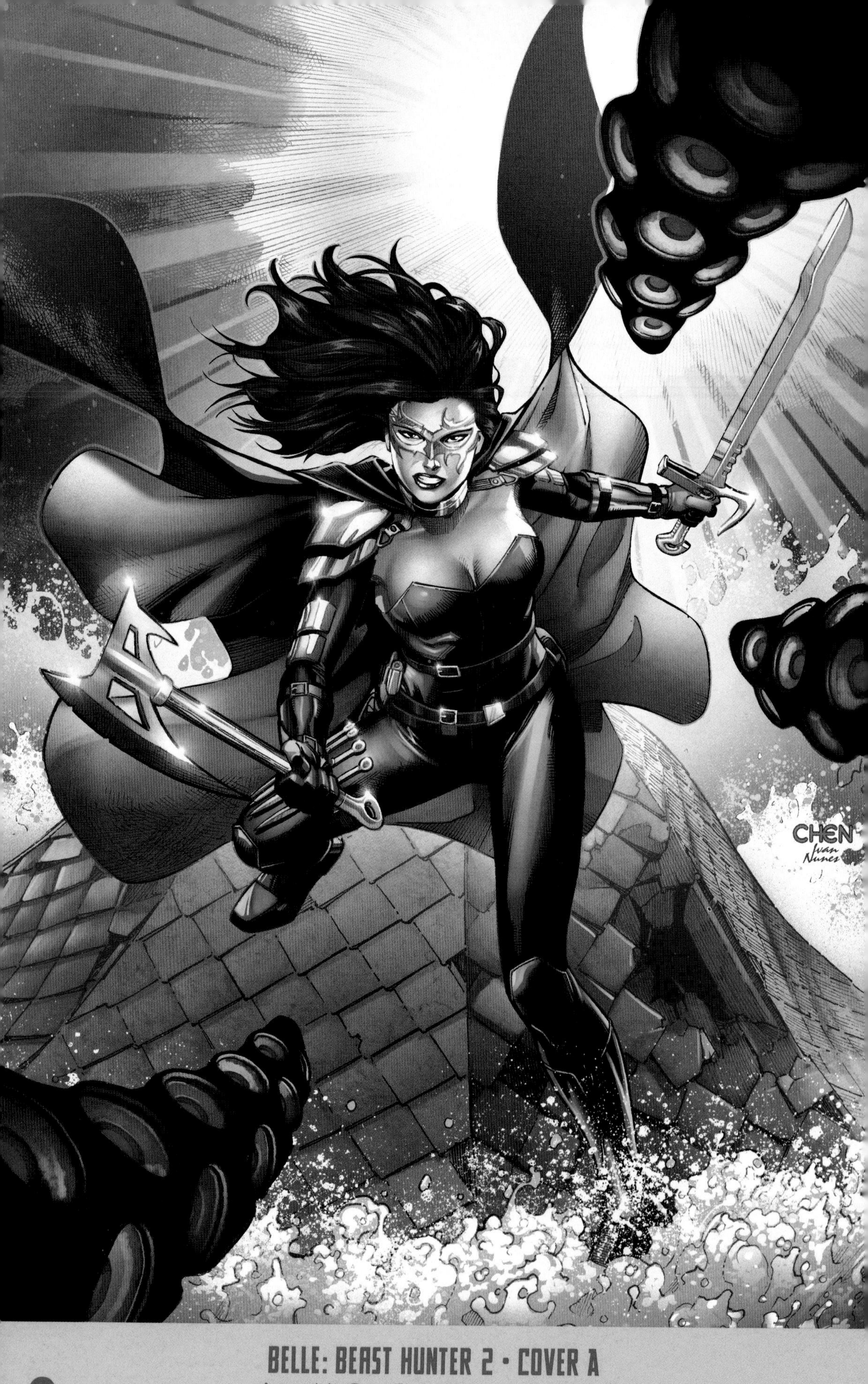
CHEN
Ivan
Nunes

BELLE: BEAST HUNTER 2 • COVER A

Artwork by Sean Chen • Colors by Ivan Nunes

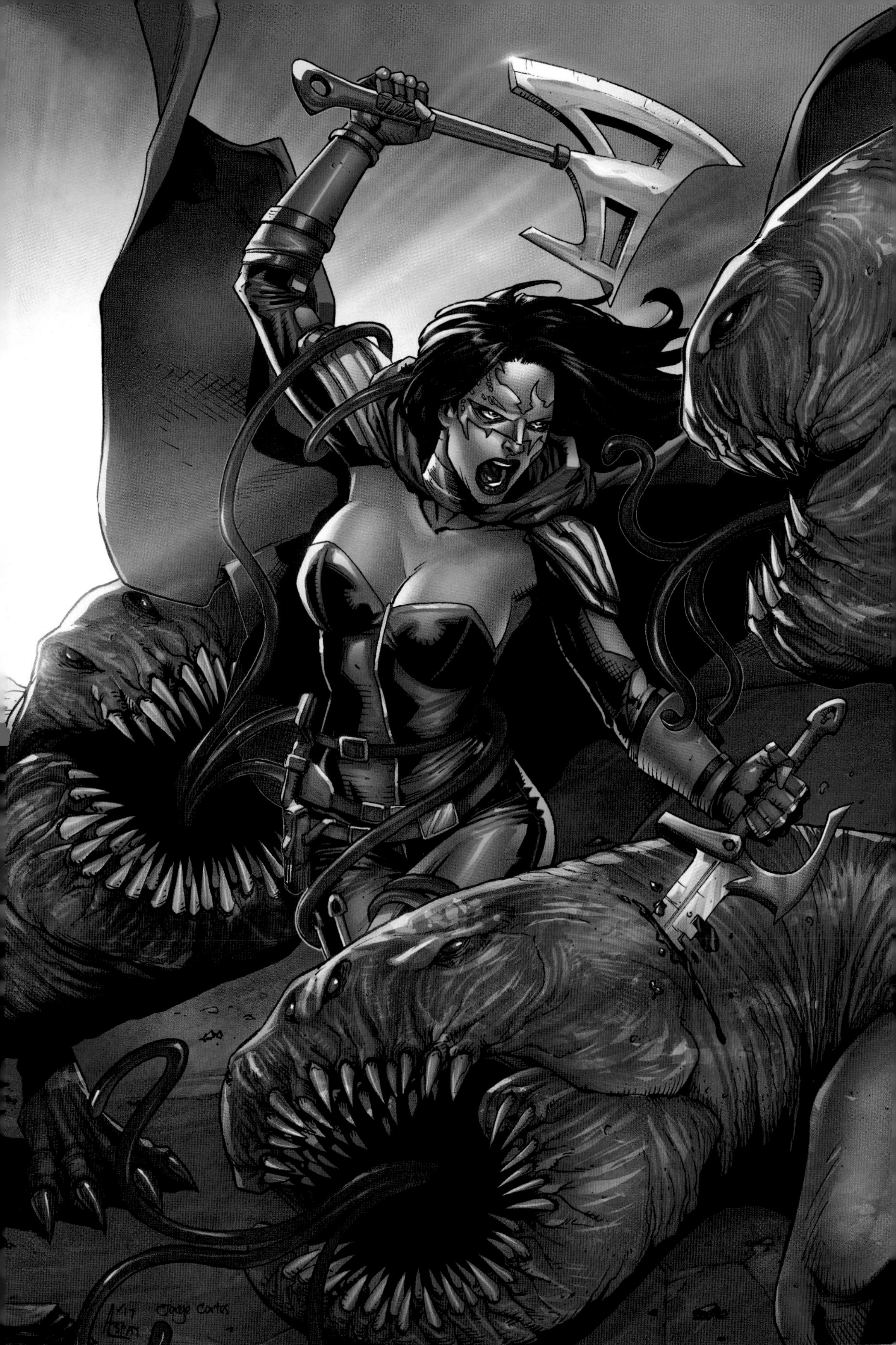

BELLE: BEAST HUNTER 2 • COVER B

Artwork by Anthony Spay • Colors by Jorge Cortes

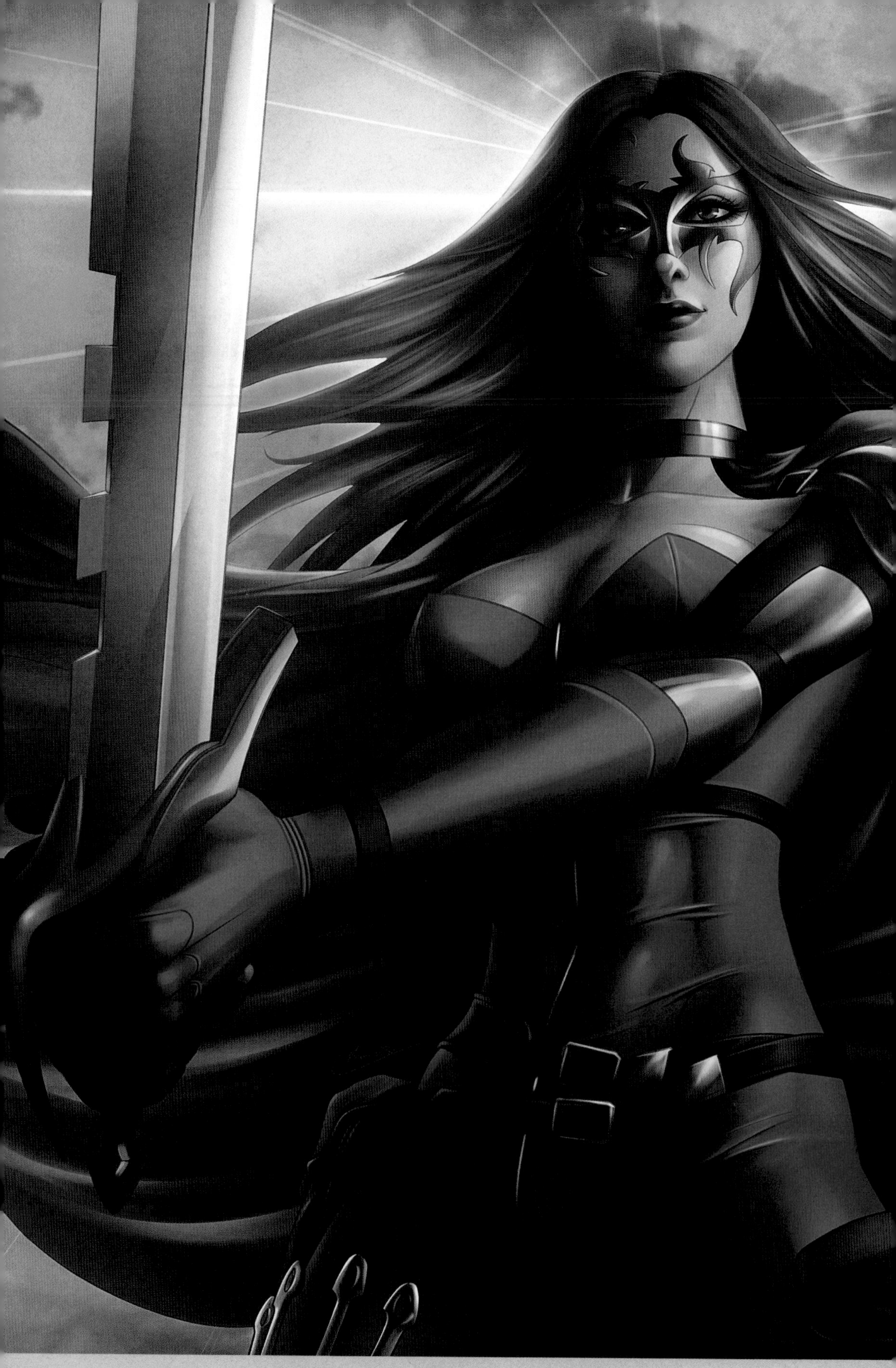

BELLE: BEAST HUNTER 2 • COVER C
Artwork by Meguro

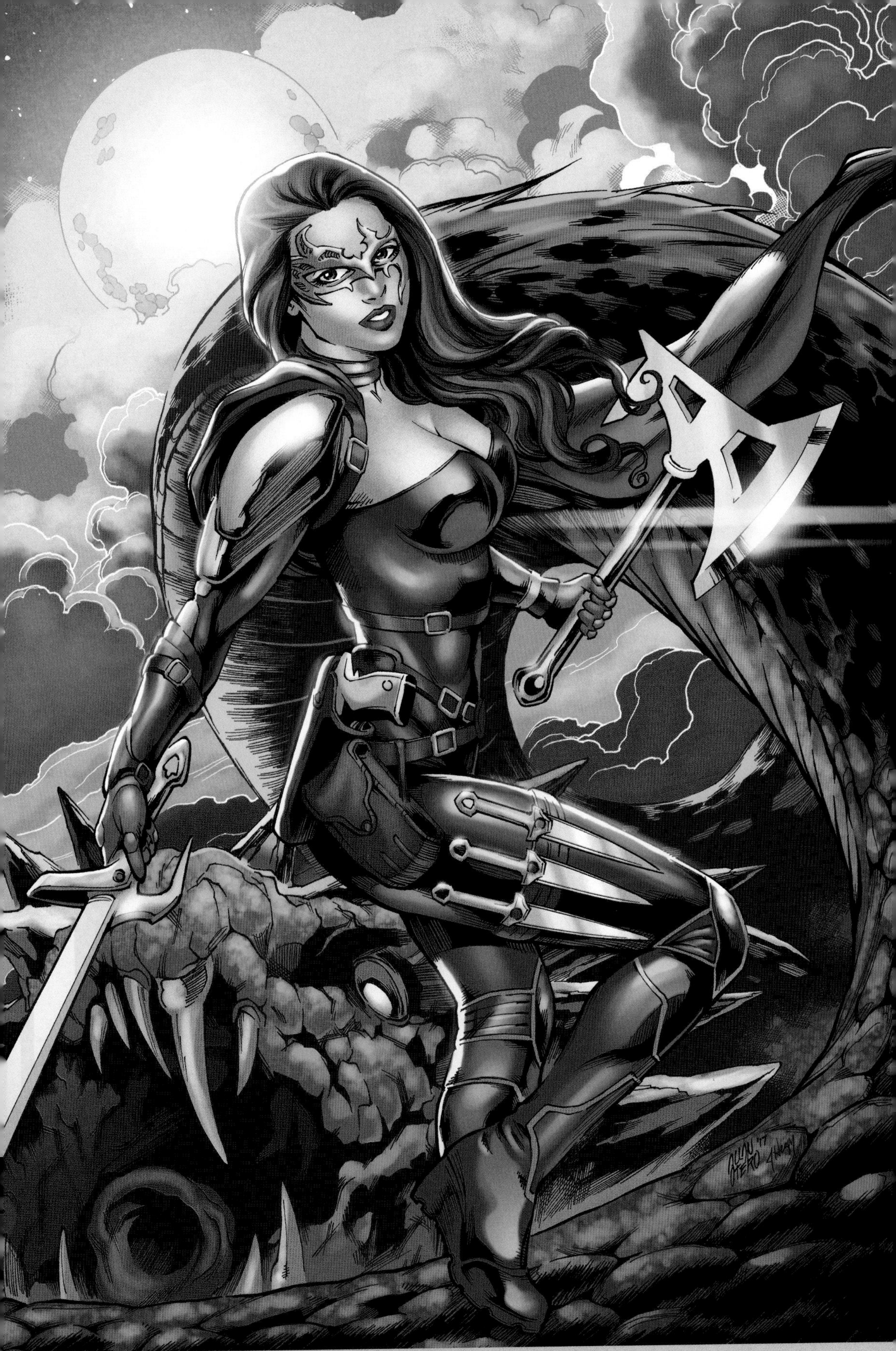

BELLE: BEAST HUNTER 2 • COVER D

Artwork by Allan Otero • Colors by Jesse Heagy

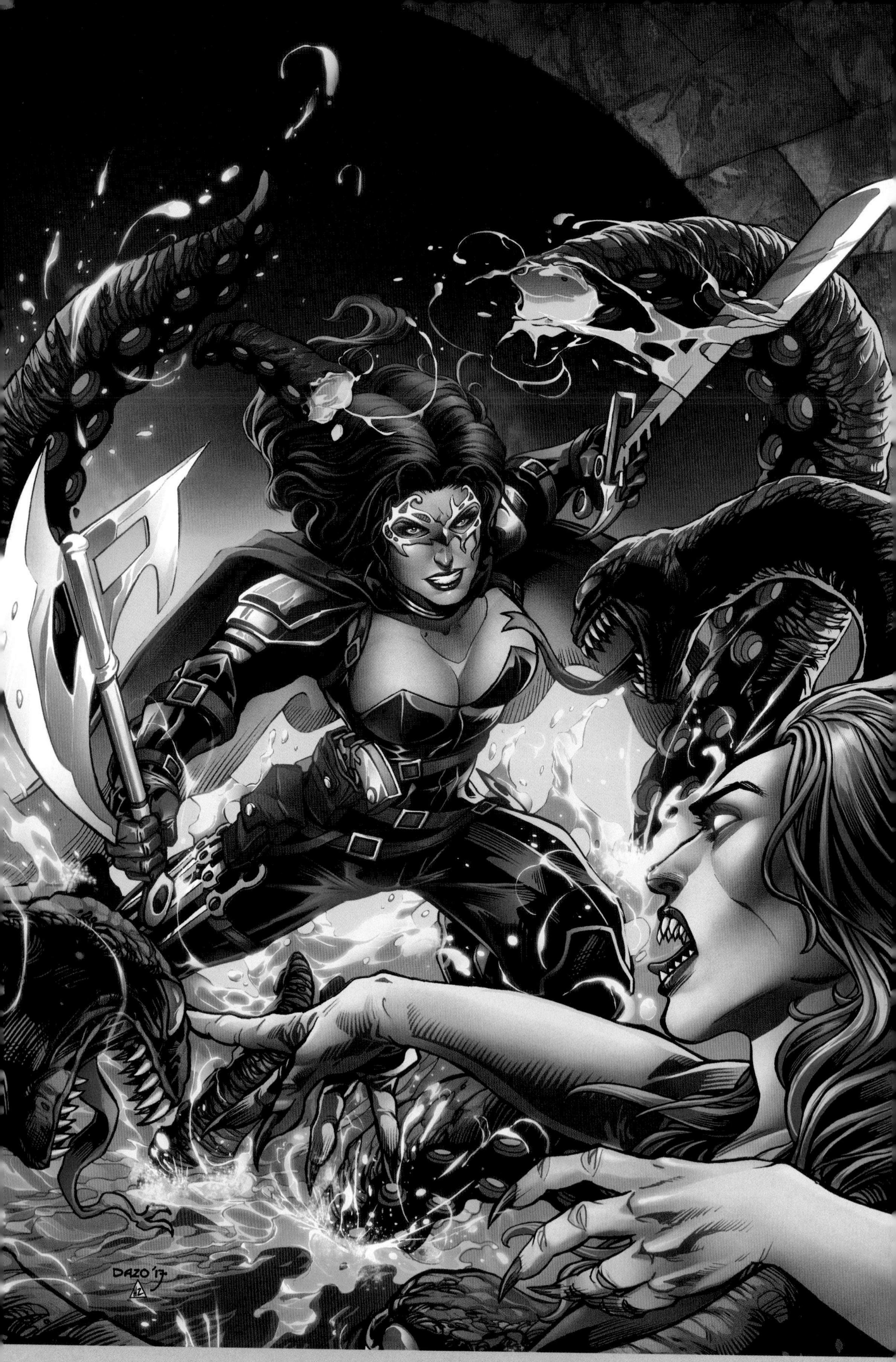
DAZO '17

BELLE: BEAST HUNTER 3 • COVER A

Artwork by Bong Dazo • Colors by Hedwin Zaldivar

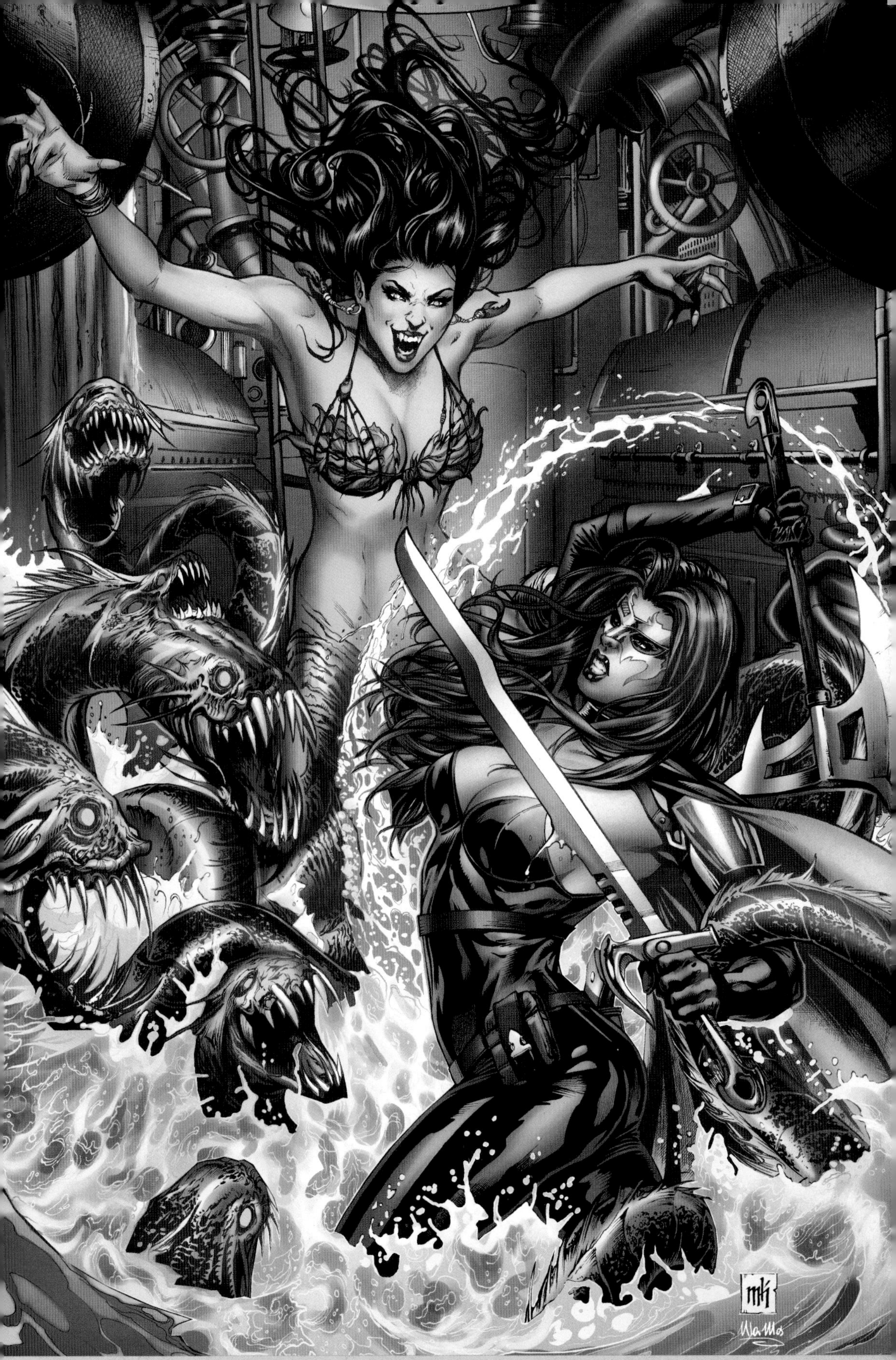

BELLE: BEAST HUNTER 3 • COVER B

Artwork by Mike Krome • Colors by Ula Mos

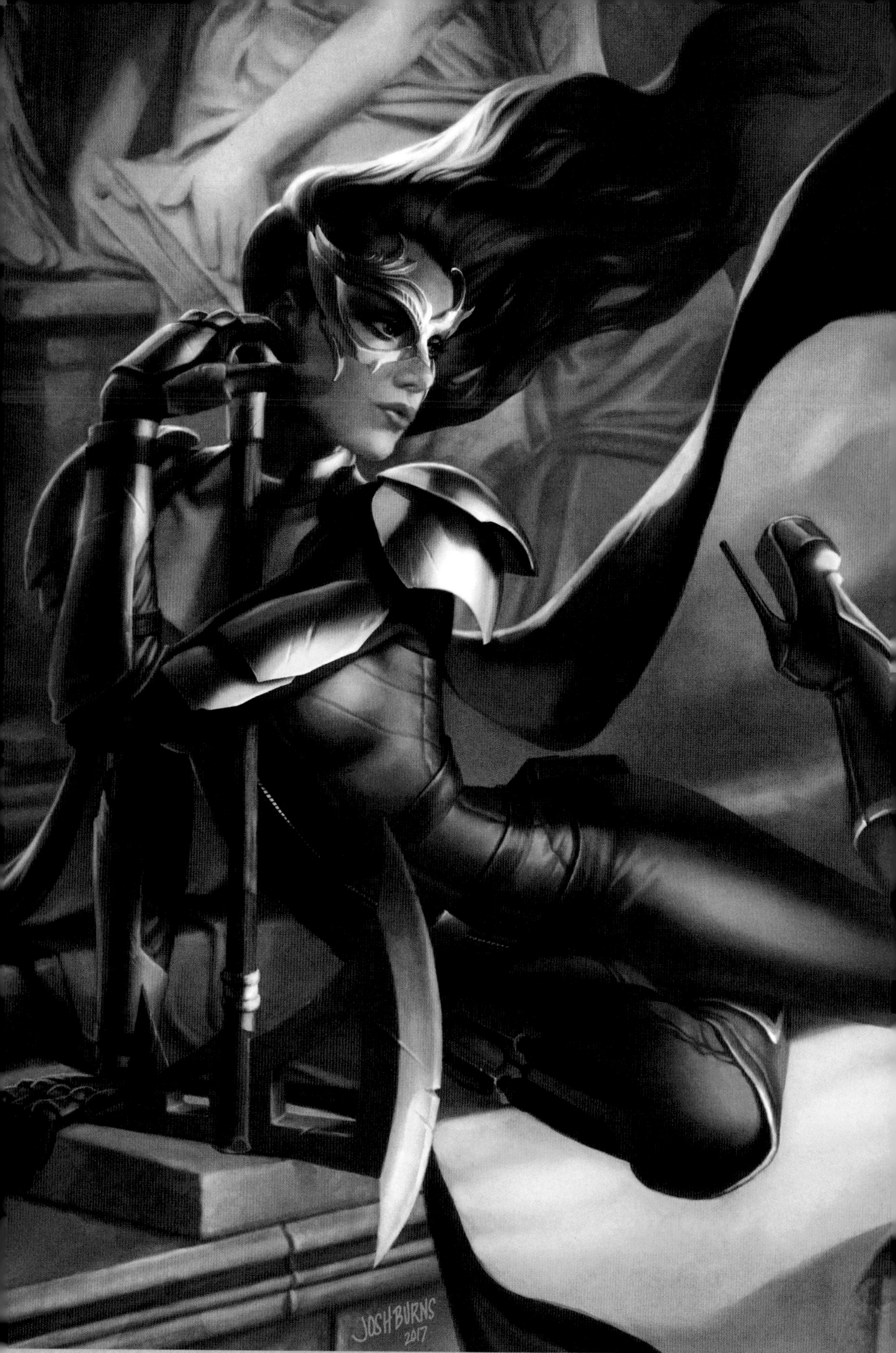
JOSH BURNS
2017

BELLE: BEAST HUNTER 3 • COVER C

Artwork by Josh Burns

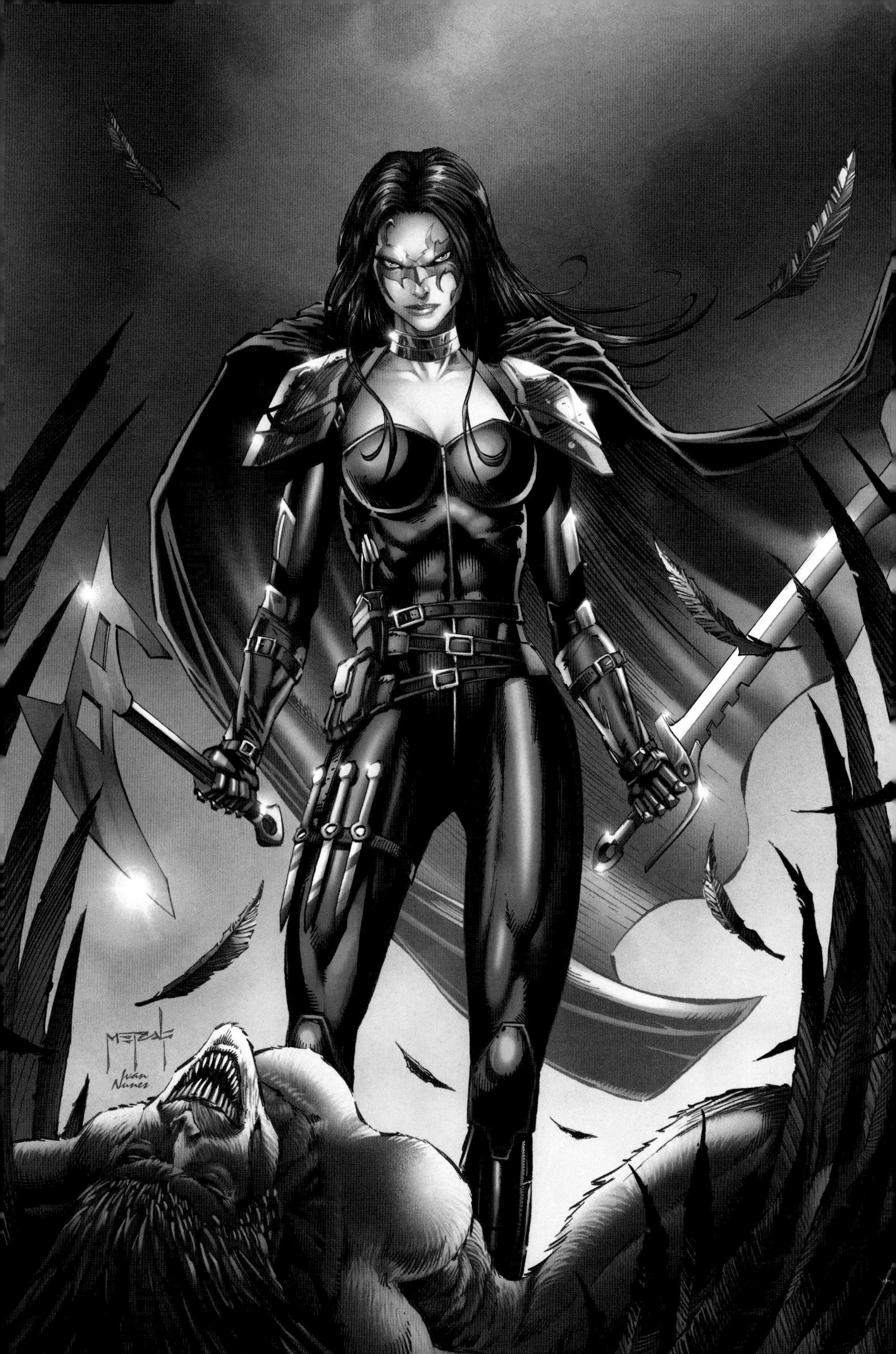

BELLE: BEAST HUNTER 3 • COVER D

Artwork by Jason Metcalf • Colors by Ivan Nunes

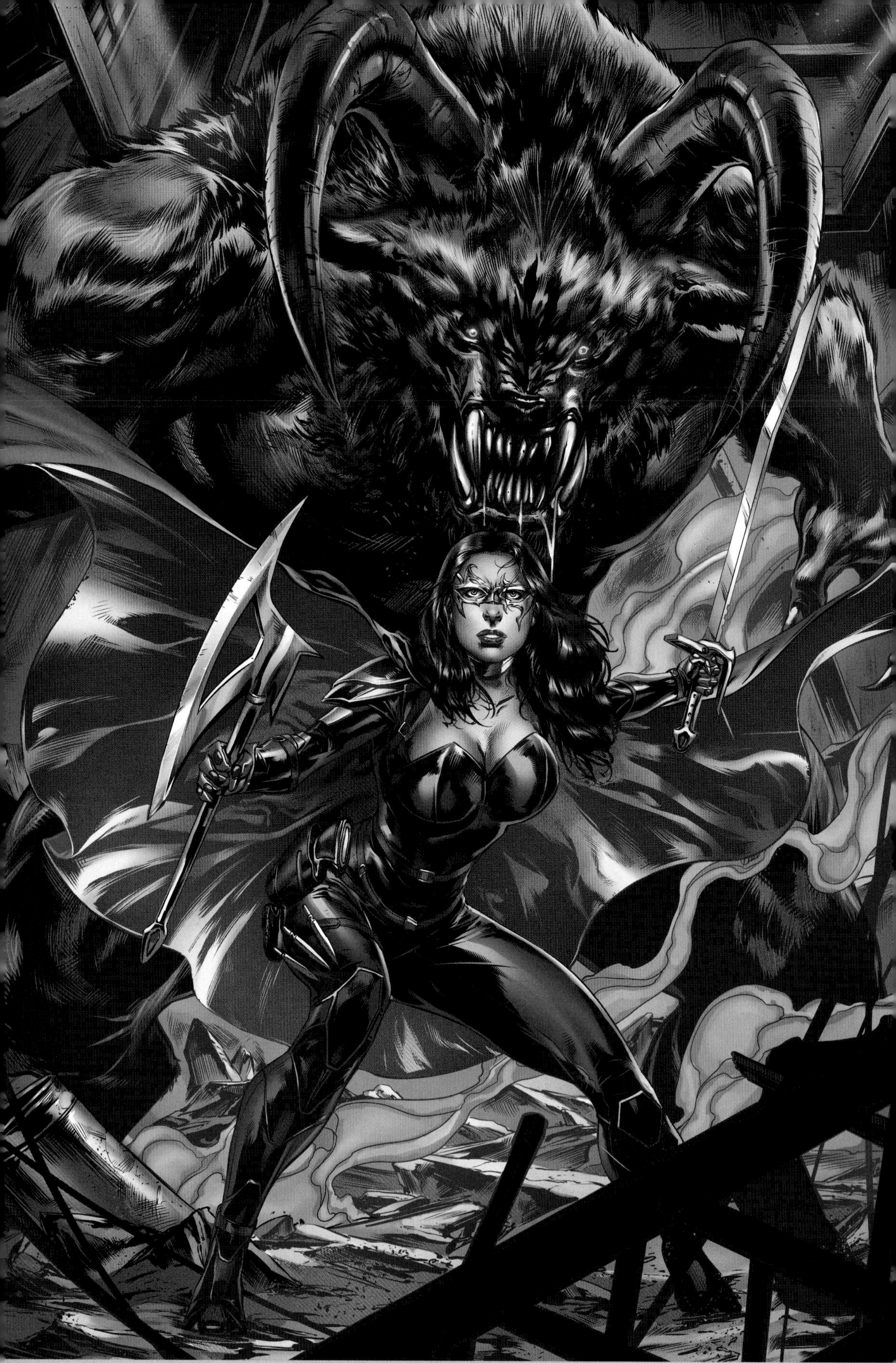

BELLE: BEAST HUNTER 4 • COVER A

Artwork by Caanan White • Colors by Ula Mos

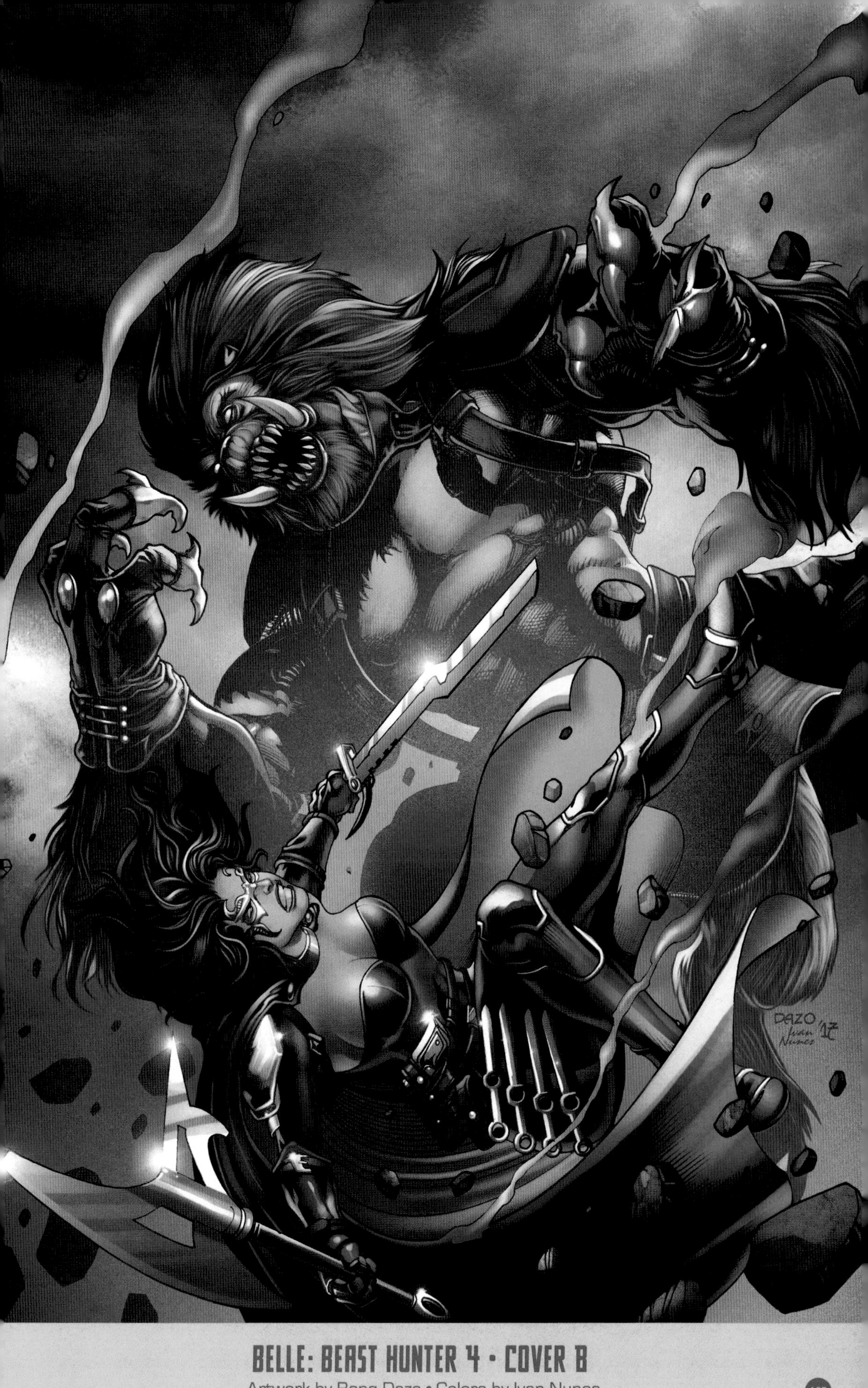
DAZO

BELLE: BEAST HUNTER 4 • COVER B

Artwork by Bong Dazo • Colors by Ivan Nunes

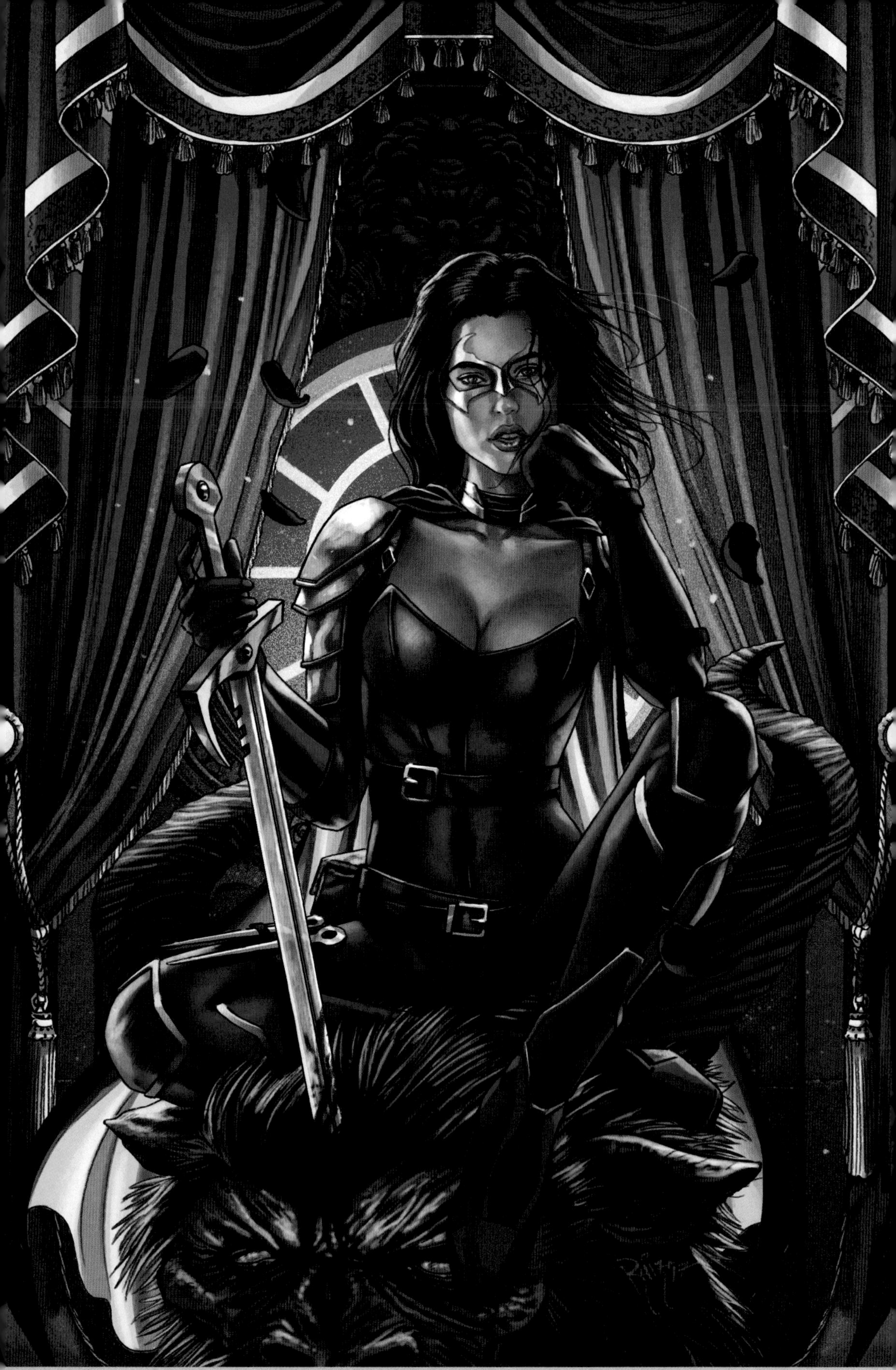

BELLE: BEAST HUNTER 4 • COVER C

Artwork by Ruiz Burgos

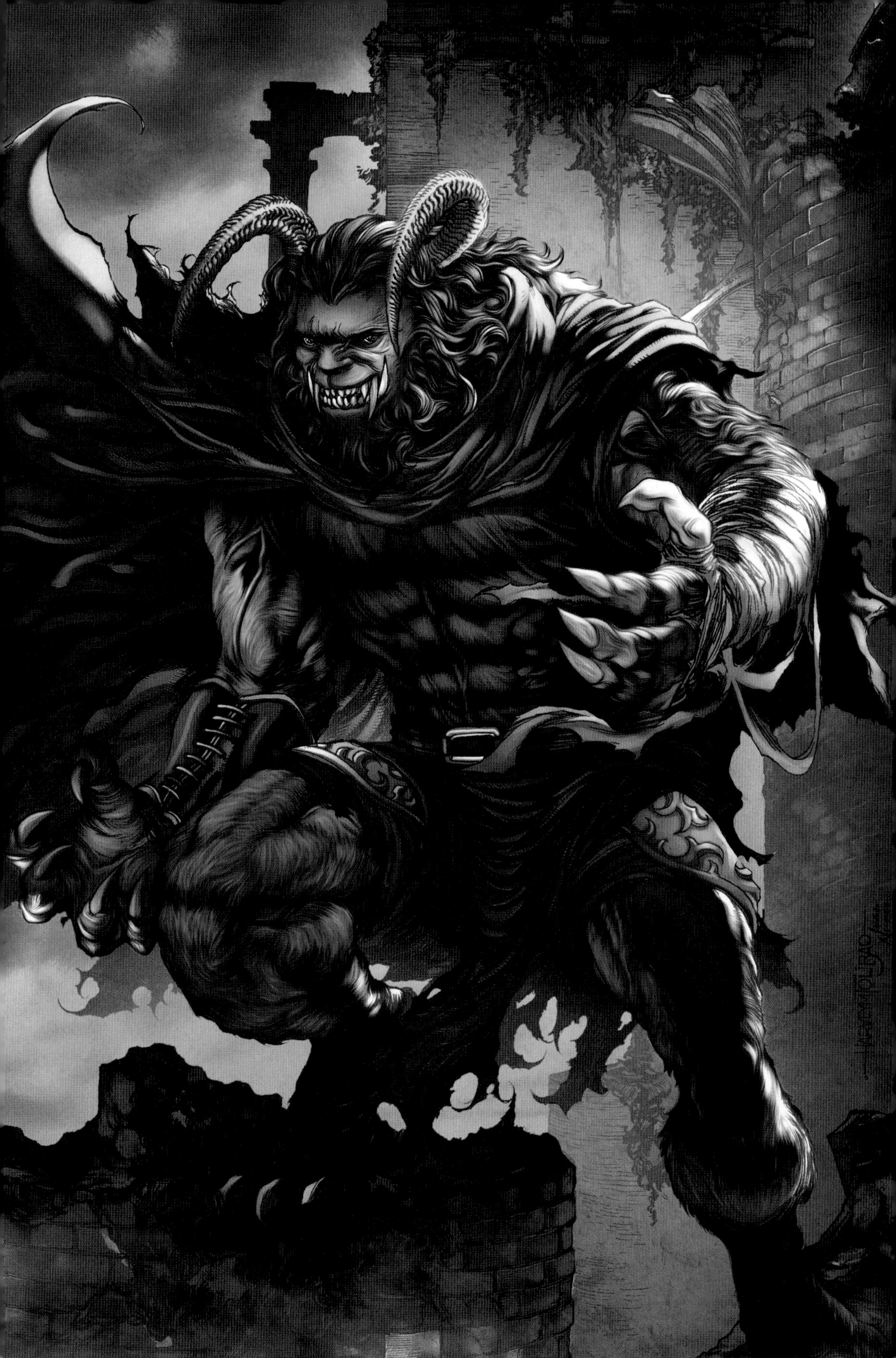

BELLE: BEAST HUNTER 4 • COVER D

Artwork by Harvey Tolibao • Colors by Ivan Nunes

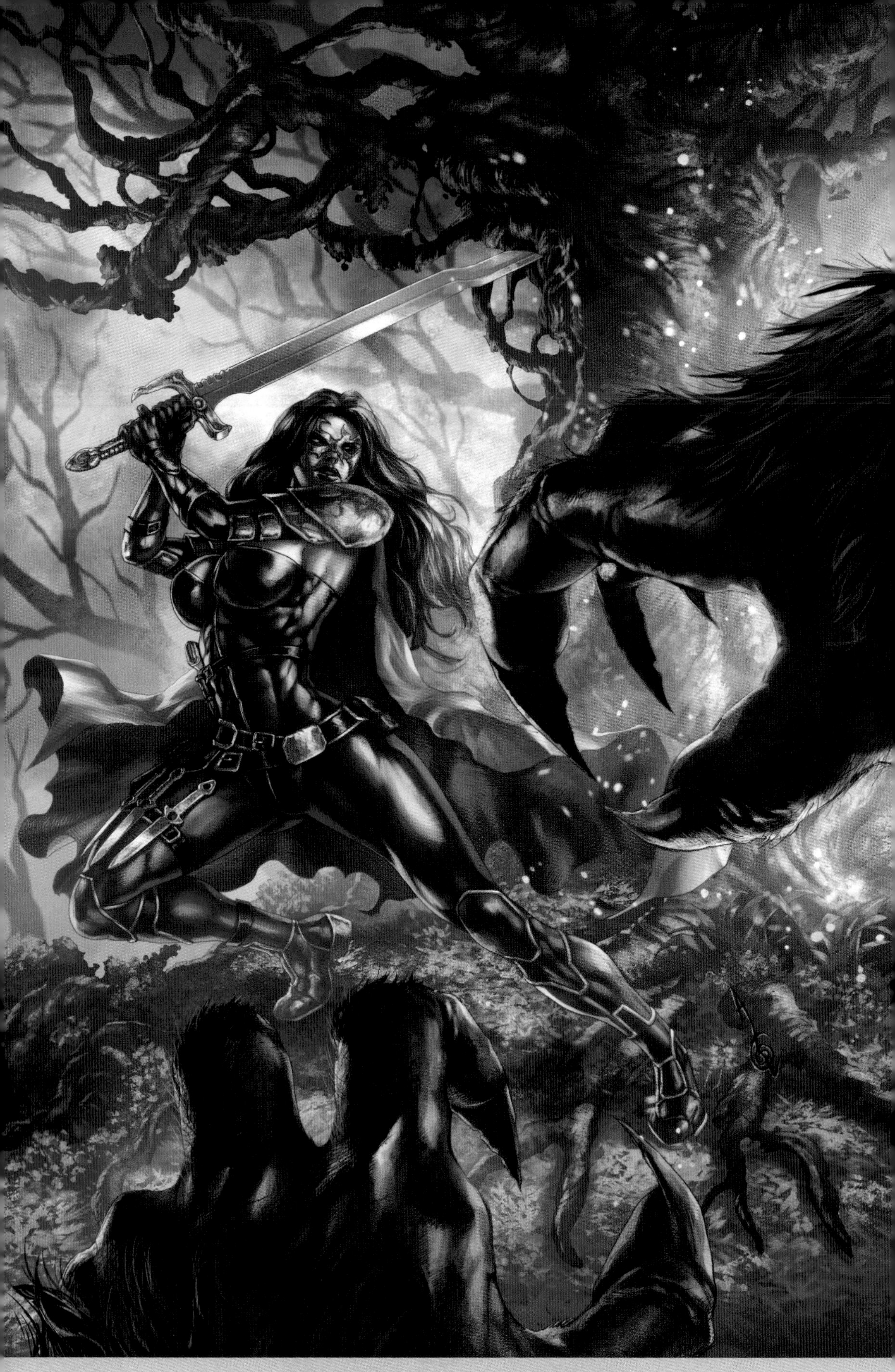

BELLE: BEAST HUNTER 5 • COVER A

Artwork by Alan Quah • Colors by Komikaki Studio (Feat. Sean Lee)

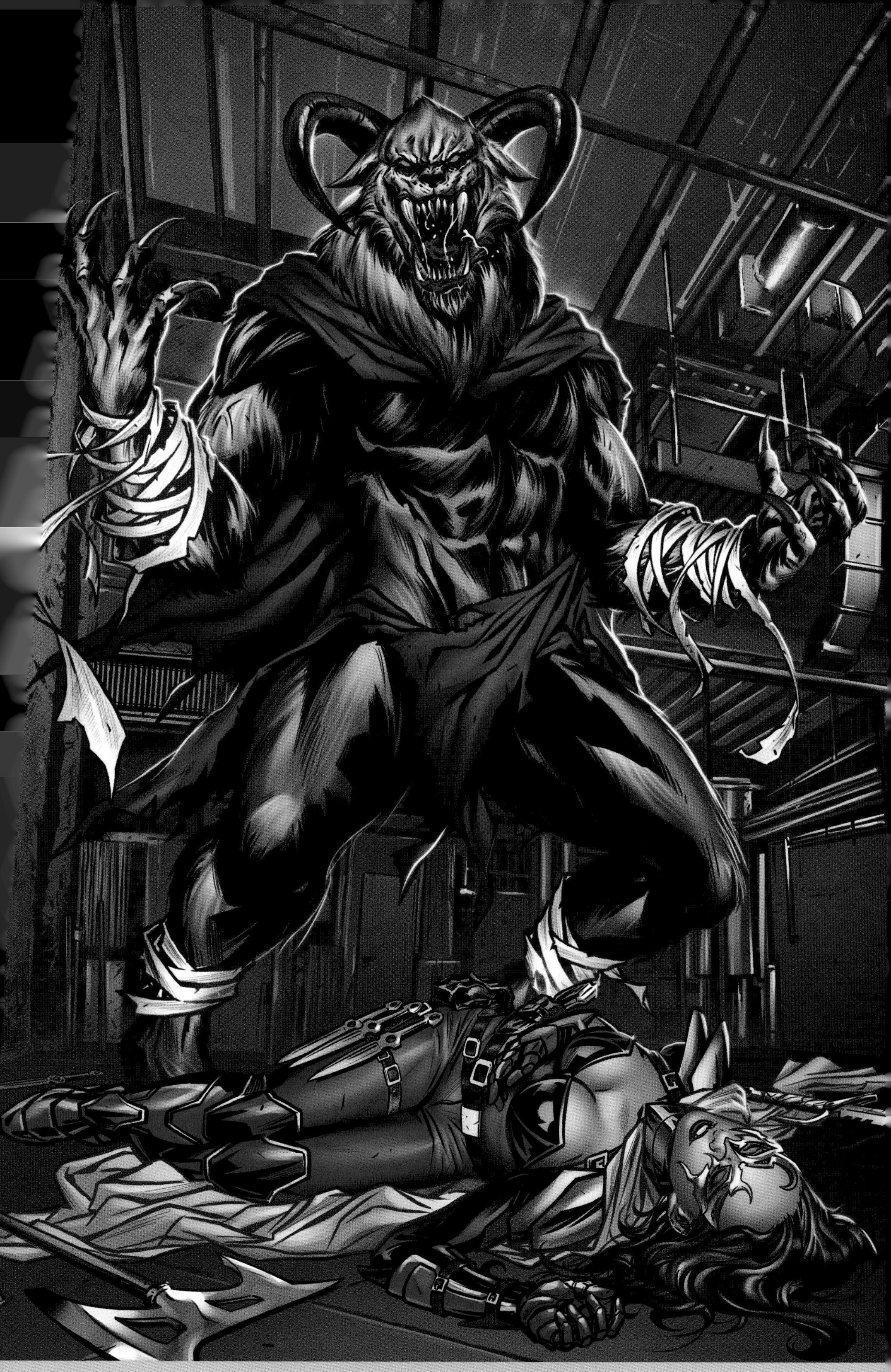

BELLE: BEAST HUNTER 5 • COVER B

Artwork by Riveiro • Colors by Ula Mos

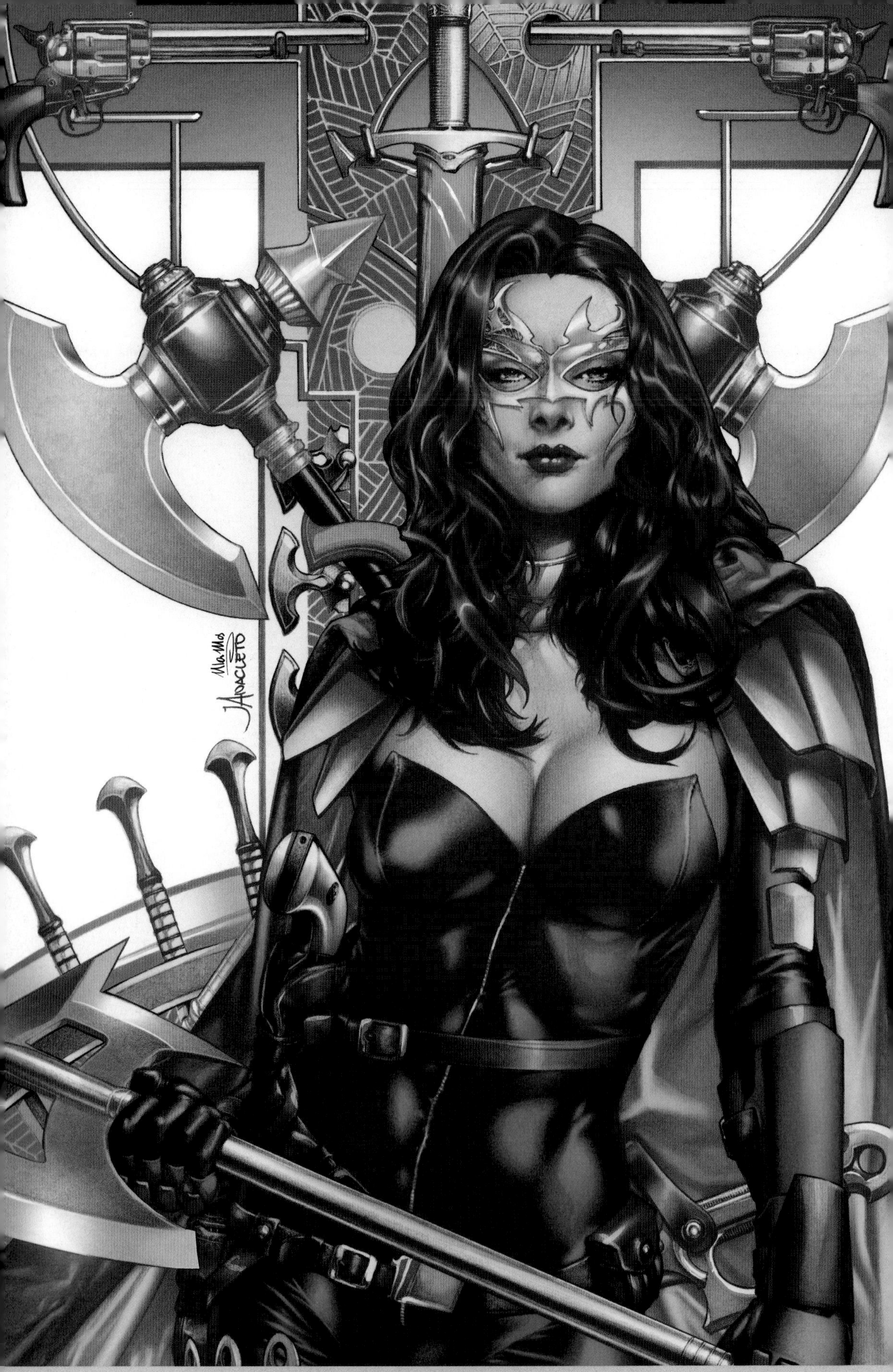

BELLE: BEAST HUNTER 5 • COVER C

Artwork by Jay Anacleto • Colors by Ula Mos

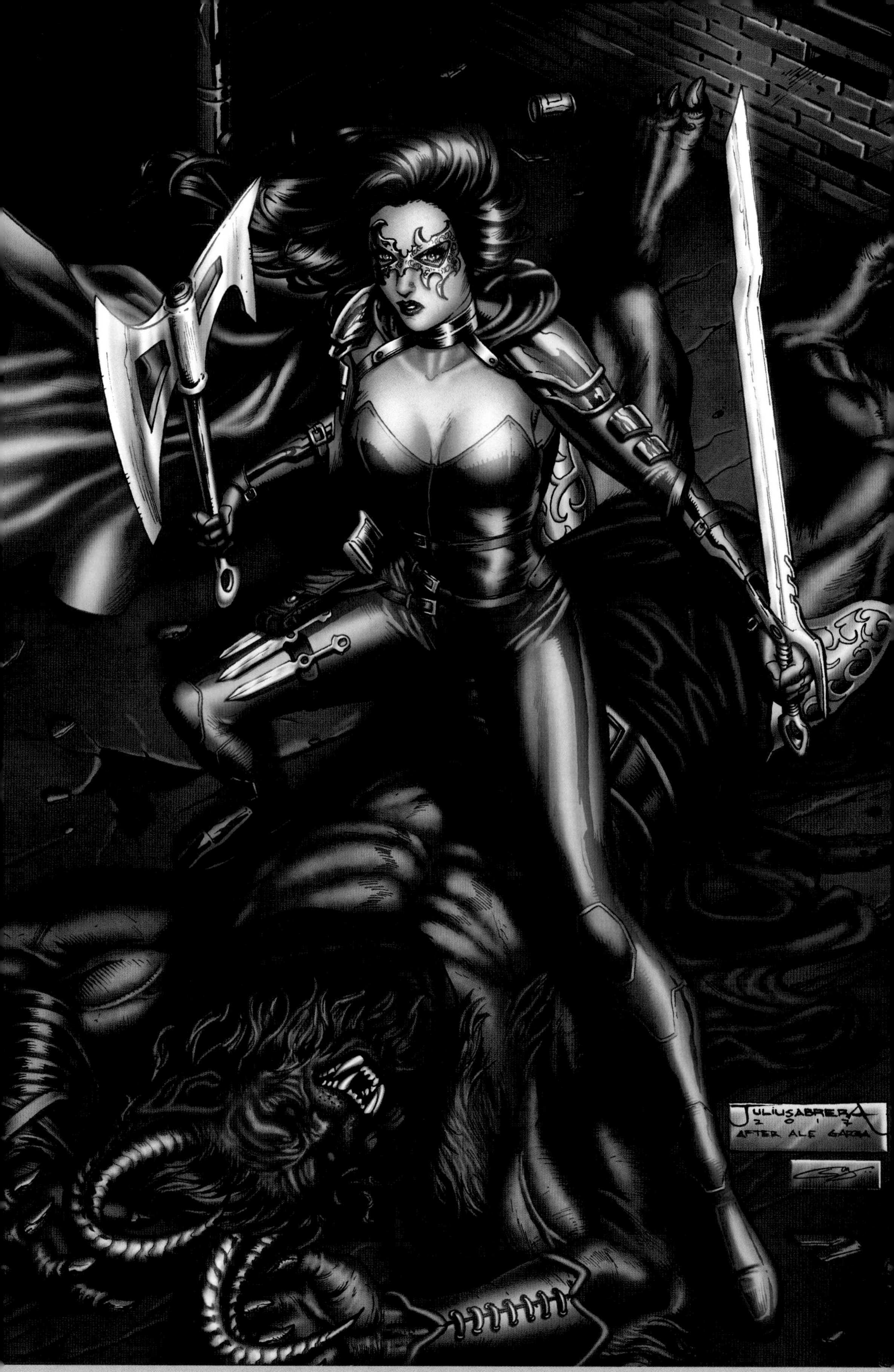
JULIUSABRERA
2017
AFTER ALE GARZA

BELLE: BEAST HUNTER 5 • COVER D

Artwork by Julius Abrera • Colors by Sanju Nivangune

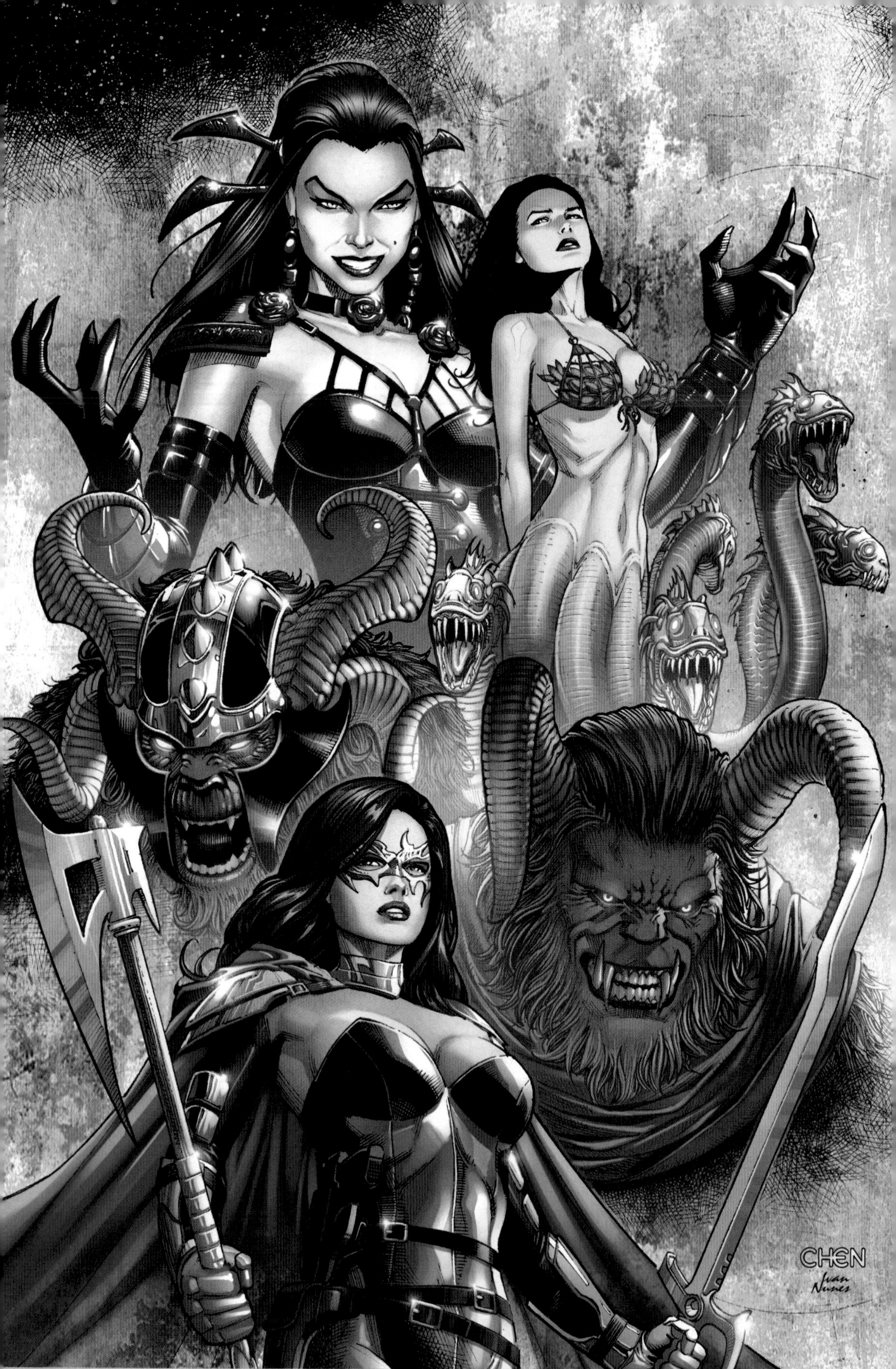
CHEN
Ivan Nunes

BELLE: BEAST HUNTER 6 • COVER A

Artwork by Sean Chen • Colors by Ivan Nunes

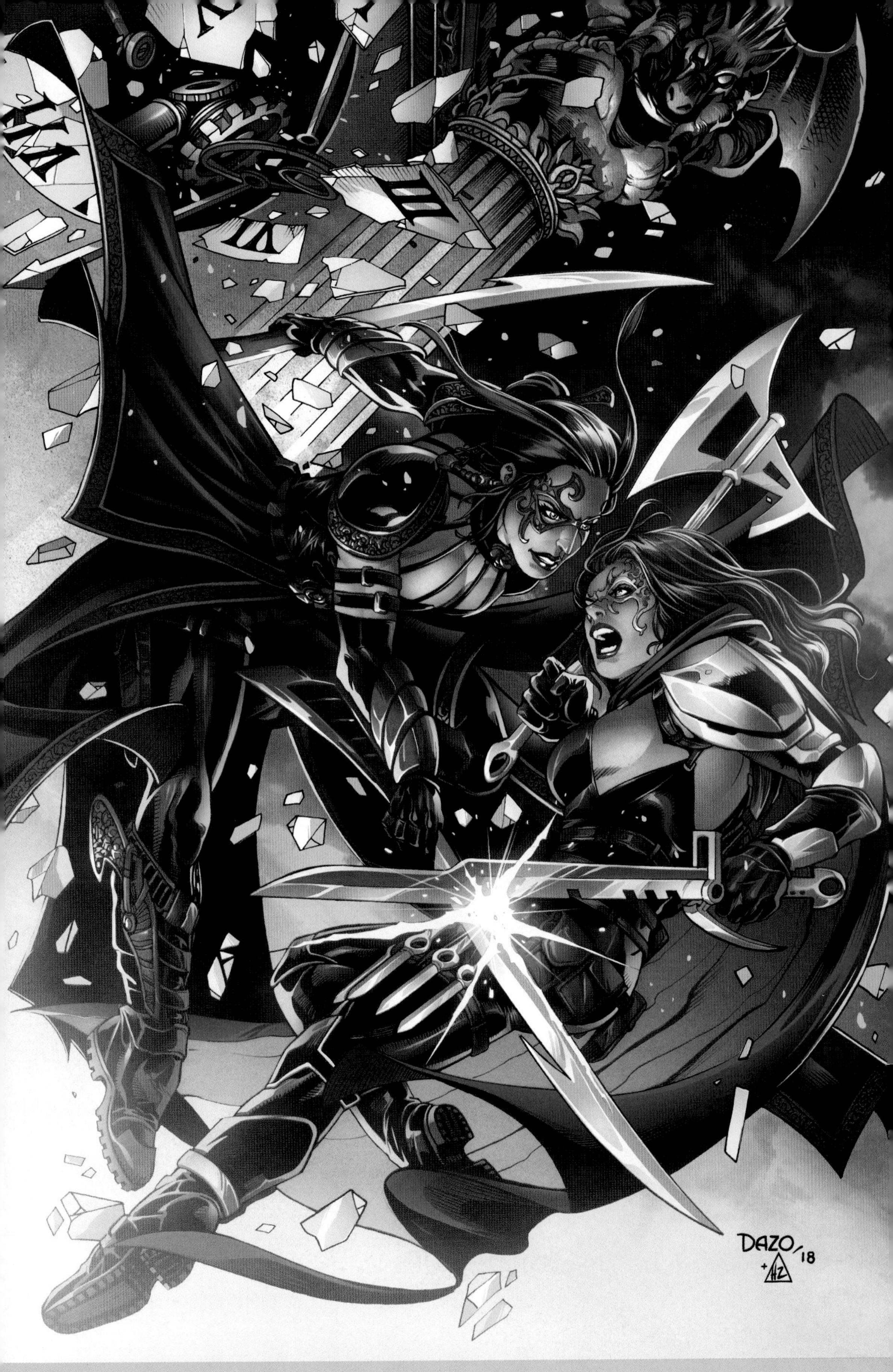
DAZO 18

BELLE: BEAST HUNTER 6 • COVER B

Artwork by Bong Dazo • Colors by Hedwin Zaldivar

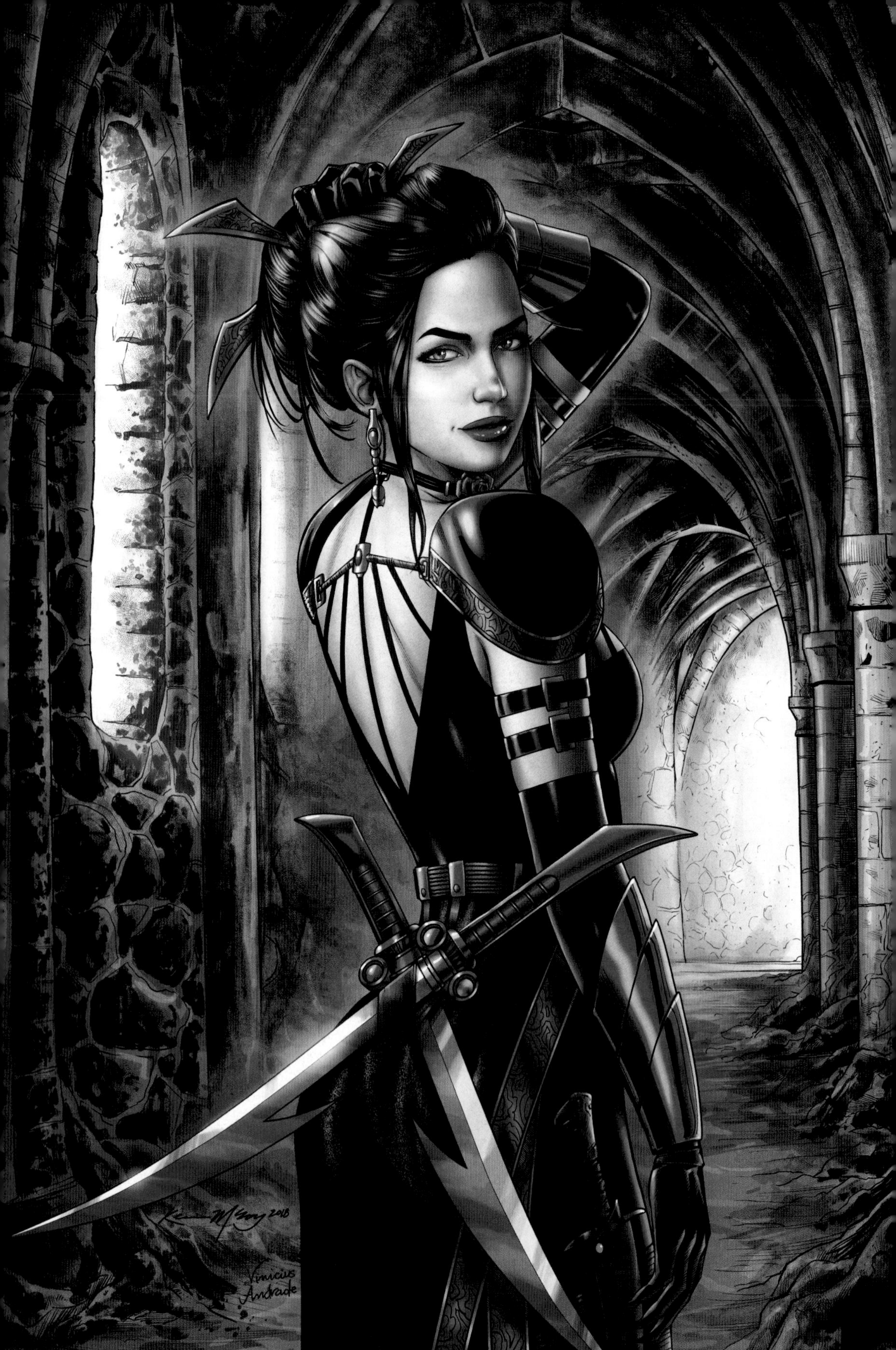
Vinicius
Andrade

BELLE: BEAST HUNTER 6 • COVER C

Artwork by Kevin McCoy • Colors by Vinicius Andrade

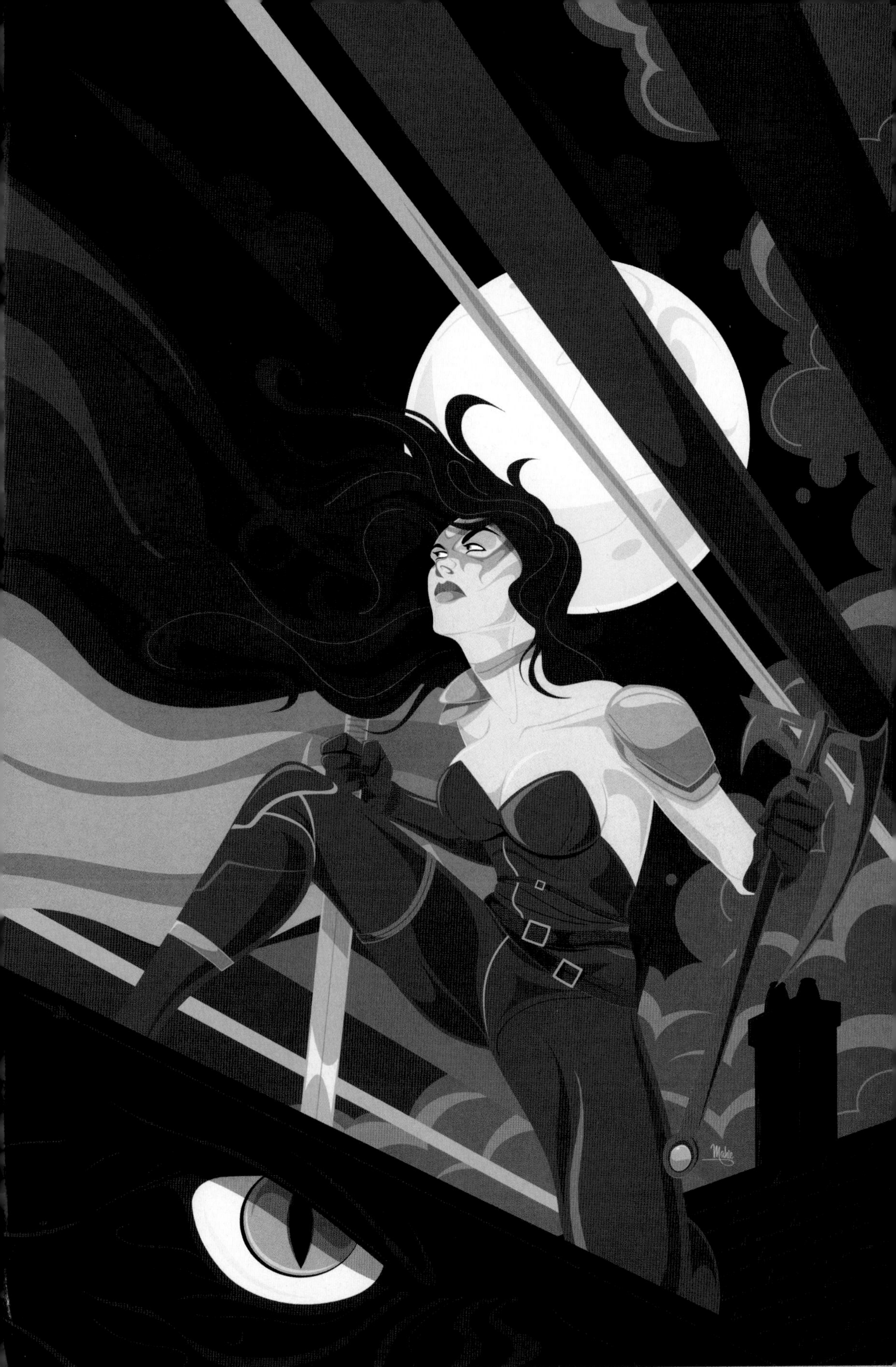
Mahle

BELLE: BEAST HUNTER 6 • COVER D

Artwork by Mike Mahle

BELLE
BEAST HUNTER

zenescope

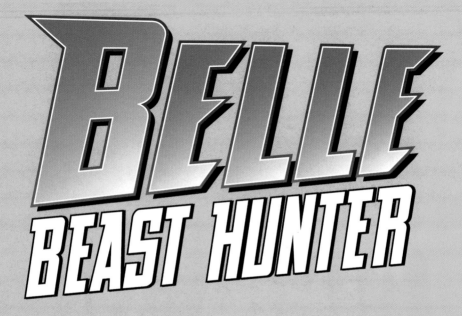

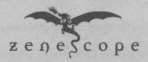